# THE DECLINE OF MAGIC

# THE DECLINE OF MAGIC
## Britain in the Enlightenment

Michael Hunter

YALE UNIVERSITY PRESS
NEW HAVEN AND LONDON

For information about this and other Yale University Press publications, please contact:
U.S. Office: sales.press@yale.edu    yalebooks.com
Europe Office: sales@yaleup.co.uk    yalebooks.co.uk

Set in Minion Pro by IDSUK (DataConnection) Ltd
Printed in Great Britain by TJ International Ltd, Padstow, Cornwall

Library of Congress Control Number: 2019946335

ISBN 978-0-300-24358-1

A catalogue record for this book is available from the British Library.

10 9 8 7 6 5 4 3 2 1

# CONTENTS

❀

# PREFACE

This book offers a fresh view of the change in educated attitudes towards magical beliefs that occurred in Britain between about 1650 and 1750. Though it is widely accepted that some kind of 'Decline of Magic' occurred at this time, its exact nature, and the reasons why it occurred, remain obscure. In the pages that follow it will be argued that

- Though it is often thought that the scientists of the early Royal Society tested magic and found it wanting, this is a misconception. In fact, the society avoided the issue because its members' views on the subject were so divided, and it was only in retrospect that this silence was interpreted as judgmental.
- The true pioneers of scepticism about magic were humanist free-thinkers, whose ideas seem more often to have been expressed orally than in printed form. The fact that such men were also sceptical about religion, however, tarnished their reputation and postponed the general acceptance of anti-magical views like theirs.
- Though eighteenth-century doctors like Sir Hans Sloane and Richard Mead might seem modern in their claim that a belief in magic was a physiological problem that they could cure, the treatments they recommended were ones like blood-letting and purging that went back to classical antiquity.
- The argument of fraud proved surprisingly inconclusive, as is illustrated by the case of the 'Drummer of Tedworth', a notorious poltergeist, on which opinions long remained divided.
- When change occurred, it did so through a kind of cultural osmosis, based as much on the legacy of classical antiquity as on the findings of science. It was a matter of assurance rather than proof, even though

the fashionable trappings of Newtonianism were often invoked in connection with it.

- The implication of such findings is that, contrary to popular belief, the Enlightenment did not reject magic for good reasons but for bad ones. This means that the validity of the phenomena involved remains as much an open question now as was the case in 1700.

These themes are dealt with in successive chapters, following a lengthy introduction which sketches the broader context within which these developments occurred, giving particular attention to the significance of the new science of the seventeenth century and the overriding anxiety about what was described at the time as 'atheism'. The book ends with a conclusion which offers an overview of the 'Decline of Magic', the way in which it came about and the legacy that it has left.

At the outset, it may be helpful to the reader to explain how the book has taken shape. Though I hope that the finished product represents a coherent whole within which the component parts echo and mutually reinforce one another, these components have been written over a long period, and it is useful to recapitulate their context. The earliest essay, which appears here as Chapter 1, was written in conjunction with the investigation of 'atheism' in the early modern period that I made in the 1980s. Chapters 3, 4 and part of Chapter 6, on the other hand, grew out of my studies of the early Royal Society and of Robert Boyle, which preoccupied me for over two decades. Only since the completion of my biography of Boyle, published in 2009, have I been tempted to take more of an interest in developments in the period after his death, and this is reflected in the most recently composed chapters of this book, namely Chapters 2, 5 and the latter part of Chapter 6: the first is based on the Roy Porter Lecture that I gave in 2011 and on my talk at the 'Priestcraft' conference held at Cambridge in 2016; the second on my Dacre Lecture delivered at Oxford in 2014; and the last on a talk given at a conference on second sight and prophecy at Aberdeen in 2013. The Introduction and Conclusion are more recent still, being deliberately conceived to bind the intervening chapters together by providing background and drawing out their implications: these incorporate and develop the arguments put forward in my paper, 'The Supernatural and the Natural in English Thought, 1650–1750', delivered at the conference of the International Society for Intellectual History at Blagoevgrad, Bulgaria, in May 2017.

I should perhaps also explain that, although the book is predominantly focused on the period *c*. 1650–*c*. 1750, Chapters 4–6 extrapolate from this to deal with developments of the later Enlightenment, taking the story up to the time of John Wesley, Samuel Johnson and Sir Walter Scott and to the dawning era of Romanticism. Hence it seems only appropriate for the subtitle to allude to the 'Enlightenment' as a whole. It is as well to add that the emphasis in the Introduction on 'atheism' is intended to make sense of the concerns of the orthodox protagonists who figure in that and other chapters of the book; although ideas of the kind that alarmed them undoubtedly became commoner in the eighteenth century, I should stress that I hold no brief for claiming 'atheism' as the philosophical outlook which typified the Enlightenment.

In writing this book I have accumulated many debts. First, I must acknowledge how much I learned from successive generations of Master's degree students at Birkbeck, University of London, who took a course that I taught on 'The "Decline of Magic": Magical Ideas in English Society 1650–1750' for many years prior to my retirement in 2011. I also owe a great deal to numerous seminar audiences throughout the world who listened to and commented on presentations in which I aired some of the ideas outlined here, going back to the 1980s. It would be invidious to try to list all these venues and the organisers responsible for the talks that I gave, but my gratitude is none the less for that. I might, however, mention the most recent such presentation, in which I outlined the thrust of the book as a whole: this took place at All Souls College, Oxford, on 25 April 2018, under the auspices of Dmitri Levitin and Philipp Nothaft, and at it I benefited from the comments of the organisers and of Robin Briggs, Keith Thomas and others who were present.

Of the various writings on my part that the current volume comprises, some have already been published. I am grateful to the publishers of the material in question for giving me permission to re-use it, namely Boydell & Brewer Ltd (Chapter 1), *The Historical Journal* (Chapter 2), *Historical Research* (Chapter 4) and *Notes & Records: The Royal Society Journal for the History of Science* (Chapter 3): for details, see Introduction, notes 109–14. Certain of these articles acknowledge my debts for access to archival and other resources that are deployed in them. In addition, the acknowledgements therein mention various friends and colleagues who read drafts of the writings in question, and to those the following must be added for their helpful comments on material hitherto unpublished: Peter Anstey, Jonathan

Barry, Stephen Brogan, Mark Dawson, John Henry, Anthony Ossa-Richardson, Lawrence M. Principe, Matthew Ramsey, Michael Riordan and Alexandra Walsham. For help with the illustrations, I am indebted to Jon Wilson. At Yale University Press, I owe sincere gratitude to Heather McCallum, Marika Lysandrou, Clarissa Sutherland, Lucy Buchan and Rachael Lonsdale.

Michael Hunter

July 2018

❀

# ILLUSTRATIONS

### In the text

1 (p. 32).  The title-page of John Wagstaffe's *The Question of Witchcraft Debated* (2nd edn, 1671). © Wellcome Collection.

2 (p. 63).  The title-page of Francis Hutchinson's *An Historical Essay Concerning Witchcraft* (1718). © Wellcome Collection.

3 (p. 124).  The title-page of John Beaumont's *An Historical, Physiological and Theological Treatise of Spirits, Apparitions, Witchcrafts, and other Magical Practices* (1705). © Wellcome Collection.

### Plates

1. The frontispiece to the second part of Joseph Glanvill's *Saducismus Triumphatus* (1681; from the 3rd edn of 1689), engraved by William Faithorne.

2. An etched portrait of Thomas Hobbes by Wenceslaus Hollar (1665).

3. A drawing of the interior of a London coffee-house (*c.* 1695). British Museum, 1931,0613.2. © The Trustees of the British Museum.

4. An engraved portrait of Henry More by William Faithorne (1675).

5. An engraved portrait of Joseph Glanvill by William Faithorne (1680).

6. A brass medal of Robert Boyle cast by Carl Reinhold Berch (1729) from a now lost ivory medallion of Boyle carved by the Huguenot artist, Jean Cavalier (1960).

7. The title-page to volume 3 of Shaftesbury's *Characteristicks* (2nd edn, 1714), embellished with a vignette criticising superstitious practices by Simon Gribelin.

8. Pages 312–13 from Martin Martin's *A Description of the Western Islands of Scotland* (2nd edn, 1716), annotated by John Toland and Lord Molesworth, C.45.c.1. © The British Library Board.

9. A terracotta bust of Sir Hans Sloane by John Michael Rysbrack (1693–1779) for the head of the marble statue formerly in the Chelsea Physic Garden. British Museum, 1756,0619.1 © The Trustees of the British Museum.

10. Fol. 8v of British Library Sloane MS 2731, a late seventeenth-century copy of the magical text *The Key of Solomon the King*. © The British Library Board.

11. A bronze medal of Conyers Middleton, made in Rome by Giovanni Pozzi (1724), with reverse depicting Cambridge University Library. British Museum 1966,0403.244. © The Trustees of the British Museum.

12. An etched portrait of Richard Mead by Arthur Pond (1739). Wellcome Library no. 6446i. © Wellcome Collection.

13. 'Dr Johnson in his Travelling Dress as Described in Boswell's Tour' by Thomas Trotter, published by George Kearsley (1786). NPG D34874. © National Portrait Gallery, London.

14. A plate from William Gilpin's *Observations, Relative chiefly to Picturesque Beauty, Made in the Year 1776, On several parts of Great Britain, Particularly the High-Lands of Scotland* (2 vols, 1789; 2nd edn, London, 1792), vol. 1, facing p. 135.

15. A stipple portrait of Sir Walter Scott by James Heath after James Saxon, from *The Lady of the Lake* (Edinburgh, 1810).

16. *Credulity, Superstition and Fanaticism. A Medley* by William Hogarth (1762).

# ABBREVIATIONS

The following abbreviations are repeatedly used in the notes to this book:

| | |
|---|---|
| Add MS | British Library Additional Manuscript |
| BL | British Library |
| *ECCO* | *Eighteenth-Century Collections Online* |
| *ESTC* | *English Short-Title Catalogue* |
| FRS | Fellow of the Royal Society |
| HMC | Historical Manuscripts Commission |
| MS | Manuscript |
| *ODNB* | *Oxford Dictionary of National Biography* |
| *OED* | *Oxford English Dictionary* |
| PRO | Public Record Office |
| RS | Royal Society |

Quotations from manuscript sources are presented according to the principles expounded in Michael Hunter, Antonio Clericuzio and Lawrence M. Principe (eds), *The Correspondence of Robert Boyle*, 6 vols (London, 2001), vol. 1, pp. xli–xlii, and Michael Hunter and Edward B. Davis (eds), *The Works of Robert Boyle*, 14 vols (London, 1999–2000), vol. 1, p. cii. Briefly, original spelling, capitalisation and punctuation are retained; standard contractions (e.g. the thorn with superscript 'e' for 'the') have been silently expanded. Underlining in the original is shown by the use of italic. Editorial insertions have been denoted by square brackets. Words or phrases inserted above the line in the original have been denoted ‹thus›, and deletions are recorded in separate notes. However, in cases where a full transcription is already available in print, insertions and deletions have sometimes been silently ignored.

# THE SUPERNATURAL, SCIENCE AND 'ATHEISM'

## *Background*

The time is ripe for a detailed re-examination of 'The Decline of Magic', or what has sometimes been described as 'the disenchantment of the world' or 'the elimination of magic from the world'. The latter phrases represent alternative translations of the concept that Max Weber expressed in German as 'Entzauberung der Welt' in his famous book, *The Protestant Ethic and the Spirit of Capitalism* (1905; English translation, 1930); it forms part of his broader claims for the ideological and cultural impact of the Reformation which continue to be discussed.[1] The phrase that precedes them and that forms the title of this book has been popularised above all by Keith Thomas in his groundbreaking study, *Religion and the Decline of Magic: Studies in Popular Beliefs in Sixteenth- and Seventeenth-century England* (1971).[2] In many ways that classic work provides the starting point for the current one, which has a good deal in common with Thomas's, including its terms of reference – though with some variations. Thus this book, like that one, concentrates on Britain, largely eschewing discussion of developments elsewhere in Europe. On the other hand, it differs from *Religion and the Decline of Magic* in dealing not only with England and (to a lesser extent) Wales, but also with Scotland, principally in connection with the phenomenon of second sight, the uncanny ability of certain individuals to foresee future events, to which a whole chapter is here devoted.

The book also adopts a similar definition of 'magic' to Thomas's. This comprises supposed intercourse with forces and powers above the course of nature, which it was thought possible for adepts to manipulate and control. At the core of Thomas's book, and occupying the largest part of its content, is a comprehensive account of witchcraft, the supposed ability of individuals to cause harm to others by supernatural means, along with the 'white magic' which was believed to provide a more beneficial complement to this, and the activities of the 'cunning folk' who purveyed the healing and divinatory powers involved. In addition, Thomas considered various ancillary beliefs presupposing intercourse with the spiritual realm, involving prophecies, ghosts, apparitions and fairies, while he also paid attention to omens, lucky times and other concepts dismissed as 'superstitious' by Enlightenment commentators.[3] It is with changing attitudes to beliefs like these that this book is concerned.

By comparison, it has rather less to say about a further belief system to which Thomas gave attention, namely astrology. In this respect, I have followed the prevailing historiography of more recent years, which has tended to eschew Thomas's pioneering breadth of focus, astrology instead being predominantly studied separately from witchcraft and related beliefs:[4] this arguably reflects the extent to which both the practice and the trajectory of that art followed separate lines from the other forms of magic with which Thomas was concerned, even if there was an element of overlap between the two. Though attitudes to astrology will feature from time to time in this book, especially in Chapter 3, I have not pursued my earlier studies of the topic at length here; instead I hope to do so separately at a later date.[5] Much the same is true of alchemy, a further set of related ideas at which Thomas merely glanced, although the subject has been of absorbing interest to many historians. Again, the topic is here referred to briefly, particularly in relation to Robert Boyle, in connection with whom I have written extensively on this topic;[6] but I have again largely eschewed detailed discussion of what is a rather separate field of study.

Thomas's work gives a brilliant and exhaustive survey of all his principal themes, providing an extraordinary insight into commonplace attitudes and activities in early modern England that had previously rarely formed the subject of scholarly study. He illustrates just how pervasive at all levels of society was belief in a universe teeming with forces and powers above the course of nature. He also lays stress (as his title implies) on the relationship between such beliefs and the religious ideas which were so predominant in every aspect of life in the period: indeed, the section entitled 'Religion' in his book occupies as many pages as that on 'Witchcraft'. On the other hand, Thomas's account of magic's 'decline' is surprisingly perfunctory. Only two chapters of *Religion and the Decline of Magic* are devoted to this topic, comprising just forty-two pages out of a book that runs to over seven hundred.[7] In this connection, it is perhaps salutary to recall that the work seems to have acquired its memorable title at a surprisingly late stage in its preparation. In the influential study, *Witchcraft in Tudor and Stuart England*, by Thomas's pupil, Alan Macfarlane, published in 1970, just one year before *Religion and the Decline of Magic*, Thomas's forthcoming work is referred to with the title: 'Primitive Beliefs in Pre-Industrial England'. It might be felt that, despite its slightly crude edge, this better describes the work's content than does the more evocative title that it subsequently acquired.[8]

Hence, although Thomas had no doubt that the eighteenth century saw increased scepticism about the beliefs and practices that had flourished earlier, describing this change as 'the most baffling aspect of this difficult subject', he arguably did less to explore why it occurred than he might have done.[9] It is as if, by illustrating the vitality of magical beliefs in early modern England to a greater extent than any previous historian, Thomas created a problem for himself in accounting for their decline which he had not anticipated when he embarked on his work. Moreover, the section dealing with their demise is not only slightly perfunctory but arguably also disappointingly inconclusive, with intellectual and technological factors left in the balance against 'new aspirations'. Concerning this section of the book, one's views might oscillate – like those of its early reviewers – between admiration for a brilliantly succinct synthesis and a sense of inadequacy and incompleteness.[10]

Since the publication of *Religion and the Decline of Magic*, the issue of how and why attitudes to magic changed has received a certain amount of attention. The leading tendency has been to stress that, at a popular level, such beliefs did not decline until much later, a point at which Thomas merely glanced.[11] Authors like Owen Davies have illustrated how central magical ideas and practices remained to the culture of the people throughout the eighteenth and nineteenth centuries and even into the twentieth.[12] Whereas in studying the period before 1700, Thomas effectively used the term 'popular beliefs' to denote ideas and attitudes shared by people from all walks of life, since the late 1970s historians have become increasingly aware of a greater bifurcation between educated and popular culture than hitherto, and magic clearly remained central to the latter long after it had been marginalised in the former.[13] Indeed, the most significant moment of transition as far as popular belief is concerned may have been the advent of universal education and the centralisation brought about by the railways in the late nineteenth century.

Yet Thomas was undoubtedly right that, as far as educated opinion was concerned, the eighteenth century saw an increased scepticism about magical phenomena, and others have tackled this issue since the appearance of his book. In particular, Ian Bostridge in *Witchcraft and its Transformations, c. 1650–c. 1750* (1997), offered an essentially political reading of the crucial changes that occurred, seeing witch beliefs as being discredited above all by their association with High Church Toryism during the Rage of Party in the early eighteenth century.[14] There have been echoes of Bostridge's views in other writings on the subject, both prior to the publication of his book and more recently.[15] However, as I will be arguing in the course of this volume, Bostridge's reading is flawed, not least because he completely ignores the role of freethinkers and Deists in pioneering scepticism about magic – something which, as this book will show, is crucial.[16]

Other approaches have been more intellectualist, particularly in the context of the history of science. Thus in a recent study focused on the learned magical traditions of the Renaissance, Brian Copenhaver has addressed the issue of the changes that occurred in the seventeenth and eighteenth centuries, giving particular attention to transformations in metaphysical ideas and also commenting on the changing role of alchemy, a topic that has been the subject of profuse study in its own right.[17] Others have sought to give an account of broader changes in attitude through an almost exclusive reliance on published treatises on related topics by contemporary intellectuals.[18] Here, by contrast, an attempt is made to use a wide range of printed and manuscript sources of different kinds to give a subtler sense of the processes by which intellectual and cultural change occurred. This bears some resemblance to the chosen method of Keith Thomas in *Religion and the Decline of Magic*, but it contrasts with that work in its detailed attention to individual cases, thereby fulfilling the wish of one of Thomas's earliest commentators, E. P. Thompson, who regretted the book's lack of case studies, its denial of 'the space for micro-study, and for exploring the inwardness – and the irregularities as well as regularities – of the evidence'.[19]

It is, of course, nearly fifty years since the publication of Thomas's classic work, and during that time studies of the earlier period on which he mainly concentrated have flourished. Almost every aspect of magical belief and practice has been the subject of intense scrutiny during recent decades, from the worldviews of intellectuals who reflected deeply on magic and its philosophical and theological implications, to the level of village beliefs and the social dynamics that underlay witchcraft accusations.[20] In particular, our understanding of the literature of witchcraft, the erudite treatises of what was known as 'demonology', has been transformed by the magisterial work of Stuart Clark, *Thinking with Demons: The Idea of Witchcraft in Early Modern Europe* (1997). This offers a profound analysis of the integral way in which approaches to witchcraft dovetailed with every aspect of the thought of the period, be it theology, politics or scholastic views of nature; this means that Clark even questions whether 'demonology' is an appropriate label for the subject matter of his book at all.[21]

As Clark makes clear in his book, witchcraft and related beliefs raised deep questions about the relationship between God and the natural world, which were intensively debated during the Middle Ages and the early modern period. Similar issues had, of course, arisen even earlier, in classical antiquity, when popular beliefs in supernatural intervention in the world were widely dismissed as 'superstitious' by intellectuals who presumed that everything in the universe formed part of 'nature'.[22] Such debates took on a new potency in the aftermath of the rise of Christianity, when it became axiomatic that, through miracles and other supernatural interventions in the world, God might pursue his purposes by interrupting the ordinary course of nature, and from the thirteenth century onwards intense debate occurred as to just how the supernatural and natural were properly to be defined.[23] In this context a new, intermediate category of the 'preternatural' emerged, describing phenomena that appeared to be above nature yet were not truly supernatural, including many strange phenomena associated with witchcraft. There was much debate as to what events should be assigned to which category, particularly the machinations of the Devil and his ancillary demons, which formed an equally central part of the Christian worldview – including the Devil's notorious ability to trick and seduce vulnerable mortals. This went along with a tradition of 'natural magic', which dealt with phenomena that existed in nature but could not be explained according to the terms of reference of scholastic natural philosophy.[24] The result of the debates that occurred on such subjects was to raise some quite acute epistemological issues, and it has even been argued that the literature of demonology itself reflected a reaction to a 'crisis of belief' among late medieval thinkers.[25]

The Reformation obviously had a major impact on ideas in this area, as was classically explored by Keith Thomas in *Religion and the Decline of Magic*. The Protestant stress on the supremacy of scripture cast doubt on many of the beliefs and practices of medieval Catholicism, which were commonly derided by the Reformers as superstitious and implicitly magical. Indeed, Max Weber in the study already cited argued that the Reformation brought about a complete change in people's religious priorities, encouraging

a 'this-worldly asceticism' that was at odds with the ethos of medieval
Catholicism and that encouraged a wide-ranging pragmatism in many areas
of life. Hardly less significant in the context of attitudes to magic was the
doctrine of the cessation of miracles which became predominant among
Protestant intellectuals during the sixteenth century.[26] Indeed, this opened
up a significant gulf between Protestant and Catholic thought on related
topics since, although Protestant thinkers attached great significance to the
miracles recorded in the Bible, they were adamant that God no longer chose
to exercise his power by such means.[27] This radically reduced the extent to
which God could be seen as responsible for one-off interventions in the
world, in contrast to the state of affairs in biblical and early Christian times;
instead, he was seen as having an ongoing, more general supervisory role
through the doctrine of providence.[28] Yet at a popular level less changed than
devoted Reformers would have liked: it seems likely that their attempts to
expel practices that they perceived as magical from the church led to a flour-
ishing of a kind of magical counterculture, while the insistence on the impossibility of miracles seems also to have been more effectual in theory than in
practice.[29] Even rites such as the 'royal touch', the ability of English monarchs
to cure scrofula by the laying on of hands accompanied by prayer, not only
survived the Reformation but flourished in a Tudor and Stuart context.[30]

In any case, the more radical forms of revolt against traditional
Christianity that flourished in Germany and the Netherlands in the sixteenth
century, and in England especially in the aftermath of the Civil War, had
rather different implications.[31] Sometimes this led to an even more extreme
rejection of practices perceived as superstitious than that of more mainstream Protestants.[32] But in parallel with this, sects such as the Anabaptists
or the Ranters routinely invoked the possibility of direct intercourse between
God and the individual believer in a manner that seemed illicit or dangerous
to more conservative thinkers; radical Protestant thinkers also sometimes
showed a sympathy towards magical practices that disconcerted the
orthodox.[33] In addition, polarisations arose between moderate and radical
Protestants over the likelihood of the Devil's active intervention in the
world, not least through 'possessing' people: this was reflected in notorious
cases where Puritans claimed the ability to exorcise the victims of such
attacks in a manner which often bore a surprising resemblance to Roman
Catholic attempts along similar lines.[34]

In intellectual terms there were parallel developments, some of them
stemming from the Renaissance which predated the Reformation and which

encouraged the revival of ideas from classical antiquity that had been lost or distorted during the Middle Ages and which challenged the Aristotelian synthesis that had dominated medieval thought. Among the most important were the neo-Platonic ideas championed by such savants as Marsilio Ficino, including the cult of Hermes Trismegistus, believed to be an ancient sage possessed of immense magical power which those who read and absorbed his writings might be able to emulate.[35] There were also novel cosmologies, like that of the Swiss iatrochemist Paracelsus, that attacked not only the views of Aristotle and the scholastics but also the views of Galen and his followers, which in many ways provided the medical equivalent of scholasticism: Galen saw the human body as comprising four humours which it was the task of the physician to keep in their correct balance by appropriate therapeutic means, usually through expelling surplus fluids from the body by bleeding or purging. By contrast, Paracelsus and his followers argued that specific medications were more effective in curing illnesses than the attention to bodily make-up as a whole that characterised the Galenists, a challenge with momentous consequences.[36] Many of the medicaments that the Paracelsians championed were made from mineral and other substances, the efficacy of which could be experientially demonstrated, thus giving a novel, empirical dimension to views of nature. In addition, theirs and other Renaissance worldviews were often strongly vitalist in tone, taking for granted the existence of hidden powers both within and above nature which the adept might be able to understand and harness. Hence at this point science itself became strongly magical, as is exemplified by the worldviews of such leading figures as John Dee in Elizabethan England.[37] Moreover the influence of such ideas remained powerful throughout the seventeenth century and even beyond.

Not surprisingly, all this resulted in polemics in the sixteenth and seventeenth centuries which form part of the background to this book. Protestantism encouraged some bold attacks on aspects of both Catholic and sectarian practices which have resonances with the critiques of magic by writers of the late seventeenth and early eighteenth centuries that we will encounter in later chapters. For instance the Anglican cleric, Samuel Harsnett, was scathing about the exorcisms that were practised in late Elizabethan England by Catholic priests and by the Puritan, John Darrell. Indeed, he was cited in this connection by Francis Hutchinson in his *Historical Essay concerning Witchcraft* (1718), who seems to have been rather fascinated by Harsnett and who noted how his predecessor 'both disproved and ridiculed these Follies

with greater Freedom than I have ventur'd to make use of'.[38] A further striking
case is that of the Kentish gentleman, Reginald Scot, whose *Discoverie of
Witchcraft* (1584) presented a systematic attack on magical beliefs and practices as at once popish and dependent on fraud and deception which typified
sceptical attitudes on such subjects and which remained unsurpassed for
over a century.[39]

Equally significant was the assault that reached its climax in mid-
seventeenth-century England on what was described as 'enthusiasm', in
other words on the extremes of the appeal to the promptings of the spirit
which were at odds with the more sober and rationalistic approaches to the
spiritual that prevailed in orthodox circles.[40] Initially, the critique of enthusiasm was primarily theological, stressing the overriding importance of
scriptural authority in response to such inspirational claims, which were
often attributed to the influence of the Devil. But in the hands particularly
of Anglican thinkers like Henry More and Meric Casaubon in the 1650s, a
different but equally powerful critique was forged which saw the appeal to
the direct promptings of the spirit and the rejection of religious authority as
reflecting a kind of mental disorder, which was alternately derided and
condemned. Moreover, this often overlapped with a critique of the magical
tendencies in the study of the natural world that had come to the fore since
the sixteenth century, in which both More and Casaubon participated.[41] The
roots of this mindset lay in the ideas of classical antiquity, and particularly
in the concept of 'melancholy' which had originated then and was elaborated by early modern thinkers, notably Robert Burton in his famous work,
*The Anatomy of Melancholy* (1621). The thrust of the argument was encapsulated in the title of Casaubon's book, first published in 1655: *A Treatise
concerning Enthusiasme. As it is an Effect of Nature: but is Mistaken by Many
for either Divine Inspiration, or Diabolicall Possession*. In his and More's
hands, this critique proved extraordinarily effective, and it continued to be
powerful up to the time of Jonathan Swift and even later.

In the hands of such protagonists the argument against enthusiasm took
on a broader philosophical veneer, but at heart it was essentially medical,
taking for granted a 'natural' state of the human body and mind which, it
was claimed, had become disrupted in enthusiasts. It thus drew on conceptions of the human body and its proper treatment that again take us back to
the legacy of classical antiquity, and particularly the ideas of Hippocrates,
who flourished in the fifth century BC, which were subsequently greatly
elaborated by Galen in the early Christian period. This basically holistic

view, which we have already encountered in connection with the Paracelsian challenge to it, took it for granted that health depended on a proper balance between the component forces which the body comprised, classically expressed through the doctrine of the four humours. Illness occurred when the balance was disrupted, and the task of the physician was to restore it by such treatments as purging or bleeding. Explanatory power was added to the system by acknowledging that the appropriate humoral balance varied between different people, so that every case had to be individually assessed, while attention was also paid to the effects of diet, of sleep and exercise, and of the environment. It was an extraordinarily capacious and satisfying system of ideas, and it is not surprising that it remained the basis of attitudes to health and medicine throughout the period covered by this book and beyond: traces of a kind of folk humoralism have been found even in the present day, while our everyday usage of concepts like 'temperament' bears witness to its continuing legacy.[42]

Moreover, within this period such ideas were marshalled in relation to magical beliefs not only by opponents of enthusiasm like More and Casaubon but also by medical men. It was a short step for those used to diagnosing bodily ailments in terms of physiological malfunction to argue for comparable explanations of phenomena that others attributed to the influence of the Devil or to supernatural forces. One figure who has long been acclaimed as a pioneer in this regard is the sixteenth-century Flemish physician, Johann Weyer, whose relatively naturalistic approach to witchcraft was once acclaimed as proto-modern, though such claims have since been modified.[43] More revealing have been the studies of Michael MacDonald, including his detailed account of the practice of the astrological physician, Richard Napier, in which there was a tension between a belief in the likelihood of diabolical influence, which he shared with his clients, and an underlying naturalism of Galenic origin.[44] Equally telling is the role of Edward Jorden in the case of the supposed possession of Mary Glover in 1602, when Jorden took a notably naturalistic line towards the symptoms thought to characterise demonic possession, which he attributed to the effects of hysteria.[45] Such attitudes sometimes even led to medical men being accused of being abnormally prone to irreligion, though this was balanced by the writings of many doctors that were notably pious in tone.[46] Again, we see the elements of tension and complexity that were to be found within the legacy of Renaissance and early modern ideas on magic and related phenomena.

## The Scientific Revolution and the Supernatural

This therefore brings us to the so-called Scientific Revolution and its role in the developments with which we are here concerned – a complicated matter, as will become apparent throughout this book. Two developments, however, were undoubtedly crucial. One was the rise of the inductive philosophy championed by Francis Bacon, Lord Verulam, who gave a methodological structure to the inchoate empiricism that had already begun to flourish in the Middle Ages and more notably in the sixteenth century. Insisting on the need to reject a priori systems like that of scholastic natural philosophy and advocating that knowledge should instead be empirically reformulated, Bacon urged that systematic 'natural histories' should be built up which would form the basis of a reliable philosophy of nature: in his words, these were 'the primary matter of philosophy, and the basic stuff and raw material of true induction'.[47] The Baconian ethos became extraordinarily influential in seventeenth-century Britain, among a wide range of thinkers, its most celebrated advocates being members of the circle of Samuel Hartlib in the Interregnum and of the Royal Society after the Restoration. The breadth of its appeal is indicated by the fact that even a divine like John Lightfoot declared himself 'very much in love' with Bacon's method, '& labour to apply it to as many things as I can: to gather experiments & matter of fact'.[48] In the Restoration period, an increasingly sophisticated version of Bacon's methodology was developed, particularly by Robert Boyle, perhaps the most influential natural philosopher of his day (Plate 6). Boyle expounded in detail the way in which Bacon's strictures on data-collecting should be applied, in doing so helping to lay the conceptual foundations for modern experimental science.[49]

More will be said about Boyle's Baconianism in Chapter 6, but equally important for him and for many contemporaries was the rise of the mechanical philosophy, the claim that everything in nature could be explained in terms of the interaction of matter and motion. There were various versions of this, including the Epicurean ideas from antiquity that were revived at this time, but the most influential was that of René Descartes, expounded most fully in his *Principia philosophiae* (*Principles of Philosophy*) of 1644. In this work, Descartes offered explanations in terms of the combination and motion of particles of matter for a vast range of phenomena, from the power of a magnet to the movements of the planets, the corollary being that a similar explanation could be furnished for everything in the universe. It was a simple yet exhilarating doctrine, and it was taken up by thinkers in Britain from the

1650s onwards as an antidote to the account of nature provided by scholasticism, with its complicated system of 'forms', 'qualities' and different types of causation. Moreover, whereas Descartes' own mechanical constructions were often rather a priori, Boyle and others with a more empirical bent sought to give them an experimental basis: thus, in his *Origin of Forms and Qualities* and his experimental histories of colours and cold, published between 1664 and 1666, Boyle sought to prove that the mechanical hypothesis made better sense of observed data than did the obfuscation of scholastic doctrine.[50]

What was the implication of the mechanical philosophy for magic? On the face of it, it might seem likely that it would banish it from the world more systematically than ever before.[51] It is certainly true that it enforced a stricter demarcation between mind and matter than had previously existed. Descartes himself was a dualist, believing that a separate spiritual realm existed in parallel with the material world in which the mechanical philosophy held sway. Moreover it was perfectly possible for mechanical philosophers to believe in the existence of a separate, supernatural sphere, over and above that to which the laws of nature applied. Indeed, Baconians like Boyle even believed that it might be possible to provide empirical proof of its existence. This was the thrust of a section of one of his most Baconian books, *Experimenta et Observationes Physicae* (*Physical Experiments and Observations*), which he began to publish in 1691, right at the end of his life, although its conception can be traced earlier. The component in question was entitled *Strange Reports*, and the first instalment of this, included in the 1691 volume, was restricted to 'things purely Natural', bizarre phenomena that could nevertheless be explained according to natural principles (effectively the realm of the 'preternatural'). On the other hand, Boyle planned a sequel, which would have appeared in a subsequent volume had the project not been interrupted by his death, and this would have been devoted to '*Phænomena*, that are, or seem to be, of a Supernatural Kind or Order'.[52]

Boyle's motives in compiling it are clear from the sections of its prefatory material of which a Latin translation survives, until recently only in manuscript. Boyle there explained how

I am well aware that we live in an age when men of judgment consider it their part to greet a report of supernatural phenomena with contempt and derision, particularly when these phenomena are spiritual apparitions and the unusual communication of rational creatures with rational creatures that do not belong to the human race.

He continued by justifying his collection of empirical examples of such occurrences on the grounds that

> if the recounted phenomena are extraordinary rather than supernatural, the naturalist will more thoroughly investigate their cause, and a new philosophical light will dawn. But if he observes some phenomena that are above nature, there will arise the humbler consideration that there are objects beyond the grasp even of a philosopher in this life, and that some truths are not explicable by the powers of matter and motion, which truth is indeed of great importance in this age, when the Epicureans use the notions of their philosophy to reject everything that is contrary to it.[53]

It is striking, and rather strange to us, how Boyle uses the Baconian ethos of natural history to argue for magical phenomena as above nature, inexplicable, and a kind of bridge to God.

We know quite a lot about the intended content of the work, which Boyle had been collecting for some years, including stories of supernatural occurrences among indigenous peoples in Africa and North America which were translated into Latin alongside the preface.[54] A putative contents list shows that the book would have included accounts of other phenomena which Boyle similarly believed to be above nature, among them reports about second sight in Scotland, a topic in which Boyle had taken a pioneering interest which turned out to be surprisingly influential in subsequent years and about which we will hear more in Chapter 6.[55] It is also revealing that in his workdiaries, the notes that Boyle kept on experiments he made and information that he received from others, he specifically refers to requests that he made to explorers whom he met, such as Pierre-Esprit Radisson, 'to tell me freely whether he had observd any thing of supernaturall among the savages he had conversd with', and a number of such stories are there recorded.[56] In addition, it seems likely that he would have drawn on evidence from the alchemical investigations in which he was engaged, which seemed to provide evidence of a kind of intermediate sphere between the natural and the supernatural.[57]

There is other evidence of such concerns on Boyle's part. One of the first publications with which he had been associated in the 1650s had been an account by his protégé, Peter du Moulin, of a famous poltergeist case, *The Devil of Mascon*.[58] Thereafter, although such subjects are not treated at length in Boyle's published *oeuvre*, they are frequently alluded to as matters that he took for granted. For instance, in his *Free Enquiry into the Vulgarly Received Notion of Nature* (1686), he referred to the 'supernatural Revelations and Discoveries [God] has made of Himself, and of His particular care of His Creatures, by Prophecies, Apparitions, true Miracles, and other ways, that transcend the Power, or overthrow, or, at least, over-rule the Physical Laws of Motion in Matter'. Similarly, in his *Some Considerations about the Reconcileableness of Reason and Religion* (1675), he wrote: 'though we ought to be exceeding wary, how we admit what pretends to be supernaturally reveal'd; yet if it be attended with sufficient evidence of its being so, we do very much wrong and prejudice our selves, if out of an unreasonable jealousie, or, to acquire or maintain the repute of being wiser than others, we shut our eyes against the light it offers'.[59]

In his conviction of the reality of supernatural phenomena and his belief that they could be empirically demonstrated, Boyle had a precursor in the Cambridge philosopher, Henry More (Plate 4). This is seen particularly in a book that More published in 1653 entitled *An Antidote against Atheism*. Book II of this work comprises a summary of the design argument – the claim that the intricacy and purposefulness of the natural world irrefutably proved the existence of God – which may be seen as the precursor of the famous work by the naturalist John Ray, *The Wisdom of God Manifested in the Works of the Creation* (1691).[60] Book III of More's *Antidote*, however, presents a complementary argument in favour of God's existence against those who doubted it, in the form of a lengthy series of detailed accounts of events which More believed could not be explained by natural means – 'supernatural' phenomena, as he sometimes describes them. As he explained at the outset:

> Hitherto I have insisted upon such Arguments for the proving of the *Existence of God*, as were taken from the ordinary and known *Phænomena* of *Nature*; For such is the History of *Plants, Animalls* and *Man*. I shall come now to such effects discovered in the World as are not deemed *naturall*, but *extraordinary* and *miraculous*.[61]

This was followed by accounts of witchcraft, apparitions, magical transformations and other supernatural phenomena, most of them taken from books though a few derived from the oral accounts of informants whom More himself interviewed. Some scholars have been rather disdainful of this exercise on More's part, but his enterprise was not without sophistication.[62] In selecting material for his 'natural history' of the supernatural, he gave clear criteria as to what accounts should be included and what should not – that there should be multiple witnesses, that those involved should have no 'interest' in the event, and that there should be tangible outcomes.[63] His sensitivity about the empirical methodology to which he was appealing is also revealed by the fact that he actually withdrew some instances and corrected his account of others in subsequent editions of the work, deploying similar practices in later writings on related topics.[64]

Equally significant is the case of the cleric and writer, Joseph Glanvill (Plate 5). Both Boyle and More encouraged Glanvill in the compilation of a collection of 'supernatural phænomena' (in Boyle's words)[65] which was ulti-mately to materialise as *Saducismus Triumphatus*, published under More's editorship in 1681, a year after Glanvill's premature death (Plate 1). ('Sadducism' is the word used to describe scepticism about the reality of spiritual beings, derived from the Sadducees of the New Testament – Acts 23:8 – so the title means 'scepticism triumphed over'.) More will be said about the genesis of this work in Chapter 4, which deals in detail with the famous poltergeist case known as the 'Drummer of Tedworth', which seems first to have stimu-lated Glanvill's interest in the subject. Initially, Glanvill wrote a brief tract entitled *A Philosophical Endeavour Towards the Defence of the Being of Witches and Apparitions* (1666), reprinted the following year as *Some Philosophical Considerations Touching the Being of Witches and Witchcraft*, but this was superseded in 1668 by a fuller version that included his account of the Tedworth case, entitled *A Blow at Modern Sadducism*, which went into two editions.[66] One component of Glanvill's book was an essay which sought to defend witch-craft in terms of the epistemology of the new science, arguing that it was unrea-sonable to deny '*matters of fact*' on a priori grounds by analogy with our nescience as to how other, provable phenomena occur:

> We cannot conceive how the *Fœtus* is form'd in the *Womb*, nor as much
> as how a *Plant* springs from the *Earth* we tread on . . . And if we are *igno-*
> *rant* of the most *obvious* things about us, and the most *considerable*
> *within* our selves, 'tis then no wonder that we know not the *constitution*
> and *powers* of the *Creatures*, to whom we are such strangers.[67]

This, however, was combined with an increasingly long series of accounts of witchcraft and the like which he perceived as demonstrating the reality of a supernatural realm, in which he enrolled the assistance of a large number of helpers; Glanvill justified this on the grounds that such empirical accounts comprised '*the proofs that come nearest the* sence'.[68] Judging by the dates of the 'Relations' that he and More received, this task began in the 1660s and continued through the 1670s, coming to fruition as *Saducismus Triumphatus* in 1681.[69]

Perhaps unsurprisingly, the evidence of supernatural phenomena as an anti-atheist argument was also invoked by More's colleague, Ralph Cudworth, in a passage in his *True Intellectual System of the Universe* (1678).[70] More revealing is the fact that Isaac Barrow, a rather different Cambridge figure who was professor of mathematics as well as an eminent churchman, devoted an entire sermon to 'The Being of God proved from supernatural Effects', in which, in addition to biblical prophecies and miracles, he also invoked 'apparitions from another world, as it were, of beings unusual', 'spirits haunting persons and places', 'all sorts of entercourse and confederacy, formal or virtual, with bad spirits' and 'the power of enchantments, implying the co-operation of invisible powers'.[71] Others engaged in similar enterprises, for instance the Presbyterian divine, Richard Baxter, in his *The Certainty of the Worlds of Spirits* (1691) – though this is more devotional in tone than the works so far described – or, to cross the Atlantic, Increase Mather in his *Essay for the Recording of Illustrious Providences* (1684), which retails a variety of similar phenomena.[72] An equally striking example is provided in Scotland by the Glasgow professor, George Sinclair, who not only produced an equivalent to Glanvill's *Saducismus Triumphatus* in his *Satans Invisible World Discovered* (1685), but had earlier devoted a section of a scientific treatise, his *Hydrostaticks* (1672), to an account of 'The Devil of *Dunluce*', the case of a house afflicted by diabolical assaults. Sinclair specifically stated in the subtitle to *Satans Invisible World* that his aim was of 'proving evidently against the *Saducees* and *Atheists* of this present Age, that there are *Devils, Spirits, Witches,* and *Apparitions*' through the use of 'Authentick Records' and 'Attestations of Famous Witnesses'.[73]

This is therefore indicative of the importance that leading natural philosophers and others in the late seventeenth century attached to the enterprise of providing empirical proof of a supernatural realm. It is all the more notable because it transcended the undoubted tensions that existed among such figures. Sinclair sparred with both Boyle and More over the interpretation of pneumatic data,[74] while equally notable were the differing reactions of the leading supernaturalists to the mechanistic theories that had been put forward, especially by Descartes. Thus More and Cudworth postulated a 'Spirit of Nature' or 'Plastick Nature', a kind of spiritual substance at work in the world which (in Cudworth's words) 'as an Inferior and Subordinate Instrument, doth Drudgingly Execute that Part of [God']s Providence, which consists in the Regular and Orderly Motion of Matter'.[75] In More's case, this hypothesis became increasingly overt in his writings, and in his *Enchiridion metaphysicum* (1671) he actually had the temerity to try to interpret Boyle's experimental findings in terms of it. Boyle reacted angrily to this, and he wrote a book-length refutation of More's interpretations. In Boyle's view, purely mechanical explanations adequately accounted for the phenomena of nature, even if these at times became increasingly attenuated to do justice to the full complexity of the world.[76] Indeed, he wrote a whole book about the proper conception of nature, his *Free Enquiry into the Vulgarly Received Notion of Nature*, in which concepts like More's were questioned.[77] On the other hand, it is worth stressing that their disagreement was about how to interpret the ordinary workings of nature: it was this that More's and Cudworth's hypothesis sought to explain just as Boyle's more rigorously mechanical theories did, and this was tangential to the issue of the existence of a supernatural realm that they could agree existed beyond it, their unanimity in trying to prove which therefore becomes all the more striking.

It is also important to note that by no means all in late seventeenth-century scientific circles were supportive of efforts like those of Glanvill and Boyle. As we will see in Chapter 3, the Royal Society as a corporate body was distinctly unhelpful to Glanvill on such issues, which it seems to have avoided in its early years due to the lack of consensus within its ranks. It is also worth noting certain authors who might have been expected to evoke supernatural phenomena as well as natural ones in their apologetic work, but who failed to do so. A case in point is John Ray, who shared many aspects of More's and Glanvill's outlook, including the notion of a 'Plastic Nature' active in the world, yet whose *Wisdom of God Manifested in the Works of the Creation* conspicuously avoids the supernatural. This was not because Ray was sceptical about witchcraft and related topics. In one of his rare comments on such subjects, he made clear his view that 'those who pervert knowledge to evil arts, or allow themselves to be deluded by the instigation of demons into peering into the secrets of the future, ought to be constrained and condemned with severity'.[78] Similarly, in commenting on a case in Wales in 1694 when haystacks caught fire in an 'unaccountable & miraculous' manner, he seems to have agreed with local people that witchcraft was the likeliest explanation – notwithstanding the rather disingenuous attempt to place a sceptical gloss on his comments by his biographer, Canon Raven.[79] Clearly it was not the case that Ray did not believe in such things, but he evidently did not consider them appropriate material for apologetics as Boyle and More did.

## 'Atheism' and its Significance

Why, however, was so much intellectual effort invested in this period in the task of opposing the threat of irreligion, whether by using purely natural evidence, as with Ray, or by making compilations of phenomena deemed to be 'supernatural', as with Boyle and Glanvill? More, who combined the two in his contribution to the enterprise, *An Antidote against Atheism*, neatly summarised the matter in his title, and this therefore raises the question of just what such authors meant by 'atheism', and why it caused them such concern. Undoubtedly, a great many books were published at the time which professed 'atheism' as their target. But does this mean that atheists in a modern sense actually existed in the late seventeenth century? If not, can we use the discourse of 'atheism' as a means of probing at preoccupations of thinkers of the day that would otherwise be ill-evidenced? These are, of course, issues that have exercised many scholars and on which very varied opinions have been expressed.[80] Their relevance to the topic dealt with in this book will become apparent over the following pages.

One possibility is that 'atheism' was an empty slur with no real meaning, which was used simply to discredit opponents in debate. It is true that a polemical element often entered into such characterisations, but they depended on a shared perception of the meaning of the concept, and many at the time would have agreed with the divine, John Edwards, in criticising 'some deluded People who are apt to censure all as *Atheists* that are not of their way'.[81] Related to this is the argument that 'atheism' was essentially an intellectual construct, used in a polemical context as a means of discrediting an opponent, often by drawing out logical implications of his argument of which he himself was unaware. This approach has been brilliantly deployed by Alan Kors in relation to late seventeenth- and early eighteenth-century France, where he has argued that a whole armoury of atheist arguments was forged by orthodox thinkers in the course of employing such tactics, leading to a degree of fratricide which itself did much to discredit religion and sow doubt about it.[82] In an English context, the matter was nicely put by the divine, Thomas Barlow, in a letter to Robert Boyle in which he discussed the assertion by another cleric, John Turner, that Descartes was an atheist (a claim often made at the time, which was as often refuted). As Barlow put it, 'I suppose he does not meane, that Des Cartes is a profess'd Atheist, soe as to deny the beeinge of a Deity; but that it will follow from his avowed principles, that there is noe God'.[83] Undoubtedly much discussion of 'atheism' was conducted along such lines, and it is therefore a rather futile exercise to try to determine whether any particular thinker was or was not a 'real' atheist; the earliest British thinker to admit to being one was Matthew Turner in 1782.[84]

But, since contemporary authors often used the concept of 'atheism' in a generic and descriptive way, the question arises of what one can learn from their usage about aspects of contemporary thought and practice that caused them concern and to which they considered it appropriate to apply this label. A related question is whether there were milieux in which they considered such opinions as likeliest to be openly and ostentatiously voiced, even if comparable views and attitudes were more widespread and insidious. It seems to me that both questions can be answered in the affirmative and that, by pursuing them, one can learn much about the tendencies in contemporary culture and ideas that caused concern among more orthodox thinkers. Let us therefore start by briefly considering the characteristics and milieu of 'atheism' as outlined by contemporaries, combining the remarks of Boyle and Glanvill with those of other, similar commentators, including those who gave sermons as part of the Boyle Lectures, the apologetic initiative founded in 1692 under a provision in Boyle's will.

Obviously, 'atheism' was first and foremost associated with the denial of the existence of God, either directly or by implication. It was taken for granted that such unbelief would be sustained by views – often materialistic – of a natural world that had originated without a beneficent creator and in which God's activity was limited or completely absent. Here we see the influence of the Renaissance revival of ideas from classical antiquity, in particular the strong naturalism of Epicurus and others, which was widely viewed as either explicitly or implicitly atheistic. But the atheist's repertoire was also seen as comprising other arguments, including some derived from such sources like a denial of the immortality of the soul and of any absolute morality; or a scepticism about the text of the Bible, often based on its supposed internal inconsistencies; or the opinion – which orthodox polemicists repeatedly tried to turn back on itself – that religion had first been introduced as '*a meer politick Contrivance*'. Indeed, all sorts of arguments were commonly associated with 'atheists'. One Boyle lecturer, Francis Gastrell, took the view 'that the *present Atheism* is a *promiscuous Miscellany* of *all the bold notions* that have *ever* been vented by those they stile Free-thinkers', and this perceived heterogeneity is significant in itself.[85]

Such breadth of argument was linked to another perceived characteristic of 'atheists', that they were intellectually shallow, grasping at an assortment of doctrines that they only partially understood. Boyle considered them 'men that have more Confidence than Knowledge', 'conversant but about the superficial parts of things, and will seldom allow themselves the patience, and perhaps have not alwayes the Capacity, to penetrate into and enable themselves to judge of, retir'd and difficult Truths'.[86] Moreover, commentators associated this trait with what they saw as the principal milieu of 'atheism', namely the culture of 'wit', an educated but not learned environment in which superficial cleverness was at a premium. This had originated in literary circles earlier in the seventeenth century, and it was seen as thriving in the fashionable atmosphere of the court and the coffee-houses of Restoration London, thus seeming all the more dangerous for its privileged, cosmopolitan status and its proximity to centres of social and political power (Plate 3).[87] It was 'especially among those that aspired to pass for Wits, and several of them too for Philosophers', that Boyle remarked on 'the great and deplorable Growth of Irreligion' in his day, and it was London, '*this Libertine City*', that he saw as its focus.[88]

A further, related aspect of the perception of 'atheists' was that they were above all 'scoffers'. It was commonly felt that what they lacked in intellectual proficiency they made up for in arrogance and iconoclasm, and sarcasm was repeatedly presented as the commonest way in which they attacked religion. Glanvill captured this in the title of the work that he appended to his *Blow at Modern Sadducism*, entitled *A Whip for the Droll, Fidler to the Atheist: Being Reflections on Drollery & Atheism*. In it, he complained how the quintessential 'wit' 'quickly *jests* at *Scripture*, and makes a *mock* of *sin*, *playes* with *eternal flames*, and *scoffs* at those that *fear* them', and he was echoed half a century later by the Boyle lecturer Samuel Clarke, who urged his 'atheist' opponents to dissociate themselves from 'all mocking and scoffing at Religion, all Jesting and turning Arguments of Reason into Drollery and Ridicule', which he considered 'the most unmanly and unreasonable thing in the World'.[89]

In addition, 'atheists' were seen as dissolute, given over to debauchery and profanity. Contemporaries were convinced that 'atheism' was as pernicious in its practical as in its intellectual manifestations, and they saw the two as inextricably connected. In part, this was due to the fact that atheists were said to succumb to unbelief because immorality gave them an interest in it, thus echoing the argument that they were not open to rational persuasion. Ralph Cudworth, for instance, thought that even 'the *Truth* of *Geometricall Theorems* themselves' could not be sustained against men swayed by 'any *Interest of Life*, any *Concernment* of *Appetite* and *Passion*'.[90] But it was also commonly believed that atheistic views justified immorality, on the grounds that only Christianity, with its promise of a future state of rewards and punishments, enforced virtue and thus guaranteed social stability. Though Pierre Bayle, in his *Miscellaneous Thoughts on the Comet of 1680* (1682), had questioned this view, the orthodox remained unconvinced: indeed, John Harris in his 1698 Boyle Lectures actually sought to refute Bayle's arguments.[91]

What, therefore, is one to make of all this? Undoubtedly the orthodox had incentives to exaggerate both the scale and the homogeneity of the threat that faced them. On the other hand, if their characterisation of it had been wholly unrelated to reality, they would have sacrificed the very appeal to plausibility on which their polemic was grounded. It therefore seems likely that, through a careful exegesis of their characterisation, we may be able to gain significant information about facets of contemporary society and ideas. First, it *does* seem likely that, perhaps particularly in metropolitan circles, it was possible to find groups of people who voiced the questionable views on religion and related topics about which contemporaries complained – whether or not they were true atheists in a modern sense – and who represent a significant element in the culture of the period.

Above all, we here need to introduce the figure of Thomas Hobbes, 'their Great Master and Lawgiver' in the words of John Edwards (Plate 2).[92] Not only was Hobbes responsible for an overtly materialist version of the mechanical philosophy, in contrast to the dualism of Descartes; in addition, especially in his *Leviathan* (1651), he had put forward a cynical, manipulative view of human nature and human institutions which was widely seen as corrosive of religion. To make matters worse, his ideas were seen as dangerously influential in late seventeenth-century Britain, in the form of what was disparagingly described as 'Hobbism'. Indeed, Hobbes himself was seen to abet this, not least due to his 'confidence to talk profanely, which Atheistical persons call Witt'.[93] It is revealing that the 1673 pamphlet *The Character of a Coffee-House, With the Symptomes of a Town-Wit* stated of its 'atheist' protagonist that he 'boasts aloud that he holds his *Gospel* from the *Apostle of Malmsbury*' (an allusion to Hobbes's birthplace) – even though the author disparagingly continued that 'it is more than probable he ne'r read, at least understood *ten* leaves of that *unlucky Author*'.[94] More than anyone else, Hobbes was central to the attitudes with which we are here concerned. But he was not alone. A generation later, a further notorious example is provided by the Deist, John Toland, who also fitted the 'atheist' model due to his manner – his 'insolent conceited way of talking' – and his proclivity to broach serious subjects in irreverent venues like coffee-houses.[95] Equally familiar is the case of the Earl of Rochester, libertine and freethinker, and the circle of court rakes of which he formed part, or, to give a Scottish example, the unfortunate Thomas Aikenhead, executed for his irreligious views in 1697.[96]

If such individuals are well known, however, others are more shadowy. One revealing figure is John Wagstaffe, whom we will encounter in Chapter 1, whose book, *The Question of Witchcraft Debated* (1669), arguably gave printed form to the kind of iconoclastic opinions that were voiced in fashionable circles and that caused the orthodox concern. Other figures expressed their views only through oral interjections rather than written ones, as we will see in later chapters, but they nevertheless contributed to contemporary perceptions of a dangerous threat. Thus Chapter 4 provides a telling instance of the role of ideas verbally expressed in its reconstruction of an otherwise lost dialogue between orthodox spokesmen and the 'wits' over the case of the 'Drummer of Tedworth'. Clearly a vigorous oral culture existed which significantly affected contemporary opinion but which is by definition underrepresented in the printed record. Indeed, here the most telling comment is that of the first Boyle lecturer, Richard Bentley, who opined that: 'Atheism is so much the worse that it is not buried in books; but is gotten εἰς τὸν βίον [into life], that taverns and coffee-houses, nay Westminster-hall and the very churches, are full of it'.[97]

Some modern scholars have been rather dismissive of such a scenario. Thus Philip Harth has remarked in connection with  this putative reaction to heterodox ideas that 'it is unreasonable to suppose that so much concern could be elicited by conversation alone', while the hypothesis that in the early eighteenth century Berkeley's *Alciphron* was partly aimed at arguments voiced orally in coffee-houses has been rather unkindly dismissed as 'an effort to reassure readers that Berkeley had not stooped to caricature'.[98] As we now know, Harth may have been at least partially right to invoke an intermediate domain in the form of texts transmitted in manuscript: but it nevertheless seems crucial, if we are ever fully to understand the intellectual history of the period, to get beyond books and to try to probe at the realm of ideas orally expressed.[99] There is a potential analogy here to the reconstruction of the oral culture of the common people to which much effort has recently been devoted, perhaps particularly by Carlo Ginzburg in *The Cheese and the Worms*.[100] Ginzburg is right to stress the need to give some benefit of the doubt to the existence and vitality of a culture which, just because it was mainly oral, is greatly underrepresented in the sources compared with the written ones with which it coexisted: such strictures are equally applicable to an 'elite' culture of the kind with which we are here concerned. Obviously there are potential pitfalls in postulating the significance of this oral realm, since we are often dependent on the testimony of hostile critics who may or may not be trustworthy. Equally, however, there is potential for evoking a whole world of ideas which would be denied us if we adhered solely to what was written in books.

There is a second point to be made about contemporary perceptions of 'atheism', and this is as follows. Though it does seem to be the case, as later chapters will show, that the most extreme emanations of heterodox opinion – on magic, as on other topics – came from advanced circles such as those identified in the previous paragraphs, it is doubtful whether it is appropriate to restrict contemporary anxiety about 'atheism' to them. Instead, it seems likely that attention focused on such circles because they seemed to epitomise in extreme form tendencies that were more widespread in contemporary society and that caused concern accordingly. Indeed, here there are echoes of the early modern literature on witchcraft, which elaborated an almost entirely imaginary conspiracy against society to which individuals who showed anti-social traits in less extreme form were assimilated; this idealised construct of evil was classically expressed by the inversion of normality represented by the myth of Satan and his dutiful human servants.[101] The 'atheist' stereotype was in various respects comparable, and it therefore seems worth attempting briefly to work out what trends were encapsulated in it.

One was undoubtedly naturalism, in other words the presumption that everything could be explained as an effect of nature which inspired the supernaturalist project of Boyle, More and others by way of reaction. Boyle considered that 'many *Atheists* ascribe so much to *Nature*, that they think it needless to have Recourse to a *Deity*, for the giving an Account of the *Phænomena* of the Universe'.[102] Obviously in a post-Cartesian context it was taken for granted that the natural explanations so invoked were likeliest to comprise some form of the mechanical philosophy. But in addition alternative naturalisms continued to flourish, many of them descended from the vitalist philosophies of the sixteenth century, while, going further back, Aristotelianism itself was fundamentally naturalistic, as was classical thought as a whole – something which is all the more significant considering the profound influence of such ideas in the context of the Enlightenment.

Equally important was the perception of a widespread cynicism, a this-worldliness and a rejection of the extremes of religiosity which had charac-terised the Civil War and its aftermath, which led to everything being assessed according to criteria of self-interest. This was the reaction against enthusiasm taken to an extreme, and it affected even orthodox thinkers of the period, encouraging them to frame their defence of religion in such functionalist terms that they often invited the challenge from their critics that they were Hobbesians themselves. A case in point is the accusation to this effect against prominent clerics like Edward Stillingfleet and John Tillotson, but again this could be seen as a telling characterisation of Enlightenment thought as a whole.[103]

Of other aspects of the 'atheist' stereotype, the association with the 'scoffing' demeanour of the 'wits' has already been noted, and again the idealised image mirrored a broader concern about the satirical and dismis-sive tone of much of the fashionable discourse of late seventeenth-century Britain, epitomised perhaps above all by some of the more extreme emana-tions of Restoration drama. And, linked to this, there is the concern about morals reflected in the accusations of 'practical atheism', a burgeoning liber-tinism which was seen as alarmingly widespread in society and which caused deep concern among the orthodox. John Harris in his Boyle Lectures saw his 'atheists' as likely – even if they refrained from more serious offences – 'to impoverish a Family by Extravagance and Debauchery, to defraud Creditors of their just Debts, or Servants of their Wages, *to Cheat at Play*, to violate one's Neighbour's Bed to gratifie one's own Lust'.[104] This is the back-ground to the crusade for moral reform that formed so important a feature of the public discourse of the period.[105]

Here, it may be added that the concern about 'sadducism' and its preva-lence may be seen as a further example of the way in which the extreme, 'atheist' stereotype encapsulated trends that appear to have been more widely in evidence in milder form. In this case, too, it seems to have been presumed that the spokesmen in fashionable circles who made the running in articulating anti-magical attitudes reflected a wider current of scepticism that was rarely so openly expressed. The point was well made by Glanvill in his *Blow at Modern Sadducism*, who explicitly claimed that:

> those that dare not bluntly say, *There is NO GOD*, content themselves, (for a fair *step*, and *Introduction*) to deny there are *SPIRITS*, or *WITCHES*. Which sort of *Infidels*, though they are not ordinary among the *meer vulgar*, yet are they numerous in a little higher rank of *understandings*. And those that know any thing of the world, know, That most of the looser *Gentry*, and the small pretenders to *Philosophy* and *Wit*, are generally deriders of the *belief* of *Witches*, and *Apparitions*.[106]

Boyle similarly took the view that 'we live in an age, and a place, wherein all stories of witchcrafts, or other magical feats, are by many, even of the wise, suspected; and by too many, that would pass for wits, derided and exploded', and much the same point was made by Richard Ward in the section of his *Life of Henry More* in which he dealt with More's supernaturalist enterprise in Book III of *An Antidote against Atheism*. In it, he defended More on the grounds that what he was out to oppose in that part of his work was 'the humour of many, not only Wits, or of the lighter sort, but even those that are graver'.[107] Here again we see how the denizens of the London coffee-houses formed a conspicuous target, providing a helpful means for contemporaries to express their concern about more general trends in contemporary thought which they found alarming although these were rarely so openly expressed.

Moreover it needs to be stressed here that for orthodox thinkers it was taken for granted that witchcraft and related phenomena were real, and hence that their denial was dangerous and (as Glanvill claimed) an implicit threat to religion. Indeed, this was arguably particularly the case in Scotland, where, more even than in England, witchcraft belief remained predominant throughout our period. We will come in a later chapter to Joseph Addison's assertion in 1711 in his fashionable journal, *The Spectator*, how 'I believe in general that there is and has been such a thing as Witch-craft', despite the problems that might arise concerning particular instances of it, and the whole matter was well summarised by John Edwards in *Some Thoughts Concerning the Several Causes and Occasions of Atheism* (1695), where he wrote:

> And here I might observe that among the Opinions which lead to Atheism, the denial of *Dæmons* and *Witches*, which of late hath so much

prevail'd, is none of the least. For besides that this is an open defiance to unquestionable History, Experience and matter of Fact, and so introduces the worst sort of Scepticism (which is the high-way to Atheism) it is evident that this supplants the belief of *Spiritual Beings* or *Substances*: for Witchcraft and all Diabolick Transactions are disbeliev'd on the account of the improbability, if not impossibility of *Spirits*. So that it is plain the rejecting of the being and commerce of Dæmons or Infernal Spirits opens a door to the denial of the Deity, of which we can no otherwise conceive than that it is an *Eternal Spirit*.[108]

The reality of magic thus remained central to orthodox thought for longer than might have been expected, and it will be the task of this book to explore how and why this gradually changed.

## *The Current Volume*

There are thus many important themes to explore in the pages that follow. First, we need to know more about the articulate challenge to accepted beliefs in magic presented by freethinkers and Deists, and the nature of orthodox response to this, not least due to the dangerous association between sadducism and religious heterodoxy outlined in the previous section. This therefore forms the subject of two chapters. Chapter 1 comprises the study of John Wagstaffe's *The Question of Witchcraft Debated* (1669) that I published in 1995, which seemed worth reprinting in close to its original form, not least due to the extent to which it has been cited by other scholars during the intervening period.[109] On the other hand, the brief postscript that I there devoted to Wagstaffe's legacy is here expanded, partly in Chapter 1 (concerning the posthumous editions of his book) but more fully in Chapter 2. This takes the story forward into the early eighteenth century, considering the comparable views that were expressed by Deists and freethinkers at that point and the way in which orthodox thought at last began to change – not least in the hands of Francis Hutchinson, whose reference to Wagstaffe's book in his *Historical Essay concerning Witchcraft* (1718) neatly encapsulates just how far the orthodox did and how far they did not follow their freethinking precursors.[110]

Chapter 3 turns to the rather paradoxical role of the early Royal Society in connection with magic, since as an institution it proved far less supportive of the supernaturalist project of Glanvill and Boyle than might have been expected, thus revealing significant fissures in scientific circles at the time which are often ignored. It was only in the early eighteenth century that the society's avoidance of magic was construed as displaying a systematically sceptical attitude which in practice had never really existed; this formed a part of the process by which the orthodox gradually began to come round to a cautiously sceptical viewpoint, and the chapter will end by considering the legacy of their misrepresentation of the society's earlier role down to the twentieth century.[111]

The next chapter focuses on the 'Drummer of Tedworth', the notorious poltergeist case that occurred in Wiltshire in the early 1660s that has already been noted in connection with Glanvill's role in relation to it. This is a case study which is initially revealing of commonplace attitudes towards witchcraft and related phenomena in the period. Thereafter, it brings out the complexity of the way in which opinion on such subjects developed – from the debate between Glanvill and the 'wits' that occurred in the 1660s and 1670s and which throws further light on the nature of sadducism, to an ongoing debate as to whether the case was fraudulent, which lasted much longer.[112]

Chapter 5 examines the state of affairs in the mid-eighteenth century and the extent to which a medical approach to magic and related phenomena became fashionable among intellectuals as part of the Enlightenment. Particular emphasis is placed on the role of doctors like Sir Hans Sloane and Richard Mead and the nature of their diagnosis of those with magical beliefs, and consideration is also given to the hitherto neglected influence of such ideas on liberal churchmen in their discussions of miracles and related topics. All this provides a means of exploring how scepticism on such subjects fits into our understanding of the Enlightenment as a whole.[113]

The final substantive chapter considers changing attitudes during the long eighteenth century to second sight in Scotland, the uncanny ability of certain individuals to foresee the future. This was a topic which fascinated Robert Boyle in the late seventeenth century, as we have already seen, and Chapter 6 illustrates how his enquiries on the subject began a tradition of empirical study of the phenomenon which continued into the eighteenth century. But then a change came, and by about 1800 the possibility of second sight was increasingly rejected among English and Scottish intellectuals on the grounds that it was incompatible with the 'principles' by which the universe operated. In parallel with this, however, a separate tradition emerged in which second sight and related phenomena were deemed appropriate for imaginative interpretation by poets and others, which is significant in itself.[114]

Lastly, the Conclusion pulls together the themes emerging from the previous chapters to offer an overview of the 'Decline of Magic'. It will canvass alternative potential explanations for this momentous change and suggest a likely trajectory for the developments that occurred, also commenting on the nature of the longer-term legacy that ensued. Its building blocks are the findings of the detailed studies that follow, so let us begin by more fully exploring the relationship between sadducism and free-thought in the Restoration period.

# CHAPTER ONE

# JOHN WAGSTAFFE, WITCHCRAFT AND THE NATURE OF RESTORATION FREE-THOUGHT

The penultimate section of the previous chapter illustrated the close connection between sadducism – scepticism about witchcraft – and the phenomena that the concept of 'atheism' was used to describe, including its association with the culture of 'wit' that flourished in educated and metropolitan circles. It also stressed the extent to which such scepticism shocked the orthodox, for whom the reality of witchcraft and related phenomena remained axiomatic. No less significant is the point there emphasised that such iconoclasm was predominantly orally expressed. In Chapter 4 we will encounter a striking vignette of sadducism in action in the form of the 'Gentlemen afarre off' who visited John Mompesson's house at Tedworth, acknowledging 'their diffidence of the being of Spirits', and who carried out a kind of rough and ready investigation of the poltergeist that assaulted the property, departing with the 'suspicion that what they heard was onely a cheat or a fancy'.[1] Much commoner, however, is testimony to the prevalence of such attitudes in Restoration London, particularly in the fashionable surroundings of the coffee-houses, the court, the Inns of Court and Westminster. The divine, Richard Baxter, expressed his anxiety about views espoused by 'the sadducees (at court and the Innes of Court)', while our chief witness is perhaps Joseph Glanvill, whose defence of the reality of witchcraft we have already encountered.[2]

In particular, in the section of the 1668 version of his work, *A Blow at Modern Sadducism*, entitled *A Whip for the Droll, Fidler to the Atheist: Being Reflections on Drollery & Atheism*, Glanvill placed articulate sadducism fairly and squarely in the context of the fashionable, scoffing attitudes that he saw as conducive to irreligion more broadly. 'SADDUCISM is the *Fashion*', he wrote, associating it with '*Quibblers* and *Buffoons* that have some *little* scraps of *Learning* matcht with a *great* proportion of *Confidence*', and adding: 'Now these, Sir, are the WITS (if we will believe them) and their admirers take every *jest* for an *argument*, and a *loud laugh* upon an idle tale of a *Devil*, or a *Witch*, for a *demonstration* of the *non-existence* of such beings'. He further complained, 'the *cheats* of *Impostors*, the *conceits* of *Melancholly*, the *credulity* of *Ignorance*, the *tricks* of *Waggery*, the more *solemn vanities* of *Superstition*, and the *tales* of *old Women*; these are excellent *Topicks* for a *frolick* and *wanton fancy*,' adding how, when the quintessential 'wit' had 'wanton'd a while, and frolickly toy'd in his *affected merriments*, his *reason* becomes an obedient servant to his *fancy*'.[3]

Glanvill's characterisation was echoed in the 1673 pamphlet, *The Character of a Coffee-House,* in which sadducism is again seen as one of the staples of the atheistical, Hobbesian 'Town-Wit' who is the hero of the piece:

> Talk of *Witches* and you Tickle him, speak of *Spirits* and he tels you he knowes none better than those of Wine, name but *Immaterial Essence*, and he shall flout at you as a dull Fop incapable of sense, and unfit for Conversation; Nor is he ever better pleas'd than when he can here hedge in some young *raw Divine* to *Bulbait* with scurrility and all kind of profaneness.[4]

Here, we seem to be in the presence of a vigorous, iconoclastic culture with real power. Indeed, the fact that the bulk of scepticism about witchcraft was expressed in such milieux makes sense of the mismatch between the scale of concern expressed by orthodox thinkers and the extent to which sadducist views are to be found in printed texts.

This is clearly illustrated by the 1660s recensions of Glanvill's book, since in these he was able to name only two sceptical authors of his own century, in addition to Reginald Scot from the previous one, whose *Discoverie of Witchcraft* (1584) had been reprinted in 1665.[5] One was Thomas Hobbes, whose trenchant opinions on this subject had been expressed in his *Leviathan* (1651), especially in chapter 45, 'Of DAEMONOLOGY, and other Reliques of the Religion of the Gentiles', which opened by providing a materialist explanation of apparitions by analogy with the way in which violent pressure on the eye produced an illusion of bright light.[6] The other was the miscellaneous writer, Francis Osborne, who had devoted a brief section to witchcraft in his *Advice to a Son* (1656), which was full of rather cynical advice to an imaginary young man just growing up; in it, he advocated a sceptical attitude towards witchcraft accusations. Significantly, this was a work which the booksellers at Oxford were ordered not to stock after country ministers complained that it fomented 'atheism' among the gentry, though we learn that it thereafter sold all the better.[7] This meagre harvest of printed opinion would hardly seem enough to justify Glanvill's onslaught on sadducism, thus illustrating all the more clearly how such published books were merely the tip of an iceberg of scepticism, the remainder of which took purely oral form.

It is true that the extended, posthumous recension of Glanvill's book on witchcraft, entitled *Saducismus Triumphatus*, brought out under the editorship of Henry More in 1681, was to include a section attacking books hostile to witchcraft that had appeared subsequent to the 1660s versions of the treatise. In particular, it responded at length to John Webster's *The Displaying of Supposed Witchcraft*, published in 1677. But it is important to make the point that, although the Glanvill–Webster debate has been of great interest to modern scholars, by definition Webster's book cannot have been responsible for Glanvill's original invective against sadducism since it was only published a decade later.[8] Instead, orally expressed opinion was clearly Glanvill's main concern.

It is also worth making the point that the very features of Webster's book which encouraged Glanvill and More to respond to it at length – and have drawn it to the attention of modern scholars – arguably make it unrepresentative of sceptical opinion in its day. (It is in any case *sui generis* in its profound commitment to the ideas of the Flemish natural philosopher, Jan Baptist van Helmont, which Webster had evidently acquired during the Interregnum, though claims that his book is to be seen as a political statement in a post-Restoration debate between an ongoing radical tradition represented by Webster and a more conservative position exemplified by Glanvill has not met with widespread support.)[9] Webster's book is a great folio, replete with biblical and historical learning, theological erudition and philosophical expertise. In it, a whole battery of sophisticated arguments is brought forward to challenge belief in witches, its most extensive sections being on the biblical passages taken to support such belief, and the potential natural explanations that could be used to account for the effects attributed to witchcraft. It is therefore clearly a 'serious' book, and authors of the day who dealt with it treated it as befitted 'a learned and laborious Volume' by a fellow member of the coterie of scholarship, even if expressing reservations about the sharpness with which Webster expressed his disagreement with his antagonists and distaste for the implications of the views he put forward.[10] Insofar as Glanvill and others were right in their perception of the centre of gravity of sadducism, then Webster is tangential to it. Indeed, he dissociated himself from the coffee-house wits who had scoffed at his earlier book, *Metallographia* (1671), claiming: 'if they can but reach some pittiful pieces of Drollery and Raillery, they think themselves fit and able to censure any thing though never read nor seen, except the Title Page'. Moreover, although such attackers of Webster as Henry More attempted to conflate him into this drolling, profane tradition, complaining of 'the elusory cavils of that profane Buffoon', these attempts have a singular lack of plausibility.[11]

## *John Wagstaffe's* The Question of Witchcraft Debated *(1669)*

Instead, it is here appropriate to look at the other main tract attacking witch beliefs dating from the Restoration period to which Glanvill replied. This has received less attention than Webster's and has sometimes been referred to rather disdainfully even when it has been noted.[12] The work in question is by John Wagstaffe and is entitled *The Question of Witchcraft Debated*; it was published in 1669 and then issued in a second, greatly extended, edition in 1671. That Wagstaffe's book has been neglected by comparison with Webster's is evidently due to the fact that it is much less impressive-looking, and that it attracted less attention from Glanvill and More.[13] But it is interesting not only in its own right, but also in that it seems to bring us closer to the otherwise elusive phenomenon of oral, fashionable scepticism about which contemporaries complained, and hence to the nature of free-thought in the Restoration period. That this is the case is further suggested by the debate between Wagstaffe and two orthodox antagonists that followed the work's initial publication, for in replying to his critics Wagstaffe enhanced the learned character of his work, and this may illustrate how printed controversy had the effect of directing intellectual discourse into predictable channels.[14]

What do we need to know about Wagstaffe's work and its author by way of background to what he says in it? Physically, the book is a small one, a dumpy little octavo, the main text of which was only eighty pages long in its first edition. Indeed, Wagstaffe admitted that it was a far from comprehensive treatment of the subject, hoping that 'those hints which I have given here, may prove useful, especially unto the ingenious Reader that can enlarge upon them with his own thoughts'.[15] That it was a book of dubious

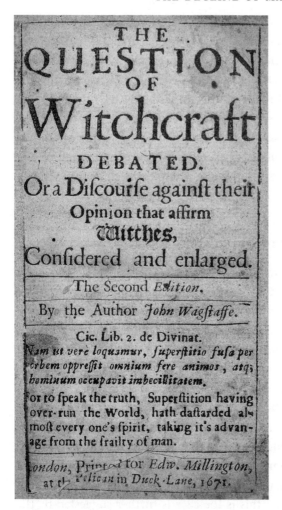

1. The title-page of John Wagstaffe's *The Question of Witchcraft Debated* (2nd edn, 1671).

orthodoxy is suggested by the fact that its first edition was provided with a duplicate title page from which the printer's name was omitted, in addition to a normal one. But we know that it was well spoken of in London circles when it appeared. This is apparent from the comments of Meric Casaubon, the venerable scholar and cleric whose critique of enthusiasm we encountered in the Introduction, and who included an attack on Wagstaffe's book in his *Of Credulity and Incredulity; In things Divine & Spiritual* (1670), one of the two attacks on the work that appeared shortly after its publication. Casaubon explained how when he first saw the book he thought that it had nothing in it to challenge the normal grounds for belief in witches, 'But since that, understanding by a learned friend, who is much conversant in

*London*, and well acquainted with all manner of books; that this *Discourse* was in no little esteem, among some: I changed my opinion'.[16]

As for its author, John Wagstaffe was born in 1633, son of a London citizen descended from a landed family in Derbyshire; he was educated at St Paul's School and Oriel College, Oxford. After taking a degree, he remained in residence at Oxford for a number of years before inheriting the family estates in Derbyshire, which enabled him to live a life of leisure.[17] The hints that we have about his career link him with the culture of 'wit' surveyed in the Introduction. The antiquary, Anthony Wood, reports jokes cracked at his expense by the Oxford wits after the appearance of his book, and he was obviously well known in such circles, while there was also a rumour that he was responsible for a pamphlet satirising the putative reformers of Interregnum Oxford, though Wood denied this. Equally telling – in view of contemporary commonplaces about the milieu and affiliations of free-thought – was Wood's report of Wagstaffe's death in 1677 aged forty-four, 'in a manner distracted, occasion'd by a deep conceit of his own parts, and by a continual bibbing of strong and high tasted liquors'.[18] This may have represented embroidery on Wood's part, since his principal informant, John Aubrey, had merely reported that Wagstaffe died of yellow jaundice.[19] On the other hand if, as seems quite possible, Wood had other sources of information, this again adds to the general plausibility of the picture, since it was commonly suspected that freethinkers were also free livers, that irreligious ideas accompanied immoral behaviour. '*Debauchery* is almost as great an enemy to mens *intellectuals*, as to their *morals*,' as Glanvill put it, 'mens *lusts* are the ground and occasion of their *scoffing*; . . . like Water and Ice they produce one another.'[20]

That Wagstaffe was a quintessential 'wit', in the sense of a sceptical commentator on controversial issues operating in fashionable milieux, is also suggested by the fact that we know that he engaged in the oral exposition of ideas of the kind that appeared in *The Question of Witchcraft Debated* before he put them into print. The lawyer and antiquary, Roger North, tells us that in 1668, shortly before the book was published, when Wagstaffe was in Cambridge to incorporate his Oxford degree, he was entertained to 'a very good dinner' by North's brother, Dr John North, master of Trinity College, at which his ideas on such subjects gained 'an express audience'. 'Much was said pro and con', North records, though he himself 'carried away little but a good meal'.[21] The context to this is provided by Roger's account of how his brother relished debates with 'young noblemen and fellow commoners, and used to say that he found more of candour and sincerity in them than in the graver sort', especially when they 'were noted for study and learning extraordinary'. In this connection, he singled out Sir Edmund Bacon, a fellow commoner whom he describes as 'a stout and early pretender to freethinking'; Dr North 'used to pump him to fetch up his most reserved reasonings, and used to say that he found such conversation profitable, because it made him digest matters in his own mind more effectually than, not being opposed, he could have done'. Unfortunately, little is known about Sir Edmund Bacon, a fellow commoner of Gonville and Caius, who came from an East Anglian gentry family and became second baronet in 1666; admitted to Lincoln's Inn in 1669, he died unmarried in 1683.[22] But we here again seem to see a typical example of oral free-thought in action.

Whether Bacon was present at the dinner with John North at which Wagstaffe held forth is unclear, but Wagstaffe would undoubtedly have relished his company either there or at the Inns of Court, a notorious haven of free-thought. Indeed, that Wagstaffe was accustomed to oral debate on such topics is suggested by his report at one point in his book that:

> 'Tis a very usual though a ridiculous thing for those who affirm Witchcraft when they are in company with others who deny it instead of arguments to tell I know not what kind of stories concerning Spirits. And when you have talkt an hour together, you shall find nothing in their discourse, that truly concerns the question of Witchcraft.[23]

Wagstaffe's literary pretensions are illustrated by his contributions to a volume of verses published at Oxford to celebrate the Restoration in 1660, which were rather unusual, comprising a Greek poem and a Latin acrostic.[24] That it is appropriate to see him as a 'wit' is also suggested by the text that he appended to *The Question of Witchcraft Debated*, a translation of one of the dialogues of the ancient writer, Lucian of Samosata, which Wagstaffe commended to his readers not only for the fact that in it the poet 'discovers the lying Spirit of Men', but also for the 'exquisite art, and delicatness of wit' with which he did so. It is worth noting that many at the time saw Lucian as a dangerously sceptical author, and Wagstaffe's inclusion of this passage itself reflects the slightly risqué milieu in which he existed.[25]

*The Question of Witchcraft Debated* was not Wagstaffe's first book but his second, and this may also be significant, since the fact that he had already broken the ice as an author may have made it easier for him to publish a controversial book on witchcraft than would otherwise have been the case. His previous work, published in 1660, was entitled *Historical Reflections on the Bishop of Rome: Chiefly Discovering Those Events of Humane Affaires which most advanced the Papal Usurpation*. This work – which Anthony Wood tells us was 'much commended' and which was based on the works of Baronius and other learned authors – argued the familiar Protestant view that the popes had originally lacked both leadership of the church and temporal power. But it gave a novel slant to this by the emphasis it placed on 'the contrived policy of corrupted men', giving a rather cynical account of the means by which papal hegemony was achieved at the expense of the susceptible barbarians in the Dark Ages through 'notorious jugling' between the popes and the Merovingian kings. Indeed, Wagstaffe looks forward to Gibbon in his scepticism about the clergy, including Gregory the Great, who, he claimed, embroidered Christianity with 'many inventions of his own, to make it more splendid and pompous in vulgar eyes'. Also telling is Wagstaffe's adulation of 'that thrice renowned *Saracenical* Empire', which he considered the victim of a conspiracy of silence among monkish historians.[26]

Comparable views are expressed in *The Question of Witchcraft Debated*, and we will assess their significance more fully in due course. Here it may be noted that his later work contains various other echoes of the earlier one, for instance when he discussed the Inquisition.[27] In addition, it displays the same sort of acquaintance with scholarship, though this is fairly lightly worn by the standards of the learned traditions of the day. Thus Wagstaffe shows some knowledge of Hebrew in discussing the terminology used to describe witches in the Old Testament. He also quoted various authors on witchcraft, including the *Malleus Maleficarum* and works by Martin Delrio and Nicholas Rémy, while he devoted a lengthy disquisition to the decrees of the Council of Ancyra in AD 314. He was also familiar with classical authors like Plutarch and patristic ones like St Augustine.[28] Indeed, Meric Casaubon admitted that Wagstaffe 'doth make some shew of a Scholar, and a man of some learning: but whether he doth acquit himself, as a Gentleman, (which I hear he is) in it, I shall leave others to judge'.[29] This was noted in reference to Wagstaffe's section on the Council of Ancyra, but it can be seen to refer to the book as a whole.

If this is the 'learned' component of Wagstaffe's work, its other character-istic is Wagstaffe's boldness and iconoclasm, in many ways its leading feature. Certainly R. T., one of Wagstaffe's antagonists whom I have not been able to identify beyond these initials, complained of 'the vast confidence which he seems to have in the strength of his Arguments'; he claimed, concerning scriptural texts, of Wagstaffe's 'making himself the only Judge in the sense of the original, and refusing any translation that suites not with his fancy, meerly for that reason'.[30] Indeed, it is perhaps not inappropriate to associate this with that 'absurd and preposterous affectation of seeming Wiser than their Neighbours' which the orthodox habitually associated with 'wit' and irreligion.[31]

Wagstaffe had no time for the argument that 'so many thousand of wise men in the world . . . could not be all deceived' on a subject like witchcraft, which he dismissed as a 'trifle'. In his peroration he appealed to 'any sober unbiased person; especially if he be of such ingenuity, as to have freed himself from a slavish subjection, unto those prejudicial opinions, which Custome and education, do with too much Tyranny impose'. Moreover he repeatedly appeals to 'reason', accusing his antagonists of 'irrationality' and having recourse to irony and sarcasm against those whom he judged deficient by such criteria.[32]

Equally symptomatic is Wagstaffe's disdain for scholasticism, already in evidence in *Historical Reflections on the Bishop of Rome*, where it is dismissed as 'the *Cobweb subtilty of a wordy nothingnesse*', and where Wagstaffe insisted on the need to reflect on 'Historical passages' rather than 'to insist upon Logical arguments either *pro* or *con*'. In *The Question of Witchcraft Debated*, he dismissed a piece of sophistry of St Thomas Aquinas with the aside: 'But what will not men of distinctions do, if you allow them their full swinge of distinguishing, they'l make any thing signifie any thing'. Moreover, apologising for his book in its second edition, he wrote, 'why should I trouble my self, to give any further satisfaction, unto a sort of men, who know nothing but a Syllogism, and whose Palats can relish nothing, which is not Metaphysically disputed on both sides of the question, with a *videtur quod sic*, and a *videtur quod non*?'[33]

This attitude is balanced by Wagstaffe's strong interest in and respect for the classics, and his scorn for 'the times of Barbarism and ignorance' which preceded 'the restauration of Learning'. This, too, is in evidence in the earlier *Historical Reflections on the Bishop of Rome*, where he bewailed 'the losse of the *Greek* tongue' in the medieval period, which led to the 'losse of all purity in the *Latine*; and consequently of *History, Geography*, skill in *Antiquity* and whatsoever savour'd of polite learning'.[34] He clearly had great respect for the 'ingenious Poets' of the Roman period, whom he quoted at length in his book, while an attack on superstition by Cicero was the motto that he selected for his title page.[35] There is a definite taste of the Augustan about Wagstaffe.

Moreover related to this and to his scepticism about witchcraft was his view that supernatural explanations had been gratuitously introduced by men in the past 'to cloak their ignorance', a theme to which we will return. Thus of ancient views concerning the falling sickness, he claimed that physicians 'pretended it came immediately from the hand of God, and therefore was to be cured with certain expiations and charms'.[36] He was equally sceptical about popular beliefs in his own time – such as 'the turning of women into cats, and their being hunted in the shape of Hares' – which he described as 'ridiculous lyes and fancies'. 'Do not our very Nurses tell us, and have we not heard from our Mothers maids such stories as these?', he asked of such 'trash', 'taken out of the very dregs of heathenism, I mean the vulgar belief'. Wagstaffe's terminology here is reminiscent of that of John Aubrey in his pioneering folklore collection, *Remaines of Gentilisme and Judaisme*, itself inspired by the view expressed by Thomas Hobbes in chapter 45 of his *Leviathan* that many superstitious practices in contemporary religion were 'Reliques of the Religion of the Gentiles'.[37] Wagstaffe probably also owed the idea to Hobbes, and his general indebtedness to Hobbes will become clear in the course of this chapter, though it should be pointed out that Wagstaffe does not explicitly cite Hobbes or the *Leviathan* at any point.

The main thrust of Wagstaffe's argument in the different chapters of his book was threefold, as summarised in his own words:

1. That the opinion of Witchcraft is not to be found in Scripture.
2. That Politique interest hath founded it on fables.
3. That those fables discover themselves to be so, by their impossibility.[38]

On the first point he took up the issue of the true meaning of the words translated as 'witch' in the Old Testament, a familiar theme since the time of sixteenth-century authors like Johann Weyer and Reginald Scot, though Wagstaffe does not in fact refer to either: with the exception of Girolamo Cardano, the only authors on witchcraft he cites are ones who defended it.[39] Wagstaffe's conclusion from a lengthy consideration of the biblical evidence on the subject was that 'those Impostures which our Translators call *Witchcraft*, signifie nothing but those arts and tricks, which were used to seduce the people to Idolatry, and to confirm them in it'. Others' views of these words, he believed, had been prejudiced by 'a præ-conceived opinion about making leagues with the Devil'. Also interesting is his dismissal of the supposed evidence of the power of the Devil in the Book of Job on the grounds that its author had decided 'to handle his subject, after the manner of Poets'.[40]

Witchcraft, Wagstaffe believed, could be explained in terms of human deceit and misapprehension, 'the folly of some, or the knavery of others'. He itemised 'the juggling delusions of confederated impostors', 'the errors or ridiculous mistakes of vulgar rumours', and the effects of torture and of 'melancholly, especially if it hath been heightned by poverty, or want of good diet, by ignorance, solitariness, and old age'. The juxtaposition of a witch's curse with harm suffered by a party against whom she might bear a grudge he dismissed as merely 'a notable concurrence of events'. All in all, the Devil's involvement became an unnecessary hypothesis. Indeed, Wagstaffe claimed that traditional witch beliefs involved the attribution of so much power to the Devil that those who subscribed to them were in danger of falling into Manicheanism. For him the issue was clear: 'it is far more easie, and far more rational to believe, that witnesses are lyars and perjured persons, than it is to believe; that an old Woman can turn her self, or any body else into a Cat'.[41]

If in this Wagstaffe was – if trenchant – not unusual among sceptics about witchcraft, what is quite novel about his book is his attempt to explain how and why witch beliefs had gained hold and the cynical construction he placed on this. He was convinced that the Papal Inquisition had had the effect of embroidering witch beliefs, adding the notions of diabolical contracts, covens and the like, not least through the extraction of confessions under torture; indeed he thought that some of the confessions that they had extracted were 'so strange that 'tis to me a wonder, if the Inquisitors can hold their countenances, and forbear from laughing at one another'. But he was also interested in the earlier history of the beliefs, and he traced their origins to a primitive attribution of misfortune to spiritual forces, thereby creating the need for agents to placate these, further arguing that witchcraft comprised attempts at such placation which had been deemed illegitimate by the authorities of the day.[42]

Moreover he placed this in the context of a cynical attitude to religion and a hostility to 'priestcraft' which is quite novel in the context of the literature on witchcraft, but which, significantly, was often identified by contemporaries as one of the characteristics of the scepticism on religious topics which caused such concern. Thus Glanvill, for instance, expostulated how irreligious attitudes were encouraged by such views: 'We see the folly and ignorance of our fore-fathers; and laugh at the Tales with which crafty Priests abused their easiness, and credulity. *Spiritual substance! Immortal souls! Authority of Scripture! Fictions, Ideas, Phantomes, Jargon*: Here is *demonstration* against the *spiritual* Trade, and *spiritual* men.'[43]

Expounding the rather Hobbesian notion that 'all men have fear implanted in them by Nature, the very strongest of all their passions', Wagstaffe explained that the 'wise Politicians [who] governed the ancient world, especially the Eastern parts thereof . . . promoted these fears of the people, and improved them for the designs of Government'. The extraordinary in nature was attributed to spirits, and 'In a word, many Religious Rites or Ceremonies of worship were instituted, with a world of variety and fancy' to remedy their ill effects. Then, 'when Hunger and Covetousness had engaged private persons, in such kind of actions as the Priests were engaged in out of policy', the priests denounced their rivals as diabolical and as acting 'contrary to the due Rites and Ceremonies', though to Wagstaffe's eyes they looked the same. 'For my part, I can see no difference between the actions of the Phylosophical Heathen Priest, and the Magician or Witch, but only this, that the one had Law or Authority on his side, the other had not.'[44]

Similar ideas recur elsewhere in the book. Indeed it opened with a cynical account of the way in which 'absolute and unlimited power' was maintained in the '*Eastern* Nations' not only by 'the force of Arms, but the craft also and tricks of superstition' and 'every particular way of delusion': 'Nor indeed were standing Armies of greater use unto the Oriental Monarchs, for keeping of their people in awe, then Idols were and Priests, and the various impostures used by them.' Elsewhere, he claimed that ideas of incubi and succubi were derived from fables of ancient heroes being begotten of intercourse between deities and humans, 'fit only to be a cloak for the Adulteries of the Heathen Priests'. It is also symptomatic that part of the reason for his rejection of the argument from authority and consensus was that 'the various Religions that have been in the world, are more than enough to convince one, how absurd and ridiculous the wisest of men are in matters of Opinion or Belief'.[45]

There was also cynicism about the early Christians, whose 'blind intemperate zeal' tempted them to forgery and whose undue openness to Platonic influence made them perpetuate the exorcising and conjuring of the heathen (Wagstaffe was especially hostile to Platonism: 'Can any one read the lives of

*Plotinus Iamblicus*, and others without amazement', he asked). Indeed, there is almost an implication of the interchangeability of paganism and primitive Christianity, since, after quoting Tacitus about how the early Christians were at first seen as witches, Wagstaffe continued: 'But on the other side when the Christians got uppermost, they were quit with the Heathens, and paid them in their own coyn: For they confidently affirmed, that the Heathen Religion was a Commerce with Devils', and the Rescript of Valentinian was required to curb the persecution that ensued.[46]

Though Wagstaffe stops short of stating it explicitly, clearly implicit in such attitudes is the kind of irreligious standpoint of which Glanvill and others were apprehensive. Moreover I think that one can detect in the book a general proclivity on Wagstaffe's part to imply a slightly more radical position than he actually stated. This is especially clear on the theme to which I have just alluded. For instance, in introducing the concept of fear as a motive force, Wagstaffe covered himself by stating, 'although it be an impious saying, and irrational, that fear was the first thing which brought Gods into the world, yet I am apt to believe, it first of all brought in these omnipotent Devils, that contract with Witches'.[47] Similarly, of the existence of spirits Wagstaffe rather ambiguously averred that this was 'a thing which no wise man can deny, though he doth not believe it: For it is one thing to doubt, and another to deny'.[48] Also potentially open to misinterpretation was his rhetorical assertion that, if witchcraft could explain so much, 'no rational man by the light of reason, shall be able to tell from the History of the Gospel, whether Christ were a Witch or no'. This was intended to attack witchcraft rather than orthodoxy, but it is symptomatic that Wagstaffe's antagonist R. T. considered the suggestion 'as malicious as it is frivolous'.[49]

How such statements should be interpreted is a little unclear. There is always the possibility of subterfuge. It has thus been argued of a number of heterodox thinkers of the early modern period that, at a time when the threat of prosecution made the open statement of atheistic opinion dangerous, the safest alternative was to imply such views without actually stating them. Figures like the Venetian historian, Paolo Sarpi, and the early eighteenth-century Deist, Anthony Collins, have been claimed to indulge in such dissimulation, and, though one has to beware of scholars indulging in wishful thinking about the 'true' radicalism of their subject, it would be naive to dismiss this possibility out of hand.[50]

Certainly Meric Casaubon seems to have suspected Wagstaffe of a certain disingenuity. Noting, concerning one of Wagstaffe's arguments, how 'this, though not expressed, must of necessity be supplyed, if you will make any thing of the inference', he continued: 'how any man that knows what belongs to sense, or reason; should thus argue, I cannot imagine; except he did it on purpose, to make himself sport, and to try to the utmost, how far the simplicity, and credulity of ignorant people will go. How, do we think, such a man doth laugh in his sleeve, when he hears himself commended?'[51]

This may help to explain orthodox overreaction to Wagstaffe. Even in his first edition he defended himself against the accusation of 'atheism' – presumably incurred in oral encounters that had already taken place – by aggressively accusing his adversaries of encouraging polytheism by attributing so much power to the Devil. In his second edition he reiterated how the accusation – which had evidently been reinvigorated by the publication of his ideas – was 'a ridiculous slander', 'not worthy to be answered'.[52]

It is also symptomatic that he felt bound to defend himself against 'some who wonder, that I would offer to annex unto my book, a *Dialogue* of *Lucian*, who as they say was a known Atheist'. As already noted, in sixteenth- and seventeenth-century Europe Lucian was often regarded as a quintessential scoffer at religion; many orthodox Christians of the day rejected his works without reading them, while his translators were repeatedly defensive on this point.[53] But Wagstaffe's defence is interesting in itself. Lucian, he claimed, was no atheist: 'he had too much Wit and Learning to be one', and Wagstaffe could draw attention to the fact that the translation he used was by no less a figure than Thomas More, who wrote before paranoia about Lucian's irreligion had reached its peak. Wagstaffe added, 'Nor did I ever meet with an Atheist in all my life, as to my own knowledge; and therefore am apt to believe, that those who are recorded such in History, were rather reputed then, real Atheists.'[54]

On the other hand, such disclaimers may be paralleled in heterodox figures like Charles Blount and John Toland, and when one considers this 'atheist' accusation in the light of what Wagstaffe said and what he implied, it is possible to understand why orthodox figures might feel anxiety – particularly in the light of another facet of their perception of the 'atheist' threat, their conviction of the progressive nature of free-thought, starting (as they believed) with a mild scepticism ironically expressed and ending in outright disbelief. To cite Glanvill again, a fashionable derision of religion could easily turn 'into a down-right, *serious* Infidelity . . . through the *witch-craft* of this *vice*, and the *secret judgement* of God'.[55] Moreover, whereas in Wagstaffe's case we have a printed text with which to collate accusations of 'atheism', it is here worth extrapolating more widely to the oral milieu in which heterodox ideas were evidently so frequently expressed. For it should be pointed out that ideas outlined in conversation were peculiarly liable to be misconstrued. One can thus well believe that a good deal of the fear of free-thought stemmed from overreaction to positions which were not really as heterodox as their adversaries made out, or which were expressed with a studied ambivalence which, in transmission, could be overlooked.

To return to Wagstaffe, it seems that, though caustic, his views were less extreme than his antagonists feared. This is seen in his discussion of spirits and their activity, where his trenchant scepticism fell short of outright disbelief. He introduced the topic by ridiculing his opponents' assertion that 'this is a question not to be disputed on, in regard it is a matter of fact, and consequently the object of sense, not of reason'. Then, referring to instances where chairs were supposed to have moved in a room without being touched, or to hearing 'Trumpets sound, and Drums beat, when neither Trumpeter nor Drummer have been near the place' – an evident allusion to Glanvill's celebrated story of the 'Drummer of Tedworth' – he dismissed such phenomena as questionable in themselves and in any case irrelevant to the issue of the reality of witchcraft. In defending this position against those who accused anyone holding it of being 'a meer Sceptick', who would deny even self-evident things, he replied that, on the contrary, 'Spirits being not the objects of sense, their actions must needs be obscure, and not so manifest unto true reason, as obnoxious unto fancy and immagination [sic]'. It was in this context that he made the agnostic remark about belief in spirits that has already been quoted.[56]

But he accompanied this by asserting that he himself did accept them – 'For my own part I firmly believe, there are many thousands of spirits, made of an incorporeal matter, too fine to be perceived by the senses of men' – the issue being whether they were active in the world 'upon the account of a Contract made with any man or woman'. Indeed, whereas Glanvill, Casaubon and others implied in their polemics that scepticism about witches was invariably associated with materialism and a denial of spiritual substances, Wagstaffe belies such an expectation: he may have learnt a cynical psychology from Hobbes, but not this.[57] Moreover, in general Wagstaffe's views on nature seem to have been orthodox and even old fashioned: in his commentary on the episode involving Pharaoh's magicians in Exodus, chapter 7, his criteria of what was and was not possible within the realms of natural causation seem to operate within the conventions of scholastic natural science.[58]

In religious matters, too, Wagstaffe can be seen as a perfectly legitimate theist, for all the subversive potential of some of the arguments he canvassed.

This is made clear by his additions to his 1671 edition on the issue of Christ's comparability to witches. For though some of his remarks seem caustic – 'What Miracle is there of Christ, which they have not equalled?', he asked – he made it clear that his concern was to protect the uniqueness of Christ: ' 'tis dangerous to depreciate the Miracles of Christ; by setting up others of equal value, notwithstanding any pretence of Holiness in the one, and unholiness in the other.'[59] Moreover it is perfectly easy to read Wagstaffe's hostility to the notion of witchcraft – like that of Reginald Scot in the sixteenth century, for instance – as perfectly theistic; this is seen in his insistence on God's overwhelming sovereignty and his resentment of the way in which the supposed initiative of the Devil and witches in spiritual affairs impinged on this, a topic on which he cited Calvin. In his view, such 'gratification of an old Womans malice, is wholy inconsistent with Divine goodness'.[60]

As with his predecessor, Reginald Scot, there is a strong humanitarian streak in Wagstaffe's thought. It was shocking, he claimed, to think how many women had died as a result of this 'pernicious and absurd error', his aim being 'to endeavour the saving of innocent persons, from torture and death it self'. Concerned to prevent unnecessary suffering, he was apprehensive about the danger of a witchcraft inquisition in the hands of 'Ambitious, Covetous, and malicious men'.[61] Indeed, this informed his convictions as to the proper end of government: 'without question, under this side Heaven, there is nothing so sacred as the life of man, for the preservation whereof, all Policies or Forms of Government, all Laws and Magistrates, are most especially ordained'.[62]

If to us this all sounds very humane and admirable, it would be wrong to underrate the heterodoxy even of notions like these in the context of late seventeenth-century Britain. Indeed, one might even detect Deistic tendencies in the remark about the role of government just quoted. Moreover, quite apart from this, I do not think that it is difficult to understand why Wagstaffe's work caused concern in its approach and its insinuations, nor to see why he tended to be conflated with more extreme positions than he actually held. It seems to me that Wagstaffe's cynical and iconoclastic manner rings very true to what the orthodox said about the characteristics of free-thought in his time.

## Wagstaffe's Impact and Legacy

We may now turn to the debate in which Wagstaffe engaged with his orthodox adversaries, R. T. and Meric Casaubon. Not entirely surprisingly, in attacking Wagstaffe these tended to concentrate on the detailed aspects of scriptural interpretation and theology which Wagstaffe raised – making some quite sound points at his expense – rather than on the broader, cynical arguments about 'politique interest' that he put forward. In part, it might be thought that this argument was a difficult one to answer in any case, being superimposed on the data rather than derived from them and deliberately intended to work insidiously like a kind of conspiracy theory. On the other hand, it could be said that if the rest of the argument was faulty and witch-craft did exist in scripture and in reality, then it became unnecessary to account for its invention, which could therefore be dismissed as 'his fancy' (to use R. T.'s words).[63]

But what is interesting is to see the effect that this had on Wagstaffe, for the second edition of his book which appeared in 1671 was extended in the light of the attacks to which it had been subjected. Wagstaffe did not retract anything; indeed, he almost flauntingly had the original chapters reprinted unchanged, adding a further commentary on each (which is sometimes a little repetitious). He also put his name on the title page for the first time, and it may be significant that he presented a copy of this edition to the Bodleian Library at Oxford. In his preface he explained how he had often read over the original treatise, 'Nor do I find any reason at all, to repent of what I have written, but to rejoyce in it rather'; at the end of the book, he issued a ringing challenge to those who disagreed with him.[64]

What is revealing is that the tendency of Wagstaffe's additions – insofar as they did not simply recapitulate his argument and clarify points that he had made – was to accentuate the 'learned' character of the work. In part this was obviously due to a need to respond to the points made by his erudite antagonists in their printed attacks. (In passing, it is worth noting that these were evidently not the only disagreements that he had encountered, but he was dismissive of the rest: 'I cannot chuse but laugh at the weakness of that objection which hath been often made against me', he wrote concerning one point, or, on another, 'I never heard any thing but canting stuff, which passeth my understanding'.)[65] But his response to the learned, published objections of Casaubon and R. T. was to add excursuses, for instance on the Inquisition, or the Rescript of Valentinian which legitimised paganism.[66] The more inflammatory points that he had made, on the other hand, were left without very much elaboration, and I would be inclined to argue that the genre itself tended to encourage this narrowing of the argument in a learned direction.

Beyond this, one comes away from an examination of Wagstaffe's and his antagonists' books with a strong sense that, though erudite points were exchanged, a proper debate did not really occur at all. On the central issues – particularly that of the Devil and his activity – the two sides merely stated their case and there the matter stood, with two incommensurate positions embattled against one another. Moreover, particularly with Casaubon, the way in which an author who was capable of quite cogent argument on other issues simply asserted the contrary to some of Wagstaffe's claims without proper documentation is telling in itself.

One such issue concerned the incidence of witchcraft. In R. T.'s words,

it is easily thought this Author would not raise a Devil which he could not lay again; and that of so many Arguments as may be brought too for the proof of Witches, he would only make choice of such as he could answer, or at least would so order the matter, as to leave out the most material circumstances, thereby to render the Argument invalid.

In particular, he reaffirmed the credibility of the witnesses in the Tedworth case, which Wagstaffe had questioned, while he reiterated the appeal to consensus as a basis for witch beliefs, on the grounds that

to imagine that whole Countries, nay, all the Christian world, should be so over-spread with folly, as to establish Laws against a sort of people which never were in being, is a madness of which whosoever is guilty, wants but one step more to become a Sceptick, and reject the Testimony of his own senses.[67]

Casaubon was a little more sophisticated on this score, modishly appealing to the evidence specifically of naturalists and physicians; on the other hand, he elsewhere rather let himself down by baldly enquiring: 'Hath he never read of any Popes, that ever were witches, or sorcerers?'[68]

As for the role of the Devil, neither R. T. nor Casaubon could see that the fact that imposture might be involved had the implication of making the Devil's involvement an irrelevance. As R. T. put it, witches might be deluded, 'but it does not follow, because they are deluded, that they are no Witches', and he answered Wagstaffe's standard rationalist argument that the Devil seemed not to reward his servants very satisfactorily on the grounds either that they might imagine benefits, or that they might have sordid expectations. He also considered it irrational 'for us to deny that the Devil can do such things, only because we cannot tell how they are done'.[69]

Indeed it is revealing that, whereas Wagstaffe had used the fact that much remained inexplicable in nature to suggest that this meant that natural effects were over-readily attributed to divine causes, R. T. used the fact that 'no man has yet attain'd to that perfection in Natural Philosophy, as to know the thousandth part of what may be done by natural means' to argue that this favoured the notion of a league with the Devil, whose skill in natural philosophy was notorious. The incommensurability of their positions was further revealed when R. T. asserted that 'we must not look for a reason of all Gods actions', on the grounds 'that many times his great wisdom sees good to do those things which seem to us very strange, and unaccountable'.[70]

It is almost as if intellectual change does not really occur through argument at all, that the detailed debates that we reconstruct from erudite tomes might as well not have happened. People just made up their minds and then grasped at arguments to substantiate their preconceived ideas, with a new generation simply rejecting out of hand the commonplaces of the old. Moreover this may help to make sense of a facet of the contemporary perception of free-thought that has been so profusely transmitted to posterity by orthodox polemicists, namely their sense of frustration that freethinkers appeared not to be susceptible to persuasion by intellectual means, or certainly not by the 'rational' arguments which the orthodox claimed so confidently as theirs.[71] Such an idea would have appealed to Wagstaffe, who argued in his *Historical Reflections on the Bishop of Rome*:

> this is palpable enough, that when the bent of our understanding, is enclined to any party, by the strong biasses of education and interest; We straightway greedily embrace, all shewes and appearances of reason, which seem to make for our side; and with abundance of selfe applause, improve a meer sneaking hint of an opinion, into a demonstrative confidence.[72]

Moving forward in time, one of the most interesting and significant aspects of Wagstaffe's book is the extent to which it had a prolonged afterlife as a bold and succinct statement of a sadducist position (though it was always the original 1669 version, rather than the extended 1671 one, that was reprinted). The year 1712 saw the notorious trial of Jane Wenham for witchcraft, which occasioned the last full-scale debate on witchcraft to occur in England and, as part of this, virtually the entire text of Wagstaffe's book appeared in serialised form in a newspaper, *The Protestant Post-Boy*. This text was then published as a book, of which a second edition came out the same year, entitled *The Impossibility of Witchcraft, Plainly Proving, From Scripture and Reason, That there never was a Witch; and that it is both Irrational and Impious to believe there ever was.*[73] Indeed, this was the most outspoken pamphlet urging *The Impossibility of Witchcraft* to come out as part of the controversy, illustrating how texts expressing such outright scepticism remained uncommon, and that, as in the late seventeenth century, a more querulous position on the overall reality of witchcraft as against the difficulties experienced in specific cases remained the norm. This is further illustrated by the reaction to Wagstaffe's book of Francis Hutchinson in his *Historical Essay concerning Witchcraft* (1718), to which we will come in the next chapter: again, as we will see, Wagstaffe's text displayed a radicalism which Hutchinson simply disavowed.

In 1736, in conjunction with the repeal of the parliamentary act against witchcraft in that year, Wagstaffe's work was reprinted yet again, this time under the title of *A Discourse on Witchcraft. Occasioned by a Bill now Depending in Parliament, to repeal the Statute made in the first Year of the Reign of King James I, Intituled, An Act against Conjuration, Witchcraft, and dealing with evil and wicked Spirits.* Indeed, this comprised the only statement of a sceptical position to be published at that point.[74] This edition of Wagstaffe has more than once been cited by modern scholars unaware of its actual authorship (as has the 1712 reprint), and it is a striking tribute to Wagstaffe that his text should enjoy success so many years after his death, even in an unsuspected guise.[75] It seems as if *The Question of Witchcraft Debated* continued for an extraordinarily long time to serve a genuine function in providing a critique of witchcraft beliefs with a punchy, cynical tone that was well suited to the taste of the period.[76] Moreover, even if this reflects the fact that no one else wanted to take the risk of framing a new version of its controversial argument, this does not detract from Wagstaffe's achievement.

This chapter has therefore attempted to do justice to Wagstaffe's 'sweepingly sceptical performance', in Keith Thomas's words;[77] its aim has been to rescue from neglect a pioneering critic of commonplace witchcraft beliefs, whose tone is often surprisingly similar to that of the early eighteenth-century Deists. Moreover, the suggestion made above about the link between Wagstaffe's work and the phenomenon of oral heterodoxy in his day implies that comparable ideas may have been more widely expressed in conversation in the Restoration period than is apparent from the printed record. Indeed, there is an interesting parallel here to what has been observed concerning the concept of 'priestcraft', which, although coined in 1657, rarely occurs in print before the 1690s, when it suddenly becomes commonplace.[78] Wagstaffe illustrates with particular clarity the importance of an ill-defined but unmistakeable 'Hobbism', something which contemporary commentators stress again and again as the intellectual core of free-thought in their day.[79] Many of the quotations that I have included in this chapter illustrate how much Wagstaffe had learnt from Hobbes's cynical view of human nature and of social and religious institutions, though it is noteworthy that he failed to combine this with a thoroughgoing materialism. What is almost more significant is Wagstaffe's manner and his approach. With his confidence and iconoclasm, his preparedness to broach controversial topics and his cynicism towards accepted beliefs, he brings us as close as we are likely to get to the true nature of that elusive phenomenon, free-thought in the Restoration period.

CHAPTER TWO

# FROM THE DEISTS TO FRANCIS HUTCHINSON

## *The Deists and Magic*

Wagstaffe's *The Question of Witchcraft Debated* may long have held the day as a full statement of a sadducist position, in part because no one else wrote a book-length work on the subject. But what is striking is how axiomatic scepticism about magical beliefs became among freethinkers and Deists during the period involved, reflecting the application of a cynical psychology to the history of religion that was typical of them.[1] Indeed, the Deists are the one group of writers who were systematically sceptical about witchcraft and related phenomena in their publications, at a time when orthodox thought remained either defensive or indecisive. One Deist author, Anthony Collins, even made a general point of this in the course of a disquisition on the changing fortunes of witchcraft beliefs in England and the United Provinces in his *Discourse of Free-thinking* (1713), arguing that the Devil's 'Dominion and Power' were 'ever more or less extensive, as Free-Thinking is discourag'd or allow'd'.[2] In the next chapter we will examine the orthodox response to this by the scholar Richard Bentley, who bombastically (and incorrectly) appealed to the influence of the new science instead. Here, it will suffice to state that Collins was essentially right, in that freethinking *does* seem to have encouraged a strong sadducism that is not in evidence elsewhere.

Neither was this phenomenon lost on contemporaries. Maximillian E. Novak has seen the stimulus to Daniel Defoe's slightly strange writings about magic of the late 1720s, which combine titillation with an underlying apologetic rationale, as being what he describes as 'the Deist Offensive during the Reign of George I'.[3] Similarly, a conservative writer, Robert Wightman, complained in 1738 'that *in proportion* as *Deism* prevails, and gets footing among Men in Power, *in proportion* the *Disbelief* of the *Being* of *Spirits*, and *their Agency* in this World takes place'.[4] It is also important to reiterate how, for more orthodox thinkers, the very fact that heterodox authors like these were so open in their denial of such phenomena continued to be problematic, in that it tainted such views with overtones of 'atheism' and made them difficult to adopt. This is seen, for instance, in one of the more sceptical pamphlets inspired by the Jane Wenham case in 1712, *A Full Confutation of Witchcraft*, the anonymous author of which specifically stated how 'in all popular Errors, if we discover the least Incredulity, we run the Risque of being taken for Men of no Religion'.[5] Indeed, this stand-off between heterodox and orthodox thinkers represents a significant episode in the history of such attitudes that has not received the attention that it deserves. Yet the stalemate only lasted a few decades, as we will see, and by about 1720 orthodox figures themselves began to put forward sceptical views about witchcraft and the like, albeit in a more restrained way than their heterodox predecessors.

Of course, there was an element of rhetoric in complaints like that of Robert Wightman about 'Deism' and its prevalence. It is certainly true that, though a number of thinkers can legitimately be brought together under this label, they tended not to identify themselves as a coterie in the way that hostile contemporaries and modern commentators often do, and the exact boundaries of the group are a matter for dispute.[6] In relation to magic, it needs to be emphasised that, although the Deists expressed strongly sceptical views on such subjects on the occasions when they discussed them, this was not a major preoccupation of theirs by comparison with their concern to reform religion and free it from priestly power. They aspired to a true civil religion, in which lay believers would be allowed to exercise rational devotion towards a supreme God, freed from unnecessary mysteries and dogma; this formed part of an aspiration to an ordered, prudentialist state which owed much to the influence of secularising thinkers like Machiavelli.[7] Magical beliefs appear mainly as the ultimate, most laughable extreme of superstition: it is almost as if, in their eyes, magic – more even than the organised paganism of classical antiquity – was the *quintessence* of superstition and to be deprecated accordingly. It is also worth placing this in the context of the anxiety about 'atheism' surveyed in the Introduction, since in many ways the Deist assault on orthodox religion and by extension on magic can be seen as an example of the way in which such thinkers adopted an extreme version of positions that were more commonplace in moderate form. In this case, we find that the staples of Protestant religious polemic, against both Roman Catholics on one side and 'enthusiasts' on the other, were now being turned against sacerdotal religion as a whole. The Deist assault on 'priestcraft' had strong echoes of the Protestant assault on 'popery' that had thrived since the Reformation, while in many ways the cynical and reductionist view of magical beliefs that the Deists adopted was a development of the critique of 'enthusiasm' by thinkers like Henry More and Meric Casaubon that we encountered in the Introduction.[8]

Moreover, as with Wagstaffe a generation earlier, it was often to the tools of humanist erudition that the Deists and related thinkers turned in order to achieve their polemical ends, and hence the influence of antiquity can be argued to have had a crucial 'modernising' effect in this area – more than the 'scientific' one to which Bentley blusteringly appealed, as we will see. It has been observed how, in the years around 1700, orthodox scholars increasingly lost interest in the broad, synthetic erudition which had characterised the seventeenth century, instead turning to minute textual studies of the kind which Bentley himself exemplified in his studies of the New Testament and other ancient writings.[9] Indeed, he sought to justify this elsewhere in his attack on Collins.[10] On the other hand, though Collins and his colleagues were undoubtedly poorer scholars than Bentley, the result of this was that (in the words of Kristine Haugen) 'the genre of the broad historical narrative began to be aggressively coopted by the unorthodox and the relatively unscholarly'.[11] In the writings of a whole swathe of ancient authors like Strabo or early Christian ones like Celsus, such men found the tools to mount a critique both of orthodox religion and, by extension, of magic and other forms of superstition.[12] They also drew on scholarly writings of the seventeenth century with a decidedly heterodox tone, perhaps most notably by the Dutch scholar, Anthonie van Dale, especially his *De oraculis ethnicorum dissertationes duæ* (1683) and his *De origine ac progressu idolatriæ et superstitionum* (1696), the former the source of Fontenelle's more famous critique of pagan oracles and also a key inspiration for the witchcraft sceptic, Balthasar Bekker.[13]

The published pronouncements by Deist authors on aspects of magical belief and practice as extreme forms of superstition start with Charles Blount, whose *Anima Mundi* (1679) expressed an artful ambivalence on many aspects of religious and related beliefs. In it, he claimed: 'Nor is a man that is incredulous in the point of Witches, without some reason on his side', on the grounds that witches' belief that they could converse with spirits or fly through the air merely reflected 'the prodigious power of . . . waking dreams'.[14] Blount pursued such matters further in his translation of *The Two*

*First Books of Philostratus, Concerning the Life of Apollonius Tyaneus*, published the following year. This deliberately incendiary work made available to an English-reading audience an account, profusely annotated from learned sources, of an ancient figure whose supernatural gifts could be compared to Christ's – whose claims to miraculous power were thereby subversively undermined. Here again, Blount exhibited a relentless hostility to 'the whole Roguery of these Priests' and the manipulation of opinion in which they indulged, which is similar to Wagstaffe's but more intense, and in which he explicitly invoked the example of Hobbes. As he put it at one point:

> Mr. *Hobbs* tells us, that in these four things, opinion of Ghosts, ignorance of second causes, Devotion towards what men fear, and taking of things casual for Prognosticks, consisteth the natural Seed of Religion; which by reason of the different Fancies, Judgments, and Passions of several men, hath grown up into Ceremonies so different, that those which are used by one man, seem ridiculous to another.[15]

He further cited Hobbes in conflating 'the greatest part of the *Gentiles* Religion in times past, that worshipp'd Satyrs, Fawns, Nymphs &c. and now adays the opinion the rude people have of Fairies, Ghosts, Goblins and Witches', providing a reductionist explanation of both.[16]

In another work Blount argued, following Spinoza, for a purely naturalistic explanation of miracles, and here he was on even more dangerous ground, since the miracles, especially of Christ, were even more central to the supernaturalist programme that Boyle and others pursued than the contemporary cases of witchcraft and the like that he and Glanvill collected. Miracles seemed to Boyle and other orthodox figures to provide such powerful evidence of God's direct involvement in the world that it was wellnigh unquestionable, and Blount's critique of them thus again exemplified the dangerous intellectual trends that caused Boyle and others such concern.[17]

John Toland was equally trenchant. In a passage in his notorious *Christianity not Mysterious* (1696), he was chary of miracles and their significance, though accepting that they might serve 'wise and reasonable Purposes', and in the same passage he went on, 'By this Rule the celebrated Feats of *Goblins* and *Fairies*, of *Witches*, of *Conjurors*, and all the *Heathen Prodigies*, must be accounted idle and superstitious Fables'.[18] He made a more substantial intervention on the subject in his *Letters to Serena* (1704), the opening chapter of which, on 'The Origin and Force of Prejudices', includes similarly hostile remarks about magical beliefs and how these were imbued even in the educated from childhood onwards, not least for manipulative purposes. The third chapter of the same work, on 'The Origin of Idolatry, and Reasons of Heathenism', comprises what is essentially a natural history of magic, including a searing critique of the priestly origins of superstition. In it, he invoked the 'numberless and superstitious Vanitys, which are continu'd in most parts of the World to this very Time, and which may be found describ'd at large in VANDALE', going on to detail the supposed results of the diabolic covenant or of divination, which he saw as 'Pranks, tedious to relate, and impossible for thinking Men to believe'.[19] Toland pursued a similar agenda in his *Adeisidaemon* (*The Unsuperstitious*) of 1709, in which he defended the ancient historian Livy from the charge of credulity, claiming that, on the contrary, Livy, like he himself, was hostile to superstition, which he saw as epitomised by belief in 'ghosts, hobgoblins, witches & spectres'.[20]

The 3rd Earl of Shaftesbury's *Characteristicks of Men, Manners, Opinions, Times* (1711) is of course notable for the many themes that it broaches, but one of the most important was his hostile attitude towards all kinds of superstition and those who abetted it, something of which he made a visual point through the book's engraved vignettes (Plate 7).[21] Shaftesbury was hostile to 'men of prodigy' in the church, who wanted to set religion

> on the foot of popular tradition and venture her on the same bottom with parish tales and gossiping stories of imps, goblins and demoniacal pranks, invented to fright children or make practice for common exorcists and 'cunning men'! For by that name, you know, country people are used to call those dealers in mystery who are thought to conjure in an honest way and foil the devil at his own weapon.[22]

What is more, the opening 'Letter concerning Enthusiasm' includes a reference to 'an eminent, learned, and truly Christian prelate', early identified as Edward Fowler, Bishop of Gloucester, whom Shaftesbury ridiculed for his interest in fairies and other supernatural phenomena.[23] It is indeed the case that Fowler was perhaps the leading clerical demonologist in the generation after Glanvill, contributing a number of stories to the posthumous edition of *Saducismus Triumphatus* and encouraging the recording and dissemination of other material of this kind, though he never published a collection like Glanvill's and only scattered hints survive of such activity on his part.[24] Shaftesbury's open attack on him is therefore all the more revealing.

A further example of hostility to such beliefs is provided by John Trenchard's *Natural History of Superstition* (1709), which has been seen by Justin Champion as a key work in the Deist critique of orthodox religion.[25] Trenchard attributed magical beliefs to fraud and manipulation by crafty impostors – a typical part of the Deist onslaught on 'superstition'. But such manipulation was only possible because of human susceptibility, and equally central to his case was a quasi-medical argument about people's proneness to delusion. As he put it: 'To these Weaknesses of our own, and Frauds of others, we owe the Heathen Gods and Goddesses, Oracles and Prophets, Nimphs and Satyrs, Fawns and Tritons, Furies and Demons, most of the Stories of Conjurers and Witches, Spirits and Apparitions, Fairies and Hobgoblins, the Doctrine of Prognosticks [and] the numerous ways of Divination', which he went on to itemise at length. In the same work, he also noted how 'It requires less pains to believe a Miracle, than to discover it to be an Imposture, or account for it by the Powers of Nature', deprecating the extent to which this had 'given opportunity to Men of Fraudulent intention, to impose upon the Ignorance and Credulity of others'.[26]

Later, Trenchard and his collaborator, Thomas Gordon, were equally scathing in their journalistic writings, in 1722 devoting three whole numbers of their freethinking journal, *Cato's Letters*, to excoriating 'superstitious Fears', including 'a further Detection of the vulgar Absurdities about Ghosts and Witches', on the grounds that (in their words) 'those stories are believed through the world, in exact proportion to the ignorance of the people, and the integrity of their clergy, and the influence which they have over their flocks'. They returned to similar issues in later numbers.[27] Further comments on such topics appeared in another joint publication by the two men, *The Independent Whig*, while Gordon's *The Humourist* (1720) included sceptical essays 'Of Witchcraft', 'Of Ghosts and Apparitions' and 'Of Credulity', in one of which he summarised his viewpoint by stating, 'In these Cases, Credulity is a much more Mischievous Error than Infidelity, and it is safer to believe nothing, than too much'.[28]

Perhaps the most remarkable instance, however, is not a published source but an as yet unpublished one, the annotations made by John Toland and particularly by his colleague, Robert, 1st Viscount Molesworth, to a copy of the 1716 second edition of Martin Martin's *A Description of the Western Islands of Scotland*, especially the account appended to that of second sight – the uncanny ability of certain individuals to foresee the future, which had fascinated intellectuals since the time of Robert Boyle and of which a fuller

account will be given in Chapter 6 (Plate 8).[29] Molesworth's and Toland's
annotations have been the subject of attention both from Justin Champion
and from me, and what is striking is not only how scathingly dismissive of
the whole phenomenon Molesworth was, but how far he associated it with
'priestcraft'; it is also revealing that the section of Martin's book dealing with
second sight is more heavily and indignantly annotated than any other.
Molesworth saw both those who believed in second sight and those who
claimed the gift as 'Credulous ignoramus's'; for him, the phenomenon was
'Contagious, as all deceits are' and he was also inclined to attribute people's
susceptibility to it to 'Hysteric fits'.[30] At one point he noted, 'See how superstition improves';[31] he further asserted that the entire belief system was
encouraged (if not brought about) by 'priestcraft' – 'the whole thing is a
meer invention of Popish preists taken first from paganism & designed to
promote the notion of Purgatory', he noted in one place, while in another he
wrote, 'Here's popery again'.[32] Elsewhere he took the view that 'As ignorance
vanishes so doe's all Spectres, Second Sights, Hobgoblins, fayries, Haunted
Houses & 100 such fooleryes & apparitions. the pretenders to such storyes
ought immediatly to be taken up, & whipp'd at a Carts tayl for Cheates &
impostors in a well Policed government'.[33] Later he reiterated concerning
another of the supposed seers: 'He ought to have bin put in Jayl for his
predictions if they were such', and his overall verdict at the very end of this
section of Martin's book was 'All impostures'.[34] Once again we see how the
Deists were at the forefront in condemning magical beliefs and using the
language of 'priestcraft' in excoriating them and accounting for them.

The vigour of Molesworth's reaction, and especially his wish to have
recourse to physical punishment for those who made such (in his view)
fraudulent claims, is striking. It is perhaps an illustration of how the Deists'
critique of 'priestcraft' would have worked in practice had they ever been in
a position to implement it: in other words, if imposters were found in action,
this is how they should be treated. In this connection it is possibly revealing
that the 1736 Act of Parliament which repealed the Jacobean legislation
against witchcraft similarly threatened those guilty of making fraudulent
claims to such powers with punishment. In its words,

> for the more effectual preventing and punishing of any pretences to such
> arts or powers as are before-mentioned, whereby ignorant persons are
> frequently deluded and defrauded . . . every person so offending . . . shall
> for every such offence, suffer imprisonment for the space of one whole

year without bail or mainprize, and once in every quarter of the said year in some market town of the proper county upon the market day there stand openly on the pillory by the space of one hour.[35]

## Free-thought and the Response to it

Returning to Molesworth, although his views on Martin were mainly expressed in his annotations to the latter's book, the two men did have a face to face encounter. At one point Molesworth wrote, 'I knew this poor ignorant Martin, & one day exposed him so much to the ridicule of very good company (whither he was brought to dine) upon the account of the second sight which he pretended to maintain, that he never afterwards durst appear again in that company'.[36] This interestingly brings us back to the oral dimension of scepticism like his, since it is clear that the critical viewpoint to which the Deists gave voice in their written comments on the subject continued to be expressed much more widely in oral form in the venues where freethinkers gathered. Here, striking testimony is provided by the Leeds antiquary, Ralph Thoresby, who recorded in his diary encounters with sceptics concerning supernatural phenomena which took place during a visit to London in the summer of 1712 and which clearly made a marked impression on him. The episodes in question took place in coffee-houses where, now as in the late seventeenth century, it was notorious that such risqué ideas were likeliest to be expressed: indeed, the first such passage has been widely cited to illustrate how shocked the orthodox were by the heterodox opinions on such subjects that they there heard.[37] On 21 August 1712, Thoresby wrote:

> Was troubled at some expressions in company, that dropped from some who would be thought the only wits, and glory in the style of Freethinkers, who deny the existence of spirits, downright affirming those expressions in Scripture, the works of the flesh, and the works of the Devil are synonymous, there being no such thing as a Devil in their opinion. The Lord enlighten their dark minds, and let not much learning make them mad! Stayed too late, being earnest in opposing them. Lord pity and pardon![38]

The other confrontation was a little earlier, on 13 June 1712, and it involved a man named Obadiah Oddy whom Thoresby had recorded meeting in a coffee-house on the previous day. Thoresby wrote:

Evening, sent for by Dr Halley, Savilian Professor, but was after troubled at an ingenious and learned gentleman, Mr Ob. Od. whom I had formerly observed very zealous in opposing even the best attested narratives of apparitions, witchcraft, &c. who now confessed he believed there was no Devil: the Lord enlighten him![39]

Quite how the June and August episodes relate to one another is unclear. The fact that no reference is made to Oddy on the later occasion suggests that on that date Thoresby encountered a separate group of thinkers expressing views that shocked him, evidently indicating how common such ideas were in the coffee-houses of the day. As for Thoresby's account of Oddy, what is perhaps most notable about it is how explicit Thoresby is about the progressive nature of Oddy's scepticism about the supernatural realm, from opposition to the truth of well-attested supernatural narratives to a complete denial of the reality of the Devil. In fact, although the diary references to Oddy occur on consecutive days, the implication is that Thoresby had been aware of him earlier, hence observing the progression from mild to extreme scepticism that he describes.

Since in this case we know the name of the sadducee who shocked Thoresby, Obadiah Oddy, it is worth focusing on him, since it is possible to find out a good deal about him although he has otherwise almost completely vanished from the historical record. Oddy's life was devoted to classical scholarship. An associate of Richard Bentley, Oddy aspired to produce a definitive edition of the ancient historian, Dio Cassius, one of the key sources for the history of the late Republic and early Roman Empire; his scholarly preoccupations are well illustrated by a series of notebooks purchased after his death by the Earls of Oxford which are now in the Harleian Collection in the British Library.[40] Oddy was also friendly with the Oxford antiquary, Thomas Hearne, who describes him in his diaries as 'a very hard Student, has Excellent natural Parts, is a great master of the Greek Tongue & very well skill'd in Sacred & Prophane History', while a number of telling letters from Oddy to Hearne and others survive, mainly in the Bodleian Library.[41] These reveal Oddy as rather a spirited, raffish figure, in contrast to the earnest, slightly humourless Thoresby: on one occasion, for instance, he sent Hearne 'A Dithyrambick Rhodomontade, as writ over a Glasse, on purpose to make you laugh'.[42] It is also apparent that Oddy, whose father had been a Presbyterian minister and who had himself once been a Presbyterian teacher, had become what Hearne calls 'an irreligious

Latitudinarian'.[43] In addition, he showed a degree of tolerance towards Islam that shocked Hearne, and the fact that he was later to commit suicide might perhaps be seen as displaying libertarian tendencies on his part of a kind which Hearne deprecated.[44]

The source of the sadducism that disquieted Thoresby is apparent from Oddy's notebooks, which are littered with anti-clerical sentiments and sceptical comments about people's credulity; they also contain notes from the iconoclastic works by the Dutch scholar, Anthonie van Dale, which were referred to at the start of this chapter and which also influenced Toland.[45] Indeed, the case of Oddy confirms the extent to which classical learning was a potential source for sadducism – as with the Deists, and as with John Wagstaffe a generation earlier – and, in the emerging Augustan age, this is a stimulus to intellectual change that we ignore at our peril. Of course, classical erudition was not new, but we have already seen how it was becoming increasingly apparent at this time that it could serve heterodox ends as easily as orthodox ones; it thus provided a potential resource for those with a proclivity to such scepticism as Oddy clearly exemplifies.[46] It is worth noting that, in addition to extracts from learned works, Oddy's notebooks also contain notes from Newton's *Principia*, which he read in a discriminating way, singling out passages that seemed to him especially crucial; in addition, it is interesting to find him making notes on the writings of the German jurist, Samuel Pufendorf, whose project for desacralising civil philosophy he evidently found attractive.[47] But there seems no doubt that his longstanding absorption in classical antiquity was the chief stimulus to his heterodox ideas. As for the metropolitan milieu in which Thoresby encountered him, Oddy's letters to Hearne suggest that he was somewhat disdainful of it, complaining how it was characterised by 'a state of Ignorance; accompanied with abundance of pride' and on one occasion reporting how 'Yesterday in Company where I was, I heard an Asse upon Record cry'd up, for a Man of the greatest learning in the World'.[48] Yet he clearly enjoyed himself there, and the likely trickle-down effect of a combination of iconoclasm and erudition like his is not to be underestimated.

Returning to Thoresby, it is interesting that he also had an epistolary encounter with none other than the arch-Deist, John Toland, in 1715. On the other hand, the edge is rather taken off this by the fact that it was Toland who contacted Thoresby in connection with his history of Leeds, *Ducatus Leodiensis*, published that year. Toland did so in order to inform Thoresby that his colleague, Pierre des Maizeaux, had arranged for a notice of the book to be placed in the journal *Nouvelles Littéraires* and, in doing so, he spoke highly of the work (possibly slightly tongue in cheek), assuring Thoresby that, since he had rendered Leeds illustrious or even immortal, his townsmen should erect a statue to him. Although Thoresby's response expressed predictable satisfaction that his book was being noticed in this way, he could not resist including a rather smug reproof to Toland for his heterodoxy: 'But you will pardon me for wishing that a Gentleman of so much humanity, learning, and curiosity, was, in one point, more of the sentiments of the Catholick Church' (by which he evidently meant orthodox Christianity). He excused this by invoking 'the affectionate desires of a simple recluse in his country cell, where he prays for peace and truth, and the welfare of all mankind', and it may be that this was as far as he felt he could go in an exchange like this (it is in any case unclear what the 'one point' on which he reproved Toland was, and it is possible that he was unaware of the full extent of Toland's heterodoxy).[49] But his relatively assured tone is notable, and it echoes his report of his encounter in 1712 with a heterodox but wholly theistic figure in the form of William Whiston, who had been ousted for his Arian views from the Lucasian Chair to which he had succeeded Newton at Cambridge. Thoresby was a great collector of autographs, and he approached Whiston to obtain his, continuing, 'yet, fearing it might harden him in his heterodoxy, after a genteel complement as a person of learning, I told him freely that, wherein he dissented from the catholick Church, I did the like from him, which seemed to startle him as a rough complement, but went off in a litle discourse'.[50]

By comparison, Thoresby's coffee-house encounters with sadducees seem to have caused him an almost visceral anxiety, as we have seen, and experiences like these appear to have impelled him to a project for continuing the supernaturalist enterprise of Glanvill and Boyle. On the very trip to London when he met Oddy, Thoresby records that he began a collection of supernatural phenomena, which is clearly described in his 'Review' (his until recently unpublished autobiography) as comprising 'some memorable, wel-attested narrativs of apparitions and preternatural occurrences' (his long-available diary is more ambiguous in its wording).[51] It is perhaps worth noting in passing how we have now come so far from the traditional, inter-mediate concept of the 'preternatural' noted in the Introduction that Thoresby uses the word as a synonym for 'supernatural', and this was symp-tomatic of the way in which the word was increasingly used thereafter.[52] None other than Edward Fowler provided Thoresby with the letter of encouragement which was prefixed to the collection, which he 'earnestly desired' Thoresby 'to publish for the conviction of sceptical people in this infidel age'; at the same time, he also gave him 'some remarkable narratives of spirits'.[53]

Sadly, Thoresby's collection no longer survives, but some idea of its likely content is available from materials that *are* extant – particularly his notes on William Turner's *A Compleat History of the Most Remarkable Providences, Both of Judgment and Mercy, Which have Hapned in this Present Age* (1697), a further apologetic work in which supernatural visitations figured, and the extracts that Thoresby made from the diaries of the nonconformist, Oliver Heywood, and the 'daybook' of Henry Sampson, which survive in the British Library (the latter is also the source of some of our knowledge of Fowler's interest in such matters).[54] The Heywood extracts include various strange and prodigious phenomena such as apparitions, while the extracts from Sampson's daybook have more of the same: premonitions of death and other apparitions; sudden deaths, deliverances and visions; cases of diabolical possession and haunted houses; and a case of witchcraft at Honiton in Devon. In addition, some accounts of prophecies, premonitory dreams and 'other supernatural occurences' that were probably destined for the work survive elsewhere among Thoresby's papers.[55] The loss of his collection is the more poignant because, had it survived, it would in a sense have been the last great English work of demonology, its apologetic purpose meaning that the accumulative skills of the scientist and antiquary were enrolled in the defence of religion itself. Thoresby was a pious, well-intentioned figure, an heir to the tradition of Puritan spirituality of the seventeenth century who straddles the nonconformist–Anglican divide (in 1699 he abandoned his dissenting roots and conformed to the Church of England).[56] It is thus revealing that he seems to have seen it almost as a public duty to undertake the defence of the supernatural realm against those who questioned its existence.

A rather different commentary on the association of sadducism with freethinking appears in the play, *The Drummer, or the Haunted House*, written by Joseph Addison possibly with the assistance of others, a romping comedy based on supposed ghostly apparitions which was put on in 1716.[57] Its ultimate inspiration was the Tedworth case to which reference has already been made and the continuing ambivalence over which will be considered in Chapter 4. Of course, in *The Spectator*, that influential arbiter of fashionable opinion, Addison had specifically advocated in 1711 that witchcraft was a subject 'in which a Man should stand Neuter, without engaging his Assent to one side or the other'. Though admitting that he could 'give no Credit to any Particular Instance of it', he nevertheless continued to aver that 'I believe in general that there is and has been such a thing as Witch-craft'.[58] As far as *The Drummer* is concerned, most of the characters in the play take it for granted that apparitions were plausible, even if the context is quite light-hearted and ambivalent: Addison seems already to have been feeling his way towards seeing the potential for a kind of suspension of disbelief concerning such phenomena in a dramatic context, a proto-Romantic attitude that befitted the author of the well-known *Spectator* essays on 'The Pleasures of the Imagination'.[59] There is, however, a striking exception to this ambivalence in the form of the character 'Tinsel', a self-proclaimed wit down from London, who promises his country hosts 'that you shall learn to think as Freely as the best of us'. He is axiomatically dismissive of apparitions of the kind around which the play revolves, explaining,

> I am convinc'd by four or five learned Men, whom I sometimes over-hear at a Coffee-house I frequent, that our Fore-fathers were a Pack of Asses, that the World has been in an Error for some Thousands of Years, and that all the People upon Earth, excepting those two or three worthy Gentlemen, are impos'd upon, cheated, bubbled, abus'd, bamboozl'd.

Of course, this is the sensible Addison's caricature, but the point is that when an apparition *does* appear – thus reflecting Addison's ambivalence about the reality of such phenomena, in contrast to the dogmatism on the subject that he attributed to Tinsel – Tinsel instantly renounces his scepticism, and flees in terror.[60]

In this connection it is worth noting a challenge issued to Addison in connection with his comments on witchcraft in *The Spectator* by the author who adapted John Wagstaffe's *The Question of Witchcraft Debated* as a commentary on the Jane Wenham case, probably William Pittis. As noted in the last chapter, these extracts from Wagstaffe's book originally appeared in the journal, *The Protestant Post-Boy*, and in one of the issues involved, the editor deliberately called Addison's bluff concerning witchcraft, aping *The Spectator* in providing a motto from Horace (in fact, a quotation that Addison had himself used in a similar context) and challenging Addison's decision to 'stand Neuter' on the subject. Instead, he argued that in such passages Horace had 'laid it down as a Mark or Token of a Man's Proficiency in *Moral Philosophy*, if he had learn'd to dispise and laugh at such kind of Fables as my last was written to expose'.[61] Indeed, the compatibility of scepticism with cosmic optimism of an essentially classical kind is well captured by Addison himself in the very issue of *The Spectator* in which he used the quotation from Horace in question. In it, he excoriated a variety of superstitions, from monitory dreams to spilled salt, reflecting 'on the Evils that attend these superstitious Follies of Mankind; how they subject us to imaginary Afflictions, and additional Sorrows that do not properly come within our Lot', and adding, 'as it is the chief Concern of Wise-Men, to retrench the Evils of Life by the Reasonings of Philosophy; it is the Employment of Fools, to multiply them by the Sentiments of Superstition'.[62] It might be felt that it was only a matter of time before the orthodox saw the incompatibility of magical beliefs with the outlook that such comments reflect.

### Francis Hutchinson and Changing Orthodoxy

In fact, gradually and slightly timidly, the orthodox *did* start to come around to adopting the scepticism that had been pioneered by the freethinkers and that they had previously rejected as dangerous, and this is the process that we must now document. Here, the key figure is Francis Hutchinson, whose *Historical Essay concerning Witchcraft* (1718) has long been acclaimed as the *coup de grâce* to witchcraft beliefs among the educated in England. It is therefore worth focusing on him both to try to understand what factors underlay this key change, and to explore how far thinkers like him *were* now speaking the language previously espoused by the heterodox.

Hutchinson seems to have drafted his *Historical Essay* long before it was finally published in 1718, exploring the possibility of publishing it in 1707 and then again in 1712 in connection with the Jane Wenham affair.[63] It is interesting that on the first occasion we learn that the book was frowned on by the church authorities. The specific reason given for its suppression at that point was that it might upset the Scots at the time of the impending Union, Scottish opinion being notoriously conservative on such matters: this was a shrewd move, since, as the author of a sermon in support of the Union, Hutchinson was hardly likely to demur. On the other hand, it seems likely that what was really at stake was a continuing belief among many churchmen in the reality of witchcraft – or at least, a pusillanimity on the subject – encouraged by the heterodox affiliations of sadducism that have been surveyed in this and the previous chapter.[64]

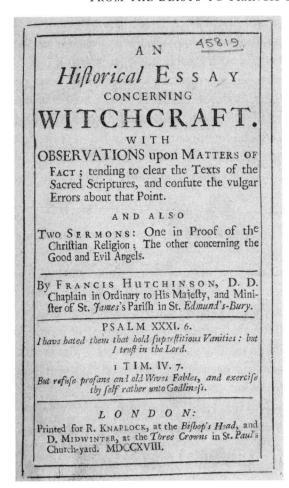

AN 45819.

*Hiſtorical* E s s a y

CONCERNING

WITCHCRAFT.

W I T H

OBSERVATIONS upon MATTERS OF
FACT ; tending to clear the Texts of the
Sacred Scriptures, and confute the vulgar
Errors about that Point.

A N D  A L S O

Two S E R M O N S : One in Proof of the
Chriſtian Religion ; The other concerning the
Good and Evil Angels.

By FRANCIS HUTCHINSON, D. D.
Chaplain in Ordinary to His Majeſty, and Mini-
ſter of St. *James's* Pariſh in St. *Edmund's-Bury.*

PSALM XXXI. 6.

*I have hated them that hold ſuperſtitious Vanities : but
I truſt in the Lord.*

1 T I M. IV. 7.

*But refuſe profane and old Wives Fables, and exerciſe
thy ſelf rather unto Godlineſs.*

L O N D O N:

Printed for R. KNAPLOCK, at the *Biſhop's Head,* and
D. MIDWINTER, at the *Three Crowns* in St. *Paul's*
Church-yard. MDCCXVIII.

2. The title-page of Francis
Hutchinson's *An Historical
Essay Concerning Witchcraft*
(1718).

The long gestation of Hutchinson's ideas on the subject make their initial
stimulus a little hard to divine. It is possible, as his recent biographer has
suggested, that he first came to feel strongly on such matters as a result of his
personal experience of a witchcraft case in 1694 while he was a cleric at Bury
St Edmunds; this might have been the stimulus to the special study that he
made of the notorious Matthew Hopkins witch-hunt in East Anglia half a
century earlier.[65] But Hutchinson's feelings were clearly enhanced by the
Wenham case in 1712, which more than ever exemplified the ignorance and
credulity that he saw as characterising popular witch beliefs, resulting, in his
view, in 'great trouble & disturbance, not only to the poor old Creatures,
but to all timerous Persons, & the whole Neighbourhoods where they are'.[66]
Some historians have seen the Wenham trial as decisive because of

the extent to which it politicised witch beliefs and thereby discredited them, and it certainly had political overtones locally, while some of the pamphlets published in connection with it were highly partisan in tone.[67] But it might be argued that what was more crucial was the extent to which it accentuated the incompatibility between traditional witch beliefs of the kind which surfaced in the trial and its aftermath and the confident and critical ethos of the period to which Hutchinson gave expression: indeed, it is thus that one could read the reference that was made to the episode by Anthony Collins in the section of his *Discourse of Free-thinking* that has already been referred to.[68]

In Hutchinson's case, further evidence on the evolution of his views is provided by his opposition to the so-called French Prophets, who had come from the Cévennes claiming miraculous powers, and who achieved a significant following in London in the first decade of the eighteenth century (though this diminished when they predicted that one of their converts, Thomas Emes, would rise from the dead and he failed to do so). Hutchinson's attack on them, entitled *A Short View of the Pretended Spirit of Prophecy* (1708), argued that 'a great part of them are crafty Impostors'.[69] The French Prophets were disconcerting not least because they did not simply represent the forces of popular superstition but gained support from people of high status; it was partly for this reason that Hutchinson went out of his way to present them as implicitly subversive and destabilising of the status quo.[70] Equally important, as Hillel Schwartz has pointed out in his study of the opposition to the Prophets, was the contrast among their critics between an older generation – including Edward Fowler – who accepted that the Prophets had supernatural gifts but attributed these to the Devil rather than God, and men like Hutchinson who combined this with a much more naturalistic line, attributing their behaviour to natural forces or to deception.[71] Indeed, Hutchinson used his book as an opportunity to try to discredit claims to supernatural powers more generally, including a lengthy section attacking a series of supposed prophets and illuminati, from John Dee to Sabbatai Ṣevi, in a manner that would have made Edward Fowler rather uncomfortable but would have delighted Deists like the Earl of Shaftesbury.[72]

As for Hutchinson's book on witchcraft, this followed his attack on the French Prophets in its emphasis on fraud – also, of course, shared with Deist commentators like Molesworth whom we have already encountered. Nearly a fifth of the book comprises 'a Collection of some notorious IMPOSTURES Detected', ranging from the Maid of Kent in the Reformation period, through such cases as those of William Sommers and the Boy of Bilson in the years around 1600, to that of Richard Hathaway, 'convicted of Imposture by the Lord Chief Justice *Holt*' in 1702.[73] The book is also notable for Hutchinson's modish appeal to 'principles' in assessing the plausibility of witchcraft and other beliefs: he used the term to denote premises to arguments, which meant that these could as easily be false as true, the principles of the witch-finders being 'unnatural, contradictory, and absurd'.[74] He has also been acclaimed a pioneer in using probability theory to assess testimony on such topics, even if it was primarily through examining historical instances that he did so.[75]

What is most significant about the *Historical Essay*, however, is the extent to which Hutchinson felt that in it he was negotiating a route between Scylla and Charybdis, between superstition on the one hand and a dangerous degree of scepticism on the other – 'an Atheistical Sadducism on one hand, and a timorous Enthusiastical Credulity on the other', in Hutchinson's own words.[76] This has been missed in most previous scholarly accounts of Hutchinson because the authors in question failed to take account of the pioneering freethinking tradition of scepticism surveyed in this and the previous chapter, and the extent to which this inhibited similar attitudes on the part of the orthodox.[77] Hutchinson's book is set out as a dialogue between a jury-man, an 'advocate' from Scotland and a clergyman who clearly speaks for Hutchinson. At the start of the 'Conclusion', the jury-man refers to one of the books published in connection with the Wenham case, *The Impossibility of Witchcraft* – in other words the reprint of John Wagstaffe's sceptical work which we examined in the last chapter – and says to the clergyman, 'I do not remember, that in any part of our *Dialogue* you have ventur'd so far: And therefore some will think that in several Parts you have been too cautious, and left Things too doubtful'. The clergyman replies, 'I had rather err on that Hand than the other . . . There is something doubtful in all Subjects', and he was at pains to stress that his argument was about the weakness of the evidence against most accused witches rather than the reality of a diabolical realm as a whole.[78] In fact, though Hutchinson did reach a sceptical conclusion, his approach was cautious – almost timid – compared with that of Wagstaffe, and his anxiety about going even as far as he did is revealed by his concern that what he had said 'may not be made an ill Use of, by those who are too apt to take Things wrong'.[79]

Indeed, Hutchinson refers more than once in his book to more extreme stances than his own, and to the extent to which a moderate position like his had formerly been inhibited by 'fear of loose People carrying the Notion too far the other way'.[80] It was 'for Prevention of Mistakes' of this kind that he appended to his treatise a sermon 'in Proof of the Christian Religion' and another asserting the existence of good and bad angels, which were explicitly aimed to refute 'the Free-Thinkers of our Age'.[81] Hence it is not surprising that the Deists John Trenchard and Thomas Gordon, in their more radical dismissal of witch beliefs in *Cato's Letters* a few years later, were rather disdainful of Hutchinson, describing him as 'the worthy Dr Hutchinson', and referring rather patronisingly to 'what he hath with great piety and judgment published upon this subject'.[82]

Hutchinson's book is therefore a testimony to a point at which a moderate scepticism about witchcraft came to be acceptable because outright belief in the phenomenon seemed more dangerous than outright disbelief in it. Hutchinson was content to go part of the way down the sceptical route of the freethinkers because the alternative was the disruptive enthusiasm represented by the popular uproar over the Jane Wenham case or that associated with the French Prophets. And this was not an act of political partisanship: it was not because Hutchinson was a Whig that he adopted this view, as has been claimed in certain recent accounts of witch beliefs in this period, which have arguably greatly overestimated their party-political nature – a point to which we will return in the Conclusion to this book.[83] Hutchinson's decision to critique witch beliefs was a matter of conviction which probably hindered his career rather than enhanced it.[84] Indeed, it is revealing that he himself rather deprecatingly described the *Historical Essay* in a letter to the Oxford scholar, Arthur Charlett, as being about 'so dark & unpopular a subject', and this letter seems to hint that he was slightly less confident in the position that he adopted in his book than he implied within its pages.[85] Nevertheless, at this stage we have arguably reached a pivotal point in terms of the acceptability of sadducism to the orthodox. We will revisit this from another perspective in the following chapter, and pursue its later trajectory in subsequent ones.

CHAPTER THREE

# THE AMBIVALENCE OF THE EARLY
# ROYAL SOCIETY

What part did the Royal Society in its early years play in the 'Decline of Magic' to which this book is devoted? On this topic, views have differed. It has sometimes been asserted, for instance by Sir Henry Lyons in his 1944 history of the society, that the body significantly undermined belief in witch-craft and the like through its efforts to 'investigate critically this and other reputed supernatural manifestations' – and we will see in the course of this chapter that such views have an ancestry going back to figures like Francis Hutchinson whom we encountered in the previous one.[1] Indeed, this might seem to be borne out by Thomas Sprat's famous *History of the Royal Society* (1667), which contains some scathing comments on magical practices, for instance regarding techniques that astrologers used 'to deceive the Ignorant', while Sprat's view of alchemy was: 'their success has been as small, as their design was extravagant. Their Writers involve them in such darkness; that I scarce know, which was the greatest task, to understand their meaning, or to effect it.' He also looked back on an age when 'an infinit number of *Fairies* haunted every house' and apparitions appeared everywhere, a state of affairs from which he claimed the new philosophy had freed people.[2]

On the other hand, we are now aware that Sprat's *History* only imper-fectly represents the corporate stance of the society on whose behalf it was composed and, after being subjected to some outspoken criticism, it was effectively withdrawn.[3] Indeed, on this particular issue his book may have expressed almost the reverse of the truth, since, in a pair of articles published in 1976, K. Theodore Hoppen took a diametrically opposite view, arguing that the society's membership in its early years was characterised by an overwhelming eclecticism, in which magical beliefs played a central role: indeed, he went so far as to assert that this represented the true 'nature' of the early Royal Society.[4]

In reconsidering this question, it is important to focus on the role of the
society as a corporate body. Although we have come to be suspicious of
manufactured statements of the society's policy like Sprat's, it remains true
that the society as an institution represented more than the sum of its parts:
it early acquired a corporate momentum which partook of the efforts of its
individual members but transcended them in a manner which is significant
in itself.[5] What is more, we can study the society's corporate life through the
extraordinarily full records of its activities which survive, particularly in the
form of its journal books, which allow us to eavesdrop on its proceedings in
a manner that is almost unique for the period.[6] We have an almost equally
rich set of records documenting the society's public role – especially the
correspondence undertaken on the society's behalf by its first secretary,
Henry Oldenburg, and the publication stemming from this that he inaugu-
rated in 1665, *Philosophical Transactions*.[7] Through such means, the society
undoubtedly had an influential institutional presence. In part, this occurred
through defining the proper method of doing science, a topic that has been
the subject of much interest in recent years.[8] But, though this has received
less attention, the society also played a key role in defining the boundaries
of the studies that fell within the remit of natural philosophy – what is nowadays referred to as 'boundary work'.[9] Arguably, the society as an institution
had a substantial influence on contemporaries' perception of just what
science did or did not comprise.[10]

This means that, in assessing the society's role in relation to magic, it is
on the society's institutional activity that we should focus. The question
cannot be answered by reference to broader intellectual trends with which
the society was associated, and which to a greater or lesser extent it exemplified – the rise of the mechanical philosophy, for instance, or the role of
Baconian empiricism – although these have often been seen as contributing
in some way to changing attitudes towards magic.[11] These would only be
relevant insofar as they were explicitly invoked by the society in this connection. Equally important is the need to consider the society as a corporate
body. Insofar as specific Fellows may have had interests which they pursued
apart from the society but which did not recur in its proceedings, these
should not form part of any assessment of the society as a whole. Indeed,
they may be significant for the disparity they may reveal between the individual's private concerns and those of the institution, which will further
help us to identify the distinctiveness of the position which the society may
have adopted in relation to magic and related topics.

This brings us to the findings adduced by Hoppen in his 1976 study and their significance. Hoppen professed to illustrate the heterogeneity of the society and the extent to which its Fellows were interested in magical and other topics that would at one time have seemed inappropriate in 'serious scientists' such as the body comprised. He did so by collecting evidence illustrating a fascination with magical or preternatural phenomena and a commitment to alchemy, astrology and other arcane pursuits on the part of many of the society's early Fellows, including such luminaries as Robert Boyle and Isaac Newton, as well as lesser figures like John Aubrey, Thomas Henshaw and Robert Plot. Hoppen's terms of reference were slightly different from those used here, in that he was interested in all evidence of 'eclecticism' on the part of Fellows, which meant that he devoted as much attention to an interest in the monstrous and the bizarre as in the magical. Yet the two are appropriately separated, since attention to the prodigious in contrast to nature 'in its ordinary course' had been advocated by Bacon as a key part of natural history; it is thus rather different from overtly magical practices, of which Bacon was more wary.[12] But, even if we ignore such concerns and concentrate on more arcane ones, we still find evidence of interest in witchcraft and comparable phenomena, as well as an active engagement with pursuits like astrology and alchemy, among many leading Fellows of the society in its early years.

What needs to be stressed, however, is the extent to which these were the *private* interests of these Fellows, on which Hoppen was able to throw light by his extensive investigation of sources other than the records of the society. At the meetings of the society, and in articles in the *Philosophical Transactions*, such matters come up tangentially, if at all. Perhaps the closest that the society came to a systematic investigation of a phenomenon central to the magical preoccupations of the day was that of may-dew in 1664–5, as studied by Alan Taylor. It was widely believed that may-dew might have mysterious, alchemical properties.[13] Thereafter, we very occasionally encounter laboratory-based investigations relating to alchemy – an area where the natural and the supernatural were notoriously intertwined – while there is also Boyle's 1676 paper in *Philosophical Transactions* on the incalescence of mercury, though this was as unusual in its subject matter as in its format (it was set in Latin and English in parallel columns, a mode of presentation never otherwise used in the journal).[14] What needs to be emphasised, however, is the sheer rarity of such excursions into the arcane in the society's corporate proceedings. Moreover, when it came to phenomena like witchcraft or astrology, the society's records are extraordinarily taciturn, as a few instances will illustrate.

## Some Examples

Such cases will also reinforce the importance of distinguishing between the activities of the society as a corporate body and the wider activities of what might be called the Royal Society circle. One famous instance concerns the Irish 'stroker', Valentine Greatrakes, whose cures by laying his hands on diseased people caused a stir when he came to England in 1666. Initially, Greatrakes was based in the West Midlands and particularly at Ragley, where he attempted unsuccessfully to cure the migraine attacks of Lady Anne Conway, but in February that year he moved to London, in the first instance at the command of the king, ministering to many in and around the metropolis. Indeed, at this point his activities were monitored by Robert Boyle, who kept a log of the healing sessions by Greatrakes that he observed between 6 and 16 April, and it was evidently at the behest of Boyle and other like-minded figures that from this point onwards Greatrakes began to keep detailed 'Testimonials' of the cures that he effected which were subsequently to be published in the *Brief Account* of himself in the form of a letter to Boyle which he published later in 1666: this represented a novel way of recording phenomena of this kind and could be seen as reflecting the Baconian ethos which was so important to the Royal Society (though, here again, broader trends should not be mistaken for specific institutional influence).[15]

Greatrakes's cures raised the issue of the nature of his powers – whether he performed Christ-like miracles, or whether a natural explanation of them could be given – and a pamphlet war ensued. This involved such figures as the controversialist Henry Stubbe who, by dedicating his 1666 pamphlet on the subject, *The Miraculous Conformist*, to Boyle, impelled Boyle to give his own view on the matter. This was that he was 'not yet fully convinc'd that there is . . . any thing that is purely supernaturall' about what Greatrakes did ('unlesse in the way wherein he was made to take notice of his Guift, & exercise it . . .) and therefore till the contrary doth appear, I hold it not unlawfull to endeavour to give a Phisicall Account of his Cures'.[16] The episode has often been seen as closely involving the Royal Society. Indeed, one recent commentator on it, Jane Shaw in her *Miracles in Enlightenment England* (2006), treats the position adopted by Boyle and others as essentially a 'Royal Society' one.[17]

It is certainly true that Stubbe appealed to Boyle and to the society for arbitration on the subject, and at one point in his *Brief Account*, Greatrakes himself referred to 'those Honourable Gentlemen of *Gresham* Colledge, who were pleased to afford me the Honour of their Company at *Lincolns-Inn-fields*, and elsewhere', though the identity of these figures and the nature of their role is unclear.[18] But it is important to stress that, as a corporate body, the Royal Society was not involved in the episode at all. Greatrakes was never mentioned in the society's minutes: during the spring of 1666, when interest in his cures was at its height, the society's proceedings were entirely devoted to 'science', to Hooke's investigations of gravity and of the rotation of the planet Mars, to various investigations of the loadstone and its powers, or to discussion of the potential for transfusing blood from one animal to another. Slightly more topical were discussions of the plague, from the outbreak of which London had only recently recovered, and there was also, of course, an admixture of more miscellaneous business, but of Greatrakes and his cures we hear nothing.[19] The nearest the society came to taking an interest in the affair was the publication of an article entitled 'Some Observations Of the Effects of *Touch* and *Friction*' in *Philosophical Transactions* in May 1666. This was clearly inspired by the Greatrakes episode, but, that being the case, it is strangely opaque, failing actually to mention Greatrakes at all.[20] In terms of its corporate role, as against the activities of individual members like Boyle, it is important to stress that the Royal Society was almost entirely uninvolved in the affair.

A comparable example is provided by the witchcraft project of the divine, Joseph Glanvill, who made much of his credentials as 'Fellow of the Royal Society' in his demonological work which went through various recensions from 1666 onwards, initially under the title *A Philosophical Endeavour Towards the Defence of the Being of Witches and Apparitions*. In it, as we saw in the Introduction, Glanvill echoed the society's methodological stance in appealing to the establishment of '*matters* of *fact*' which it was unreasonable to reject on the grounds that we cannot explain the phenomena involved, invoking our nescience as to the formation of a foetus in the womb or a plant in the earth to justify a similar open-mindedness towards the realm of spirits. In providing detailed narratives of witchcraft cases, he also profess-edly deployed the kind of approach used by Boyle and other members of the Royal Society, of not only invoking such 'matters of fact' but also appealing to the 'credit' of their 'Relators' in order to prove beyond doubt the reality of the Devil's activity in the world.[21]

Glanvill even went so far as to suggest that the Royal Society might itself investigate witchcraft, calling on the society to take up the study of such phenomena in a dedication to William, Viscount Brereton, in the 1668 edition of his work, now entitled *A Blow at Modern Sadducism*. Urging that 'the *SOCIETY* of which your Lordship is an illustrious Member, direct some of its *wary*, and *luciferous* enquiries towards the *World* of *Spirits*', Glanvill explained how:

> as things are for the present, the LAND of SPIRITS is a kinde of *AMERICA*, and not well discover'd *Region* . . . For we know not any thing of the world we live in, but by *experiment*, and the *Phænomena*; and there is the same way of *speculating immaterial* nature, by *extraordinary Events* and *Apparitions*, which possibly might be improved to *notices* not *contemptible*, were there a *Cautious*, and *Faithful History* made of those *certain* and *uncommon appearances.*[22]

In fact, however, the society as a corporate body took not the slightest notice. It may be true, as Charles Webster has written, that 'individual initiative more than made up for the lack of formal commitment of the Society to this project', and certainly not only Glanvill and his mentor, Henry More, but also Robert Boyle and other Fellows were active in collecting material of this kind, as we saw in the Introduction.[23] But this surely misses the point. What is significant is the fact that, corporately, the society had no time for Glanvill's suggestion at all.

Insofar as the society *did* take a corporate line on witchcraft, it was ironically to give its imprimatur to a sceptical treatise, *The Displaying of Supposed Witchcraft* (1677), by the Yorkshire physician, John Webster. The minutes record that the manuscript of Webster's book was presented at a meeting on 4 March 1675, the author desiring 'that the Society would give their sense of it'; three Fellows, Sir William Petty, John Pell and Daniel Milles, were thereupon asked to report on it, and some notes on the work survive among the papers of Pell, now in the British Library, including a transcript of the dedication to the Royal Society that formed part of the manuscript. We also know that Webster (who was not himself a Fellow) had approached his Yorkshire contact, Martin Lister, to see if the society would license the book since it had been rejected by the ecclesiastical censors on the grounds not least that it 'attributed too much to naturall causes', and Lister seems to have been instrumental in arranging for it to be put before the society. After a substantial delay, it was indeed provided with the society's imprimatur, but in a very abnormal manner. Previously, the imprimatur had always been authorised by the President at a meeting of the society's council. In this case, on the other hand, the recently elected vice-president, Sir Jonas Moore, a former contact of Webster's, issued the imprimatur on a day when neither the society nor its council met, a unique and highly irregular procedure. It seems to have been a case of slipping the book through as a personal favour when other censors had rejected it, rather than representing any considered stance on the society's part. Indeed, it is revealing that, as published, the book lacked the dedication to the society, instead being dedicated to five Yorkshire JPs (it is perhaps also significant that no copy of the book is now to be found in the society's library). In all, though the episode provides a telling commentary on the dysfunctional state of the society in the late 1670s, it says little about the institution's attitude to magic.[24]

Later in the century, witchcraft and related phenomena were mentioned at the society's meetings on just a couple of occasions. On 28 March 1688 a letter was read about a case of supposed bewitchment in Ireland, which stimulated reference to a comparable case. But the comment elicited by the initial instance was sceptical – 'It was supposed that this might be carried on by confederacy as severall things of the like nature had upon examination been found to be' – and the exchange was rounded off by an anecdote from a further Fellow about a 'cheat' in medicine.[25] Then, in March 1691, a case was reported of a woman said to be possessed by the Devil, and an implicitly sceptical tone is apparent from the view that was expressed that the idea of possession worked on her 'fancy' and had a harmful effect on her health.[26] These were typical of the kind of miscellaneous reports with which the society's minutes in these years are full, and they do not suggest that witchcraft was more than a minor preoccupation. It is perhaps revealing that the documents divulged on these occasions do not appear to have been registered in the society's records, and neither were the matters pursued. Again, we see a position in which phenomena that Glanvill and others considered crucial and worthy of serious investigation were simply sidelined by the society as a corporate body.

A third example concerns astrology, and especially the society's relations with John Goad, headmaster of Merchant Taylors' School, and his attempt to reform the art by a meticulous study over many years of the relations between the weather and the movements of the planets, ultimately published in his *Astro-Meteorologia* (1686). This was a highly Baconian project which was again in the spirit of the Royal Society, and in which the society could easily have taken an interest if it had seen such topics as within its remit.[27] Certainly Goad circulated his monthly weather predictions to individual Fellows of the society – Boyle in 1678 and perhaps over a longer period, and Elias Ashmole for more than a decade.[28] In addition, Goad's project was briefly discussed at a meeting of the society on 16 January 1679, when the president, Sir Joseph Williamson, inquired, whether Dr Goad had perfected his theory of predicting the quarter and strength of the winds from astronomy. To which Sir Jonas Moore answered, that Mr Flamstead had examined several of Dr Goad's predictions, but had not found one of them true. But Mr Henshaw had examined them continually for about two years about a month since, and had found not above one of four false.[29]

That was it: the discussion started and ended there, and was never pursued. It is as if the Royal Society as a body did not want to get involved in such issues. Thereafter, a copy of Goad's book was presented to the society by the then secretary, Thomas Gale, on 5 May 1686, but no discussion ensued.[30] There are complications about this matter. In particular, Flamsteed's own attitudes – towards both astrology and Goad – were more ambivalent than the passage above implies, as I have shown in my study of his critique of astrology and the reasons why he never published it. There is also evidence for open-mindedness towards or support for astrology among various other Fellows.[31] But what is significant is that, insofar as the society as a corporate body could have associated itself with an empirical assessment of the validity of astrology in relation to the weather as represented by Goad's project, it failed to do so; it had even less association with other attempts to reform astrology along empirical, Baconian lines.[32]

Astrology recurred in the society's proceedings in 1697, when an anonymous correspondent wrote to the society 'containing some assertions of the said authors abilitys & designs to promote & perfect Astrology if he could procure some sutable incouragement and by this perfect Astrology to perfect Astronomy also'. Interestingly, the society responded to this, not with a doctrinaire dismissal, but the desire that he should produce proof of his ability by attempting some prediction.[33] Yet that is again as far as the matter went. If it suggests an ambivalence not dissimilar to that seen in the discussion of Goad, it also implies a lack of strong interest in the subject on the society's part. Such matters were evidently seen as dispensable from its remit, and figured only in a marginal way in its proceedings.

### The Society's 'Policy' and its Rationale

Why was this so? Up to a point, it may have been due to the role of individuals, especially those central to the institutional life of the society in its early years, at least two of whom seem to have been distinctly anti-magical in their attitudes. One was Henry Oldenburg, first secretary of the society and inaugurator of the *Philosophical Transactions*, whose attitudes as divulged in his assiduous correspondence did more than anything to define the early Royal Society's official line. Oldenburg's comments in a letter to Boyle of 10 October 1665 suggest that he might have been responsible for the society's lack of corporate interest in Greatrakes, while in April 1669, when the virtuoso Joshua Childrey offered Oldenburg 'the fullest, & most particular account of Sorcery ... that ever I met with', Oldenburg noted concerning his response, 'said nothing of MS. of Sorcery'.[34] This seems to have typified his attitude on such matters, and he was evidently also sceptical about astrology.[35] Indeed, it seems possible that correspondents to the society from New England who were inclined to supernaturalist interpretations of phenomena – like some of the commentators on Greatrakes – tended to write to like-minded Fellows such as Lord Brereton or Theodore Haak rather than to Oldenburg, though Oldenburg's growing monopoly over the society's correspondence made this increasingly marginal.[36]

The other central figure who was outspokenly hostile to magic was the society's curator of experiments and Cutlerian lecturer, Robert Hooke. Hooke's views on such subjects have recently been the subject of scrutiny and it turns out that he had some sympathy for figures in the 'natural magic' tradition such as John Dee, from whose writings he thought valuable truths might be recovered. In addition, certain of his notions had definite non-mechanical overtones, perhaps particularly the significance that he attached to 'harmony' in his views on the congruity of particles, or his invocation of 'active principles' both in the animate and the inanimate creation. He certainly illustrates how we need a definition of the mechanical philosophy broad enough to encapsulate this.[37] Yet what needs to be emphasised in Hooke's case is that he was explicitly anti-magical. In a lecture that he gave to the Royal Society in 1676, he strongly criticised Henry More's invocation of a so-called 'Hylarchick Spirit' 'to perform all those things which are plainly and clearly performed by the common and known Rules of Mechanicks'. Hooke saw mechanical principles as providing a perfectly adequate explanation of such phenomena, and he considered it unhelpful for More to 'perplex our minds with unintelligible Idea's of things'. Of course, as we saw in the Introduction, More's 'Spirit' was intended to encapsulate God's vicarious power in the world, but Hooke mocked him by conflating it with superstitious magic of a kind that he scorned. He wrote:

For supposing the Doctor had proved there were such an Hylarchick Spirit, what were we the better or the wiser unless we also know how to rule and govern this Spirit? And that we could, like Conjurers, command this Spirit, and set it at work upon whatever we had occasion for it to do. If it were a Spirit that Regulated the motion of the water in its running faster or slower, I am yet to learn by what Charm or Incantation I should be able to incite the Spirit to be less or more active, in such proportion as I had occasion for, and desired; how should I signifie to it that I had occasion for a current of water that should run eight Gallons in a minute through a hole of an Inch bore?[38]

No less revealing is a lecture that Hooke delivered in 1690 in which he claimed that the diaries in which John Dee recorded his supposed intercourse with spirits must be written in code since they seemed to him to comprise 'a Rhapsody' of 'unintelligible Whimsies', whereas in Hooke's view Dee was 'a very extraordinary Knowing Man in his time, and not to be suppos'd capable of such incoherent ridiculous fancies, as are in appearance contained in that Book'.[39] Equally telling is a letter about alchemy from Hooke to the Somerset virtuoso, Andrew Pascall, an avowed devotee of such studies, in which, though pleading his 'dulnesse' and 'Ignorance in this matter' in an evident attempt to avoid hurting Pascall's feelings, Hooke made it clear that he thought the entire business a waste of time.[40] His comments on Goad's attempts to provide an astrological account of the weather are equally caustic: 'Made Jupiter cold and malignant and many other whims about the weather', he wrote in his diary.[41] Since Hooke dominated the business of the society's meetings much as Oldenburg dominated its external relations, they might have been expected to be influential in such matters.

On the other hand, since both men were subordinate to the 'grandees' who actually directed the society, particularly its honorary officers and Council members, this does not seem a sufficient explanation. Instead, we need to revert to the corporate identity of the society and the way in which this actually operated, with a role being played by these and other active Fellows.[42] Here, various factors were arguably involved. One was the range of Fellows' opinions about magic in a private capacity which has been illustrated by the work of Hoppen and others: in the light of this, one would simply not expect the kind of anti-magical party line that Sir Henry Lyons evidently took for granted in the passage quoted at the start of this chapter (to the rationale of which we will return). In fact, what is likelier is a kind of stalemate, with the scepticism of Oldenburg and Hooke being balanced by ambivalence towards or enthusiasm for magic on the part of others.[43] In such a situation, there was clearly something to be said for avoiding the topic as one likely to lead to disagreement which a focus on 'safe' science would avoid.

A further, related complication was the extent to which magic may have had controversial overtones in connection with religious debates in late seventeenth-century England, especially the reaction against 'enthusiasm' and the concern about 'atheism' that were surveyed in the Introduction. It is true that certain prominent early Fellows of the society had been associated with the rejection of magical ideas as an adjunct of religious radicalism in the 1650s, while by this time matters were complicated by the extent to which men like Glanvill wanted to defend the reality of phenomena like witchcraft as a defence against the 'atheism' which was seen as rampant.[44] The polemical overtones of such enterprises, too, might have encouraged the society to avoid such issues.

Equally important was a factor which I have invoked in relation to Robert Boyle's behaviour concerning magic, and particularly his prevarication over publishing the now lost second part of his *Strange Reports*, in which he would have divulged various empirically substantiated supernatural phenomena. The reason he gave was: 'Discretion forbidding me to let that appear, till I see what Entertainment will be given to the *I. Part*, that consists but of Relations far less strange than those that make up the other Part.'[45] This reflected the concern about his 'reputation' that Boyle expressed in the prefaces to various of his books – we know from contemporary sources that 'Some condemns him for being too credulous and giving too much heed to the relations of his informers in philos[ophical] matters'[46] – and similar considerations may have affected the Royal Society as well. Certainly there were those who were concerned about the society's 'reputation' – such as the unidentified 'A. B.' in his commentary on the state of the society in 1674, who saw this as the key to its obtaining the support it needed to be effective in its mission. As A. B's anxieties underline, it is easy in retrospect to forget how marginal and lacking in support the society was in its early years, and the extent to which it therefore had to mind its Ps and Qs in relation to public opinion.[47]

As far as magic was concerned, there was a particularly potent body of public opinion in terms of the fashionable discourse of the London intelligentsia, represented by the 'wits' of the play-houses and the coffee-houses.

As we saw in Chapter 1, with particular reference to the most strikingly
sceptical text from this era, John Wagstaffe's *The Question of Witchcraft
Debated* (1669), *they* seem to have been in the forefront in rejecting magic
at this time, when more serious-minded figures like the clerics and profes-
sionals who made up the Royal Society were more divided in their views.
Indeed, partly due to such iconoclasm, men like Wagstaffe were in the forefront of the 'atheism' about which orthodox spokesmen like Glanvill
expressed such concern, as surveyed in the Introduction. It is also worth
noting that, in this milieu, the science of the Royal Society was already a
joke, as witnessed in satires by Samuel Butler, author of *Hudibras*, or in
Thomas Shadwell's notorious play *The Virtuoso* (1676).[48] As Boyle found,
public engagement with the realm of magic was a dangerous hostage to
fortune, encouraging an impression of credulity to which his scientific
concerns were less vulnerable. To suggest this may seem to privilege a part
of the contemporary intellectual milieu that some would see as marginal,
but, as has been argued throughout this book, the critical and self-confident
culture of the wits represented as significant a modernising impulse in the
thought of the day as the science of the Royal Society. Moreover, the satire
that emanated from such circles had undoubted potency. In attempting to
vindicate the society against the wits in his *History of the Royal Society*,
Thomas Sprat tellingly described them as 'these terrible men', adding: 'I
acknowledge that we ought to have a great dread of their power.'[49] Hence it
seems only likely that, as with Boyle, one factor in the society's ambivalence
towards such topics may have been fear of the adverse effect that engagement with them would have on the society's public image.

There may thus have been various, mainly negative reasons for the early
Royal Society's avoidance of such matters. But the effect was a cumulative
and significant one, namely of marginalising magical pursuits in relation to
the study of natural philosophy of which the society was the public champion. Individual Fellows might dabble in alchemy or astrology, or promote
miraculous cures, or compile accounts of witchcraft; but they left such
pursuits behind when they attended meetings of the society. Hence, so far
from investigating such phenomena and discrediting them, the society
simply avoided them. But it could be argued that this very avoidance was
itself significant. Such demarcation was not inevitable – even if it may seem
so in retrospect – yet boundary work of this kind *did* do much to define the
proper subject matter of science and, in the case of magic, to lead to a reduction in the intellectual respectability of the pursuits which the society thus

sidelined, from which they arguably never recovered. If the society had taken an open-minded interest in serious and empirically precise appraisals of astrology of a kind exemplified by John Goad and perhaps by their anonymous correspondent in 1697, such men might have become the Michel Gauquelins of their day;[50] it might similarly have vindicated the therapeutics of Greatrakes. Yet the society's attitude instead helped to relegate such investigations to the realm of pseudo-science, and there they have remained ever since.

Moreover, by the eighteenth century, this attitude had been institutionalised, as may be illustrated by a single example. This concerns the phenomenon of second sight in Scotland, the ability of certain individuals to foretell future events, something which had fascinated Boyle as a strange power which was empirically verifiable but seemed above the forces of nature (as we saw in the Introduction, this was to have been one of the themes of the postponed part of *Strange Reports*, and we will return to it in Chapter 6). The subject had also arisen at a meeting of the Royal Society in 1698, when a paper on it was read, stimulating one Fellow, William Bridgeman, to note a further instance.[51] However, in the 1740s, when another Fellow, Henry Baker, became deeply interested in the topic, it is revealing that he made it clear to his Scottish correspondents on the subject that this was a *private* concern on the part of himself and other Fellows 'in their private & separate Capacitys', which could not 'be brought before us as a Society not coming within the Design of our Institution'.[52] By now, the piecemeal decisions of the late seventeenth century had effectively resulted in an official line of demarcation. Even if not intentionally, by thus ostracising it from science, the early Royal Society apparently did play a significant role in the decline of magic.

### The Royal Society in Eighteenth-century Debates

Equally interesting is the fact that, in parallel with this, one sees the emergence of unsubstantiated claims for a more positive role on the part of the society which are the likely source of assertions of the type made by Sir Henry Lyons. The context is the debate over witchcraft and related phenomena which took place in the early eighteenth century, as surveyed in the previous chapter. Initially, there is evidence that people were perplexed as to where the Royal Society stood on such matters. Thus in a revealing exchange concerning the witchcraft controversy in Daniel Defoe's journal,

*The Review*, in 1711, an anonymous contributor (possibly an alter ego of Defoe himself) complained about the imprimatur granted by the society to Webster's 1677 volume on the grounds that it attacked the beliefs of Glanvill, 'one of the same Society'. 'To what purpose is the *Imprimatur* of a Society to a Book', the author wrote, 'if it be not that such Books being approv'd by those Societies, as the best Judges of Matters relating to their own Professions, the Vulgar Readers may the better believe them?'[53]

More significant is an exchange two years later between Anthony Collins, the Deist, and Richard Bentley, the conformist scholar and Master of Trinity College, Cambridge. By this time, as we have seen, the tradition of the Restoration wits had been taken up by the Deists, and Collins was keen to assert that freethinking had had a beneficial effect in relation to belief in witchcraft and the like, arguing in his *Discourse of Free-thinking* (1713) that there was a direct correlation between the rise of the one and the decline of the other.[54] In his view of the link between free-thought and articulate scepticism, Collins was arguably correct, thus creating a dilemma for more orthodox thinkers in that the very fact that heterodox authors like Collins were so open in their sadducism had the effect of tainting such views with overtones of potential 'atheism' and making them difficult to adopt.

By now, however, as we saw in the last chapter, the orthodox were gradually coming round to sharing the scepticism that the freethinkers had pioneered and which they had previously rejected as dangerous. This is seen in Bentley's response to the passage in Collins's book just cited, for he would have none of Collins's claim, and it is interesting to find that a part in his argument was played by a kind of myth of a positive role on the part of the Royal Society – as echoed by Lyons. As Bentley retorted to Collins: 'What then has lessen'd in *England* your stories of Sorceries? Not the *growing Sect* [of freethinkers] but the Growth of Philosophy and Medicine. No thanks to Atheists, but to the Royal Society and College of Physicians; to the *Boyle*'s and *Newton*'s, the *Sydenham*'s and *Ratcliff*'s.'[55] Clearly he was referring to the post-*Principia* consensus in which he and his contemporaries gloried, and it is revealing how often this passage has been quoted by historians of ideas of the period as evidence of the positive role for the Royal Society which has been questioned here.[56] Yet it deserves careful scrutiny and various points may be made about it.

The first is that, of the figures whom Bentley specifically named in this connection, we have already seen how Boyle took a diametrically opposite position. As for the others, Bentley would have been hard put to cite public utterances on the subject by them at all. Indeed, insofar as men like Sydenham, Radcliffe or Newton might have been tempted to a sceptical view, it would not be fanciful to suggest that this was due less to their medical or scientific credentials than to the fact that they were closet freethinkers, as with certain medical men to whom we will come in Chapter 5.[57] It is equally noteworthy that, although Bentley's assertion has usually been cited in connection with the role of the Royal Society and the new science, in fact he gives the College of Physicians an equally prominent billing, going on, 'When the People saw the Diseases, they had imputed to Witchcraft, quite cur'd by a course of Physic; they too were cur'd of their former Error'. We will return to the role of physicians in encouraging scepticism about magic in Chapter 5, but here what is significant is that this was linked with a regime of purging and blood-letting rather than with incipient modernity. Indeed, it is notable that even the author who has given the fullest recent account of the relevant passage in Bentley's tract, David Wootton, is forced to fall back on a rather bland asser-tion that his meaning was that 'the new sciences had undermined credulous belief', with an aside to the effect that, though Bentley may have believed that medicine was improving in his time, 'this belief now seems unjustified'.[58] In truth, the significance of Bentley's assertion was in providing a blustering, rhetorical claim to an establishmentarian pedigree for what might otherwise have seemed dangerously heterodox ideas.

Much the same is true of Francis Hutchinson in his *Historical Essay concerning Witchcraft* (1718) – long acclaimed, as we saw in the last chapter, as a turning point in being a book by an orthodox thinker which took a sceptical line regarding witchcraft. In fact, as we saw there, although Hutchinson made much of his empirical credentials, he was rather a timid thinker.[59] He consciously held back from the degree of scepticism repre-sented by John Wagstaffe and his book is throughout salted with allusions to more radical stances than that which he adopted and the extent to which even the moderate position that he took had in the past been inhibited by 'fear of loose People carrying the Notion too far the other way'.[60]

Yet what is revealing is how Hutchinson, like Bentley, found it comforting to be able to enrol an august public body like the Royal Society on his side. As Michael Winship has nicely put it, Hutchinson 'rewrote Restoration intellec-tual history by crediting the decline of witchcraft to the influence of the Royal Society'.[61] In a slightly odd digression to the account of the Jane Wenham case of 1712 in his *Historical Essay*, Hutchinson waxed enthusiastic about the society and its role, giving a narrative of the foundation of this and comparable bodies, and adding: 'Since that hath been founded, not only our Witchcrafts have been banish'd, but all Arts and Sciences have been greatly improv'd'.[62] Hutchinson also provided an example of 'scientific' discrediting of magical beliefs which he associated with such an institutional milieu, though it is revealing that he had to have recourse to an Italian rather than English example, in the form of Francesco Redi and the Accademia del Cimento.[63]

Hutchinson too, therefore, was keen to propagate the Royal Society myth as part of his case. Indeed, in this he was wresting the society's authority away from the author whose book stimulated the publication of his own, *A Compleat History of Magick, Sorcery, and Witchcraft* (1715–16) by Richard Boulton – who could in fact claim closer links than Hutchinson with the milieu of the Royal Society (though he was never a Fellow), having previously published editions of Boyle. On the other hand, though following Glanvill and More in seeking to use narratives of witchcraft to confute sadducist claims, Boulton's work was of no great depth. The bulk of its content comprised reprints of published witchcraft cases, with introductory material which includes lengthy extracts from works on related topics, one of them Locke's *Essay concerning Human Understanding*.[64] It seems likely that, as with his Boyle editions, it was a compilation that the author, an impoverished medical man, made at the behest of the booksellers, and Hutchinson's reference to it in his own work may have made it seem more significant than it really was.[65]

### The Making of a Myth

Hutchinson's paean of the Royal Society was almost certainly one of the principal sources of the assertion of the society's significance for the decline of magic made by C. R. Weld, the society's assistant secretary, in his *History of the Royal Society* of 1848, in the course of which Hutchinson's *Historical Essay* is cited among other works. At the end of Chapter 4 of his book, Weld gave an extended appraisal of the society's role in which he focused on precisely the kind of topics that have been itemised here – witchcraft, Greatrakes's supposed cures and the like.[66] He also referred to the curing of scrofula by the royal touch, noting that William Becket, author of *A Free and Impartial Enquiry into the Antiquity and Efficacy of Touching for the Cure of the King's Evil* (1722), was described as F.R.S. on the title page – although the book, which explains the touch in terms of the iatromechanical theories fashionable in the wake of the *Principia*, was not otherwise connected with the society.[67] Though Weld acknowledged that some Fellows believed in phenomena of these kinds, he used this as evidence of the general prevalence of such beliefs at the time, before continuing:

> It was a labour well worthy the men who met avowedly for the investigation and developement of truth, to inquire into these superstitions, and patiently and dispassionately to prosecute such experiments as should tend to eradicate them. It would indeed be difficult to over-estimate the great benefit that accrued to society by their destruction, and a lasting debt of gratitude is due to the Royal Society, for having been so essential an instrument in dispelling such fatal errors.[68]

Of course, as we have seen, this was precisely what did not happen. The society did not inquire into these phenomena and discredit them: it simply avoided them – even if, as has here been argued, this very avoidance was influential in itself.

But this did not stop Sir Henry Lyons from almost exactly echoing Weld's evaluation of the society's early achievement in *his* history a century later, though with some embellishments. Lyons wrote:

> The object for which the Society was founded is defined in the Charter as being for 'the improving Natural Knowledge by experiment'. The word 'natural' is here used as excluding all that is 'supernatural'. Sprat speaks of 'Experiments of natural things as not darkening our eyes, nor deceiving our minds, nor depraving our hearts'; and elsewhere he describes the Society as 'following the great precept of the apostle, of trying all things, in order to separate superstition from truth'. Belief in witchcraft and divination as well as superstitions of all kinds were rife in the seventeenth century and instances, for which irrefutable evidence was claimed, were constantly being brought before the early meetings of the Society to be examined in order to see whether any reasonable explanation for them could be found. Sir Walter Scott, in his *Demonology*, records his conviction that the belief in witchcraft decreased materially after the Royal Society began to investigate critically this and other reputed supernatural manifestations.[69]

This passage, though based on Weld, deserves a detailed commentary in its own right. First, it is almost certainly not true that 'natural' was used in the society's charter to exclude the 'supernatural': rather, it was meant to denote natural knowledge as against humane learning (the incorrect interpretation came from Weld, who had in turn taken it from the 1831 *Life of Sir Humphry Davy* by the doctor and chemist, J. A. Paris).[70] Second, although Lyons and Weld were right to look to Sprat's *History* for an expression of anti-magical views, we have already seen that these are of questionable reliability as an index of the society's actual policy (it is perhaps also worth noting that the quotations are slightly adapted, and the final phrase – about separating superstition from truth – is an embellishment in which Lyons followed Weld and which again does not appear in the original).[71] The next sentence paraphrases and extrapolates from Weld, but it is worth pausing over Lyons's citation of Scott's *Letters on Demonology and Witchcraft* (1830), which Weld had also noted to similar effect (again following Paris).[72] We will be hearing more about Scott's views on related topics in Chapter 6, but here it is worth noting that, contrary to what Lyons states, these words related not to witch-craft but to astrology: Scott justified bringing this into a treatise on witch-craft on the grounds that the two were interconnected. Having given a critical account of William Lilly and other seventeenth-century astrologers, Scott went on:

> The erection of the Royal Society, dedicated to far different purposes than the pursuits of astrology, had a natural operation in bringing the latter into discredit; and although the credulity of the ignorant and unin-formed continued to support some pretenders to that science, the name of Philomath assumed by these persons and their clients began to sink under ridicule and contempt.[73]

Once again, we have a very generalised claim reminiscent of Bentley's and Hutchinson's, and it is ironic that this should have formed the basis of a canonical but unfounded claim concerning the early Royal Society's actual activities on the part of both Weld and Lyons. Yet what is important is that such accounts are simply untrue. As has been shown here, the society did not carry out investigations of this kind: as a corporate body, the society simply ignored such studies. Yet we have also seen how such boundary work *was* significant in defining science and excluding magic from it.

Hence the early Royal Society played a rather paradoxical role in relation to magical beliefs. Through its negative institutional stance in relation to magical phenomena, the Royal Society had an important – if probably unwitting – definitional significance in this area. But what is curious is the permutation through which the society's role then went, in the context in which orthodox thinkers began hesitantly to follow in the footsteps of the freethinkers who had pioneered sceptical attitudes in the late seventeenth and early eighteenth centuries, having previously been inhibited from doing so by the heterodox affiliations of such scepticism. Ironically, it was a great consolation to men like Bentley and Hutchinson to be able to invoke the institutional lead of the Royal Society, albeit on the shakiest of evidence. They thus founded a myth of the confrontation between the society and such ideas which, through Weld and Lyons, has survived into our time.

# CHAPTER FOUR

# THE 'DRUMMER OF TEDWORTH'

## CONFLICTING INTERPRETATIONS AND THE PROBLEM OF FRAUD

The episode in the early 1660s known as the 'Drummer of Tedworth' – when strange and violent disturbances afflicted the house of John Mompesson in Wiltshire – has been described as 'perhaps the best-known of all poltergeist hauntings'.[1] This is largely due to the central position that it occupied in Joseph Glanvill's *A Blow at Modern Sadducism. In some Philosophical Considerations about Witchcraft* (1668), subsequently adapted into his oft-reprinted *Saducismus Triumphatus: or, Full and Plain Evidence Concerning Witches and Apparitions* (1681).[2] Indeed, the engraved frontispiece to the latter book includes a dramatic vignette of the Mompesson house with a devil with a drum and ancillary demons in the air above it (Plate 1). Glanvill's work was one of the chief emanations of the supernaturalist project referred to in the Introduction to this book, the whole point of which, as we saw, was to provide empirical proof of the reality of witchcraft and other phenomena deemed to be above the normal course of nature, preferably attested to by as many and as reliable witnesses as possible. As will become apparent in the course of this chapter, this is precisely what Glanvill and others believed the Tedworth case offered – indeed, that it even seemed to display the potential for testing, like a Boylian experiment – thus giving it a central role in the enterprise of vindicating the reality of magic.[3]

But the incident is also interesting for other reasons. For one thing, as we will see in this chapter, the almost triumphalist championship of the Tedworth case by Glanvill and others had been preceded by an earlier, more querulous phase in its interpretation which has been neglected and which is revealing in itself. In particular, the reaction of the principal victim, John Mompesson, seems to have evolved from an initial, rather puzzled and anxious one to a more assured position as he was offered models of response and explanation that helped him to cope with the disorder in his house. The case thus valuably illustrates the process of constructing 'narratives' of witchcraft and related phenomena by which historians have become preoccupied in recent years, especially the way in which a plausible rationale was sought for events, and how this might change.[4] Equally significant is the extent to which Glanvill's own position evolved, as revealed by the differences between the earlier and later recensions of his published account, which have also hitherto gone unnoticed. Having initially embroidered Mompesson's account to present the poltergeist at times almost flippantly as evidence of the reality of the diabolical realm, Glanvill later removed the light-hearted passages that he had inserted. This was evidently in response to the scepticism – predominantly orally expressed – with which his book was received in certain quarters. Almost from the outset, there were those who suspected that the whole affair was 'onely a cheat or a fancy', and the debate as to its genuineness was to continue for a perhaps surprisingly long time afterwards.[5]

Indeed, the accusation of fraud that long hung over the Tedworth case reflected one of the key problems of the supernaturalist project as a whole. Robert Boyle, for instance, was only too aware of the damage that fraudulent instances could do, urging Glanvill in his 1678 letter to him about witchcraft cases to be

> very carefull to deliver none but well attested narratives. The want of which Cautiousnes's has justly discredited many Relations of Witches & Sorceries & made most the rest suspected since in such stories, the number ‹of the whole› can no way compensate the want of truth or of proofe in some of the Particulars, & a few narratives cogently verifyd will procure greater credit to the cause they are brought to Countenance than a far greater number of Stories wherof some tho never so few are false, & others ‹tho perhaps not many› suspitious.[6]

Ironically, as we will see, in the Tedworth case accusations of fraud were answered equally vigorously by those who believed in its verisimilitude. It is thus apparent that the supposed 'proof' of fraud in relation to witchcraft and related phenomena was less straightforward than modern historians have often presumed, and we will explore the implications of this at the end of this chapter.

## *John Mompesson and the Poltergeist*

First, however, we must recapitulate the Tedworth case. John Mompesson, its victim, was a landowner, excise officer and commission officer in the militia, who lived at North Tidworth on the Wiltshire–Hampshire border.[7] Born in 1623, he was the son of a clergyman of the same name who had held the parish of North Tidworth in plurality with that of Codford St Mary, and who had been called before the parliamentary authorities for royalist sympathies in 1646.[8] His uncle was the notorious Jacobean monopolist, Sir Giles Mompesson, while his cousin, Thomas Mompesson, was a Wiltshire landowner who, on his father's early death, had been entrusted to the guardianship, among others, of Sir Edward Nicholas, secretary of state to Charles I and Charles II, whose seat was at Winterbourne Earles in Wiltshire. In 1655 Thomas Mompesson had raised a force in support of the royalist rising led by John Penruddock and he thereafter went into exile in France prior to returning to England at the Restoration, when he regained his estates, became MP for Wilton, and in 1662 secured a knighthood for himself and the Wiltshire excise farm for his cousin, John.[9] Apart from the episode with which we are concerned, John Mompesson, who was buried at North Tidworth on 29 May 1696, is a rather shadowy figure, but he clearly played a significant role in the affairs of the village and its neighbourhood, for instance arranging a levy on his neighbours for poor relief in 1656.[10]

In March 1662, Mompesson intervened in the case of a drummer, William Drury, who had requested money from the local constable at the neighbouring village of Ludgershall on the basis of a pass which proved to be counterfeit. It later turned out that Drury had been in the parliamentary army (hence perhaps explaining the royalist Mompesson's initial suspicion of him). Mompesson had him arrested and his drum confiscated, a slightly capricious act which he may later have regretted; subsequently, in April, it was sent to Mompesson's house at Tedworth, and this is when the disturbances began. At first they occurred outside the house and attempted burglary was suspected. But they then moved inside, focusing on the room occupied by Mompesson's widowed mother, who was evidently permanently domiciled with the family, and who encouraged the children to play with the drum. It was at this point that the drumming came to the fore, often taking the form of tattoos to which Mompesson initially warmed with the enthusiasm of a militia officer ('as truely and sweetly as ever Drum beat in this world', he wrote in his account of the events). But the strange noises became more and more overt, varied and perplexing, including thumping on the outside of the house, the sound of sawing and the shoeing of a horse, and 'a perfect hurling in the aire over the house' which made the windows and beds shake.[11]

There was an intermission while Mrs Mompesson was in labour and following the birth of her child, but thereafter the disturbances recurred, being targeted particularly on the children of the house. The spirit would 'runne under the bed-teeke, and scratch as if it had iron talons, and heave up the children in the bed, and follow them from roome to roome and come to none else but them'. Now, the thumpings and other noises became even more pronounced. Mompesson specifically singled out the events on 5 November, when a servant had a tussle with a board which moved in a strange way and when the occupants of the house were affected by a strange sulphurous smell, of which Mompesson wrote, 'I must confesse I never doubted whether I should be able to stand my ground till that time'. He added, presuming that a spirit was responsible,

It has taken our servants up in their beds, bed and all, and hath lifted them up a great height, and layd them down softly again, and layes often on their feet with great weight, sometimes the candles will not burn in the roome where it is, and though it come never so loud and on a sudain, yet no dog will bark: it hath been often so loud that it hath been heard into the fields and has wakned my neighbours in the towne.

In addition, 'in our presence and sight the chaires did walk about, the childrens shooes were tost over our heads and every loose thing throwne about the roome', including a bedstaff, although when this hit someone it proved as soft as wool. Further developments included the appearance of strange lights, one of them seen by Mompesson's wife, which was 'very blue and glimmering, and caused as she thought some stiffnesse on her eylids'; another was the perception of a ghost in rustling silk. As we will see, these disturbances continued through 1662 and into 1663, despite (or perhaps because of) the fact that Mompesson had 'long agoe' taken the drum out of the house and burnt it.[12]

All this was reported by Mompesson in a series of letters dating from December 1662 and January 1663 to William Creed, a Wiltshire cleric who was regius professor of divinity at Oxford from 1660 until his death on 19 July 1663, and who was also related by marriage to Mompesson.[13] These letters, which have recently been published in full, are obviously of immense value because they give an exactly contemporary report on the events that occurred by the man most directly involved in them; they are also significant because copies of them were in the hands of Glanvill when he wrote his published account of the affair, for which they formed the main source, as we will see. On the other hand, what is no less revealing about them, and particularly the first, is the initial strong sense that comes across of anxiety, almost of strain, about these strange phenomena, especially those that occurred from 5 November onwards – something that in the Glanvill version is completely elided. Apart from the noisome smell, Mompesson's querulous response to which has already been noted, we learn of recourse to repeated prayer sessions, involving the local minister, as a way of trying to remove the poltergeist. Mompesson was aware that 'many I suppose may be ready enough (and have been as I am told) to judge that this comes upon me for some enormous sin or other', answering them with a lengthy passage expressing his humility before God – 'I know I have deserved far greater punishments at the hand of God then these have yet been' – yet acknowledging God's mercies to him: it was by his 'mighty hand' that they were defended, and by his 'grace and power' that they were strengthened against these assaults. He also warned others to 'take heed how they censure others in these or the like cases, lest they prove themselves not so good as they should be', while his view of 'the Devil roaring and raging' echoed that in 1 Peter 5:8.[14]

In their initially querulous tone, the letters bear some relation to the earliest published source concerning the poltergeist, which itself bears witness to the notoriety that the case quickly acquired. This was a ballad by Abraham Miles which came out in February 1663, entitled *A Wonder of Wonders; Being A true Relation of the strange and invisible Beating of a Drum, at the House of John Mompesson, Esquire, at Tidcomb* [sic] *in the County of Wilt-shire*, which recounted a selection of the events that had transpired, presumably from oral testimony, and which opened by urging repentance on the grounds that such occurrences 'shew Dooms-days nigh'.[15] This rather apocalyptic attitude towards the case was echoed in a memorandum written a little later by the Oxford antiquary Anthony Wood, who kept various documents relating to it and who noted this and other instances of 'the devill let loose to possess people' along with prodigious births and other unusual events and developments which he clearly found unsettling.[16] Indeed, the apprehensive tone is reminiscent of the famous *Mirabilis Annus* tracts of the early Restoration, in which abnormal events were reported in an atmosphere of anxious expectation. Moreover, whereas the motivation for reporting such cases in those publications was clearly subversive, the fact that Mompesson and Wood shared this unsettled attitude is revealing of the prevalence of a similar mindset in the early years of the Restoration.[17]

On the other hand, what the letters also reveal is how Mompesson's own attitude seems to have become more assured as he was offered strategies for attempting to deal with the strange occurrences that had afflicted him and his family. In part, these stemmed from commonplace preconceptions of the period, in part from the comments of those who learned about the affair or who visited the house. Most obviously, there was the suspicion that witch-craft was involved. At one point the words 'a witch, a witch' were heard 'many times' in the house, and it was taken as axiomatic that the Devil was responsible for what occurred. This was later confirmed when ashes that were strewn round the house had the appearance of a claw mark in them, while a bible that they covered was found to be open at the passage in St Mark's Gospel concerning Christ casting out evil spirits.[18] There was also a curious episode in the form of a kind of seance carried out at Mompesson's house in the presence of two gentlemen from Wiltshire and Oxfordshire, when those present responded to the knocking that occurred by saying: 'Satan, If the Drummer set thee on worke, let us understand so much by giving three knockes and no more', which duly took place, and the proce-dure was then repeated for confirmation.[19]

Mompesson's commentary on this is revealing, illustrating how these phenomena were being interrogated in terms of standard early modern views about supernatural intervention in the world. 'This I suppose . . . may be an argument that this Spirit comes not to discover any murthers committed, Treasures hidden, or the like', he reflected; he also noted of the interrogatory knocking how it was 'no evidence to a Jurie, for the Devil ought not to be believed'. But this aside confirms how he had by now resolved to prosecute William Drury, the drummer, as a witch who was responsible for the disturbances that had taken place. Mompesson's enquiries revealed that Drury did indeed have an existing reputation as a 'cunning man'. Though a tailor by trade, he 'went up and down the Countrey to shew Hocas pocas feats of activity, dancing through hoops and such like devices'. It was also reported that he had been a retainer to a local cleric, Woolston Miller, who had been accused of practising magic, and that after Miller's death Drury 'often repaired to his Widow, and has reported that Mr Miller had gallant Bookes which he had seen, and understood by them how to tell fortunes, which he practiced &c'.[20] Mompesson's suspicions would also have been aroused by the fact that, although released after Mompesson's arrest of him in March, Drury was subsequently incarcerated at Gloucester for some months in 1662 on a charge of theft unrelated to the Tedworth affair, and during this time, he was reported to have said, 'Although the Drum be burnt, the Devil is not dead; and that he had been better let me and my Drum alone'. This was reported in the account of the legal proceedings that appeared in two newspapers at the time, *Mercurius Publicus* and *The Kingdoms Intelligencer*, which provides our main evidence on this aspect of the case.[21]

Drury's case came up at the Gloucester assizes on 31 March 1663, where he was found guilty of stealing two pigs, successfully sought benefit of clergy, was ordered to be branded but had this remitted when he was sentenced for transportation.[22] However, when he and others were put on a barge to be carried to the vessel in which they were to be transported, Drury jumped overboard and escaped back to Wiltshire, where he purchased a new drum, perhaps to torment Mompesson all the more (though the fact that he had been in prison for much of the period when the disturbances at the house occurred shows that he personally cannot have been the sole cause of them).[23]

Mompesson had actually gone to Gloucester to learn the outcome of the case, and was on his way home when he learned of Drury's escape.[24] In April 1663 he therefore had him indicted as a felon under the Jacobean witchcraft statute 'with suspicion of practising Witchcrafts, and so causing the troubles that had been in his house for above these twelve months'. This makes sense of his speculation on the validity of spectral evidence which has already been noted, and he recapitulated this evidence in his deposition which was included in the newspaper reports already noted.[25] The evidence against Drury was heard before a Wiltshire JP, Isaac Burgess, and Drury's and Mompesson's depositions were published in the newspapers already referred to in April 1663.[26] The case came up at the Wiltshire assizes at Salisbury on 3 August. No official records survive, but Mompesson gave a fuller account of Drury's trial in a letter to the bookseller, James Collins, dated 8 August 1674 which was published in *Saducismus Triumphatus* in 1681, in which he explained how 'the Grand Jury found the Bill upon the Evidence, but the Petty Jury acquitted him, but not without some difficulty'.[27] However, Drury was still in trouble over his previous conviction and escape from custody; on his acquittal, he was not released but removed back to Gloucester gaol by a writ of habeas corpus to await the arrival of the judges of the Berkshire circuit on 19 August and an arraignment for his escape. He was again sentenced to transportation, and presumably began a fresh life in the New World. After this, we hear no more of him.[28]

Thus the prospect of prosecuting Drury as a witch, which presumably would have been the most satisfying outcome for Mompesson, failed to materialise. Meanwhile, however, other strategies had emerged by way of response to the disturbing events that had occurred. To reconstruct these, we must return to the end of 1662, around the time when Mompesson initially reported on the affair to William Creed in Oxford. Mompesson's letter to Creed was conveyed via his cousin, Sir Thomas Mompesson, and was accompanied by a letter of the same date from Mompesson to Sir Thomas which does not survive. However, what *does* survive is the latter's response, dated 11 December, evidently because John Mompesson later enclosed it with a further letter to Creed.[29] Sir Thomas's letter is revealing in illustrating the acceptance of the reality of witchcraft, and the degree of knowledge about it, to be found among the landed classes at the time – thus highlighting a further contemporary consensus which it is easy to underestimate in retrospect.[30] He reported that he had consulted his mentor, Sir Edward Nicholas, on the subject, who, on the basis of a similar occurrence that he had heard about in France, offered an elaborate strategy for trying to flush out the witch (who, tellingly, Sir Thomas presumed to be female). This involved a large number of men slashing into the air at random with their swords in the hope of wounding her: it was possibly a garbled recollection of this piece of advice concerning the case to which John Aubrey later referred in connection with the question of whether spirits could suffer bodily harm, writing how 'one advised Mr Mompesson of Tydworth, to shoot suddenly and at randome in the aire.'[31] Sir Thomas made two further related points: first, that the plan should not be discussed in or near the house, since the witch was probably invisibly present even when it was not audible; and second, that more than one witch might be involved in a 'Rendezvous.'[32]

This crucial letter seems to have suggested to Mompesson both a strategy for dealing with the phenomenon and a set of explanations to be tested which affected his behaviour over the next few weeks. The result was to give him a more confident and positive attitude, which is reflected in his second letter to William Creed, dated 26 December. This letter also suggests that the reaction to events of Mompesson and his family was galvanised by suggestions made by those who came to the house at this stage; these, too, seem to have influenced perceptions of the events that took place, and the language used to describe them. In particular, Mompesson mentioned near the start of his letter how 'A neighbour coming and discoursing with my Mother, told my Mother that she had heard storyes of Fayries, that did use to leave money behind them in Maydens shooes, and the like'.[33] This again seems crucial, since, if Sir Thomas had invoked the commonplaces of demonology in relation to the affair, this was supplemented by a folkloristic dimension of fairies and goblins and the stories of their erratic intervention in human affairs that circulated widely in early modern Britain.[34] This, too, was reflected in the developments that followed.

Evidently due to the provision of these more positive agendas, Mompesson's tone in his letter to Creed of 26 December 1662, though still ambivalent, became markedly more optimistic. The letter also reveals the extent to which the family's perceptions were affected by the advice they had now received. It told how, after Mompesson's mother sardonically riposted to the neighbour's story about the fairies that the poltergeist should 'leave us some money to make us satisfaction for the trouble and charge it putts us to', the drumming had been replaced by a strange jingling of money round the house. Mompesson also reported an armed confrontation between the spirit and his servant John, introducing it with the phrase, 'I shall acquaint you with some Mirth we have with it'. Mompesson actually used the term 'Goblin' to describe John's invisible adversary, while it seems likely that Mompesson approved of his servant's martial encounter with the spirit not least because of the extent to which it cohered with the strategy that Sir Thomas had advocated. In addition, the way in which the chinking of money at night picked up on a conversation at noon the same day clearly reflected Sir Thomas's comments about the spirit's being present and alert even when not audible. His words were reflected even more clearly in Mompesson's statement that they had discovered a 'Rendezvous' of spirits, exactly echoing his cousin's terminology, while also relevant was Mompesson's statement that they had 'discoverd' the spirit's fear of weapons and of 'much light', again suggesting an investigative attitude based on the agenda that Sir Thomas had set.[35] Indeed, Mompesson subsequently sent his cousin's letter to Creed to illustrate how many details had been 'experimentally found to be true as the Letter mentions' (this may have been partly because the Oxford dons had shown slight disapproval of the antics of John).[36] It is perhaps also revealing that the discovery of Mompesson's mother's bible in the ashes of the chimney was seen as a 'trick', whereas earlier it might have been taken as a more sinister anti-Christian gesture.[37]

## Early Reactions to the Case

The further significant development that is in evidence concerns Mompesson's realisation of the apologetic purposes to which the strange events at his house might potentially be put. Even in 1662 many 'strangers' had started to visit Mompesson's house to witness the occurrences for themselves: indeed, in his letter to Creed of 26 December 1662 he specifically commented on 'the great concourse of people that break in upon me and almost devoure me, to see this', noting in the same letter how 'I have now three Letters from persons of great quality that they may be admitted'. The visitors included 'Divines and others, persons of judgment, who doe all conclude it to be witchcraft', thus commencing the process of making sense of the phenomena which Sir Thomas Mompesson and others continued. In a postscript to his first letter to Creed, Mompesson wrote, 'I have often thought that if any learned man had made these observations that I have done, he might have discovered much of the nature of these spirits', and his motive in sending Creed a narrative of the events was possibly to encourage him to provide just such an analysis (which he might well have done but for his premature death in July 1663).[38] Indeed, Mompesson requested advice on the matter not only from Creed but also from another Oxford don, Thomas Pierce, president of Magdalen College, who had bought a large estate at Tedworth earlier that year, and whom Mompesson asked Creed to show what he had written, stating how he would be glad to receive 'what rules or directions you shall vouchsafe me, and I shall be carefull to follow them'.[39]

By the time of Mompesson's letter of 4 January 1663, he had evidently received responses from Creed and Pierce: unfortunately, neither of their letters is extant, but it seems possible that they requested more detailed information for use in a putative account, and it may have been in response to this that Mompesson prepared a further extant document, which gives a matter-of-fact narrative of the events at his house on a daily basis from 10 to 21 January. It is almost like a kind of 'natural history' of the phenomena, intended to be kept as a record; it is perhaps revealing that in his 4 January letter to Creed, Mompesson requested in a postscript, 'keep I pray my Papers together'.[40] The document divulged additional revealing details, giving the names of further visitors, in this case members of Wiltshire gentry families related to the Mompessons. It described Sir Thomas Mompesson's strategy being tried, with the spirit in Mompesson's daughter's bed being threatened by 'naked swords' – 'but it was so swift that we could not thrust it without indangering her'. It also recorded the tormenting of a smith who shared Mompesson's servant's chamber and the strange heat by which the children's bedroom was affected.

At this stage, Mompesson was convinced that the events proved the indisputable reality of a supernatural, diabolical realm. Indeed, although he complained in his letters about the problems caused by incessant visitors, telling Creed how these intrusive visits 'have troubled me half as bad as the spirit', he reconciled himself to this by the fact that 'there were never any yet that came to see it, but were satisfied, which is strange to me that the Devill should have no more witt'. Indeed, he took the view:

> I am of opinion the Devill hath done himself a great hurt by this, for I am
> confident here have been some that were convinced of the being of spirits
> by what they have here seen, which is to me an ample satisfaction for all
> the trouble it putts me to, and makes me more willing to admitt strangers
> to the sight of it.[41]

Unfortunately, however, this was not to last, since Mompesson's letter to Creed of 4 January contains a lengthy account of some visitors – 'Gentlemen afarre off' – who, in contrast to all their predecessors, were sceptical about the affair. They smiled when the spirit initially failed to appear on cue, and they declared to two ministers who were present 'their diffidence of the being of Spirits'. When the knocking ultimately did occur, they searched the room for crannies where someone might hide, and they requested Mompesson's permission to take up the floor-boards, which he refused. They also 'calld out, Satan, Doe this, and that, and, Whistle if thou canst, or let us see where [whether] thou canst tell money, or make chaires dance, as we have heard, let us see it'. Mompesson's reaction was revealing of the difference between his attitude and that of these sceptics, who he thought were inviting God's wrath by their rather frivolous attitudes: 'I protest I was afraid at their cariage, and begd of them to be more sober and to withdraw themselves', he observed, although they took no notice, and he told Creed that 'I shall be more carefull how I admit strangers for the future'.

Worse still, they 'departed with some kind of suspicion that what they heard was onely a cheat or a fancy' for which Mompesson, as householder, was implicitly responsible. He therefore ended the letter by protesting the truth of what he had reported, since 'I should tremble to lay in my house, and think that I put (as much as in me lays) a Mockery upon God and the passages of his providence', continuing, 'I trust that all this will tend to no other end but the setting forth of Gods goodnesse and rich mercy, and the shaming of the devill, and the conviction of all uncharitable and misbelieving people'.[42]

This, therefore, introduces us to the history of the interrogation of the affair by more or less sceptical outsiders, to which we must now turn. The visitors in evidence before the end of 1662 have already been mentioned, while in the next section we will see how Joseph Glanvill paid a visit to Tedworth in January 1663. In addition, in a letter of 24 February that year to his friend Sir John Brooke, the London virtuoso Abraham Hill reported that 'many hundreds are witnesses' to the strange events in Wiltshire, and that the eminent cleric and natural philosopher John Wilkins was considering a visit, though whether he actually went is unknown.[43] We also know of two such expeditions through the account of them included by John Aubrey in his *Natural History of Wiltshire*, though unfortunately without indicating exactly when they occurred. Aubrey told of visits to Tedworth, first by his close friend, the lawyer Anthony Ettrick, and Ettrick's patron, the Dorset landowner Sir Ralph Bankes, and second by Sir Christopher Wren and an unnamed companion. Bankes and Ettrick 'lay there together one night out of curiosity, to be satisfied. They did heare sometimes knockings; and if they said "Devill, knock so many knocks," so many knocks would be answered. But Mr Ettrick sometimes whispered the words, and there was then no returne.' Aubrey himself interjected at this point: 'but he should have spoke in Latin or French for the detection of this' (a standard trope of demonology). Wren also

lay there. He could see no strange things, but sometimes he should heare a drumming, as one may drum with one's hand upon wainscot; but he observed that this drumming was only when a certain maid-servant was in the next room: the partitions of the rooms are by borden-brasse, as wee call it. But all these remarked that the Devill kept no very unseasonable houres: it seldome knock't after 12 at night, or before 6 in the morning.[44]

Wren's suspicions about the role of servants in the affair is perhaps confirmed by one of Mompesson's complaints in his letters to Creed, namely about 'the unrulynesse of Servants who apprehend that if they leave me, none other will come to me, and so they are become my Masters'. The surmise that the servants may have been complicit in the disturbances was also voiced at a later date by the writers Balthasar Bekker and John Beaumont, to whom we will come later in this chapter.[45]

The Tedworth case also attracted interest in London and at the royal court. A letter from Henry More to his confidante, Lady Anne Conway, of 31 March 1663, not only recorded how 'A gentleman that lives near the place and slow enough from believing any such things' had affirmed 'that this is certainly true, and that hundreds and hundreds of men could witness it', but also reported that Lord Robartes, later Earl of Radnor, 'carryed Mr Montpesson himself to the King who heard all the story, my Lord being by, who after by Dr Carr a fellow of our Colledge, sent me particular notice of it, with the assurance of the truth thereof'.[46] The case is also referred to in the second part of Samuel Butler's satirical poem, *Hudibras*, first published in 1664 and evidently reflecting fashionable gossip of the previous year, which told how 'some/ Have heard the Devil beat a Drum'.[47] It also featured in a conversation about spirits with the courtier and diplomat Lord Sandwich 'both at and after dinner' on 15 June 1663, recorded by Samuel Pepys in his Diary. Pepys noted that Sandwich was

> very scepticall. He says the greatest warrants that ever he had to believe any, is the present appearing of the Devil in Wiltshire, much of late talked of, who beats a drum up and down; there is books of it, and they say very true. But my Lord observes that though he doth answer to any tune that you will play to him upon another drum, yet one tune he tried to play and could not; which makes him suspect the whole, and I think it is a good argument.[48]

It is revealing that, in a slightly later letter to More, Glanvill acknowledged that 'I perceive the Story is not beleiv'd by the Courtiers; And perhaps no evidence will convince them'. In the same letter he also noted another sceptic he had recently met, the London-based physician and virtuoso Walter Charleton, who 'laughes att the Notion of Spirrits, and perticularly att this story. Which I somewhat wonder att in one that hath writ a booke of our Immortality'.[49]

It was perhaps to adjudicate such conflicting opinions of the Tedworth affair that two courtiers were sent down to Wiltshire 'to examine the truth of it', the queen's chamberlain, Philip Stanhope, 2nd Earl of Chesterfield, and Charles Berkeley, Earl of Falmouth, on behalf of the king. We have a retrospective account of the episode by the Earl of Chesterfield, who was clearly unconvinced. It is perhaps revealing that, although in his Memoir he had expressed a degree of ambivalence about the reality of two incidents of premonition which he had himself earlier experienced, which 'might have probably convinced any one (who had been witness to them) of the reality of the appearing of spirits', Chesterfield rehearsed for himself various sceptical arguments, and his considered verdict was that 'mankind loves to be deceived by strange stories of supernatural accidents; and is very unwilling to have the mistake or deceit of them found out'.[50] In the passage of his Memoir dealing with his trip to Wiltshire to investigate the Tedworth case, he curtly noted that 'wee could neither see nor heare any thing that was extraordinary, and about a year after his majesty told mee that hee had discovered the Cheat, and that Mr Monpesson (upon his Majesties sending for him) had confes'd it to him', expressing indignation that Mompesson was later to deny this.[51] We will hear more in a subsequent section about the rumours that circulated at the time concerning Mompesson's confrontation with the king: on how many occasions the two men met, and exactly when, is not entirely clear. Chesterfield went on to note Joseph Glanvill's subsequent publication of 'the strang things that he saw, felt and heard there', adding, 'where probably having been frighted and deceived, he hath by his book endeavoured to deceive Posterity'. It is to Glanvill's pivotal role in relation to the Tedworth affair that we must now turn.

### Enter Joseph Glanvill

We know that Glanvill visited Mompesson's house in January 1663, since a letter is extant from him to the Presbyterian divine, Richard Baxter, dated 21 January, which explains, 'I came yesterday from Mr Mompesson's house at Teidworth'. Although it lacks a year, the letter is addressed to a house where Baxter resided only in January 1663.[52] Glanvill noted that he had heard that Baxter would like an account of the case so that he could publish it, evidently alluding to Baxter's known interest in such matters: this reached its climax in his *Certainty of the Worlds of Spirits* (1691), but he had included briefer sections on related matters in earlier books.[53] Glanvill added, 'I came thither upon the same designe, & was an eye & eare witnesse of many thinges which the Infidell world will scarce beleive', a narrative of which would prove 'as palpable & convictive a Testimony against Atheism as this age hath afforded'. Indeed, he reported – perhaps consciously echoing the sentiments of Mompesson – that 'some Hobbists who have been there, are already convinced, and those that are not so are fain to stick to their opinions against the evidence of their sences'. Though he added, 'My occasions will not give mee leave at present to informe you of perticulars', stating that Mompesson himself was 'not willing to have a Narrative publish't, till the disturbance bee over', it is clear that he was already at work on an account of the affair.

In fact, it is highly likely that Glanvill was the author of a description of the case that survives among the State Papers, and which must date from very early in 1663, despite the fact that it is filed under 1667.[54] This gave prominence to the same events of 5 November as did Mompesson's first letter to Creed, but it went on to summarise some more recent developments, most, though not all, overlapping with the events recounted in Mompesson's subsequent letters. On the other hand, it was evidently based on oral testimony rather than on those letters, since events were presented in a different order and certain of them were conflated together. (In this respect, it is perhaps to be compared with Abraham Miles's ballad, published in February 1663.)[55] Although the author of the paper is not identified, and although the extant copy is not in his handwriting, Glanvill is a strong candidate for its authorship, since the State Papers account includes details of a visit to Tedworth by its author, who had witnessed the poltergeist in the children's bed. Moreover various aspects of the experiences in the children's bedroom reported in this paper recur in almost identical autobiographical terms in Glanvill's published account of the case, of which the State Papers text may even represent the initial recension. Though the events described overlap with those in Mompesson's letters, the tone of the piece is rather different: it is written in an impressionistic, almost journalistic way, describing the events, though 'strange', as 'tricks', and giving an impression of a 'boisterous' yet intriguing atmosphere. It also gave a more self-conscious gloss on one episode – namely the tormenting of a smith who visited the house, whose nose was snipped as if with pinchers – in the form of an allusion to the legend of the Devil and St Dunstan. The presence of the document in the State Papers implies that it was sent to court, perhaps with a view to arousing interest in the affair there: in this connection, it may be significant that the most notable topic mentioned in it which is not to be found in Mompesson's letters to Creed is the episode when the phantom drummer was puzzled by a new tune, on which Lord Sandwich picked up in his conversation with Pepys.

Be that as it may, Glanvill's interest in the matter is not surprising, since in 1662 he had published *Lux orientalis*, in which he argued in favour of the Platonic doctrine of the pre-existence of souls, and hence an imminent and populous spirit world, a topic which established an immediate rapport between him and Henry More, whose interest in the Tedworth case we have already encountered. Glanvill had already established himself as a philosophical sceptic with particular reference to the prevailing Aristotelian philosophy in *The Vanity of Dogmatizing* (1661); in that work he made various respectful references to More but showed no evidence of acquaintance with him.[56] Their friendship probably began when he sent More a copy of *Lux orientalis*, for which More immediately became an enthusiast.[57] More had long been interested in witchcraft cases as evidence of the reality of the spiritual realm, and, as we saw in the Introduction, had devoted Book 3 of his *Antidote against Atheism* (1653) – dedicated to Lady Conway – to a series of lengthy accounts of such phenomena. At least in part it seems likely that this was the inspiration of Glanvill's own comparable writings. From More's letter to Lady Conway of 31 March 1663, cited above, we know that by then he had received 'a narration' of the Tedworth case 'from a very sober hand, an eye witness of part of those feats' – almost certainly Glanvill: indeed, it might have been a copy of the text surviving in the State Papers.[58]

It also seems likely that it was later that year that Glanvill set to work on the fuller narrative of the case that he was to publish in 1668. As we have seen, although William Creed apparently intended to write an account of the affair, his death that July prevented him from doing so, and instead it was Glanvill who inherited the task.[59] In a further letter to Henry More of 13 November, without year but evidently dating from 1663 (as is confirmed by a report of it in a letter of similar date from More to Lady Conway), Glanvill explained that Mompesson 'was pleased to give mee all his letters, which were sent to the Doctor of the Chaire att Oxford, that contained an account of all the remarkeable particulers of the whole disturbance'. On the basis of these he now sought to compose 'a perfect Narrative with some of my Remarques', and in his published account he specifically stated that his narrative was 'extracted from Mr *Mompesson's* own Letters. The same particulars also he writ to the Doctor of the Chair in *Oxford*.'[60]

It is perhaps worth noting here that, although the bulk of Glanvill's later account was based on Mompesson's letters to Creed, the latter part of it included some information not to be found therein, covering events of which one was dated 'About the beginning of *April*, 1663'. In addition to extra details concerning events that *were* dealt with in the letters, some entirely new occurrences were described. These included an occasion when Mompesson shot at a pile of wood that appeared to move and blood was found; further assaults on the children of the house; a sighting by his servant of 'a great body, with two *red* and *glaring* eyes'; the appearance of spikes in Mompesson's and his mother's beds; a story of a gentleman's money turning black in his pocket; and an occasion when a horse was found with one of his hind feet caught in his mouth, which had to be levered out by several men.[61] These could derive from a further letter from Mompesson to Creed that is now lost, or they could derive from a letter from Mompesson to Glanvill himself. That his source was a written one is suggested by Glanvill's concluding comment: 'After this there were some other remarkable things; but my *account* goes no farther: Only Mr. *Mompesson* told me, that afterwards the house was several nights beset with 7 or 8 in the shape of men, who as soon as a Gun was discharged, would shuffle away together into an Arbour'.[62]

The exact date of these events is unclear, however, as is the question of how much longer disturbances at Mompesson's house continued. In his letter to More of 13 November 1663, Glanvill reported that, in response to More's enquiries about the case, he had 'very lately' visited Mompesson, and had learned from him 'that the Drummer was banished, and that since his banishment his house had been very quiet'. His report to this effect had been delayed by illness, and he went on to state that the day before writing to More he had received a letter from Mompesson

to desire mee to come over to speake with him about his old Troubler, which he sayes hath now invaded him againe. The house had been quiet 9 weekes during the absence of the Drummer; but he escaping as soon as he was come home, the disturber returned, but playes other kind of tricks then formerly . . . Strange thinges are reported of the Drummer's escape, but I can yet give you no certain account.[63]

The chronology of this is puzzling: Glanvill also described 'one perticular passage' with which Mompesson had acquainted him and which he specifically noted occurred the night before he wrote the letter – the horse with its hind leg in its mouth – yet this was recorded in Glanvill's 1668 account in conjunction with an event dated to April 1663. This could be due to careless drafting, but it tallies better with what is known about Drury's movements from the legal records.

It is also slightly odd how slow Glanvill was in producing his account of the case, considering his concern to refute the scepticism about both the Tedworth poltergeist and such phenomena more generally that was evidently widespread, as exemplified by Lords Sandwich, Chesterfield and others. The Tedworth case was not included at all in the first version of Glanvill's *A Philosophical Endeavour Towards the Defence of the Being of Witches and Apparitions* (1666), which was reprinted in 1667 as *Some Philosophical Considerations Touching the Being of Witches and Witchcraft* following the destruction of the bulk of the first impression in the Fire of London. Only in the 1668 version, now entitled *A Blow at Modern Sadducism*, did an account of the events at Tedworth finally appear, and the fact that the narrative peters out at the point early in 1663 noted above may reveal not that the events really ended then but that Glanvill had given up hope of the further particulars that he had been importuning Mompesson to provide. In part, this may have been due to reluctance by Mompesson who, Glanvill told Henry More in a further letter dated 13 March 1667, 'is, for reasons which I doe not know, grown cold & backward in the buisiness. I earnestly sollicitt him by all opportunityes for the remaining particulars, but receive no answere to my importunityes, or such as are dilatory putt offs'; even later than this, he told More in another letter dated 25 September that he had paid an abortive visit to Mompesson and had also sent him 'a Letter to desire his further informations in order to the compleating of my Narrative; but have yett heard no more from him'.[64]

Finally, however, the 1668 recension dealt with the case in full, and it did so in two sections. One was Glanvill's narrative of it, presented with a separate title page, *Palpable Evidence of Spirits and Witchcraft: In an Account of the Fam'd Disturbance by the Drummer, In the House of M. Mompesson*, with the running head, 'The Dæmon of *Tedworth*'. It was introduced by a dedication to the virtuoso and Fellow of the Royal Society, Lord Brereton, in which, as we saw in the last chapter, Glanvill urged the Royal Society to conduct 'a *Cautious*, and *Faithful History*' of spirits, of which this would doubtless have formed part.[65] In addition, in the accompanying section, which in a further edition of the work issued later in 1668 was given a separate title page, *A Whip for the Droll, Fiddler to the Atheist: Being Reflections on Drollery & Atheism. Sent, upon the occasion of the Drummer of Tedworth, In a Letter to the most Learned Dr. Hen. More, D.D.*, Glanvill responded to sceptical arguments about the case, going on from this to attack 'the *Reasons* men are so apt to cavil at this kinde of *Relations*', which 'are chiefly, I think, an *affected humour* of *Drollery*, and *Scoffing*, and a *worse* cause, *ATHEISM*'.[66]

That the published version was based either on Mompesson's letters or on virtually identical texts is shown by the exactness with which the two match one another. (In addition, as already noted, the narrative of the encounter with the poltergeist in the children's bed closely echoes that to be found in the State Papers.) On the other hand, Glanvill elaborated the earlier texts in various ways. To some extent he wrote in a more literary manner, elucidating matters for the benefit of the reader. In the case of a door catch striking one of Mompesson's young sons when he went to relieve himself during the night, Glanvill not only bowdlerised the purpose of his mission, but also slightly embellished the story, invoking a '*waggish Dæmon*' in connection with the boy's injury.[67] In addition, at the end of this section of the book he added a lengthy disquisition on issues arising from the case. Thus the probity of the witnesses, including Mompesson himself, was strongly emphasised on the grounds that 'the credit of *matters* of *fact* depends much upon the consideration of the *Relators*; and if *They* cannot be *deceived* themselves, nor supposed any wayes interessed to *impose* upon others, we *may*, and we *ought* to acquiesce in their *reports*'. There was also a riposte to the argument that the failure of Chesterfield and Falmouth, the emissaries from the king and queen, to encounter the spirit proved that it did not exist. By way of response Glanvill noted how unwise it would be to presume that there were no robbers on Salisbury Plain just because you often travelled there and had never met one, while he also invoked the absurdity of a Frenchman who concluded that '*There was no Sun in* England, *because he was 6 Weeks here, and never saw it*'. In all, Glanvill's account made a point of describing everything that transpired with the greatest possible verisimilitude, on the grounds that '*matter* of *Fact* is not capable of any proof besides, but *that* of *immediate sensible Evidence*'.[68] In other words, what we have is very much the discourse that we have come to see as characteristic of Restoration science, here put to strongly apologetic purposes in emphasising the reality of the spirit realm against sceptics.[69]

Yet what is striking is how both the anxious, evangelical tone of Mompesson's initial account and the strategy suggested in Sir Thomas Mompesson's letter to him are almost entirely elided. The 'great mercy' of the intermission of the spirit's activity during Mrs Mompesson's childbirth became a '*civil cessation*'; the recourse to prayer just one detail out of many; while Mompesson's anxiety that some might see the affair as 'the *Judgment* of God upon him, for some *notorious impiety*' was mentioned only as further evidence of how this honest man had suffered, in conjunction with being accused of fraud.[70] Even more striking is the way in which, at the points where Mompesson's account included codas recording recourse to prayer or querulous self-doubt, Glanvill instead introduced slightly whimsical asides, for instance suggesting that a temporary intermission in the spirit's activity occurred because 'perhaps the Laws of the *Black Society* required its presence at the general *Rendezvous* elsewhere'.[71] On the other hand, Glanvill took up and elaborated Mompesson's account in his second letter of the confrontation between the demon and Mompesson's servant John, which (echoing his source) Glanvill introduced by begging leave 'to be a little less solemn'. But he made it more literary in tone, altering the order of Mompesson's narrative to conflate different passages, and embellishing the whole episode in terms of mock heroic:

> There was *John engarison'd*, and provided for the assault with a *trusty* Sword, and other implements of War. And for some time there was scarce a night past, without some doubty action and encounter, in which the success was various . . . And for the most part, our Combatant came off with honour and advantage, except when his enemy outwatch'd and surprized him, and then he's made a prisoner, bound hand and foot, and at the mercy of the *Goblin* . . . But enough of *plaisance* upon the occasion of *John's Chivalry*, and *Encounters*.[72]

This elision of the serious tone represented by Mompesson's initial reaction to the case, and the complementary intensification of the more confident attitude reflected by his subsequent letters to Creed, reveals a telling shift in religious sensibility on Glanvill's part. What we see is a rejection of the pious introspection which we might be inclined to describe as 'Puritanical', but which clearly reflected a broader mentality insofar as it was shared by a loyalist family like the Mompessons, in favour of a more assertive, self-confident attitude – cheerfully accepting and almost celebrating the reality of a divine dispensation in which God was pitted against a diabolical realm, and able to joke about it. Indeed, it is interesting that both Glanvill and his mentor, More, happily talked about 'tricks' and 'pranks' in this context, meaning not that these had anything to do with the human fraud that sceptics invoked in such cases, but that such trickery was what was to be expected of the Devil.[73] Hence, it seemed only appropriate to use wit to give a little light relief to a narrative vindicating the reality of the phenomena involved, evidently reflecting the rhetorical use of humour to 'salt' a more serious argument.[74]

### Glanvill versus the Wits

In addition, as already noted, in the annexed *A Whip for the Droll, Fiddler to the Atheist: Being Reflections on Drollery & Atheism*, Glanvill sought to refute various arguments that were current, evidently in oral form, against the verisimilitude of the events. He refers to a whole string of these '*murmures, and petty evasions of wilful Unbelievers*' (to use his words), which almost read like the inventory of questions by a sceptical investigator of a modern psychic phenomenon.[75] The first was that '*The House is rented, and that this is a device to beat down the value of it*', the second that '*It is a trick to get money from those that come to see the Prodigy*', both of which Glanvill was able categorically to deny. He was equally confident in dealing with the objection '*That there was no Drumming in the midst of any Room, but only a striking on the Boards as it were with a Hammer, in a corner of the outsides of the House*', while he went on to assert how the chief victims of the assaults 'were little, harmless, modest Girles, that could not well have been suspected guilty of the confidence of such a juggle, had it been possible they could have acted in it'; he added that their hands were above, rather than below, the bedclothes when the disturbances occurred.[76]

Glanvill stated that these were objections that More had heard at Cambridge, but a different gloss on them was given by a pamphlet entitled *The Drummer of Tedworth* issued in 1716 in connection with Addison's play of that year, *The Drummer*, which we encountered in Chapter 2. This stated in connection with Chesterfield's and Falmouth's visit to Tedworth in 1664 that 'unluckily, for the Credit of the *Dæmon*, no Noise, no Disturbance happen'd that Night; and upon this, the Earl of *Rochester*, and other Wits of the Age, endeavour'd to turn the whole Story into ridicule'.[77] The author then exactly cited the first two of the sceptical arguments refuted by Glanvill in his *Whip for the Droll*, as if it was to Rochester and his friends that he was responding. It is, of course, quite possible that this simply represents a hack writer's embroidery of the earlier work, perhaps also extrapolating from a reference to 'something that passed between my Lord of *R*— and your self about my troubles, &c.' in a letter from Mompesson to Glanvill of 8 November 1672 that was included in *Saducismus Triumphatus* in 1681 which it is otherwise unfortunately impossible to elucidate.[78] On the other hand, it may represent a genuine memory of Rochester's active role in promoting scepticism about the affair, which would be wholly in character; it is reminiscent, for instance, of Rochester's satire of quackery through adopting the persona of 'Dr Bendo'.[79]

That someone, whether or not it was Rochester, was making witty mischief at Glanvill's expense both before and after the appearance of the 1668 version of his book is, however, clear. By the time that a revised version of Glanvill's account came out in *Saducismus Triumphatus* in 1681, it had been significantly altered, and this appears to reveal the extent to which articulate sadducism had been at work in undermining his enterprise over the intervening period and the way in which Glanvill reacted to this. We have already noted how, even when he was writing *A Blow at Modern Sadducism*, Glanvill had confided to More that he knew that the story was rejected by the courtiers, 'And perhaps no evidence will convince them'. It is also worth noting Samuel Pepys's opinion of the published work as 'well writ in good style, but methinks not very convincing', while, of Glanvill's account of the events at Tedworth, John Aubrey wrote: 'as he was an ingenious person, so I suspect he was a little too credulous'.[80] Now, Glanvill faced an even greater threat.

Though *Saducismus Triumphatus*, the revised version of Glanvill's book, was not published till 1681, in the aftermath of a published assault on the veracity of the affair in John Webster's *Displaying of Supposed Witchcraft* (1677) to which we will come shortly, the preface to the new recension of Glanvill's work made it clear that this had been prepared some years earlier, reflecting Glanvill's reaction to the view that the whole thing was 'a Delusion and Imposture' that can only have been orally expressed.[81] In a letter to Glanvill of 18 November 1670 Richard Baxter told him that:

> Some gentlemen of quality and parts coming purposely to me, to heare what more instances I could give them of Apparitions and Witches than I have printed, (telling me of the very great increase of sadducees that will beleive no other evidencies, & importuning me (in vaine) to print the instances I gave them), when Mr Mompessons story (published by you) was mentioned on the by, they assured me that it goeth currantly now among the sadducees (at court and the Innes of Court) that

Mr Mompesson hath confessed that it was all his own jugling done onely that he might be taken notice of &c. I intreate you (from them) to acquaint him with the report, & wish him if it be false (not for his own honour so much as for their sakes that are hardened by it) to publish some vindication or contradiction.[82]

The reports to which Baxter was referring seem to be based on Mompesson's supposed meeting with the king – either as reported by More in 1663 or Chesterfield in 1664 or at some later date – at which it was said that he had confessed to the king that the whole thing was a fraud. Moreover knowledge of this seems to have become increasingly common, perhaps encouraged (as the 1716 pamphlet claimed) by Rochester and his friends. Whether such a confession did actually occur is, of course, impossible to know: the strongest evidence for it is Chesterfield's direct statement to this effect, which has already been quoted and which the report that Baxter heard echoed.[83] On the other hand, it seems perfectly plausible: one can imagine how difficult it would have been for a loyal subject like Mompesson to stick to his normal account of the strange events at Tedworth when in the presence of a monarch who was intent on extracting a confession of fraud. One is reminded of Charles's predecessor, James I, who (in the words of the miscellaneous writer, Francis Osborne) was 'gratified by nothing more, then an Opportunity to shew his Dexterity in Discovering an Imposture, (at which, I must confess Him, the Promptest Man Living)', as illustrated by his success in extracting confessions of fraud from the supposed witchcraft victims Anne Gunther in 1605 and John Smith in 1616.[84] In the latter case, Osborne specifically notes how during the boy's confrontation with the king, '(possibly daunted at his Presence, or Terrified by his Words) he began to faulter, so as the King discover'd a Fallacy', and Mompesson possibly suffered the same fate.

Be that as it may, Glanvill felt it essential to refute such reports. He even took the trouble to solicit a letter from Mompesson dated 8 November 1672 which was published in *Saducismus Triumphatus* in 1681, in which Mompesson acknowledged

that I have been very often of late asked the Question, Whether I have not confessed to His Majesty or any other, a Cheat discovered about that affair. To which I gave, and shall to my Dying-day give the same Answer, That I must bely my self, and perjure my self also to acknowledge a Cheat in a thing where I am sure there was nor could be any.[85]

But worse was to come, since word seems to have got around that Glanvill himself no longer believed in the veracity of the affair. Now, there is not the slightest evidence that Glanvill ever had any such doubts; instead, it is tempting to see this as a clever ploy by the sceptics – and here one could well imagine the artful involvement of Rochester – which stimulated the serious-minded king's chaplain to telling exasperation as he sought to rebuff them, thus no doubt adding to the joke from their point of view. In the preface to the new edition of his book, in answer to the accusation 'that *Mr. Mompesson* and my self, have confessed all to be a cheat and contrivance', Glanvill wrote:

> Concerning this, I have been asked a thousand times, till I have been weary of answering, and the *Questionists* would scarce believe I was in earnest when I denied it. I have received Letters about it from known Friends and Strangers out of many parts of the Three Kingdoms, so that I have been haunted almost as bad as *Mr. Mompesson*'s House. Most of them have declared that it was most confidently reported, and believed in all the respective parts, that the business was a Cheat, that *Mr. Mompesson* had confessed so much, and I the same: so that I was quite tired with denying and answering Letters about it. And to free my self from the trouble, I at last resolved to re-print the Story by it self with my Confutation of the Invention that concerned me, and a Letter I received from *Mr. Mompesson* (now printed in this Book) which cleared the matter as to him.[86]

Moreover, it is worth noting that similar rumours seem to have been spread concerning a more august figure who had long been associated with the defence of the reality of witchcraft, the aristocratic natural philosopher, Robert Boyle (who Rochester and his friends, incidentally, are known to have found something of a joke).[87] In 1658, Boyle had orchestrated the publication of an English translation of an account of one of the most famous poltergeists in early seventeenth-century France, *The Devil of Mascon*. Yet in January 1678, when asking Boyle for additional cases of witchcraft to include in the extended version of his book then in preparation, Glanvill wrote:

> I have bin often told of late that you do now disown the story of the *Devill of Mascon,* & that a clear imposture hath bin discover'd in it. The like hath very falsly bin reported of Mr Mompesson, & my self, in relation to that

story. So that I am apt to think that this also concerning you, may bee a contrived falshood, (for by such, ‹some› men endeavour to run down all things of this kind) & therefore I most humbly begge you would please to lett mee know, if there bee any truth in this so confident a report.

Of course, Boyle replied that, on the contrary, he believed as strongly in the Mascon story as ever, indeed that its truth had been confirmed by his conversation with 'a learned & intelligent Traveller' who had been there more recently.[88] But what is clear is the effectiveness of the 'contrived falshood', in Glanvill's phrase. It seems likely that – inspired by the story of Mompesson's supposed confession to the king – someone was cleverly spreading such rumours. Moreover, Glanvill had no doubt that those responsible were the leaders of fashionable opinion whom he associated with the court and the coffee-houses in London, and especially with the circles of 'wit'. He saw these as having a vested interest in presuming that all cases like that at Tedworth were fraudulent, and that it was inconceivable that God or the Devil could intervene in the world in so direct a way. What is more, the rumours worked, in the sense that clearly the credibility of such beliefs was seriously undermined by them. This aspect of the case thus reveals the crucial role in bringing about cultural change of fashionable opinion; by comparison, the writings of a man like Glanvill were arguably more peripheral.[89]

Here, it is interesting to study the reaction to this counter-attack on the part of Glanvill and his posthumous editor, Henry More, as illustrated by the 1681 and subsequent editions of *Saducismus Triumphatus*. Apart from the inclusion of the letters and preface already referred to, the other principal changes were as follows.[90] Firstly, the elaborate dedicatory epistle to Lord Brereton was removed; Brereton had died in 1680, but, since the Royal Society had never responded to Glanvill's fulsome request for a natural history of 'the LAND of SPIRITS', this might have seemed something of a hostage to fortune in any case. More striking was the excision of the various direct and slightly whimsical allusions to the Devil and his minions which Glanvill had introduced in place of Mompesson's outbursts of piety in the 1668 version, thus making a marked change to the overall tone of the text.[91] Glanvill had himself complained in his 1668 text how his antagonists bolstered their case by 'a *loud laugh* upon an idle tale of a *Devil*, or a *Witch*',[92] and it is almost as if he had now come to feel that the use of mirth as a weapon by the sceptics made it less appropriate for a humorous element to appear in his own, orthodox account of the case.

On the other hand, Glanvill strengthened up the detail on 'matters of fact', giving the names of certain people who had witnessed the strange events at Tedworth;[93] a similar motive impelled him and More to include more and more 'relations' of demonic activity in the world in the book as a whole. Equally interesting, additional detail was added concerning Glanvill's own experience of the poltergeist and his attempts to establish that what he felt and saw could not be explained away by fraud or panic on his part. He explained how

> This passage I mention not in the former Editions, because it depended upon my single Testimony, and might be subject to more Evasions than the other I related; but having told it to divers Learned and inquisitive Men, who thought it not altogether inconsiderable, I have now added it here. It will I know be said by some, that my Friend and I were under some Affright, and so fancied noises and sights that were not. This is the Eternal Evasion.

More striking still, in the course of giving extra detail about the strange scratchings that he witnessed, he stressed how he

> searcht under and behind the Bed, turned up the Cloaths to the Bed-cords, graspt the Bolster, sounded the Wall behind, and made all the search that possibly I could to find if there were any trick, contrivance, or common cause of it; the like did my Friend, but we could discover nothing. So that I was then verily perswaded, and am so still, that the noise was made by some *Dæmon* or *Spirit*.

In addition, Glanvill included extra information such as that his horse, which had been stabled at the Mompesson house, went lame and subsequently died.[94]

Though the extra stress on fact was perhaps only to be expected, it is nevertheless interesting how the abandonment of wittiness was accompanied by this greater accent on verisimilitude and integrity. Arguably, Glanvill's emphasis on his own experiences, and the way he had been convinced by them, is indicative of a further trend in Restoration Anglicanism – the increased stress on sincerity and moral earnestness which was to become typical of Latitudinarian divines.[95] Equally revealing is the way in which, although Glanvill had initially believed that his juxtaposition of a confident,

rhetorical appeal to 'matters of fact' with a comfortably ironic tone in relation to the reality of the Devil and his works would be effective, instead it
proved unstable, as more extreme forms of rationalism of the kind that
Glanvill attacked in *A Whip for the Droll* undercut the assertion of factuality
which lay at the heart of his case. It is thus interesting how, in evident
response to this, Glanvill abandoned the less serious passages with which he
had salted his original account, instead adopting the persona of injured
truth-teller in his continued attempt to vindicate the reality of the phenomena
against their fashionable detractors. From these permutations, we learn
much about the history of Restoration thought.

## The Aftermath and the Problem of Fraud

But the story did not end with Glanvill's death in 1680 and the appearance
of *Saducismus Triumphatus* under More's editorship the following year.
Details of the Tedworth case were further propagated by subsequent, more
derivative demonologists such as the New England cleric, Increase Mather,
in his *Essay for the Recording of Illustrious Providences* (1684) or the
Scot, George Sinclair, in his *Satans Invisible World Discovered* (1685).[96] In
addition, Richard Baxter reiterated the story in his *The Certainty of the
Worlds of Spirits* (1691), asserting how it was 'all undoubtedly true' on the
basis of a conversation he had had with a local attorney 'within this
Month'. Also interesting was his answer to the objection that 'when some
unbelievers went from *London* to be satisfied nothing was done when they
were there', on the grounds that 'as God oweth not such Remedies to
Unbelievers, so Satan hath no desire to cure them'.[97] The extent to which the
affair had become a commonplace at the time is illustrated by an episode in
1676 when Robert Hooke's coffee-house companion, Francis Morgan, tried
to interest him in a strange apparition in Northamptonshire (a difficult task,
since it was just at this time that Hooke was penning his sarcastic attack on
Henry More as a quasi-magician), quipping, 'I beleeve we shall putt
down your Drumming Devill of Tedworth'.[98] Equally interesting is the case
of a haunted house at Cambridge recorded by the diarist Abraham de la
Pryme in 1694, which many considered to evidence the activity of the Devil,
since this was in many ways a copy-cat version of the Tedworth affair, the
strange occurrences including echoes of such aspects of it as objects being
thrown about, the jingling of money, 'a great hollow noise' and a sulphurous
smell.[99]

But scepticism also continued. The Cambridge case just mentioned elicited a critical response from none other than Isaac Newton, 'fellow of Trinity
College [and] a very learned man', who, as de la Pryme specifically noted,
said to those waiting outside the haunted house: '"Oh! yee fools . . . will you
never have any witt, know yee not that all such things are meer cheats and
impostures? Fy, fy! go home, for shame", and so he left them, scorning to go
in.'[100] As for Tedworth, in addition to the similar oral scepticism to which
Glanvill had had to reply, there were now printed treatises which used the
evidence of fraud there as part of a more general assault on the reality of
witchcraft, and to these and the responses to them we must now turn.

First, we have John Webster's *Displaying of Supposed Witchcraft* (1677),
which, after nearly three hundred pages of learned argument on the subject
from biblical and philosophical evidence, has a whole chapter devoted to the
issue of imposture, in which Webster argued that the presumption was that,
since many cases of witchcraft and demonic possession had been shown to
involve fraud, it stood to reason that others did too. In his elaborate exposition he invoked various cases going back to the sixteenth century, arguing
that it was more plausible to find an explanation in terms of 'meer natural
causes'. He then specifically went on, concerning the Tedworth affair,

> Must not all persons that are of sound understanding judge and believe
> that all those strange tricks related by Mr. *Glanvil* of his Drummer at
> Mr. *Mompessons* house, whom he calls the Demon of *Tedworth*, were
> abominable cheats and impostures (as I am informed from persons of
> good quality they were discovered to be) for I am sure Mr. *Glanvil* can
> shew no agents in nature, that the Demon applying them to fit patients,
> could produce any such effects by, and therefore we must conclude all
> such to be impostures.[101]

An even more elaborate argument of a similar kind was mounted by the
Dutch sceptic, Balthasar Bekker, in his classic exposé of witch beliefs, *Der
Betoverde Weereld (The World Bewitched)*, published in 1691–3, which
created a furore in Europe, though only part of the work was ever translated
into English – perhaps because of the extent to which it replicated the
current of mainly oral sadducism that has been surveyed here.[102] In the
fourth volume of the work, which appeared in 1693 – perhaps encouraged
in part by the issue of a Dutch version of the relevant part of Glanvill's
*Saducismus Triumphatus* by Jacobus Koelman in his response to the initial

volumes of Bekker's work published two years previously – Bekker gave a lengthy account both of the Tedworth case and that at Mascon about which Glanvill had queried Boyle a quarter of a century earlier.[103] Bekker expressed profound scepticism about the role of Glanvill as commentator on the episode, on the basis not least of the oral testimony of an English 'homme d'esprit' whom he had consulted, who explained how 'gens d'esprit' like himself were sceptical about the whole affair. After quoting Glanvill's entire narrative of the case, Bekker proceeded to point to various suspicious circumstances about it, including the haphazardness of the occurrences and the extent to which they seemed most easily explicable in terms of the antics first of the disgruntled William Drury himself and then of Mompesson's servants – hence implying that fraud was the likeliest explanation of the events at Tedworth. In all, he concluded that it was 'a piece of nonsense' ('fadaise'),[104] unworthy of serious discussion.

Bekker's book has often been acclaimed as a decisive intervention in the witchcraft debate, and it has always seemed axiomatic that the demonstration of fraud in cases like this was fundamental in discrediting witchcraft beliefs and hence in bringing about their decline.[105] However, what needs to be stressed is the extent to which the argument that the Tedworth affair was fraudulent was resisted, not only by Glanvill up to his death in 1680, but by others thereafter. Thus Richard Bovet, in his *Pandæmonium* (1684), specifically referred to the Tedworth case in his response to the 'sort of Witty and (otherwise) Ingenious, Persons' who 'openly, and with great zeal profess a disbelief of the Existence of Dæmons, and Witches':

> such was the bold confidence of some of these Witch Advocates that they durst Effront that Relation of the Dæmon of *Tedworth*, published by the Ingenious Mr. *Glanvil*, and Attested by Mr. *Mompesson*, a Gentleman, and a Divine, who (to all that knew them) were never over fond of crediting stories of that kind; Yet (I say) had some of this sort of men the impudence to declare to the World that that whole *Relation* was but a Figment, or Forgery, and that Mr. *Mompesson*, and Mr. *Glanvill* had retracted, whatever they had published touching that Transaction.[106]

Bovet was reassured that in the 1681 edition of *Saducismus Triumphatus* 'both Mr. *Glanvil*, and Mr. *Mompesson*, again renew, and confirm the Truth of their former Testimony, thereby giving the world a just Occasion to detest the base Artifices of such bold Impostors'. He objected to the way in which 'they oppose their simple *Ipse dixit*, against the most unquestionable Testimonies, of persons of the greatest Integrity and Generosity'. He equally deprecated their 'peremptory and staring confidence, which must Huff and swagger down all the most undeniable proofs', notwithstanding the fact that their arguments had 'been sufficiently refuted and baffled, by those Learned and Ingenious Pens who have still made it their business to Vindicate and Rescue substantial Truth, from the Attacques of Atheists, and Scepticks'. His characterisation of his opponents is a revealing one to which we will return.

Equally striking was the line taken by the Somerset geologist and spiritualist John Beaumont in his *Historical, Physiological and Theological Treatise of Spirits, Apparitions, Witchcrafts, and other Magical Practices* (1705). By this time, Bekker's critique had also appeared, and Beaumont was at pains to refute the arguments contained in that, as was specifically noted on the title page of his book. He accused Bekker of flying in the face of the evidence, in the case both of Tedworth and of Mascon.[107] He wrote:

> Dr *Bekker* rejects all the Facts alledg'd for proving the Operations of *Dæmons*, and among others the Facts of the *Dæmons* of *Mascon* and *Tedworth*, as being done by Combinations of Servants, or others; and would have the World acquiesce in his Arbitrary say so, without any manner of Proof, only alledging this frivolous Pretence, that there have been Impostures in that kind, and therefore those must be so; a notable consequence which should a School-Boy infer, he would deserve lashing.

Beaumont was perfectly aware of the story that Mompesson had 'own'd privately to the late King *Charles* the Second, that all that pass'd at his House at *Tedworth* was done by Contrivance'. He added how: 'another Person has told me, it was done by two Young Women in the House, with a design to scare thence Mr. *Monpesson*'s Mother'. But he considered that, balanced against the testimony of the 1672–4 letters of Mompesson (which he cited at length) and the account of the case as published in Glanvill's book, such views would only be held by 'obstinate Opposers of the Truth':

> After the foregoing Declaration of Mr. *Mompesson*, I must freely tell all Men, that shall pretend a Cheat in the Transaction at *Tedworth*, that till they fairly make appear to the World, by whom the Cheat was play'd, and how the Facts Sworn to were perform'd, the Imposture must lie at their Door.

Earlier in the passage he had explained: 'I know not what may be offer'd to Men of such obstinate Prepossessions, who will have all things done by Imposture, which seem strange to them, and interfere with their Belief'. Though he acknowledged that if a single person told a strange story it might seem suspect, this was not the case when it was a matter of such consensus. In his view, 'the Facts of the *Dæmons* of *Mascon* and *Tedworth*' could be left 'to Men of unbyass'd Thoughts to judge of them as they see cause: These Relations seeming to me well attested, and as well examin'd as if the Critical Dr. *Bekker* had been a Party concern'd on that Account'. Indeed, he remained convinced that the events that occurred were 'above all Humane Performance', going so far as to say, 'I think it a violation of the Law of Nature, to reject all these Relations as fabulous, meerly upon a self presuming Conceit, unless a Man can fairly shew the things to be Impossible, or wherein those Persons were impos'd on'.

A similar and equally interesting commentary on the case is to be found much later, in the journal of John Wesley under 27 May 1768, in connection with an account of Elizabeth Hobson, a woman in Sunderland who claimed abnormal visionary powers. Wesley had of course long been aware of similar events, not least the strange disturbances at Epworth Rectory, his father's house, in 1716–17 (which, as with the 1694 Cambridge case, also had echoes of the Tedworth episode).[108] Later, he was to reprint Glanvill's account of Tedworth in the *Arminian Magazine* in 1785.[109] In his journal account, Wesley acknowledged that it was widely and confidently alleged that such occurrences were 'the mere contrivance of artful men', continuing:

> The famous instance of this, which has been spread far and wide, was the drumming in Mr. Mompesson's house at Tidworth, who it was said acknowledged, 'It was all a trick', and that he had 'found out the whole contrivance'. Not so. My eldest brother, then at Christ Church, Oxon, inquired of Mr. Mompesson, his fellow-collegian, whether his father had acknowledged this or not. He answered, 'The resort of gentlemen to my father's house was so great, he could not bear the expense. He therefore took no pains to confute the report that he had found out the cheat, although he, and I, and all the family knew the account which was published to be punctually true'.[110]

In fact, Wesley got his Mompessons confused, and the man whom his brother Samuel had known at Oxford came from a different branch of the family from the Tedworth Mompessons involved in the case of the drummer. But this illustrates once again how the imputation of fraud could be effectively sidestepped by those who wished to believe in the reality of the phenomena involved. Indeed, there is a certain plausibility in Wesley's account of Mompesson wanting to avoid the nuisance of the visitors who plagued his house in pursuit of the sensation, although this is not referred to in any other account of the affair.

In Wesley's case, as with Bovet and Beaumont over a generation earlier, his defence of the case formed part of his reaction to the way in which 'the English in general, and indeed, most of the men of learning in Europe, have given up all accounts of witches and apparitions as mere old wives' fables', summarising the manner in which this had been achieved with the words, 'the infidels have hooted witchcraft out of the world'. It was in this connection that he made the celebrated remark:

> They well know (whether Christians know it or not) that the giving up witchcraft is in effect the giving up the Bible. And they know, on the other hand, that if but one account of the intercourse of men with separate spirits be admitted, their whole castle in the air (deism, atheism, materialism) falls to the ground. I know no reason therefore why we should suffer even this weapon to be wrested out of our hands.

He went on to answer the question, 'Did you ever see an apparition yourself?' His reply was:

> No. Nor did I ever see a murder. Yet I believe there is such a thing; yea, and that in one place or another murder is committed every day. Therefore I cannot as a reasonable man deny the fact, although I never saw it and perhaps never may. The testimony of unexceptional witnesses fully convinces me both of the one and the other.[111]

Yet the truth is that, in the Tedworth case in particular, scepticism does seem by this time to have become the order of the day. Thus Joseph Addison's play, *The Drummer, or the Haunted House* (1716), which was inspired by Tedworth, took it for granted that the events were contrived, despite the slight frisson of fashionable horror that sets off the extreme scepticism expressed by the freethinker as examined in Chapter 2. The pamphlet issued in conjunction with Addison's play, *The Drummer of Tedworth* of 1716, was more overt in its scepticism, seeing 'the Pranks which were play'd' as 'not so mischievous as they were merry, and such as we commonly call *Christmas Gambols*'.[112] A similar attitude underlay William Hogarth's famous print, *Credulity, Superstition and Fanaticism. A Medley* (1762), in which a thermometer calibrating enthusiasm is surmounted by the figure of a drummer on a plinth with the legend 'Tedworth' (Plate 16).[113] Hogarth's targets also included yet another, more topical, poltergeist case which *was* proved to be fraudulent, that which occurred at Cock Lane in London in 1762. This again had echoes of the Tedworth affair in the interrogatory knockings that were involved in it, and it is perhaps revealing that it stimulated a revival of Addison's play.[114] Hogarth's print also overtly associated such views with Methodism, reflecting his scorn for Wesley's support for such beliefs (he would not have been at all surprised by Wesley's championship of the Tedworth case had he known about it). A similar presumption of fraud appears, for example, in the physician John Ferriar's brief account of the Tedworth affair in a lecture on demonology in 1786, or, a generation later, in Charles Mackay's fuller one in his *Memoirs of Extraordinary Popular Delusions* (1841), which wrote off the whole episode as a 'trick', most notable for the extent to which it was 'cleverly managed'.[115]

Yet what is important here is that the invocation of fraud in this case was by no means as straightforward as might be expected. As will be apparent especially from the comments of Richard Bovet and John Beaumont, such men, who believed in the intrinsic likelihood of supernatural occurrences like those that were supposed to have occurred at Tedworth, contested the claim of imposture. In their view, those who invoked fraud did so on a priori grounds, arguments of imposture acting as a defence mechanism which enabled them to deny the reality of phenomena with which they were uncomfortable. Thus we have Bovet's characterisation of the 'great zeal' of these 'bold Impostors' and Beaumont's view of them as 'Men of such obstinate Prepossessions, who will have all things done by Imposture, which seem strange to them, and interfere with their Belief'. Effectively, the accusation of fraud was simply a weapon in the battle between believers and sceptics, and it seems unlikely that the invocation of fraud, in itself, made many converts to the sceptical cause of people who had reasons to believe in the reality of the phenomena in question.

Here, it is interesting to recall Lord Molesworth's rather blustering critique of Martin Martin's narratives of second sight as 'All impostures' which we encountered in Chapter 2.[116] It is no less interesting to note earlier analogues to the dismissal of the argument of fraud by Bovet, Beaumont and Wesley, even during the period when witchcraft was being actively prosecuted. This may be illustrated by a single example from Restoration England, since a confrontation of just this kind occurred at the famous Bury St Edmunds witch trial of 1662, presided over by Sir Matthew Hale. At it, on the initiative of 'an ingenious person', an empirical test was devised to ascertain the genuineness of the fits that were supposedly induced in five local girls by the touch of the accused witches, Rose Cullender and Amy Duny – namely of blindfolding one of the girls and allowing her to be touched by someone else. This had the same effect as when she was touched by one of the witches, whereupon some of those involved in the trial protested that 'the whole transaction of this business was a meer Imposture'. But what is equally interesting is that others argued that the fact the girl might be deceived into thinking it was the witch who had touched her when it was really someone else was irrelevant to the overall plausibility of the accusations against the witch,

> for say they, it is not possible that any should counterfeit such Distempers, being accompanied with such various Circumstances, much less Children; and for so long time, and yet undiscovered by their Parents and Relations: For no man can suppose that they should all conspire together, (being out of several families, and, as they Affirm, no way related one to the other, and scarce of familiar acquaintance) to do an Act of this nature whereby no benefit or advantage could redound to any of the Parties, but a guilty Conscience for Perjuring themselves in taking the Lives of two poor simple Women away, and there appears no Malice in the Case.[117]

A supposedly impartial empirical test thus proved less decisive than it should have done.

Much the same is true of supposed confessions of fraud, and here it is interesting to go back to an even earlier date and to the famous possession cases involving the Puritan, John Darrell, in the Elizabethan period, when confessions of fraud were made under duress which were subsequently retracted. Thus Thomas Darling, the 'Boy of Burton', wrote to Bishop Bancroft claiming that 'he had beene drawne on by subtilties' to make his confession, while Darrell's subsequent protégé, William Sommers, alternately simulated his fits before sceptical onlookers to show that they were false, and reasserted their genuineness; it is also notable that Darrell accused Samuel Harsnett of selectiveness as to when he adduced fraud accusations in his powerful polemic on the subject.[118] Here, one is reminded of the case of John Mompesson himself and his supposed confession to Charles II, as noted earlier in this chapter, including the analogy with the comparable activities of James I. It does seem likely that, as with confessions of witch-craft, confessions of fraud could be manufactured, not least due to the social dimension by which pressure could be put on those of lower status to admit imposture to satisfy their social superiors.

Indeed, certain historians of witchcraft have perhaps seen the accusation of fraud as more straightforward than it really was. For instance, in his *The Realities of Witchcraft and Popular Magic in Early Modern Europe* (2008), Edward Bever has noted the increasing frequency with which cases that came before the authorities in the Duchy of Würtemburg were put down to 'conscious fraud', particularly in relation to offences like seeking hidden treasure, echoing his Enlightenment predecessors in finding fraud a reas-suringly straightforward explanation of witchcraft and related phenomena.[119] Bever problematises many of the other explanatory categories that he uses, but fraud is treated as self-evident, requiring no discussion. Yet it could be argued that the suspicion and unmasking of fraud was by no means as uncomplicated as a treatment like his implies.

This therefore brings us back to the fundamental point about the Tedworth case, that the accusation of fraud was not really decisive at all. As we will see in the Conclusion to this book, belief in the authenticity of the phenomena that occurred at Tedworth has continued among students of psychical research to the present day and it really does seem as if it was a predisposition to believe or to disbelieve, rather than any decisive piece of evidence, that was fundamental in dictating people's response to what occurred. Leaving aside Beaumont's comment about their 'obstinate Prepossessions', there is much truth in his view of his opponents' invocation of imposture to account for things 'which seem strange to them, and interfere with their Belief'. This obviously takes us back to the underlying preconceptions that made people defend or reject supposedly supernatural phenomena, and to the broader issues concerning intellectual change and its stimuli with which this book has throughout been concerned, to which we will return in the Conclusion. The case of the 'Drummer of Tedworth' gives a rich and vivid view of these debates in progress over more than a century.

# CHAPTER FIVE

# THE ENLIGHTENMENT REJECTION
# OF MAGIC

## MID-CENTURY SCEPTICISM AND ITS MILIEU

On 12 May 1786, Dr John Ferriar read a paper to the Manchester Literary and Philosophical Society entitled 'Of Popular Illusions, and Particularly of Medical Demonology'.[1] Ferriar was a typical Enlightenment figure, the 'premier physician' of Manchester in his day, who not only had an extensive and successful practice but also played a leading role in measures aimed to improve sanitary conditions in the city and to provide humane treatment for the insane.[2] His paper, published in the society's *Memoirs* in 1790, gave a learned account of beliefs in witchcraft and related phenomena, remarking particularly on the 'passion for mysticism' which characterised many Renaissance and early modern authors. As he approached his own day Ferriar commented in almost shocked terms on various examples of the 'credulity' that he was surprised to find still in evidence, including the acceptance of traditional demonology by the early eighteenth-century medical progressive, Friedrich Hoffmann, or the notorious convulsions at Saint-Médard in Paris in the 1730s, which showed how 'illusions scarcely credible may prevail in the brightest periods of science and art'.[3] Coming forward to the time when he was writing in the 1780s, Ferriar similarly instanced the widely publicised magnetic cures of Franz Mesmer in Paris, while in a postscript to the published version of his lecture he gave an account of the dispossession of George Lukins at Bristol in 1788, commenting: 'Is it for the credit of this philosophical age, that so bungling an imposture should deceive seven clergymen into a public act of exorcism?'[4] Ferriar's amazement at the continuing prevalence of such beliefs was interspersed in his paper by piecemeal explanations of why people were susceptible to such erroneous views, and he was later to develop a systematic account of one such belief system in his *Essay towards a Theory of Apparitions* (1813), often acclaimed as a pioneering work of its kind, in which he argued that apparitions and related phenomena could be attributed to purely physiolog-ical causes: they were 'spectral impressions', mere illusions 'composed of the shreds and patches of past sensations'.[5]

Yet it is extraordinary how, in recent studies of the fortunes of magical beliefs in the eighteenth century – books like Paul Kléber Monod's *Solomon's Secret Arts: The Occult in the Age of Enlightenment* or John V. Fleming's *The Dark Side of the Enlightenment: Wizards, Alchemists, and Spiritual Seekers in the Age of Reason*, both published in 2013 – the views of sceptics like Ferriar have been sidelined. Instead, emphasis has been placed on the very beliefs and practices that he found so out of place in his enlightened age; the argu-ment is that occult thinkers attached themselves to the ethos of the Enlightenment and that such beliefs flourished as much as ever during that period.[6] Indeed, books like Monod's and Fleming's perhaps raise the question of how the Enlightenment ever gained its reputation as an age characterised by its scepticism about magical and related modes of thought, suggesting that critical attitudes like Ferriar's, which once seemed so commonplace that they were almost taken for granted, deserve fresh scrutiny in their own right.

It is perhaps in the nature of occultist commitment of the kind that Monod and Fleming have studied to leave profuse archival traces on which historians can fasten. Yet that does not prove that it was the preoccupation of more than a minority, at a time when most may have rejected such beliefs. Indeed, if anything this makes it more, rather than less, necessary to eluci-date the alternative, sceptical position. On the other hand, though Ferriar's comments typify the dismissive outlook that became increasingly predomi-nant as the period progressed, at an earlier date it is more elusive. Even if the Enlightenment saw an increasing naturalism and an increased reluctance to accept the possibility of supernatural intervention in the world of the kind which magical beliefs took for granted – as we have seen in previous chap-ters – published critiques of such beliefs like Francis Hutchinson's *Historical Essay concerning Witchcraft* (1718) are surprisingly rare. For this reason, it seems worth considering who was in the forefront of rejecting such beliefs, particularly in the middle years of the eighteenth century, and why. Who followed in the footsteps of the Deists in being axiomatically hostile to magic and occasionally taking the trouble to say so, at a time when orthodox figures were more likely to be defensive or pusillanimous? What can we learn about the affiliations and rationale of such articulate scepticism? A reconsideration of this may help us towards a better understanding of Enlightenment thought.

## John Beaumont and Sir Hans Sloane

We may begin by considering a figure who well illustrates the occultist milieu about which Monod and Fleming have written, namely the Somerset naturalist, John Beaumont, who died in 1731, whose *Historical, Physiological and Theological Treatise of Spirits, Apparitions, Witchcrafts, and other Magical Practices* (1705) we encountered in the last chapter.[7] Beaumont's book provides an encyclopaedic account of beliefs in the existence of '*Genii or Familiar Spirits*' from antiquity to his own time, arguing the reality of such phenomena against those who were sceptical about them and modishly organising his material in terms of each of the five senses by which such supernatural beings could be apprehended, in an evident attempt to align his ideas with those of John Locke. Not only did Beaumont provide an account of the experiences of such spirits on the part of others; he also told of his own encounters with them. On the first occasion, he only heard them: they 'kept at my Chamber Windows . . . called to me, sung, play'd on Musick, rung Bells, sometimes crowed like Cocks, &c'. Subsequently, however, hundreds of spirits appeared 'and I saw some of them Dance in a Ring in my Garden, and Sing, holding Hands round, not facing each other, but their Backs turned to the inner part of the Circle'. Thereafter, he was mainly visited by just two spirits, both 'in Womens Habit, they being of a Brown Complexion, and about Three Foot in Stature', whose costumes he described in detail, and who sometimes had three male companions. Mostly they came to him when he was in bed and encouraged him to dream, during which they suggested various actions that he subsequently took – including courting the member of a local gentry family who became his wife. On the other hand, on one occasion they threatened to kill him if he went to sleep or told anyone about their presence, while in general their visitations led to diarrhoea and other physical side effects, which caused him to describe 'this state of conversation with spirits as the most vexing thing in the world'.[8]

The earliest printed reaction to Beaumont's book appeared in 1709, in John Trenchard's *The Natural History of Superstition*, one of the Deist critiques of magic and related ideas that we encountered in Chapter 2.[9] Trenchard was typical of such authors in his outspoken hostility to magical beliefs, which he blamed on 'priestcraft', on fraud and manipulation, though he argued that this itself depended on human proneness to delusion. As he wrote, ' 'Tis this Ignorance of Causes, &c. subjects us to mistake the

AN

Hiftorical, Phyfiological and Theological

# TREATISE

OF

# SPIRITS,

Apparitions, Witchcrafts,

and other Magical Practices.

CONTAINING

An Account of the *Genii* or *Familiar Spirits,* both Good and Bad, that are faid to attend Men in this Life; and what fenfible Perceptions fome Perfons have had of them: (particularly the Author's own Experience for many Years.)

Alfo of Appearances of Spirits after Death; Divine Dreams, Divinations, Second Sighted Perfons, &c.

Likewife the Power of Witches, and the reality of other Magical Operations, clearly afferted. With a Refutation of Dr. *Bekker's World be- witch'd*; and other Authors that have oppofed the Belief of them.

By *JONH BEAUMONT,* Gent.

*Praeftat aliqua probabiliter noffe de rebus fuperioribus & Coelefti- bus, quàm de rebus inferioribus multa demonftrare.*
Arift. Moral. 9.

*London:* Printed for *D. Browne,* at the *Black Swan* without *Temple-Bar* ; *J.Taylor,* at the *Ship* in *St.Paul's Church-Yard;* *R.Smith,*at the *Angel* without *Temple-Bar* ; *F.Coggan,* in the *Inner-Temple Lane*; and *T.Browne* without *Temple-Bar,*1705.

3. The title-page of John Beaumont's *Historical, Physiological and Theological Treatise of Spirits, Apparitions, Witchcrafts, and other Magical Practices* (1705).

Phantasms and Images of our own Brains (which have no existence any where else) for real Beings, and subsisting without us', and it was in connection with this quasi-medical argument that he adduced the testimony of John Beaumont, one of the few actual instances that he cited in the course of his work. Trenchard wrote, 'A Gentleman now Living has given an account in Print of his Conversation with Spirits for several Years together, and closes his Account with a distrust of the reality of their Conversation with him, though he had said before that *they appeared* to him *to be real*'.[10] In fact, this is slightly unjust to Beaumont, since in the passage of his book that Trenchard cited he reaffirmed the reality of the apparitions, presumably in response to sceptical views like Trenchard's which he had earlier encountered orally.[11]

We do in fact know of one such encounter, which took place at a dinner party organised by the physician and collector, Sir Hans Sloane, one of the best-known medical men in eighteenth-century Britain (Plate 9). Sloane was acquainted with Beaumont, and he wanted to give him the opportunity to explain about his 'extraordinary case' to a group of men 'distinguished both by birth and by their liveliness of mind and knowledge in every genre of erudition'.[12] One of those present was a figure with freethinking proclivities, John Sheffield, Duke of Buckingham, and, when the issue of Beaumont's actions with spirits arose and he 'related many of these conversations he had had with them without reserve', Buckingham responded:

> I can well see, Sir, that you are a person of great curiosity, and I do not doubt that on meeting a traveller from a far away and unknown country, you would wish to be told about the inhabitants' customs, about their food, drink, habits, methods of procreation and so on. You will thus do us a great service by giving us the fairies' replies to these questions.

At this, Beaumont 'remained silent for some time' before replying 'that he was not at all informed about these kinds of things'. Buckingham thereupon apologised for the overt scepticism that he had displayed, as if he had seemed to believe that Beaumont 'was only dreaming up or dreaming of these conversations'. This is an intriguing episode, because it is to be seen in the context of the fashion in coffee-houses at the time for 'shamming', for telling tall stories and encouraging listeners to challenge the credibility of the tale. Buckingham clearly believed that he was being treated to a 'sham' and responded accordingly, whereas this was at odds with the deadly seriousness of Beaumont's belief in his spiritual encounters.[13]

Returning to John Ferriar a century later, he included a long account of Beaumont's visions in his *Essay towards a Theory of Apparitions* (1813). He considered that they 'shew in a most astonishing manner, how far the mind may be deceived, without the occurrence of actual derangement'. Ferriar continued: 'Had this man, instead of irritating his mental disease, by the study of the Platonic philosophers, placed himself under the care of an intelligent physician, he would have regained his tranquility', though he admitted that as a result 'the world would have lost a most extraordinary set of confessions'.[14] In fact, unbeknown to Ferriar, Beaumont *had* consulted an eminent doctor, in this case Sloane, and we know about the encounter between the two men because Sloane wrote it up after Beaumont's death.[15] This took the form of a manuscript memoir of Beaumont that Sloane sent to the French savant, the abbé Jean-Paul Bignon at the Académie des Sciences, ostensibly as the possible basis for an *éloge* of Beaumont. Since, in addition to his treatise on spirits, Beaumont had made a significant contribution to the geological debates of the day, this was not an implausible ambition.

If this was Sloane's aim, however, the text that he compiled was a strange one, since, after just a few paragraphs outlining Beaumont's geological writings, he moved on to a lengthy description of his encounters with spirits. Sloane then devoted the rest of his text – by far the bulk of it – to other cases of supposed spiritual intercourse which he saw as comparable to Beaumont's experiences, in the course of doing so giving a medical disquisition on the mental disorder that he saw as involved in such cases. We will return to that shortly, but here it is worth pointing out the extent to which the cases that Sloane described were ones that related to manuscripts that he treasured in his massive collection of curiosities of different kinds that was to form the basis of the British Museum. These were items associated with figures like the Elizabethan occultists John Dee and Simon Forman, with the seventeenth-century astrologers William Lilly and Elias Ashmole, and with other, more shadowy figures in Restoration London whose books Sloane acquired. The memoir of Beaumont, which I have now published, thus constitutes an important personal testament on Sloane's part as to why he collected material of this kind, and it may even have been for this reason that he wrote it.

This is important, since it has often been supposed that, in his assiduous activity in collecting magical manuscripts, Sloane himself displayed a closet enthusiasm for the kind of practices that they chronicled, thus exemplifying the occultism of the period which John Fleming and Paul Monod have studied.[16] In fact, however, Sloane took exactly the opposite view. In his opinion, these manuscripts exemplified the folly of those who had compiled them. In the case of one text by Simon Forman, which he had seen but not managed to obtain, he considered that it 'would be worth procuring to see the madness contained within it'. Moreover, his accounts of the magical seances and the like that lay behind books that he acquired were retailed in a flippant, dismissive manner. For instance, one story that he told of 'something rather entertaining that happened here several years ago' concerned 'A Catholic priest, a Presbyterian minister and a bankrupt prosecutor, who had little money and a lot of faith in these mystic sciences', who rented a house in Clerkenwell 'in order to discover hidden treasures using these sorts of practices'. Since they failed to pay the rent, the owner of the house evicted them and sold the furniture along with their books, which included an elaborate copy of the famous magical text, *Clavicula Salomonis,* that Sloane himself acquired (Plate 10).[17] As he explained, this book had been placed on a table

> positioned at the centre of the room, the floor of which was covered in white satin, on which someone had traced several concentric circles, and between these circles the names of God were written in several languages (mainly oriental ones) to prevent the spirits coming too close and harming the magician, who was sat at the centre or in the middle, wearing a pair of slippers that were blessed and bore a cross.

This led on to further stories about treasure seeking by magical means. One was at Southwark, but it came to a bad end when the people involved were attacked by a guard dog, while another was at Westminster Abbey and involved William Lilly. In this case, the escapade was terminated by a violent storm, on which Sloane drily noted: 'They imagined that this had happened because they had not carried out their fumigations in the proper manner'.

This brought him to an even stranger story concerning Lilly's associate, Elias Ashmole, perhaps the leading seventeenth-century collector of magical manuscripts, whose huge assemblage of material of this kind survives at Oxford. It involved a visit to Ashmole in 1682 by the Moroccan ambassador, Muhammad ibn Haddu, then on a state visit to London, who, when Ashmole showed him some of the manuscripts of John Dee's supposed seances with angels,

> asked Mr Ashmole to make some of these spirits appear so that he could speak to them about some events that were taking place in his country at the time. Mr Ashmole declined, in order to avoid, he said, the disturbances that they might cause. So the ambassador asked him at least to show him how to make them appear, saying that he would risk the trouble that it could cause, but he was never able to persuade him [Mr Ashmole], even though he offered to convert himself and several of his fellow countrymen to Christianity and relinquish substantial business interests in his home country, if Mr Ashmole would only show him these spirits.[18]

It is also interesting that, in the course of his memoir, Sloane extrapolated to other related beliefs, including witchcraft, which he clearly saw as having characteristics and stimuli similar to such magical encounters. He explained how, by taking drugs, people dreamed of being present at witches' sabbaths, and that they believed so strongly that their experience was real that they were prepared to be condemned and executed for it. In Sloane's view, those who believed in magic were deluded, and his text represents an almost uniquely overt indictment of the beliefs and practices involved.[19]

What is more, Sloane believed that those who suffered from such delusions could be diagnosed and treated by a doctor like himself. He explicitly told Beaumont of his supposed visions 'that what he believed to be real with regard to the fairies was only imaginary, or a strong impression of a dream'. With reference to Beaumont's case he commented more generally: 'I have treated several kinds of disorders of the mind or the brain and I believe that some of them stemmed from the fact that these people dream while awake; [a state] from which it becomes necessary to bring them back, by giving them very strong, powerful and harsh purges'. In the memoir of Beaumont he collected other, similar cases of 'those who are afflicted by this misfortune', including that of a 'young, very rich gentleman who had been tormented by this illness seven to eight months', believing that to do so would 'be useful to those who want to understand illnesses of the head and of the mind'. This text therefore presents a compendium of such cases that would otherwise be hard to locate in Sloane's profuse surviving medical correspondence.[20]

Basically, Sloane seems to have seen such figures as suffering from what was defined at the time as hypochondria, a disease stemming from the lower belly or spleen which affected the body as a whole and the symptoms of which overlapped with the traditional ailment of melancholy, so that it was sometimes referred to as 'hypochondriack Melancholy'.[21] It was generally accepted that these symptoms could include delirium, which comprised 'the *Dreams of waking Persons, wherein Ideas are excited without Order or Coherence, and the animal Spirits are drove into irregular Fluctuations*', in the words of Archibald Pitcairne, a pioneering mechanistic physician whom we will encounter later in this chapter.[22] Moreover, Sloane believed that there were appropriate therapies for dealing with the illness, and he particularly advocated blood-letting and the use on such patients of strong emetics like crocus metallorum or juice of asarum (the former was the name given to a chemical preparation, antimony sulphide, while the latter was a herbal one, made from the very bitter juice of the leaves and roots of the asarabacca plant). He found that, when administered to his patients, these 'have rarely been unsuccessful in curing them within a sufficient length of time', even though the side effects of such severe treatment often 'causes a lot of embarrassment', presumably because of the repeated evacuations that resulted. Sloane's conclusion was, 'Experience has absolutely convinced me that those who are afflicted by this misfortune can be cured just as well as those suffering from pleurisy, colic or other similar illness'. In the case of Beaumont, Sloane stated how his patient was 'very happy to be freed' from his spiritual intercourse 'by the vomits and natural purgatives that delivered him'.[23]

## Magic and the Doctors

In a follow-up note on Beaumont's case, Sloane made it clear that he conflated magical phenomena like those that Beaumont and others claimed to have witnessed with the claims to ecstatic experience of members of religious sects in the period. He reported that Beaumont 'told me a few years before his death that in a new sect called Philadelphians there was a brass basin which when placed beneath the bedhead would never fail to produce this kind of (dreams or) conversations'.[24] In fact, this reference has proved hard to substantiate from the writings of Jane Leade and the sect of 'Philadelphians' of which she became leader (named after one of the churches mentioned in the Book of Revelation): if anything, the idea of brass vessels having a special role seems to be one that Beaumont promoted himself.[25] But this link is significant because it aligns the diagnosis of magic on Sloane's part with the explanation of religious 'enthusiasm' as the result of mental disorder that, as we saw in the Introduction, had been commonplace since the mid-seventeenth century, as exemplified by the writings of Henry More and Meric Casaubon.[26] 'Enthusiasm' played a similarly prominent role in John Trenchard's critique of traditional religion in his *Natural History of Superstition*, and it is worth noting that medical arguments like those that both he and Sloane used were also deployed by more orthodox controversialists in the pamphlet war that greeted the French Prophets in the early years of the eighteenth century, which we briefly encountered in Chapter 2.[27]

Sloane's overt invocation of such reductive explanations in relation to magic thus had a clear pedigree, but what is notable here is the rather taken-for-granted way in which he put them forward, a trait that he shared with his medical contemporaries, as we will see. Equally important is the accompanying belief of such men that they had the wherewithal to *cure* such distempers, a power which neither seventeenth-century philosophers like Henry

More nor Deists like John Trenchard had ever claimed, although this does follow a tradition of medical reductionism towards such beliefs with a pedigree going back to the seventeenth century if not earlier, as we saw in the Introduction.[28] The physician, Nicholas Robinson, for instance, opined that the French Prophets 'would have done much better under the Hand of the Physician, than the secular Arm. Strong Purgatives, Bleeding often repeated, and the Discipline and Management necessary in such Cases, would much easilier have pull'd down that over-weaning Opinion of Self-holiness'.[29] Another eminent doctor, Richard Mead (Plate 12), devoted a chapter of his *Medical Precepts and Cautions* (1751) to conditions straddling those dealt with by Robinson and those covered by Sloane, from those who fancied they were haunted by hobgoblins to those suffering from 'vain terrors, and notions of divine vengeance', all of whom were to be treated by blood-letting, vomits and the like.[30] Indeed, a rare vignette of how those with such beliefs might become patients at the hands of medical men is provided by the record of cases kept by Dr John Woodward and published after his death, which includes detailed accounts of two patients suffering from 'Hypochondriac Disorders' whom he treated, who turn out to have been suffering from melancholy linked to a heightened religious sensibility which he analysed in purely physiological terms and 'cured' by the use of clysters and purges.[31]

In one of these cases, Woodward included a section comprising 'An Attempt to explain the Phænomena mechanically',[32] and it is important to acknowledge the extent to which doctors like these believed that medicine had been revolutionised in their era by the application of models stemming from the mechanical philosophy of the seventeenth century. Various authors published elaborate tomes which offered a rationale of the workings of the human body and the proper treatment of ill health according to mechanistic principles, with the aim of creating a '*Theory of Physick*' with 'the same certainty as *Geometry*'.[33] The origins of the tradition go back to authors like Giovanni Alfonso Borelli and Lorenzo Bellini in Italy and Pierre Chirac in France in the late seventeenth century, who sought to produce a medical system based on essentially Cartesian principles, and their ideas were invoked by some adherents of the tradition.[34] But increasingly it was Isaac Newton who came to the fore, and this represents a key example of the power of Newton's influence and the extent to which the method used in his *Principia* (1687) and his *Opticks* (1704) was seen as providing a model for intellectual enquiry which was equally applicable to all aspects of nature.

The explicitly Newtonian version of the tradition began with the Scottish physician, Archibald Pitcairne, in the lectures that he gave while professor at Leiden in the early 1690s; his Newtonian view of the human body and its workings was divulged in various writings, notably his *Philosophical and Mathematical Elements of Physick*, posthumously translated into English in 1718.[35] Pitcairne was followed by various others, including George Cheyne, John Freind and others such as Richard Mead, who declared in his *Mechanical Account of Poisons* (1702) his aim of 'introducing *Mathematical Studies*, that is, Demonstration and Truth, into the Practice of Physick', or Nicholas Robinson, even the title page of whose *New Theory of Physick and Diseases* (1725) explicitly stated how it was 'Founded on the Principles of the Newtonian Philosophy'.[36] To contemporaries, such aspirations seemed to align medical men with intellectual modernity, giving them real ideological power. Indeed, doctors were arguably among the leading 'public' intellectuals in Enlightenment Britain, comparable in significance to the academics and clerics who tend to dominate accounts of the history of ideas in the period.

On the other hand, in many ways it might be felt that mechanical medicine was one of the more bizarre intellectual developments of its time, a modish attempt to climb on the Newtonian bandwagon which hardly signals medical progressiveness on the part of those engaged in it (it is perhaps notable that the ever discreet Sloane was less overt in his espousal of it than many of the others itemised here).[37] I have some sympathy with the views of the medical historian, Lester S. King, who went so far as to describe the originator of the doctrine, Pitcairne, as 'highly rationalistic', if not 'rather puerile in his approach', discerning 'a certain scholastic quality' in some of his arguments.[38] The artificiality of the stance is also suggested by the fact that those who adopted mechanistic theories of this kind all strongly disagreed with one another, viciously criticising each other's views in their books.[39] In Richard Mead's case, he completely changed his Newtonian rationale over the course of his career, initially invoking a fairly simple form of mechanism as the basis of his system, but subsequently laying a more modish stress on a '*universal elastic Matter*'.[40] And the reason for this was not least the fact that these fashionable theories really only represented window dressing. They were imposed on a therapy which remained almost entirely traditional, including purges, bleeding and the like. Though such theorising might be useful in differentiating doctors from quacks, in terms of medical practice it made very little difference at all.[41]

What is more, it was from their practice rather than their theoretical writings that the grandees of medicine in the period gained their reputation and thus made their fortunes. Indeed, some of the most successful such practitioners published hardly any books at all. This includes Sloane, whose only significant publication was his *Voyage to . . . Jamaica*, stemming from the time he spent in the West Indies at the very start of his career: the Beaumont memoir which is so revealing of his attitude to magic failed to see the light of day until the twenty-first century, and his views are often rather elusive.[42] Perhaps the classic example of medical celebrity unaccompanied by publication is provided by the famous Dr John Radcliffe, whose practice was so successful that he amassed a vast fortune which he left to the University of Oxford, yet who published no books at all apart from a brief set of prescriptions.[43] Radcliffe was notorious for his wit and sarcasm, which he often deployed at the expense of wayward patients; he was also openly hostile to quacks, and it seems quite plausible that he accompanied this by an openly anti-magical line like Sloane's.[44] But this is frustratingly hard to substantiate, since it was clearly in the interest of such men to keep a low profile on matters that were peripheral to their main professional commitments. This means that in general we are left to use hints of the kind that have been accumulated here to reconstruct an outlook that, though probably widely expressed in oral form and hence influential in proportion to the high public profile of these leading medical figures, is nevertheless disappointingly elusive.

## Debates on the Miraculous

This makes it all the more striking that there is one analogue to Sloane's memoir of Beaumont that is highly relevant to the theme of this chapter and that *was* published at the time. This is Richard Mead's *Medica Sacra; or, a Commentary On the most remarkable Diseases, Mentioned in the Holy Scriptures*, published in Latin in 1749 and translated into English in 1755, which dealt directly with ostensibly supernatural phenomena of the kind with which we are here concerned.[45] As its title suggests, it did so primarily in connection with the Bible, and for this reason it was a slightly surprising book for Mead to have written at all, since by doing so he stepped right into the middle of deep theological controversy. Miracles represented a somewhat problematic topic for thinkers of the day, raising issues concerning the likelihood of supernatural intervention in the world that were similar to those that arose in connection with magical beliefs.[46] Obviously, Protestants were united in rejecting the possibility of contemporary miracles such as those that were supposed to have occurred at Saint-Médard in the 1730s. But even the miracles of Christ had been the subject of debate between radical and orthodox figures since the publication of Thomas Woolston's notorious *Discourses on the Miracles of our Saviour* between 1727 and 1729, while in the year in which Mead's book was published a similar controversy had arisen, stimulated by the iconoclastic *Free Inquiry into the Miraculous Powers, Which are supposed to have subsisted in the Christian Church, From the Earliest Ages through several successive Centuries* (1749) by the liberal divine, Conyers Middleton.[47] In the meantime, in the 1730s a further controversy had arisen over the nature of the demoniacs whose healing by Christ was retailed in the gospels, of which the cleric, Arthur Ashley Sykes, gave a naturalistic explanation about which more will be said shortly, which unsurprisingly brought on him the ire of more orthodox churchmen.[48]

By writing on these and related topics, Mead was asking for trouble: indeed, he was attacked alongside Middleton by one guardian of orthodoxy, Thomas Church, vicar of Battersea and prebendary of St Paul's, and the episode begs the question of what he thought he was doing.[49] The answer seems to be that he genuinely meant to do well. Though he came from a strongly nonconformist background – he was the son of a dissenting minister and laterally related to the famous Puritan divine, Joseph Mede – Mead seems to have become a Latitudinarian if not a kind of Deist. He evidently believed that, by offering an up-to-date medical account of relevant matters in the scriptures, he would increase their credibility against their detractors, and he disavowed any irreligious intent.[50] This was exactly the line that men like Sykes and Middleton took, and Mead thus further illustrates the spectrum between Anglican orthodoxy and Deist heterodoxy that is now commonplace among intellectual historians of the period, even though none of these has thought it appropriate to include him in their account of such developments.[51]

Here, it is appropriate to revert to Sloane since, although his religious views have been little studied (apart from his almost clichéd conviction that his collections manifested God's glory as displayed in the natural world), he too seems to have been of a somewhat Deistic tendency.[52] It is thus revealing that he gave a copy of Toland's *Christianity not Mysterious* to one of his French correspondents, and that he had links with the mortalist thinker, William Coward; it has also been observed that, whereas his library contained relatively few theological books, he seems to have shown a disproportionate interest in works of religious heterodoxy.[53] In addition, it is interesting to find him named as part of a group described as 'talking strangely about religious topics' in 1736; another member of this was the notoriously heterodox Martin Folkes, who on this very occasion spoke of his receptiveness to the views of the Deist, Anthony Collins.[54] Beyond that, Sloane's assiduity as a collector could almost be seen as a surrogate for religious commitment and it is revealing to note the reaction of the arch-advocate of soul-religion, John Wesley, when he visited the British Museum. Though he was impressed by the vast range of books and objects that Sloane had accumulated, Wesley could not resist adding: 'But what account will a man give to the Judge of quick and dead for a life spent in collecting all these?'[55]

Returning to Mead, there can be no doubt that, although his *Medica Sacra* is not as directly concerned with magic as Sloane's memoir of Beaumont, it displays a similarly naturalistic and reductionist approach.[56] Though Mead accepted that some miracles might be genuine, he believed that the bulk of the events that were seen as supernatural in the Bible had been interpreted thus due to ignorance of their true natural causes. Moreover, the book is in passing as overtly dismissive of commonplace magical beliefs as Sloane's, as in the preface where Mead expressed himself pleased to have seen the witchcraft statute abolished in 1736, claiming that witches 'had no compacts with devils, as they themselves imagined, but were really mad, so as openly to confess that they had done such feats as are impossible in the nature of things'. 'Error generally begets superstition, and superstition cruelty', he added, in relation to the role of men like Nicholas Rémy in the witch-hunts, which he strongly deprecated.[57] Most of his text was devoted to offering a naturalistic, medical account of the various diseases and supposedly supernatural afflictions that were described in the Bible, often naming the actual complaint that he thought was involved and sometimes even suggesting the remedies that might have been used to cure it.

In the case of Saul, for instance, Mead's view of the diagnosis that he was 'troubled' with 'an evil spirit' was that 'this king's disease was a true madness, and of the melancholic or atrabilarious kind, as the ancient physicians called it', claiming that the direct effects of divine wrath did not need to be invoked if natural causes were sufficient.[58] Moreover, having invoked melancholy as the explanation of many ailments recorded in the Bible, he included a disquisition on madness, again invoking witches and continuing: 'Nor is their case different, in my opinion, who persuade themselves that they see ghosts and hobgoblins'. He then went on to use almost exactly the same language as Sloane in explaining, 'For deliriums are a kind of dreams of people awake; and the mind in both cases affects the body differently, according to the nature of its objects'.[59] He similarly explained away the symptoms of the supposed demoniacs of the New Testament as 'nothing but what may arise from a natural indisposition of body', an argument in which he could in fact claim the authority of his ancestor, Joseph Mede, while in relation to epilepsy he could quote an even older authority in the form of the Hippocratic treatise on *The Sacred Disease*, the foundation text in Western culture for a naturalist as against supernaturalist approach to affliction, which it is not surprising that men like Mead took to heart, as later did John Ferriar.[60]

As already noted, in writing *Medica Sacra* Mead was using his medical credentials to enter a debate that had long been fought over by theologians, and what is notable in returning to *that* in the light of what has been said so far is the extent to which clerics who took an iconoclastic line used medical arguments. This is certainly true of the author who started the debate about the Gospel demoniacs, Arthur Ashley Sykes, in both his *Enquiry into the Meaning of Demoniacks in the New Testament* of 1737 and the *Further Enquiry* on the subject that he published in response to his critics later in the same year. Sykes was, of course, a learned theologian and active controversialist who had been involved in many published debates on doctrinal and other topics in the course of his career (though it is perhaps surprising how little modern study there has been of him, and particularly of the demoniacs controversy that he started).[61] But what is striking about the 1737 tracts that began the controversy over demoniacs is the extent to which, in addition to learned classical, biblical and patristic allusions, Sykes also cites medical arguments and medical books in support of his case.

Thus, like Mead, Sykes saw Saul's ailment as 'nothing else but natural *Melancholy*', while he argued that the invocation of demons in cases of madness seemed to be particularly associated with victims 'who were affected with an Alienation of Mind, where no Fever attended them', for which he used the medical term 'Atra bilis'. In response to some of his critics he took them to task for their evident ignorance of what was commonplace to those 'that are acquainted with *Physick* at all'.[62] The books that he cited included the writings of the celebrated seventeenth-century doctor, Thomas Sydenham, and John Freind's *History of Physick* of 1725–6 as well, of course, as Galen and Hippocrates, *The Sacred Disease* being central to his claims.[63]

It was on such grounds that he came to his forceful conclusions concerning the natural causes of many of the supposedly miraculous events with which he dealt, and it is striking how often, like Mead, he used a dismissive language concerning magical beliefs when making his case, for instance using almost exactly the same words as Mead in comparing a belief in demons to that in hobgoblins and spectres, or seeing supposed exorcisms as being akin to witchcraft. As he concluded at one point: 'What is there so wild or so extravagant that Superstition has not thought of?'[64]

What is significant here is that it was on naturalistic, and not least medical grounds, that Sykes decided that a literal interpretation of the gospel miracles was impossible. It was essentially this that led him on to the accommodationist conclusions that he drew and that were to prove so influential on later biblical criticism; in other words the view that Christ could only be expected to speak the language of his own time in describing the ailments that he cured as representing demonic possession. Christ's role was comparable to that of 'the best and wisest Physitian', and, like any other doctor, his task was 'to prevent or cure' diseases, not to 'rectify Notions about them'. As Sykes put it: 'no Man conceives the Design of the sacred Writings to be to correct the Mistakes of Men in *Physick*, more than it is in *Astronomy*, or any other Art'.[65]

With Conyers Middleton and his brilliant and controversial *Free Inquiry into the Miraculous Powers, Which are supposed to have subsisted in the Christian Church* (1749), there is a somewhat similar state of affairs (Plate 11). Primarily, Middleton's book is a hatchet job on the early Church Fathers, whom he excoriated as '*Enthusiasts, Cheats* and *Forgerers*', in the words of one of his early critics; it was not least Middleton's hostile characterisation of men like Justin Martyr, Tertullian and Cyprian that caused the outrage with which his book was greeted.[66] His confrontational manner perhaps makes it unsurprising that Middleton caught the interest of the historian, Hugh Trevor-Roper, who clearly relished the way he championed 'all free inquiries into opinions' against 'all the opposition, that prejudice, bigottry, and superstition are ever prepared to give'.[67] It should also be made clear that Middleton's primary argument in doing down the Fathers was that of fraud, which had run alongside the reductive medical argument that has been dealt with here since the time of Deists like John Trenchard – the argument that magical and related beliefs were deliberately fostered by priests and others to delude the people and thereby increase their power. Since Middleton learned so much from the Deists, with whom he is sometimes

conflated, it is not surprising that he should echo anti-magical arguments of
this kind that had long been commonplace among them.[68] Middleton's aim,
in his words, was 'to expose the vanity of all those popular systems and
prejudices, which are to be found in every country; derived originally from
error, fraud, or superstition; and craftily imposed upon the many, to serve
the interests of a few'.[69]

In addition, however, when discussing the miracles that patristic authors
claimed had taken place after the apostolic age, Middleton, too, used medical
arguments. For instance, he invoked 'many learned men of modern times'
in seeing supposed possession as epilepsy, retailing modern cures of a viper's
bite by oil to show that there was nothing supernatural about the matter, and
claiming that supposed miracles might in fact be due to the common experience of diseases curing themselves. Indeed, he similarly saw the credit of
miracles in general as being inflated by 'ignorance of the powers of nature'.[70]
Middleton also, like Sykes, cited recent examples of phenomena like ventril-
oquism to explain away events to which significance was attached in his
sources, and he likened the enthusiasts of the early church to the French
Prophets, Moravians and Methodists of his day.[71]

Equally interesting was a long excursus in which Middleton used belief
in *witchcraft* as part of his claim for the overall need for an accommodationist position. This is a highly significant passage in relation to the subject
of this book as a whole since, in it, he claimed that 'the case of witchcraft
affords the most effectual proof of the truth of what I am advancing'. As he
pointed out,

There is not in all history any one miraculous fact, so authentically
attested as the existence of witches. All Christian nations whatsoever have
consented in the belief of them and provided capital laws against them: in
consequence of which, many hundreds of both Sexes have suffered a
cruel death. In our own country, great numbers have been condemned to
die, at different times, after a public trial, by the most eminent Judges of
the Kingdom: and in some places, for a perpetual memorial of their
diabolical practices, anniversary sermons and solemnities have been
piously instituted, and subsist at this day, to propagate a detestation of
them to all posterity. Now to deny the reality of Facts so solemnly attested,
and so universally believed, seems to give the lie to the sense and experience of all Christendom; to the wisest and best of every nation; to public
monuments subsisting to our own times: yet the incredibility of the thing

prevailed and was found at last too strong for all this force of human testimony: so that the belief of witches is now utterly extinct, and quietly
buried without involving history in it's ruin, or leaving even the least
disgrace or censure upon it.[72]

The implication was, as with Sykes, that it was necessary to take into account
the ideas that had prevailed in past periods in order to understand what had
once seemed plausible but no longer did. Thus, concerning miracles – and
implicitly, a whole swathe of ostensibly supernatural phenomena – it was
only to be expected that erroneous views would prevail until, thanks to 'the
gradual improvements of science, and the successive efforts of reason . . .
they have fallen at last into such utter contempt, as to make us wonder, how
it was possible for them, ever to have obtained any credit'.[73]

A further statement of a similar position was made by one of Middleton's
few supporters in the debate, the Hampshire cleric Frederic Toll, who also
commented on the support that 'the silly groundless Stories of Witches and
Witchcraft' had had in the sixteenth century from eminent churchmen like
John Jewel and even in parliament, by way of illustrating how a belief in
miracles in the post-apostolic period could be accounted for 'upon the same
*Principle of Credulity*'.[74] In Toll's case, he also instanced the royal touch as
a comparable belief system that had once been widely accepted but which
was similarly unworthy of credit. In passing, it is perhaps worth noting that
Toll, too, used medical arguments in support of his position, claiming of
the patristic period that 'Physick was at that Time, as it were, in a State of
Infancy'.[75]

## Scepticism and the Enlightenment

Hence there is a surprising degree of overlap between the doctors and the
progressive clerics whose views on ostensibly supernatural phenomena have
been considered here, and it is perhaps interesting to find that there is some
evidence of links between these clerics and the medical men and Deists on
whom I focused earlier. Arthur Ashley Sykes was a patient of Sir Hans
Sloane's and a handful of letters from him to Sloane survive.[76] It is interesting that at one point in his *Enquiry*, Sykes cited a conversation he had
with 'an ingenious Physician' about the meaning of a key biblical text to
which he attributed a sceptical meaning, and one wonders whether this
could have been Sloane or someone like him.[77] Here, it is perhaps also worth

noting that it was from Sloane that the cleric, Francis Hutchinson, had requested advice concerning the publication of his sceptical *Historical Essay concerning Witchcraft* some years before it actually appeared in 1718.[78] In the case of Sykes and Mead, though I am not aware of any direct links between the two, in 1749 Sykes expressed his support for Mead's *Medica Sacra* in a letter to the cleric and intelligencer, Thomas Birch. Invoking Hippocrates and others, he agreed with Mead's view that 'Demoniacs' were 'Madmen', adding: 'All the Old Physitians knew the meaning of that Word, as well as any modern Divines; & can explain it as well, if I do not very grievously mistake'.[79]

As for Middleton, we know that he consulted Sloane concerning his eyesight, while on one occasion he dealt with a scholarly enquiry on Sloane's part.[80] With Mead, on the other hand, his relationship was positively antagonistic, since in the 1720s Middleton had demolished the claim made by Mead in a public oration that doctors enjoyed high status in ancient Rome; Middleton illustrated that, in fact, doctors were of servile status.[81] But the notorious combativeness of doctors at this time over their versions of a mechanical theory of medicine has already been mentioned, and Middleton's attack on Mead aligned him with Mead's medical antagonists, and especially with John Woodward, with whom he enjoyed a friendly relationship that led to his being appointed the first Woodwardian Professor of Geology at Cambridge in 1731.[82] In addition, one of Middleton's closest friends, who became his executor after his death, was a medical man, William Heberden, and it is interesting to find Middleton recalling in a letter to Heberden 'those easy & philosophic conversations, which I used so frequently to enjoy with you', promising in another that he would 'now reserve to a personal conference & open to you perhaps at the same time, in our old free manner, what new heterodoxies I have bin meditating & sketching out in the interval of your absence'.[83] Even more interesting are Middleton's links with Thomas Gordon, the Deist collaborator of John Trenchard in such publications as the notoriously heterodox *Cato's Letters*. Many years after Trenchard's death in 1723 Gordon married his widow, and one of Mrs Gordon's closest friends became Middleton's wife, forming a group which spent much time together in music-making and other social activities.[84]

In slightly more general terms, one might also instance the overlap between Newtonian medicine and Deism, as in the case of the original advocate of the former, Archibald Pitcairne, who proves to have held deeply heterodox religious views, or of Thomas Morgan, whose books alternated between medicine and Deism – though it is hard to find much in the way of articulate anti-magical statement on the part of either.[85] What is important, however, is the nexus we seem to see in the circle described in the previous paragraphs, comprising fashionable doctors with somewhat iconoclastic views (if comfortingly traditional therapy) and clerics who flirted with free-thinking ideas, together with the men and women with whom they mixed in the fashionable, cosmopolitan circles to which they belonged. If we are trying to understand the rejection of magic that is taken for granted, for instance, in Hogarth's famous *Credulity, Superstition and Fanaticism* of 1762, it is surely among people like *these*, whose attitudes on such topics were likely to be disproportionately influential, that we should be looking.[86] Here, we encounter that assurance of the utter implausibility of magical phenomena that one might expect in an Enlightenment setting.

This may be illustrated by an anecdote recorded by the antiquary, William Cole, concerning Conyers Middleton's response when he learned that a prominent Cambridge academic, John Whalley, Master of Peterhouse,

> who was terribly afflicted with the stone, and at last died of it, had made use of a charm, by burying a certain number of bottles of water under-ground, in order to remove or allay it; which he not only greatly ridiculed, as it might deserve, but expatiated upon the absurdity of all sorts of charms and supernatural effects, but especially that the King's Professor of Divinity in a famous university should be weak enough to believe any such method could be effectual to relieve him, and that he deserved to be stigmatized for being such a fool.[87]

It is equally revealing to find Arthur Ashley Sykes making purely metaphor-ical use of the demonic in a bantering letter to his correspondent, the medi-cally trained cleric and antiquary, Cox Macro in 1737: Sykes complained to Macro about a word he had used, 'which some Demon or Other must explain, unles you'le be so kind as to recollect the English word design'd, & let me know its meaning'.[88]

Of course, this milieu co-existed with others, and justice needs to be done to them, too. As the furore over Sykes's and Middleton's books shows, for many churchmen ideas like theirs were dangerously radical, and their trea-tises were greatly outnumbered by orthodox attacks on them – though, here as elsewhere, one should be wary of measuring the significance of ideas by the extent to which they were regurgitated in print. Clearly for orthodox clerics, the kind of naturalistic and accommodationist views that such men put forward were wholly unacceptable. Indeed, it is interesting that, in the course of his attack on Middleton and Mead, Thomas Church also adopted a more conservative position on witchcraft, countering Middleton and Mead's outright rejection of its reality by citing the more neutral position that Joseph Addison had espoused in *The Spectator* in 1711 – in other words, affirming his belief 'in general that there is and has been such a thing as Witch-craft', though admitting that he could 'give no Credit to any Particular Instance of it'.[89] Indeed, it could even be argued that orthodox churchmen were badly placed to take the lead on a matter like the rejection of magic, because there is so much magic in the Bible whose literal truth they so strongly asserted.[90]

In the case of medicine, too, not all were as radical as Sloane and Mead. An example is provided by the debate over the views of the surgeon William Becket, whose sceptical work on the royal touch, *A Free and Impartial Enquiry into the Antiquity and Efficacy of Touching for the Cure of the King's Evil* (1722), was dedicated to Sloane. In his book, Becket explained the phenomenon in naturalistic terms, seeing its promotion as 'nothing more than Impositions on the People', and he accompanied this by rhetoric that aligned him with the Deists, glorying in the fact that, although

> such has been the Depravity of some former Ages, that a Freedom of Thought has been misconstrued as a Design to bring about some sinister Ends ... happy is it for us now, that our Minds are free from these Incumberances; an unrestrained Freedom of Thought, and a right Method of Reasoning, are become the happy Characters of this Age; and as we have learn't not to suffer our Senses to be imposed upon, so we likewise have to reduce every Thing to the Standard of Truth.

(Interestingly, there are echoes here of Mead's comment, 'if I may be allowed to declare my thoughts with freedom', when invoking natural causes concerning possession in *Medica Sacra*.)[91] For Becket was attacked by another doctor, Daniel Turner, in a lengthy excursus to his *Art of Surgery*, published in the same year as Becket's book, in which he not only vindicated the royal touch but also deprecated the 'present Indulgence of *Free-Thinking*'. In this he was echoed by John Freind in his *History of Physick* (1725–6), who complained how 'the darling notion of free-thinking carried beyond its bounds, has done a great deal of mischief in Physick, as well as in Divinity' and in which he also took an affirmative line towards the royal touch.[92]

Even the legacy of Newton was more mixed than my account of it so far may have made it appear. Here, a key figure is William Whiston, Newton's successor as Lucasian Professor at Cambridge until he was expelled from the university for heresy. For as the years went by Whiston became more and more of a mystic, and he lined up with the orthodox to attack both Sykes in the demoniacs controversy and Middleton in that over miracles, believing strongly in the active power of the Devil in the world as much in his own time as in antiquity, and complaining how: 'what Degree of ridiculous Scepticism may of length be arrived at by our present Free-thinkers, I do not fully know'.[93] It is interesting to find a mocking attitude towards Whiston on the part of Arthur Ashley Sykes, another Newtonian who was entrusted with the task of examining Newton's theological papers after his death and who later defended Newton's *Chronology of Ancient Kingdoms* (which he quoted in his *Further Enquiry*) against the criticism of it by William Warburton.[94] In his *Further Enquiry*, Sykes scorned Whiston for invoking '*Spirits* playing in the Air' to explain the characteristics of the *aurora borealis* of 1716 – as indeed he did – seeing this as unbecoming a figure who 'would take it ill not to be deemed a tolerable Mathematician and Philosopher'.[95] Other Newtonians promoted ideas of the kind surveyed by Paul Monod in *Solomon's Secret Arts*, including George Cheyne and William Stukeley – indeed, Monod has a whole chapter on 'The Newtonian Magi' – and here it is perhaps worth noting the conviction of another recent historian, David Katz, that 'we need to give Isaac Newton a much bigger place in the genealogy of the occult'.[96] So predominant was the influence of Newton on eighteenth-century thought that it led in all sorts of mutually contradictory directions.

Hence the broad conclusion of this chapter is to reinforce the stress on pluralism that has come to be seen as characteristic of Enlightenment thought.[97] Of course, this was to develop even more in the later years of the eighteenth century and the early years of the nineteenth, with the rise of Methodism and the occult revival, but it is important to ensure that revisionism is not allowed to give us a lopsided view of the period by attaching excessive emphasis to certain facets of it at the expense of others. It is all very well to hear about the *Wizards, Alchemists, and Spiritual Seekers* who feature in John Fleming's and Paul Monod's books, but it is equally important to do justice to the rival, more sceptical traditions in the thought of the period, the milieu of which has been sketched in this chapter. The voice of the more sceptical of medical men, in particular, needs attention, and it has also been interesting to find how their attitude to magic resonated with some of the more radical ideas that emanated from clerical circles. Indeed, through the controversies that Sykes and Middleton started, even orthodox clerics may have been forced to reconsider their ideas on such subjects, as suggested by the citation by their leading antagonist, Thomas Church, of authors like the Dutch witchcraft sceptic, Balthasar Bekker.[98]

What is more significant, however, is the extent to which we can hear the voice of a significant portion of eighteenth-century educated opinion which may have been disproportionately influential, even if it is elusive in the sources. Moreover, to return to John Ferriar writing in the years around 1800, with whom this chapter began, it has been no less important to discover a prehistory to the sceptical and reductionist attitudes towards magical phenomena voiced by men like him. This has hitherto been almost entirely overlooked by historians, who have traced Ferriar's sources no further than to Christoph Friedrich Nicolai and his well-known paper to the Royal Society of Berlin in 1799.[99] Such an exploration helps us to understand the way in which magic came to be axiomatically discarded in significant sections of Enlightenment thought.

# CHAPTER SIX

# SECOND SIGHT IN SCOTLAND

## BOYLE'S LEGACY AND ITS TRANSFORMATION

### Boyle and Second Sight

This chapter takes us back once again to Robert Boyle, who played a pivotal role in stimulating a long-running interest in the phenomenon known as 'second sight', the uncanny ability of certain individuals to foresee the future, which was not uncommon in the Highlands of Scotland, but rare elsewhere.[1] Boyle's interest in the subject was stimulated by a conversation that he had on the afternoon of 3 October 1678 with the Scottish aristocrat, George Mackenzie, Lord Tarbat, at the house that Boyle shared with his sister, Lady Ranelagh in Pall Mall. Boyle had evidently heard about stories of such matters that Tarbat had told members of the entourage of the Secretary of State for Scotland, John Maitland, Duke of Lauderdale, earlier that year, and, on Tarbat's coming to London, had summoned him to learn about them for himself. Boyle subsequently solicited a follow-up letter from Tarbat, which, although long unpublished, became widely known at the time, making second sight a topic of interest to intellectuals and thus leading to various investigations of the subject which I collected together in my 2001 volume, *The Occult Laboratory*.[2]

At the outset, it is worth underlining the extent to which, in their methods and their motivation, Boyle's investigations and the subsequent ones that he inspired typified many facets of the science of his period; they also further illustrate the apologetic motivation that we have already encountered in Boyle's writings on the supernatural. By contrast, in the later eighteenth and early nineteenth centuries a different, more sceptical attitude to second sight was expressed in a number of publications, and this chapter will go on to indicate the reasons for this, showing how it can be directly linked to changing intellectual attitudes, including a contrasting style of science that came increasingly to oust that of Boyle in the century following his death.

All this was to have a marked effect in redefining the milieu in which a belief in second sight subsisted in the context of the dawning Romantic era.

First, however, let us revert to Boyle's initial interview with Tarbat and the stories that were told at it, by way of illustrating what the phenomenon involved.[3] These related to the time during the Interregnum when Tarbat had been on the run from invading English forces in the Scottish Highlands. On one occasion, Tarbat and a colleague came across a turf digger who was looking intently at a neighbouring hill and suddenly burst into laughter. When asked why, he explained that he had seen 'a gread body of English horse' coming down the hill, and, when questioned by Tarbat – who could see nothing, and knew that there were no English troops in the vicinity at the time – he confirmed this 'because they had not Coats and bonnets the habit of that Contrey bot Cloaks and Hats'. He had laughed because he saw the horses feeding on ripe barley, whereas it was then early May and the barley was only just being sown. Four months later, Lord Tarbat heard that events had turned out at that very spot exactly as foreseen.

The second instance occurred when Tarbat joined two men sitting by the fire at a house in 'the remoter part of Scotland' where he was staying. As he sat down, one of them 'looked wery stedfastly att him' and advised him to move, 'and being asked why, he replyed':

> becaus I see in the nixt chair that is just by you a dead man with ‹his› head hanging carelesly backward, and yet his hatt upon it, the blood runs from him, one of his arms hangs broken ower one of the Arms of the chair and one of his legs is broken too.

Shortly afterwards, the house was invaded by English troops carrying in a comrade who had fallen off his horse when it slipped in the ice. They placed him in the very chair specified, where his appearance was just as the second-sighted man had described. Fortunately, however, though 'caried in for dead', his condition was not so serious, 'and by the help of Aqua vitæ and rubbing and such other ordinary means was after a while brought to himselfe'.

These were typical of the kind of low-key, yet slightly sinister premonition of future events that was involved in second sight. Other instances involved similar matters, and in a number of cases death was successfully foretold. Clearly Boyle was impressed by what Tarbat told him, since he not only dictated full notes on the interview to his amanuensis later that day but subsequently requested a further written account which Tarbat supplied in the form of the letter that has already been referred to, which gave more examples and speculated as to how the phenomenon might be explained.[4]

Boyle's meeting with Tarbat formed part of a typical activity on his part, in that he frequently interviewed travellers and others about phenomena in distant places that he was not able to visit himself. In Boyle's own words, he sought 'to make Physica peregrinare' by recording the 'Answers given to Severall Questions propounded by the Author to Navigators & other Travellers in remote Countreys'.[5] He did so in pursuit of authentic knowledge about all aspects of the world, since he followed his intellectual mentor, Francis Bacon, in believing that a true understanding of nature's laws was dependent on the compilation of a great bank of data in the form of a natural history. Boyle saw the profuse information that he gained by interrogating trustworthy witnesses of far away events as no less crucial than that which he acquired for himself through his painstaking experiments, and in his books he drew on both. It is also important to stress that the information that Boyle gleaned from travellers covered an astonishing range of phenomena, and the same was true of his profuse writings. The topics on which he interrogated his informants ranged from native medicines or abnormal atmospheric conditions to strange plants and animals, and the topics covered by his books ranged from the nature of the air to that of colours or cold, from hydrostatics or the structure of crystals to the workings of the human body. Such omnivorousness was typical of Boyle and his fellow members of the Royal Society in its formative years, and this is a highly significant aspect of the science of his day.

The appetite of such scientists for exact information was equally crucial, because this was part of a reaction against the prevailing Aristotelian system of natural philosophy, which was widely seen as having had a stultifying effect due to its doctrinaire and a priori approach. Since Aristotelians presumed that everything in nature could be explained by invoking established principles about how the world worked, there seemed no point in accumulating empirical data which merely confirmed what was already well known. By contrast, the Baconian ethos meant that a high value was placed on accumulating information almost for its own sake, since it might result in new discoveries concerning the workings of nature. Theory was not wholly proscribed: indeed, Boyle himself was tireless in promoting the mechanical hypothesis, the view that everything in nature could be explained in terms of matter in motion. He in any case thought it important that the natural philosopher should be aware of alternative theories as to how things worked, which could encourage the recording of data that might otherwise be neglected.[6] But reliable information was the key desideratum, and Boyle and his peers insisted that 'matters of fact' were to be established which might then be accounted for according to various theories. Boyle often presented '*Historical*' data without 'any Reflections on them', leaving others to evaluate them 'according to the differing *Hypotheses* and Inquisitions, to which men are inclined'.[7] Moreover, he and his colleagues also believed that nature might be surprising, that empirical inquiry might reveal it as operating in ways that were counterintuitive: yet, if something was proven as true, it had to be accepted, however difficult it was to reconcile with existing knowledge. Hence in Boyle and his colleagues there is a breathtaking sense of potential, a belief that, through such painstaking investigation, a true understanding of nature would emerge of a kind that had never previously existed.

Boyle's interest in second sight fits into this setting. Second sight was a bizarre phenomenon which deserved to be tabulated and understood regardless of how it was to be explained – thus exemplifying the insistence of Baconians like Boyle that the reality of phenomena should be established even if they were hitherto unheard of and even if their causation was unclear. As Boyle put it concerning second sight in his notes on his interview with Tarbat, it was 'a thinge, that not only is not to be meet with in the course of Nature bot is not to be matched in the books of Magick, I have hitherto read'.[8] Boyle was perfectly happy to see 'the books of Magick' as a legitimate source of information, since these might draw attention to phenomena which could be empirically verified, thus contributing to the challenge to a priori views of what was and was not possible that was central to his intellectual agenda. Equally, the apparent verisimilitude of the accounts of second sight that he received was significant in presenting a challenge to existing views of the world.

And linked to this was the further motive on Boyle's part that we encountered in the Introduction, namely his conviction that, in addition to the realm of nature, it might also be possible empirically to verify a separate, supernatural realm. Second sight, although well attested by reliable witnesses, seemed to be above nature: it thus appeared to provide evidence of the existence of the supernatural and hence of the plausibility of the existence of God in answer to those tempted to deny this. This was an important consideration for Boyle, who was always anxious to use the findings of science in defence of religion. Indeed, second sight was to have figured in the compilation entitled *Strange Reports* which we have already encountered.[9] Though the relevant section remained unpublished at his death, its avowed intention was to use authenticated examples of supernatural phenomena to refute reductionist, materialist views of the world, and this was an apologetic motive which Boyle shared with contemporaries like Joseph Glanvill, whose *Saducismus Triumphatus* (1681) collected witchcraft narratives, as '*proofs that come nearest the* sence', for exactly this purpose.[10]

Yet, as we saw in Chapter 4, the 1681 recension of Glanvill's witchcraft book itself stemmed from something of a crisis in the 1670s, in that sceptical 'wits' had ingeniously spread rumours that Glanvill had himself become sceptical about the most notable case in his book, that of the ghostly 'Drummer of Tedworth', and that Boyle was no longer convinced of the authenticity of the comparable 'Devil of Mascon'. The reaction to this on the part of Glanvill and of Henry More, who brought the book to fruition after Glanvill's death, was to pile up more examples than ever of witchcraft and other apparently demonic activity in the world. Boyle, on the other hand, seems to have been encouraged to look for new sources of evidence to prove the reality and elucidate the workings of the supernatural realm. For this, second sight, about which he first learned just at this time, must have seemed ideal. For one thing, it was empirically verifiable, often by people of high status, some of whom turned out to have the gift themselves. In addition, its sober accounts of premonitions of often commonplace future events lacked the rather lurid and implausible detail of traditional witchcraft narratives.

## Boyle's Legacy

It probably added to the appeal of second sight that it was to be found in a slightly exotic location in the form of the Scottish Highlands, which few seventeenth-century Englishmen knew much about. Indeed, the investigation of second sight formed part of a broader opening up of the Highlands at this time. Boyle himself owned the manuscript of a pioneering 'Collection of Highland Rites and Customs', which retailed a wide range of data about the inhabitants of the area and their beliefs and practices.[11] It is also revealing that in the 1680s the Oxford Philosophical Society – a kind of satellite of the Royal Society – attempted to open up links with Scotland, and one topic which interested them was second sight: indeed, a paper on

1. The frontispiece to the second part of Joseph Glanvill's *Saducismus Triumphatus* (1681), engraved by William Faithorne. Various scenes of diabolical activity are shown, including (in the top left-hand panel) the notorious poltergeist known as the 'Drummer of Tedworth', the subject of Chapter 4 of this book.

2 & 3. Left, Thomas
Hobbes, widely suspected of
fomenting the rising tide of
sceptical opinion.Below, the
interior of a London coffee-
house (*c.* 1695), where it was
widely believed that such
ideas were likely to be voiced.

4, 5 & 6. Clockwise from left: the 'supernaturalists' Henry More, Joseph Glanvill and Robert Boyle, who sought empirical proof of a realm above the purely natural.

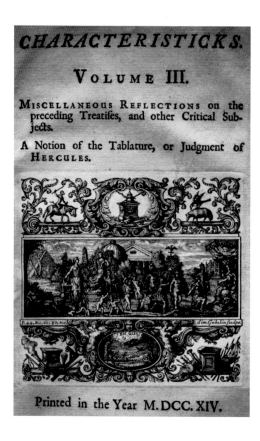

CHARACTERISTICKS.

VOLUME III.

MISCELLANEOUS REFLECTIONS on the preceding Treatises, and other Critical Subjects.

A Notion of the Tablature, or Judgment of HERCULES.

Printed in the Year M.DCC.XIV.

7. The title-page of the third volume of the Earl of Shaftesbury's Characteristicks with an elaborate vignette by Simon Gribelin criticising the superstitious practices of ancient Egypt and Rome and of the Roman Catholic church.

8. Pages 312–13 of the copy of Martin Martin's *A Description of the Western Islands of Scotland*, read by John Toland and Lord Molesworth, with its margins filled by their scathing annotations.

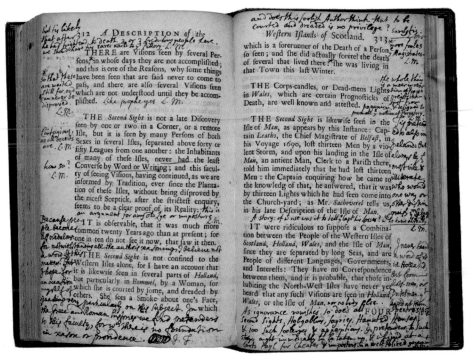

9. A statue of Sir Hans Sloane, formerly in the Chelsea Physic Garden.

10. A page from British Library Sloane MS 2731, an elaborate copy of the magical text *The Key of Solomon the King*, which is probably the one acquired by Sloane when the landlord foreclosed on its devotees (see pp. 126–7).

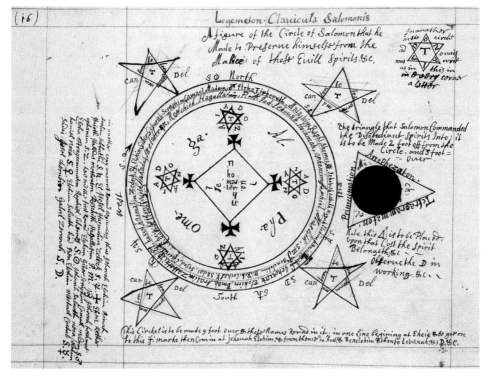

11. A bronze medal of Conyers Middleton with its reverse depicting Cambridge University Library, of which Middleton was librarian.

NON SIBI SED TOTI.
R.M.

12. Richard Mead, whose *Medica Sacra* (1749) was trenchantly sceptical of supposedly supernatural phenomena. This Rembrantesque portrait of him by Arthur Pond (1739), though effective, was not much liked by its sitter; the motto paraphrases Lucan's description of Cato ('Not for himself but the world').

13. Samuel Johnson on Mull; a caricature by Thomas Trotter (1786) capitalizing on the interest generated by Boswell's *Journal of a Tour* (1785). During his visit to the Hebrides in 1773, Johnson searched diligently for evidence of second sight.

14. A plate from William Gilpin's *Observations, Relative chiefly to Picturesque Beauty... Particularly [in] the High-Lands of Scotland* (1789), illustrating the wild terrain which James Beattie thought made people susceptible to second sight (see p. 165).

15. A portrait of Sir Walter Scott from *The Lady of the Lake* (1810): in that book, Scott rejected second sight as inconsistent with the 'laws of nature' but nevertheless considered it suitable 'to the use of poetry' (see Chapter 6).

16. William Hogarth's famous satirical engraving, *Credulity, Superstition and Fanaticism. A Medley* (1762).

the subject which was read at one of their meetings has recently come to light and is published as Appendix II of this book.[12] Such investigations were subsequently followed up by the Oxford savant, Edward Lhuyd, who briefly investigated the phenomenon in conjunction with his philological investigations in Scotland, and more fully by the virtuoso and antiquary, John Aubrey, who solicited a lengthy series of letters on the subject from a Scottish informant, Dr James Garden of Aberdeen, which he published in his *Miscellanies* (1696) – the first publication in which an account of second sight featured.[13]

Aubrey initially looked to Scotland for data on megaliths: he had written a monograph on these, inspired primarily by Stonehenge and Avebury in his native county of Wiltshire, which he thought would be enhanced by comparative data from the Highlands.[14] But, having established contact with Garden in this connection, Aubrey continued the liaison by requesting information on other phenomena, including second sight. Aubrey was a typical exponent of the Baconian science of his day, collecting vast quantities of empirical data about all aspects of the natural world, not least for his *Natural History of Wiltshire*, a typical example of the genre of county natural histories that flourished at the time, covering everything from rivers and fossils to human longevity and the clothing trade.[15] One chapter dealt with 'Accidents', comprising the typical mixture of unusual and clearly non-natural phenomena that had traditionally been encapsulated by the intermediate concept of the 'preternatural'.[16] In 1694, however, Aubrey removed this from the work on Wiltshire in order to make it into a separate book, his *Miscellanies* (1696), which was devoted to examples of phenomena like omens and portents, apparitions, prophecies, magic and 'Transportation by an Invisible Power', derived from a wide range of sources.[17] Interestingly, Aubrey had clearly come to think that these had a commonality in distinction from the rest of the subject matter of a 'natural history' like his *Natural History of Wiltshire*. The book was subtitled 'A Collection of Hermetick Philosophy', and in his dedication to it, Aubrey explained: 'The Matter of this Collection is beyond Humane reach: We being miserably in the dark, as to the Oeconomie of the Invisible World, which knows what we do, or incline to, and works upon our Passions, and sometimes is so kind as to afford us a glimpse of its Præscience'. Clearly the slightly mysterious phenomenon of second sight, which was elucidated in detail by Garden's answers to the 'queries' on the subject that Aubrey sent him, fitted perfectly into this context.[18]

A perhaps slightly more surprising collector of material relating to second sight was another virtuoso, Samuel Pepys – though his interest in the subject again shows the typical characteristics of the pursuit of natural philosophy in Restoration England. Pepys was a devotee of the new science, attending meetings of the Royal Society and reading scientific books, which he understood better than he is often given credit for: various authors have picked up on his comment on Royal Society discussions that 'I do lack philosophy enough to understand them, and so cannot remember them', but in fact he found that, if he persevered, he could master quite complex texts such as Boyle's *Hydrostatical Paradoxes* (1666).[19] Boyle was very much Pepys's scientific hero: Pepys had the completest collection of Boyle's rather diffuse publications of any contemporary, even devoting a special section to Boyle's books in the classified catalogue of his library that he had made, with an index to their content (Boyle was the only author for whom he did this).[20] Boyle appealed to Pepys for his empiricism and for the sheer range of his interests: in many ways, he seemed to Pepys to epitomise the goals of science (which makes it the more ironic that, as President of the Royal Society, it was Pepys who gave the imprimatur to Newton's *Principia*, which represented a rather different style of science that was largely to supersede Boyle's, as we will see later in this chapter).

One interest that Pepys and Boyle shared was in second sight, since in 1699–1700 Pepys obtained from the Scottish aristocrat, the 3rd Lord Reay, a Fellow of the Royal Society like himself, a copy of Tarbat's unpublished letter to Boyle, adding further material to form a collection of 'Papers between Lord Reay & Mr Pepys &c touching the Second Sight'.[21] This put on record some key findings on the subject, not least the recollections of the Anglican divine, George Hickes, to whom Pepys forwarded a copy of Tarbat's letter in order to solicit his further comments, and who did indeed provide Pepys with a lengthy account of various cases that he had witnessed when he was in Scotland in the late 1670s which he might otherwise never have recorded. Indeed, Pepys showed himself truly Boylian in the course of his enterprise when he assured one of his correspondents, the 2nd Earl of Clarendon, how 'uncontestable' he found one 'instance of Fact' concerning a premonition of this kind that Clarendon reported to him.[22]

Pepys had in fact shown an interest in related matters at an earlier date, if from a more sceptical viewpoint. This is in evidence both in comments in his famous diary and in discussions that he had with the divine, Thomas Ken, in Tangier in 1684, in which he displayed an iconoclastic attitude concerning miracles.[23] In addition, when in Spain en route home from Tangier, he had met one of the so-called *saludadores*, who claimed hereditary healing powers and witch-finding abilities; Pepys challenged the man to confess to fraud, which he duly did.[24] Pepys's Spanish experiences were reported by his friend, John Evelyn, in connection with a discussion about supernatural phenomena involving King James II and others at Winchester on 16 September 1685, at which the king explained how 'he was so extreamely difficult of Miracles, for feare of being impos'd on, that if he should chance to see one himselfe, without some other wittnesse, he should apprehend it some delusion of his senses'. In the conversation of which this formed part, various examples of ostensibly supernatural phenomena were given, including both second sight and the activities of the *saludadores*, though Evelyn added that Pepys 'did not conceive it fit, to interrupt his Majestie, who told what they pretended to do, so solemnly'.[25] On the other hand, by the time he made his collection about second sight fifteen years later, Pepys seems rather to have revoked his earlier scepticism and to have acquired the receptiveness of his mentor, Boyle, towards the verisimilitude of phenomena of this kind. In his letter to Lord Reay acknowledging the copy of Tarbat's letter and other material that Reay had sent him, Pepys professed himself convinced by the instances of second sight there recorded. As he put it, 'I little expected to have been ever brought so near to a Conviction of the reality of it, as by your Lordship's & the Lord Tarbutt's Authoritys, I must already own myself to be'.[26]

By this time, the curiosity about second sight in evidence south of the border had begun to affect the Scots themselves, most notably Robert Kirk, author of the deservedly famous work, *The Secret Commonwealth*, which is largely about the rationale and legitimacy of second sight. Kirk is an intriguing figure, educated at the universities of Edinburgh and St Andrews, who spent the bulk of his adult life in the remote parishes of Balquhidder and Aberfoyle in the Trossachs, the most southerly part of the Highlands. Here, he clearly absorbed much of the folklore of the local inhabitants, and his work can be seen at least in part as an attempt to reconcile this with his intellectual beliefs. His role as a go-between between the native population and the intelligentsia is also reflected in the fact that, as a fluent Gaelic speaker, he was employed to produce a version of the Gaelic Bible in Roman script, an evangelical effort aimed at the Highlands for which Boyle was responsible (this followed earlier initiatives on Boyle's part to make the scriptures available in the languages of the mission field).[27] Kirk spent several months in London in 1689 seeing the Bible through the press, and it is quite possible that Boyle personally gave him the copy of Tarbat's letter about second sight that Kirk was to include in *The Secret Commonwealth* and which was to form a central component of that work, as we will see.[28]

Indeed, this exemplifies a further facet of the intellectual life of Boyle's period, since, in addition to interviewing people and gleaning information from them which he then dictated to the amanuenses that he employed, Boyle also used these same amanuenses to make multiple copies of texts so that these could be distributed to interested parties.[29] It seems clear that Lord Tarbat's letter about second sight was the subject of such circulation – on the part both of Boyle and others with related interests, as illustrated by the source of Pepys's copy.[30] Indeed, it must have been by such means that a copy of the letter fell into the hands of the Somerset naturalist, John Beaumont, whom we encountered in Chapters 4 and 5. It was Beaumont who first published the content of Tarbat's letter in his *Historical, Physiological and Theological Treatise of Spirits, Apparitions, Witchcrafts, and other Magical Practices* (1705), where it is juxtaposed with his account of his own contact with supernatural beings, for which he perhaps thought it provided something of a mandate – though he failed to state that it had been solicited by and was addressed to Boyle and hence the identity of the text has until recently been overlooked.[31]

Returning to Kirk, he may have begun *The Secret Commonwealth* before his London visit, but it is clear that his experiences in the metropolis had a significant influence on him: various discussions of second sight and related topics are recorded in the fascinating diary that he kept while he was there, including one on 6 October 1689 with the Latitudinarian divine Edward Stillingfleet, then bishop-elect of Worcester, and these form the basis of significant sections of *The Secret Commonwealth*.[32] The book itself, finished shortly before Kirk's death in 1692, is a curious mixture, reflecting his ambivalent background. Much of it comprises an account of the fairies, or 'Co-walkers', whom he associated with second sight in that he believed that those with this gift obtained it through contact with this race of supernatural beings who lived in parallel with humankind and whose lifestyle and economy he therefore sought to elucidate.[33] In a way, this was the logical corollary of the conviction of Boyle and other contemporaries of the reality of a supernatural realm, though Boyle himself shunned such contact on moral grounds, fearful that the beings he encountered might be servants of the Devil rather than of God.[34] In Kirk's case, on the other hand, his detailed account of the fairy realm has meant that his book has proved an invaluable source for folklorists and others ever since it was first published in the early nineteenth century.[35]

Yet he combined this with an attempt to give a rational, almost academic, account of the subject. At the core of his book is a transcript of Lord Tarbat's letter to Boyle and the latter part of the book forms a commentary on this, canvassing biblical quotations and learned opinion to deal with various objections to the reality and legitimacy of the phenomenon of second sight. These included the argument that he had encountered from Bishop Stillingfleet in London, that the foreknowledge that second-sighted people apparently had might be of diabolical rather than divine inspiration, a further illustration of the moral dilemmas arising from acceptance of a supernatural realm which affected Boyle. Yet Kirk also saw the value of second sight for vindicating the supernatural against 'atheists' – indeed, the title page of one version of his book makes a special point of this – again echoing a key aspect of Boyle's interest in the phenomenon. Above all, his book reflects a genuine attempt to understand this interface between the natural and supernatural, and it is once again Boylian in its acceptance that things might be true even if we could not fully understand their rationale, and its celebration of the discoveries of his age, in the form of the findings of microscopes and the like, 'which were sometimes as great a wonder, and as hard to be beleiv'd' as the strange phenomena divulged in his book.[36]

A similar blend of description and analysis is to be found in another full-length treatise on second sight written in Scotland at this time, Δευτεροσκοπια, or a Brief Discourse of the Second Sight, Commonly so called (1707) by John Fraser, Dean of the Isles. Fraser was another university-educated man who spent his working life in a remote area, in this case the Western Isles, who had earlier contributed to the opening up of the area by providing an account of the Isles for the great description of Scotland planned by the Edinburgh savant, Sir Robert Sibbald. In Δευτεροσκοπια, Fraser had no truck with Kirk's fairy theory: indeed, there is no evidence that he was aware of it. But, after recounting a number of instances of second sight (also invoking what he had learned about similar incidents on the Isle of Man), he gave a careful analysis of the subject, defending its legitimacy and explaining it in terms of a theory of vision and the way in which this was affected by bodily humours which in fact went back through Renaissance scholars to the ideas of the thirteenth-century Oxford scientist, John Pecham.[37]

Yet another account of second sight appeared as part of the Description of the Western Islands of Scotland by Martin Martin, first published in 1703, which went into a second edition in 1716 and has been twice reprinted this century; it thus achieved a wide circulation that eluded Fraser's scarce pamphlet. Martin's *Description* is a typical regional natural history in the tradition of Aubrey and others, proffering a wide-ranging collection of 'things useful and curious in their kind, several of which have not hitherto been mention'd by the Learned'. As Martin put it in his preface, 'if I have been so happy as to oblige the Republick of Learning with any thing that is useful, I have my Design', and his work exemplifies the Boylian tradition of Baconian science in its stress on collecting reliable data, its nescience about causation, and its apologetic motivation.[38] Martin, himself of island origin, had been taken up by London intellectuals like Sir Hans Sloane in his capacity as secretary of the Royal Society, and he acted as a useful intermediary in supplying the society with information about the remote parts of Scotland, even if his work was received with scorn by intellectuals like John Toland and Lord Molesworth, as we saw in Chapter 2.

The lengthy section of Martin's book dealing with second sight was specifically advertised on its title page. In it, Martin recounted various cases, received 'from Persons of as great Integrity as any are in the World', and he gave the fullest account of the phenomenon yet available, which was widely drawn on by later writers on the topic, whether favourable to it or not. Thus he addressed the issue of how people obtained the gift, the form that visions took and the way in which they were divulged; he also answered a series of 'Objections that have lately been made against the Reality of it'.[39] In contrast to Kirk and Fraser, however, he completely eschewed explanation, instead insisting that the instances that he retailed offered indisputable proof of the existence of non-material forces in the world, and leaving it at that. His rationale was clear from what he said about the botanical part of his survey:

> I hold it enough for me to furnish my Observations, without accounting for the Reason and Way that those Simples produce them: this I leave to the Learned in that Faculty; and if they would oblige the World with such Theorems from these and the like Experiments, as might serve for Rules upon Occasions of this nature, it would be of great advantage to the Publick.

Specifically in relation to second sight, he justified his account as such 'as the Nature of the thing will bear', claiming that 'for those that will not be so satisfy'd, they ought to oblige us with a new Scheme, by which we may judg of Matters of Fact'.[40] As for how its operation was to be explained, he alluded to magnetism and other phenomena that were well proven 'tho we can give no satisfying account of their Causes', adding: 'And if we know so little of natural Causes, how much less can we pretend to things that are supernatural?' – an almost exact echo of Boyle and Glanvill.[41]

Moving forward in time, a comparable rationale underlay the *Treatise on the Second Sight, Dreams and Apparitions* published by 'Theophilus Insulanus' in 1763, the author of which is now thought to be William Macleod of Hamer on Skye, rather than the Revd Donald McLeod, as traditionally identified. This retailed numerous accounts of individuals who had experienced second sight, many of whom had confided this personally to the author, thus providing 'a cloud of witnesses' in support of the reality of the phenomenon and against those who were sceptical about it. In addition, in this work the apologetic motive that had been present in Boyle and others came more than ever to the fore. 'Theophilus Insulanus' engaged in various excursuses along such lines, repeatedly insisting:

> My inference from the Second Sight, dreams, and apparitions, of the existence of spirits, and the immortality of the soul, though obvious, will, I apprehend, be against the creed of our modern Free-thinkers, who treat that awful truth, in their hours of mirth and vanity, as the subject of profane mirth and raillery, as phantoms, or the idle dreams of superstitious brains.[42]

Interest in the subject also continued in England, where a Baconian ethos similar to Boyle's underlay the enquiries into second sight of Henry Baker and other Fellows of the Royal Society in the late 1740s, which we encountered in Chapter 3 in connection with the Royal Society's disavowal of it. Baker, well known as a microscopist, sought to obtain information on the subject from a Scottish informant, Archibald Blair, and he made it clear in his letters to him how, in such matters, 'a Number of Proofs may supply the Inability of our Reason to discover all the Powers and Operations of the Mind of Man', stressing how 'in such Cases I think Nothing but Facts well attested deserve to be regarded'. Professing a Boylian nescience concerning causation, he reflected how 'Our being uncapable of accounting for any Thing, is with me but a very feeble Argument against its real Existence; for if we would ingeniously confess our own Ignorance, we must own how very little we know, even of those Things we seem to know the best'.[43] The cases that Blair reported included topical ones, not least since one of the questions that Baker had asked him was: 'Did any of these second-sighted People foresee and foretell the Miseries that have lately befallen your poor unhappy Country?' and Blair was indeed able to respond with instances relating to the '45.[44] It is possibly not irrelevant to Baker's own curiosity about second sight that he was son-in-law of Daniel Defoe, who had taken an interest in second sight, though in a slightly different manner from the earnest virtuosi whom we have so far been considering. In *The Second-Sighted Highlander* (1713, 1715), Defoe capitalised on the interest in second sight stimulated by Martin's *A Description of the Western Islands* to attribute essentially journalistic predictions to a Scotsman with supposed prophetic powers; this looks forward to the rather titillating way in which he was to exploit magical beliefs in his books on the Devil, magic and apparitions in the 1720s, giving a sense of the imaginative potential of the motif which foreshadows future developments, as we will see below.[45]

Returning, however, to the Boylian ethos in relation to second sight, the final, perhaps most famous instance of this is to be found in Samuel Johnson's *Journey to the Western Islands of Scotland* (1775) (Plate 13). This work has been seen as exemplifying Johnson's scientific outlook in its indebtedness to the Baconian tradition and the way in which it 'not only calls many things in doubt but relies on exact observation for the establishment of truth'.[46] Johnson had been introduced to Martin's *Description* by his father, and he took a copy of the book with him on his tour.[47] Concerning second sight, Johnson wrote:

> particular instances have been given, with such evidence, as neither *Bacon* nor *Boyle* has been able to resist; that sudden impressions, which the event has verified, have been felt by more than own or publish them; that the *Second Sight* of the *Hebrides* implies only the local frequency of a power, which is nowhere totally unknown; and that where we are unable to decide by antecedent reason, we must be content to yield to the force of testimony.

(It is curious that he here implies that Bacon as well as Boyle had taken an interest in second sight, since there is virtually no evidence of Bacon taking an interest in the subject, but the methodological point is clear.)[48] In a conversation on the subject during his Hebridean tour Johnson challenged a sceptic about second sight with an argument that again directly echoed the ethos of Boyle and his peers, arguing that:

There are many things then, which we are sure are true, that you will not believe. What principle is there, why a loadstone attracts iron? why an egg produces a chicken by heat? why a tree grows upwards, when the natural tendency of all things is downwards? Sir, it depends upon the degree of evidence that you have.[49]

Johnson began his account of second sight by stating, 'it is desirable that the truth should be established, or the fallacy detected', ending it with the poignantly nescient conclusion, 'I never could advance my curiosity to conviction; but came away at last only willing to believe'. What is perhaps most significant here, however, is that his approach is characteristic of the tradition surveyed at length so far in this chapter.[50]

## Second Sight Debunked

If, on the other hand, we now fast-forward a few decades, we find that, when second sight was discussed, its genuineness was almost invariably questioned. This is particularly true of a burgeoning literature, generally by men with medical qualifications, which questioned the reality of apparitions and related phenomena in general, attributing them to purely physiological causes. Thus John Ferriar, whom we encountered in the last chapter, devoted several pages to second sight both in his 1790 paper, 'Of Popular Illusions, and Particularly of Medical Demonology', and in his *Essay towards a Theory of Apparitions* (1813). The entire thrust of Ferriar's 1813 book was to see all dreams and other forms of supposed pre-knowledge as illusions based on the mind's misdirection of 'recollected images', and second sight was placed firmly in this category.[51] In his 1790 paper he wrote: 'it appears highly probable that the Seers are hypochondriacal persons. Their insular situation, their solitary employments, their oppressive poverty, added perhaps to the wild, uncultivated scenes of their country, are sufficient to produce a depraved state of body, and consequently of imagination, in those who are at all pre-disposed.'[52]

A fuller account occurred in Samuel Hibbert's *Sketches of the Philosophy of Apparitions; or, an Attempt to Trace such Illusions to their Physical Causes* (1824), based on a paper on 'spectral impressions' read to the Royal Society of Edinburgh. Indeed, Hibbert rather perceptively introduced the relevant section of his book by blaming the apologetic motives of the heirs of Boyle for perpetuating a belief in the reality of such phenomena at a time when this might otherwise have died out. Hibbert was thus scornful about 'the researches of the gentlemen who consulted the Highlanders for the purpose of confuting the freethinkers'.[53] He was convinced that all supposed instances of second sight – as also stories of monitory dreams and apparitions to which he saw them as closely related – could be explained by purely physical principles, in terms of the mental suggestibility of those who believed they had such powers. In one case he noted that someone who experienced a vision had shortly before had a severe fall from his horse, and he speculated: 'Did the brain receive some slight degree of injury from the accident, so as to predispose him to this spectral illusion?' He also attributed to coincidence the fact that supposed premonitions sometimes seemed successful, on the grounds that unsuccessful ones were ignored, concluding: 'Thus, it is the office of superstition to carefully select all successful coincidences of this kind, and to register them in her marvellous volumes, where for ages they have served to delude and mislead the world'.[54]

In fact, although second sight was grist to the mill of sceptical writers like Hibbert and Ferriar, they were not the first to express such attitudes. First, there is the tradition that has already been referred to in relation to Boyle's own original apologetic intent, as echoed by Theophilus Insulanus and others, namely the role of the freethinkers, to the refutation of whose scepticism Hibbert rightly attributed Boyle's and others' concern to vindicate the reality of second sight. This is most clearly exemplified by John Toland and Lord Molesworth, whose scorn for the phenomenon is apparent from their scathing annotations to the account of second sight in Martin's *A Description of the Western Islands of Scotland*, as quoted in Chapter 2.[55] As we saw, Deist thinkers blazed a trail in expressing outright scepticism about ostensibly supernatural phenomena which the orthodox only slowly followed, and there is at least one other early sceptic concerning second sight who arguably exemplifies this tradition, namely Edmund Burt in his *Letters from a Gentleman in the North of Scotland, To His Friend in London*, written in the 1720s although not published till 1754. Like Toland and Molesworth, Burt saw second sight as a 'Cheat', a 'ridiculous Notion' 'begotten by *Superstition*' and fathered on credulous people prone 'to be gull'd by such Impostors'.[56] In this as in other aspects of Burt's book we distinctly hear the critical and anticlerical accents of the London fashionable elite, and this almost certainly explains his views on the subject. As an aside, it is worth noting that Burt was also sceptical about witchcraft beliefs, in contrast to the accepting attitude that he encountered in most of those whom he met in Scotland.[57]

Others expressed similarly overt sceptical attitudes towards the phenom-enon at the time when Theophilus Insulanus and Samuel Johnson were writing. For instance, the minister Donald McNicol, in his 1779 critique of Johnson's *Journey to the Western Islands of Scotland*, was amazed 'with what a credulous weakness he endeavours to defend so visionary an opinion . . . absurd in itself, uncountenanced by any decent authority, and to which only a few of the most ignorant vulgar give the least faith'. Indeed, he took note of Johnson's role in investigating the Cock Lane ghost of 1762, the notorious London poltergeist case which ultimately proved to be a fraud but to the validity of which Johnson was long committed, to imply that the great lexi-cographer's attitude to second sight was similarly questionable.[58]

Comparable views were expressed by various travel writers of the later years of the eighteenth century and early decades of the nineteenth. For instance, in his *A Tour in Scotland, and Voyage to the Hebrides; MDCCLXXII* (1774), the topographer Thomas Pennant wrote scathingly of 'these pretenders to second sight', concluding, 'but enough of these tales, founded on impu-dence and nurtured by folly', while in his *A Description of the Western Islands of Scotland* (1819) the geologist John MacCulloch was similarly dismissive, considering that second sight 'has undergone the fate of witchcraft; ceasing to be believed, it has ceased to exist . . . since the second sight has been limited to a doting old woman or a hypochondriacal tailor, it has become a subject for ridicule; and, in matters of this nature, ridicule is death'.[59] A particularly inter-esting example is provided by the medical student Jacob Pattison, who toured the Highlands in 1780, shortly before his premature death. In his manuscript account of his journey, he expressed a strong curiosity about second sight, 'of which we had heard, & expected so much', and he retailed a couple of instances about which he was told. But he was unimpressed by those who defended the phenomenon on the grounds that 'it was in vain to argue against matters of Fact'. Observing how 'no conquest is so pleasing as that of Infidelity', his own comment was, 'we smiled, & disbelieved the whole'. Overall, his verdict was that belief in second sight was 'credited in proportion to the distance, & obscurity of the places, & the consequent ignorance of the People'.[60]

So what had happened? How and why had this relentless scepticism come to replace the accepting attitude of Boyle and his successors? Here, various possibilities need to be canvassed and their relative significance adjudicated. One possible source of antagonism to second sight may be suggested by the fact that, as Samuel Johnson and James Boswell found when they visited the Hebrides, the leading opponents to a belief in it whom they encountered were members of the local clergy, 'who seemed deter-mined against it'.[61] This might be linked to a contrast between English and Scottish attitudes towards magical phenomena that Paul Monod has observed in his *Solomon's Secret Arts: The Occult in the Age of Enlightenment* (2013). He there argues that Scottish Presbyterianism encouraged a consis-tently more negative attitude on such subjects than existed in England during the period covered by his book.[62] However, whatever the case earlier, by this time it seems doubtful if such a hypothesis is pertinent. Boswell considered that the reason for the clerical attitudes that he encountered was (as he put it to his local interlocutor, Revd Donald McQueen of Skye) a wish on the part of the clergy to vindicate themselves: 'The world, (say they,) takes us to be credulous men in a remote corner. We'll shew them that we are more enlightened than they think.'[63] The attitude towards second sight of Johnson's critic, Revd Donald McNicol, was similarly motivated, as when he associated such beliefs with 'a few of the most ignorant vulgar', and how 'it is to be hoped a few years more will extinguish the very memory of so great a reproach to the human understanding. In proportion as the light of knowledge has dawned upon mankind, their eagerness for wonders and belief in supernatural endowments have gradually abated.'[64]

Like the comments of Thomas Pennant, John MacCulloch and Jacob Pattison already quoted, these views represent a generalised Enlightenment ethos. Indeed, it is revealing that the accusation of ignorance and fraud is central, as in men like Toland with their hostility to priestcraft and their story of an inexorable transition from superstitious ignorance to educated enlightenment, and we will return to the significance of this in the Conclusion.[65] Here, however, it is worth pausing over the extent to which various of the late eighteenth- and early nineteenth-century authors who have been quoted asserted that second sight was disproportionately a *popular* belief and to be deprecated accordingly, which seems to have been a corollary of such sceptical views. Boyle and other investigators, on the contrary, seem to have been impressed at how second sight was not neces-sarily a prerogative of the common people but was a gift that was equally likely to be found in people of high status, a fact which added to the credi-bility of the phenomenon in their eyes; this is especially true of the newly discovered account of it by Joshua Walker (see Appendix II).[66] The point that is worth making here is that in this instance the accusation of vulgarity seems to be a secondary one, a consequence of the dismissal of second sight rather than a cause of it, and this may have significant implications for

broader claims about the role of the elite–popular divide in changing attitudes towards long-established beliefs.[67]

But can we say more about the rationale of the Enlightenment rejection
of second sight, beyond the tropes of ignorance and imposture that have
already been cited? Here it is interesting to note the exact language used by
some of those who were critical of the phenomenon. Boswell records
concerning one of his clerical informants, the Revd Martin McPherson of
Slate, that 'he was *resolved* not to believe it, because it was founded on no
principle', and an even more telling remark comes from Sir Walter Scott in
one of his notes to his epic poem, *The Lady of the Lake* (1810) (Plate 15). He
there made the striking statement, 'If force of evidence could authorise us to
believe facts inconsistent with the general laws of nature, enough might be
produced in favour of the existence of the Second Sight'.[68] These comments
are worth teasing out, because their invocation of 'principles' and of the
'general laws of nature', and their rejection of 'facts' on that basis, aligns such
spokesmen with an alternative scientific paradigm to that of Boyle and his
heirs, and this contrast is crucial.

Such views reflect a quite different worldview, stemming from Sir Isaac
Newton and his *Principia* and his *Opticks*, which we encountered in connection with medical Newtonianism in the last chapter and which became
increasingly influential as the eighteenth century progressed. Since one of
the places where the new, Newtonian ethos had its greatest influence was in
Enlightenment Scotland, as seen in such figures as Archibald Pitcairne,
Colin Maclaurin or Thomas Reid, it is perhaps unsurprising that it should
have had an impact on belief in second sight.[69] Moreover, in a Scottish
context, such attitudes were echoed and reinforced by the sceptical ideas of
David Hume, not least in relation to miracles and the criteria by which these
should be evaluated.[70] The Newtonian outlook shared with Boyle and his
peers an insistence on the importance of empirical evidence as the ultimate
arbiter of scientific truth, even if it now appears that this came to prominence in Newton's ideas later than has sometimes been thought.[71] But it
rejected the nescience about explanations that characterised Boyle and his
like, instead using 'definitions' and 'axioms' to establish indisputable 'principles' in an essentially mathematical mode to which Boyle was somewhat
alien, with 'propositions' which were the subject of empirical verification
following from these. In other words, such 'principles' were taken for granted
as the essential postulates of how the world worked; they were seen as
encapsulating the general laws of nature, and this reduced the stress on the

value of serendipitous experiments and observations, and the suspicion of scientific systems, that had characterised Baconians like Boyle. The result was to make it easier to reject phenomena a priori due to their incompatibility with the worldview thus expressed: ironically, this could be seen as representing something of a return to the intellectual outlook associated with scholasticism that Boyle and others had worked so hard to supersede.

It is worth adding that this was often also accompanied by a degree of intellectual arrogance about the infallibility of this paradigm which contrasted with the rather humble sense of the provisional nature of knowledge that had characterised Boyle and various of his followers whom we considered earlier in this chapter; in this respect, there is some similarity to the attitudes of the doctors and theologians whom we encountered in the previous one. It is true that the *Principia* and the *Opticks* were succinct and focused in their method, whereas Boyle had often been diffuse and serendipitous – as seen in the vast range of phenomena in which he and other Baconians had taken an interest, of which second sight was one. It is equally true that a vision of science which placed emphasis on the relentless pursuit of truth by a remote and single-minded genius by implication made Boyle and other precursors seem like dilettantes, incapable of the profound insights which rewarded the intensity of scrutiny in which Newton – or the eighteenth-century image of him – engaged. For better or worse, the new scientific worldview challenged both the inclusiveness of the Boylian style of science and the rather heroic open-mindedness that Boyle displayed about the causation of phenomena.[72] (It should be emphasised that Boyle, too, was seeking principles, but he thought that these were premature until the experimental and observational work to which he was committed was nearing its conclusion: otherwise the resulting philosophy would be as speculative as ever.) Yet as an ethos it became increasingly predominant, bringing about attitudinal shifts in ancillary areas such as those with which we are concerned in this book, despite the fact that the data involved remained the same.

In the case of second sight, it was on precisely these a priori grounds that the phenomenon was increasingly rejected. Even if ostensibly empirically proven, it might now be rejected because it was not explicable according to accepted 'principles': Scott could hardly have summarised the matter more succinctly than he did in commenting that second sight was impossible because it was 'inconsistent with the general laws of nature'. Moreover there is an important corollary to this, since it could be argued that this rejection of the possibility of the phenomenon invited an essentially reductionist explanation of *why* those who believed in it did so. Here, we may return to the medical writers like John Ferriar and Samuel Hibbert whom I mentioned earlier, since, as we have seen, they invoked purely physiological explanations for people's susceptibility to such apparent delusions, often using the language of 'principles' in doing so. Not only did Hibbert offer a 'physical explanation' of the phenomenon in terms of mental residues; he also deployed quasi-Newtonian language in the course of doing so, invoking 'those pathological principles relative to spectral illusions which I have endeavoured to establish'.[73]

In fact, as we saw in the last chapter, men like Ferriar and Hibbert were not original in offering such explanations, as has sometimes been thought.[74] Instead, they were the heirs to the reductionist approach to magic of the British physicians of the early and mid-eighteenth century whom we there encountered, who espoused the new Newtonian ethos and sought to apply it to medicine. Although men like Pitcairne, Mead and Sloane never actually discussed second sight, it is easy to see how their theories would have accommodated it. We have already seen how John Beaumont warmed to second sight because of its resonances of his own experience of the supernatural realm, using Tarbat's letter to Boyle about second sight in his 1705 *Treatise of Spirits* as the context for an account of his own encounters with fairies. There can be little doubt that, just as Sloane took a brutally reductionist attitude towards such visions, explaining to Beaumont how 'what he believed to be real with regard to the fairies was only imaginary, or a strong impression of a dream', he would have applied a similar explanation to those who claimed the power of second sight.[75] Moreover, although there is no evidence that anyone attempted a medical treatment of second-sighted people by purging and bleeding like that which Sloane prescribed in cases like Beaumont's, what is crucial is the potency of these reductionist explanations of such phenomena as the 'dreams of people awake'. This complemented the more conspiratorial view of second sight inherited from the Deists, which saw it as a deliberate pretence. Instead it was not an imposture but a mistake, potentially even a well-meaning one, which was a more congenial, if equally negative, explanation for a phenomenon which had earlier attracted so much sympathetic attention.

## The Realm of the Imagination

But did this mean that second sight was finished? On the contrary, it now took on a new lease of life, but in a separate sphere. Here we may revert to Scott's comments in *The Lady of the Lake*, where, following the remarks already quoted about its incompatibility with 'the general laws of nature', he gave various particulars about second sight from Martin Martin's account of the topic, concluding: 'But in despite of evidence, which neither Bacon, Boyle, nor Johnson were able to resist, the *Taisch*, with all its visionary properties, seems to be now universally abandoned to the use of poetry'.[76] To illustrate this, he cited Thomas Campbell's 'exquisitely beautiful poem', 'Lochiel's Warning' – an allusion that in fact echoed the naturalist Sir John Carr's account of second sight in his *Caledonian Sketches, or a Tour through Scotland in 1807* (1809), who similarly combined a rather hostile account of the phenomenon with a quotation from Campbell's poem.[77] What is significant, however, is this sense that the apparently prophetic power that second sight represented belonged to the realm of poetical fantasy. What is more, this is something that by this time already had a history, running in parallel with the rationalistic rejection of it which may be seen as typical of the Enlightenment, and it is this that we must now explore.

We have already encountered Defoe's appreciation of the way in which second sight could be deployed in a literary context, and Addison's use of the frisson of apparitions in *The Drummer* is perhaps comparable.[78] In general, however, this conviction of the potential of such beliefs to form the proper subject matter of the literary imagination seems to have developed a little later. One pioneer was the poet, William Collins, whose 'Ode on the Popular Superstitions of the Highlands of Scotland, Considered as the Subject of Poetry', written *c.* 1749 though not published till 1788, used material from Martin's *A Description of the Western Islands* about second sight and related belief systems to paint a picture of the denizens of the Highlands as living in close harmony with nature.[79] Collins depicts a world where (in the words of one commentator) 'the marvellous is quotidian and "superstition" becomes a privileged object of poetic knowledge'. Collins himself revelled in the wonderful world of 'the Boreal Mountains', with their 'old Runic Bards' and 'Sturdy Clans', and he took the view that

> Scenes like these which daring to depart
> From sober Truth, are still to Nature true.[80]

What might almost be seen as a commentary on this was provided by James Beattie, professor of Moral Philosophy and Logic at Marischal College, Aberdeen and an associate of Thomas Reid and others, who devoted a passage to second sight (accompanied by a three-page footnote) in his essay

'On Poetry and Music, as they Affect the Mind', part of his collection of essays published in 1776.[81] Beattie's text comprises an interesting mixture of the critical Enlightenment attitude that we have just surveyed and a more receptive one that echoes Collins. Some of Beattie's arguments are similar to those of Sloane or Hibbert: he thought that second sight 'may be nothing more, perhaps, than short fits of sudden sleep or drowsiness attended with lively dreams, and arising from some bodily disorder, the effect of idleness, low spirits, or a gloomy imagination', adding 'that in them, as well as in our ordinary dreams, certain appearances should, on some rare occasions, resemble certain events, is to be expected from the laws of chance'. He also took the critical line, 'That the Deity should work a miracle, in order to give intimation of the frivolous things that these tales are made up of . . . is like nothing in nature or providence that we are acquainted with'.

Yet this was combined with a kind of environmental determinism that was proto-Romantic: 'Nor is it wonderful', Beattie wrote, 'that persons of lively imagination, immured in deep solitude, and surrounded with the stupendous scenery of clouds, precipices, and torrents, should dream, even when they think themselves awake, of those few striking ideas with which their lonely lives are diversified'.[82] This must be the source of the comparable sentiments expressed by John Ferriar in the passage quoted on p. 157 above, while it is also interesting to note that Beattie's comments on the sublime qualities of the Highlands were quoted by the great advocate of the picturesque, William Gilpin, in his *Observations, Relative chiefly to Picturesque Beauty . . . Particularly [in] the High-Lands of Scotland* (1789), based on a tour of 1776 (Plate 14). This forms part of the discovery of the otherworldly qualities of the Highlands at this time which is another facet of this developing ethos (it also, of course, helps to explain the fascination of the age with the poems of Ossian).[83] Beattie concluded his account of second sight with the prescient note that 'what in history or philosophy would make but an awkward figure, may sometimes have a charming effect in poetry', thus looking forward almost exactly to the sentiment expressed by Scott. Moreover he, too, exemplified this by quoting a poem, in this case a lengthy passage about a prophet from the anonymous work *Albania*, of 1737, which ended:

Nor knows, o'eraw'd and trembling as he stands,
To what, or whom, he owes his idle fear,
To ghost, to witch, to fairy, or to fiend;
But wonders; and no end of wondering finds.[84]

Returning to Scott, he, of course, was subsequently to exemplify the potential for the use of second sight to provide atmosphere in a fictional setting: this and other supernatural tropes are to be found not only in poems like *The Lady of the Lake* or *The Lay of the Last Minstrel* but also throughout his novels.[85] Scott also added to the available literature on second sight (up to that point dominated by Martin Martin) by orchestrating the first publication of Kirk's *Secret Commonwealth* in 1815, including Tarbat's letter to Boyle.[86] More important, we now enter the era when second sight became part of the culture of Romanticism, and a typically Romantic blending of fact and fiction created a powerful image that was elaborated during the Victorian period and that continues to have resonances today. This is seen particularly in the notorious case of the so-called Brahan Seer, who was supposed to have dramatically foretold the demise of various aristocratic dynasties.[87] That, however, is another story, and so is the history of the reception of second sight, especially among French and German writers, in the early nineteenth century, a context in which a receptive attitude towards the phenomenon received a new lease of life, which was to continue among literary and other devotees of the occult in Victorian England, as we will see in the Conclusion.[88]

In this chapter, we have observed two key developments. The first is the way in which attitudes towards second sight changed as a result not only of scepticism like that of the Deists but also of the momentous change in fashion that affected science in the course of the eighteenth century, meaning that, whereas it had fitted naturally into the Boylian paradigm, it was fundamentally ill at ease with the Newtonian one that challenged it. Yet it is equally interesting how this did not prevent such beliefs taking on a new, parallel lease of life in the world of the imagination. Arguably, this is paradigmatic of the entire legacy of the period that has been examined in this book, and we will draw out its implications in the Conclusion that follows.

# THE 'DECLINE OF MAGIC'
# RECONSIDERED

We have covered a good deal of ground in the course of this book, chronologically from the Restoration to the high Enlightenment, and geographically from Wiltshire to the Scottish Highlands, even if we have probably throughout heard more about metropolitan developments than any other. There has also been an attempt to span a variety of different types of phenomena, from the fortunes of books and institutions to specific cases of witchcraft and apparitions, using the widest possible range of evidence in order to understand them. This has been deliberate. In trying to penetrate an undeniably complicated topic like the 'Decline of Magic', it is crucial to attempt to do justice to all its complexity. In particular, as will have become apparent, though much use has been made of printed books of the period, it is not adequate to try to write an account of a subject like this solely by recourse to them, and too great an emphasis on specific controversies can sometimes prove a distraction from a true understanding of broader currents of thought.[1] As has become apparent again and again in the preceding pages, much of the intellectual life of the period transcended the printed page and got 'εἰς τὸν βίον', 'into life', in Richard Bentley's memorable phrase.[2] Unless this elusive oral dimension to the intellectual life of the day is taken into account, it is doubtful if we will ever truly understand it, or the changes in it that took place. It is also desirable to see the interconnections between different types of thinkers, for instance doing justice to the role of medical men in broader controversies, as was the case in Chapter 5.

In addition, an attempt has been made throughout to avoid the simple pigeonholing that can all too often occur in the study of intellectual history. Here, I have tried to follow my earlier strictures as to how the history of ideas should be written, acknowledging that the intellectual life of the day was dominated by stereotypes to which individuals reacted – the most significant in this case perhaps being the fear of 'atheism', as outlined in the Introduction – and adopting what is essentially a biographical approach in trying to understand the discrete 'bundles' of ideas that each of them formed in response.[3] What is required is great sensitivity towards the subtlety of the intellectual positions that often evolved by such means, and hence the way in which intellectual change came about. Development was not necessarily continuous or homogeneous. Indeed, in relation to magic it has been argued here that there was a time lag in the occurrence of change due to the dangerous associations that sadducism early acquired through its association with freethinking tendencies which orthodox thinkers deprecated, from which it only slowly freed itself.

Nevertheless, there can be no doubt that a transition did occur during the period surveyed by this book, that magical ideas that had been widely accepted among the educated at the beginning of my chosen period had become marginalised by its end. As far as educated opinion was concerned, there undoubtedly *was* a 'Decline of Magic' at this time, at some date which it is hard to fix exactly, but which seems to fall in about the second quarter of the eighteenth century, so that by 1750 the position was dramatically different from that in 1700. This may be epitomised by the contrast between two passages quoted earlier in this book, both written by eminent clerics of their day. On the one hand, we have John Edwards's 1695 condemnation of 'the denial of *Dæmons* and *Witches*', on the grounds that 'besides that this is an open defiance to unquestionable History, Experience and matter of Fact, and so introduces the worst sort of Scepticism (which is the high-way to Atheism) it is evident that this supplants the belief of *Spiritual Beings* or *Substances*'. On the other, we have Conyers Middleton's confident view in 1749 that 'the belief of witches is now utterly extinct, and quietly buried without involving history in it's ruin, or leaving even the least disgrace or censure upon it'.[4] The transformation is almost total, but what have we learned about how and why it occurred?

Since it is commonly presumed that the decline of magic must in some way have been linked to the rise of science, it seems natural to begin by assessing the findings of this book about the connection between the two. In fact, as we have seen throughout, this is a far from straightforward matter. The obvious starting point is the supernaturalist enterprise of Boyle, Glanvill and More surveyed in the Introduction and, as a pendant to this, the investigation of second sight considered in Chapter 6. Both were genuinely empirical projects, and it is revealing that More used the concept, 'Mr Glanvil's

*Experiment*', to describe one of the key occurrences at Tedworth.[5] Indeed, in many ways, this represents the closest that anyone came in our period to an impartial investigation of magic – almost like a precursor of the inquiries made by the Society for Psychical Research in the late nineteenth and early twentieth centuries – although the apologetic motives of those involved meant that they were hardly disinterested parties in the endeavour.[6] In addition, as we saw in Chapter 3, they failed to gain the support from the Royal Society for which Glanvill hoped, and the sceptical tones of the likes of Robert Hooke are a reminder of the lack of unanimity on such matters in scientific circles in the late seventeenth century.

It is also worth noting that the supernaturalist project was surprisingly short lived. As we go into the eighteenth century there is a distinct dearth of books like those by More and Glanvill and that planned by Boyle. There *are* a few later examples, such as the project of Ralph Thoresby referred to in Chapter 2 and the investigations of second sight by Martin Martin and others described in Chapter 6. But in general the principal later equivalents are works of a rather derivative kind by populist writers like Richard Boulton and Daniel Defoe, who retailed accounts of supposed poltergeists and the like in a somewhat salacious way and who lack the intellectual seriousness of their seventeenth-century predecessors.[7] What, therefore, had gone wrong? One problem was the suspicion of fraud, which was an undoubted staple of early sadducees, as has been illustrated over and over again in this book: as Glanvill put it, 'The frequent *impostures* that are met with in this kinde, beget in some a belief, that all such *relations* are *forgeries* and *tales*', and this was something that especially worried Boyle.[8] On the other hand, we saw in the last section of Chapter 4 how opinions on this issue effectively cancelled each other out and, even if the accusation of imposture was satisfying to those predisposed to scepticism, we will explore its explanatory limitations below. It was also a problem for such apologists that supernatural events were not replicable like scientific experiments, though Boyle had an answer to this:

To those that say by way of objection that they would give any thing to see a Spiritt, but could never find any that could show it them. It may be answered that a man may be willing to give any money to see a Comett, but could meet with no body that could shew it him. For as those lights appear but very seldome, and upon conjunctures of Circumstances that we can neither foresee nor command[,] so those Angels of darkness appeare but rarely to the eye, and the times [and] places of their Apparitions are not before hand knowable to Us.[9]

On the other hand, what was more damaging was the argument of such men that the plausibility of a supernatural realm was enhanced by the fact that there were so many phenomena in nature which were empirically proven but for which no explanation could be given. Glanvill's analogy with our ignorance as to how the foetus is formed in the womb or a plant grows in the earth was quoted in the Introduction – yet of course the logical corollary of such nescience was that the most plausible explanation of things that *seemed* to be beyond the normal course of nature was that we had not yet understood the natural causes by which they occurred. This was stated clearly by John Webster in his *Displaying of Supposed Witchcraft* (1677), who argued that

> hitherto we have been ignorant of almost all the true causes of things, and therefore through blindness have usually attributed those things to the operation of Cacademons that were truely wrought by nature, and thereby not smally augmented and advanced this gross and absurd opinion of the power of Witches.[10]

Moreover this was abetted by the supernaturalists themselves insofar as they sought to avoid making excessive claims for supernatural activity. Since they were natural philosophers, concerned with secondary rather than primary causes, they always strove to provide explanations in entirely natural terms, only invoking supernatural ones when these seemed inadequate: had they not done so, they might have been seen as betraying their natural philosophical credentials and displaying undue credulity. In his *The Excellency of the Mechanical Hypothesis* (1674), for instance, Boyle stated concerning illnesses that if a doctor were told that symptoms were produced by a witch or the Devil, 'he will never sit down with so short an account, if he can by any means reduce those extravagant Symptoms to any more known and stated Diseases, as *Epilepsies, Convulsions, Hysterical Fits, &c*.'[11] Much the same is true with the Irish 'stroker', Valentine Greatrakes, whom we encountered in Chapter 3, since, although it was Greatrakes's own view that his cures occurred through 'an extraordinary Gift of God', Boyle was unconvinced that there was anything 'purely supernaturall' about them, preferring to give 'a Phisicall Account'.[12] Matters were further exacerbated by the extent to which such thinkers used parallels with natural phenomena to make sense of how the otherwise inscrutable realm of the supernatural might operate. This motive underlay one of Boyle's more bizarre works, his *Some Physico-Theological Considerations about the Possibility of the Resurrection* (1675), in which he rather ingeniously argued that the redintegration of particles of physical bodies provided a clue to what God would be able to achieve through his superior power at the Last Judgment, and much the same was true of Glanvill's use of the 'analogy of nature' to explain the workings of the supernatural.[13]

On the other hand, although the naturalist alternative may seem to us 'scientific', it was not necessary to be a natural philosopher to claim that many ostensibly supernatural phenomena could be explained by purely natural means. Such naturalism was commonplace in the intellectual culture of the period, and not least among the coffee-house wits and Deists who, as we saw in the Introduction and in Chapters 1 and 2, were in the forefront of denying the reality of witchcraft and related phenomena. Moreover, although More and Glanvill were liable to see their antagonists as Cartesians or Hobbesian materialists, in fact it seems likely that a wider range of naturalistic outlooks were involved. In a curious passage in his *Blow at Modern Sadducism*, Glanvill recounts a conversation with a sceptical interlocutor who seems to have espoused a kind of Platonic world soul, while John Wagstaffe, whose *The Question of Witchcraft Debated* we examined in Chapter 1, seems to have had a fundamentally Aristotelian outlook.[14] Indeed, Aristotelian naturalism had long been a source of scepticism about witchcraft, and naturalism was a key part of the legacy of classical antiquity which was so influential in this period. On the other hand, since the sixteenth century alternative naturalisms had flourished in the hands of critics of Aristotle and, by one means or another, almost anything could be explained away on naturalistic grounds. Hence, in this particular confrontation, the scientific protagonists of the reality of the supernatural were on the losing side, and the principal victors were the humanist sceptics who have been so much in evidence throughout this book. As John Trenchard put it in *Cato's Letters* in 1722: 'there can be no occasion of recurring to supernatural causes, to account for what may be very easily accounted for by our ignorance of natural ones, by the fraud or folly of others, or by the deception of ourselves'.[15] We will return to the significance of such views later in this Conclusion.

Of course, as has become apparent in this book, sceptical attitudes like Trenchard's could be given a scientific veneer. In particular, we saw in

Chapter 3 how, in the early eighteenth century, the rather opaque attitude towards magic of the Royal Society in its early years – when such topics were simply ignored, largely due to the differences in opinion among its members – was given a positive slant by orthodox writers like Francis Hutchinson and used to support the rather cautious version of the freethinkers' scepticism that he and others purveyed. Equally significant, as we saw in Chapter 5, was the extent to which the trappings of Newtonianism were used to give a fashionable gloss to the essentially traditional therapy that doctors deployed, including the naturalistic view of magic that they purveyed. Moreover, as was demonstrated in Chapter 6, an almost neo-scholastic presumption of what was and what was not possible according to the supposed mode of operation of the Newtonian universe was used to dismiss the very empirical observations concerning second sight by which Boyle and his ilk had been so impressed. Undoubtedly, a more or less sophisticated version of the Newtonian ethos became increasingly predominant in every area of thought in the course of the eighteenth century, including those with which we are concerned in this book. But it is important to note that the attitudinal shifts which this brought about had no link to any process of evaluation or adjudication of the evidence involved. Indeed it might be felt that there was an element of the emperor's new clothes about the growing predominance of this ideology, just as there was about the rather spurious claims made for the role of the early Royal Society in connection with the 'Decline of Magic'.

Recently, David Wootton has made a disappointingly Whiggish attempt to assert a direct role for the new science in the 'disenchantment of the world' in his *The Invention of Science: A New History of the Scientific Revolution* (2015) – the weakest chapter in what is otherwise a rather brilliant book.[16] When closely examined, however, this amounts to little more than an echo of the rhetoric of contemporaries like Richard Bentley that we examined in Chapter 3; the shortcomings in this that were there exposed included at least one that even Wootton was forced reluctantly to acknowledge.[17] Indeed, it is striking how little Wootton there has to say about the humanist tradition on the significance of which stress has been laid here, despite the prominence of this in his earlier writings on the intellectual history of the period.[18] Instead, with reference to the transformation of ideas about magic with which this book has been concerned, it is more appropriate to quote the prescient words of Charles Webster in *From Paracelsus to Newton* (1982): 'We must look in places other than science for the explanation of these changes'.[19] Where, therefore, should we look?

One possibility that has been canvassed in recent years lies in the role of party politics in the early eighteenth century. In particular, as was explained in the Introduction, this was the argument of Ian Bostridge's *Witchcraft and its Transformations c. 1650–c. 1750* (1997). More recently, the same theme has been taken up by Peter Elmer in his *Witchcraft, Witch-Hunting, and Politics in Early Modern England* (2016), which he opens by expressing his debt to Bostridge, seeing himself as following in his footsteps, although in his own book he deals with a much longer period, going back to the Elizabethan age.[20] Bostridge's book is undoubtedly very sophisticated and acute – in fact, at times its arguments become so subtle that they are hard to follow – but its overwhelming thrust is that the key to understanding the decline of witchcraft beliefs is the 'Rage of Party' in the early eighteenth century, and this is seriously problematic.[21] There is, of course, much of value in his book, as there is in Elmer's. Both painstakingly investigate the political affiliations of those involved in witch-hunting and those who opposed it, and Bostridge's is especially salutary in demonstrating how mainstream an acceptance of the reality of witchcraft remained throughout the seventeenth century and into the eighteenth. But it is in his treatment of events in the second decade of that century, particularly in connection with the notorious trial of Jane Wenham for witchcraft and its context, that his rather tendentious party-political interpretation kicks in. Now it is undoubtedly true, as was acknowledged in the discussion of this episode in Chapter 2 of this book, that the Wenham trial had a party-political dimension, especially at a local level. But this does not justify the extrapolation to the role of party politics in changing attitudes to witchcraft as a whole in which Bostridge indulges. A number of examples of his rather tendentious, political interpretations of evidence have been noted above, particularly in the footnotes to Chapter 2.[22] Here, however, it is perhaps appropriate to focus on a single counterweight to his argument that it was effectively because of his Whig politics that Francis Hutchinson became a witchcraft sceptic.

This is provided by an analogue to Hutchinson's book that has recently come to light in the form of a bibliographical account of witchcraft which bears some similarity to the relevant sections of his, comparably associating such beliefs with ignorance and superstition: yet this was written not by a Whig but by a Jacobite, the scholar and book collector, Thomas Rawlinson.[23] The surviving manuscript is in the Morrab Library, Penzance, and it represents a slightly surprising initiative on Rawlinson's part, since, although he furnished materials for use by others, he never published a book of his own;

this makes it all the more striking that he was apparently inspired to do so on the subject of witchcraft, though the extant text is unfortunately inexplicit about his motives in this.[24] Rawlinson's text was compiled after Hutchinson's, which had gone into a second edition in 1720 and to which Rawlinson refers, and it is possibly because it covered some of the same ground that Rawlinson's work never got into print – though, since only a fragment survives, comprising two sections of text describing witchcraft publications of the 1640s and a more expansive preface, it may never have been completed.[25] In a letter to Rawlinson dated 17 September 1722 which is quoted in Rawlinson's preface, however, Samuel Weller, vicar of Maidstone in Kent, told him not only that he was 'extreamly pleas'd with the reading of' Hutchinson's book, but also that the volume that Rawlinson hoped to publish would do 'a great deal of real Service to the World'.[26] Like Hutchinson's, the tone of Rawlinson's text is sceptical: 'the unhappy notions of the absurd Power of Witches to hurt both Man & Beast' that had flourished in the mid-seventeenth century were associated with 'the credulous & weak Teachers of those Times'.[27] Though the scale of Rawlinson's extant effort is minor compared with Hutchinson's, this unanimity of a nonjuring Jacobite with a Whig bishop illustrates how by this point scepticism about witchcraft had escaped from its dangerous affiliations with freethinking to become an acceptable viewpoint for orthodox thinkers of various hues. The truth is that party politics were tangential to the major attitudinal change towards magic that was now coming about: one is here reminded of the rather fruitless debate over the party-political affiliations of Newtonianism in the same period that occurred some years ago, which ended in almost total stalemate.[28]

Yet what is most extraordinary about Bostridge's book is not so much its overemphasis on party politics as its complete neglect of the theme that has been so prominent here, namely the role of freethinkers and Deists in pioneering the scepticism which orthodox thinkers like Hutchinson and Rawlinson were belatedly to adopt. This tradition in the thought of the period is simply elided in Bostridge's book: Anthony Collins and Thomas Gordon are briefly introduced only for their polemical conflation of devotees of witchcraft and high-flyers, not for their overall sceptical stance, while Charles Blount, John Toland and John Trenchard are not mentioned at all.[29] To a small extent, this neglect has been rectified by Peter Elmer, who, in the comparable section of his more recent volume, devotes a few pages to the role of Deism, or, as he tends to describe it, 'radical deism' – which might be seen as an attempt to politicise what was not necessarily a political phenomenon.[30] Yet Elmer follows Bostridge in failing to explore the significance of the chief motive of those who defended witchcraft and related beliefs in this period, namely that sadducism was symptomatic of the broader canker of 'atheism', and that the most articulate sceptics about magical phenomena, in the form of freethinkers and Deists, represented a disturbing symptom of wider cultural shifts that were explored in the Introduction to this book. As we there saw, the anxiety about 'atheism' focused on a range of tendencies that were seen as corrosive of traditional values, instead encouraging more iconoclastic, secular ones, and this rather broad and inclusive concern arguably encapsulated key long-term trends, by comparison with which party politics was mere froth.

As to *why* the orthodox came to follow the path which the freethinkers had pioneered and which initially repelled them due to its heterodox connotations, an attempt was made to address this in relation to Hutchinson and his generation in Chapter 2. As we saw there, it became increasingly apparent that to abandon a belief in magic did not necessarily entail any damage to the fabric of Christianity, and the context of this seems above all to have been a growth of assurance – of confidence in a serene and stable world in which the disruptiveness of magic no longer seemed to have a place. Insofar as there was a political dimension to this, it was arguably not in the struggles of Whigs and Tories but in the inexorable growth of the state and the establishment in this period of what J. H. Plumb aptly described as 'political stability'.[31] And this went with an increasing emphasis on the pursuit of an essentially civil religion which Deists like John Toland had pioneered, so that (in the memorable words of his biographer, Robert E. Sullivan), 'Historians in search of Toland's monument will find it in Georgian Anglicanism'.[32] In general, one sees here the significance of a crucial, humanistic tradition in early modern thought, going back to Machiavelli and Hobbes, which arguably deserves an equal billing with the rise of science in the origins of modernity. Moreover, it might be added that this was true not only of Britain, but of Enlightenment Europe more generally.[33]

On the other hand, the later chapters of this book have also illustrated a significant change in the nature of anti-magical arguments during the period when they were achieving hegemony among the educated. As will have become apparent in Chapters 1 and 2, central to the critique of magic by thinkers like Wagstaffe and the early Deists was the argument of conscious manipulation, of 'imposture', as the root of magical and other beliefs. Yet alongside it ran a parallel argument as to why people were susceptible to such manipulation – namely that they were ignorant, or physiologically vulnerable, or even simply the victims of psychological malfunction. Thus Blount spoke of 'the prodigious power of . . . waking dreams', Trenchard blamed our proneness 'to mistake the Phantasms and Images of our own Brains (which have no existence any where else) for real Beings', while Molesworth invoked 'Hysteric fits'; it is similarly interesting that, although Toland considered superstition especially common among the vulgar, he had no doubt that it also affected people of higher rank when they were physically or mentally ill.[34]

Of course, such arguments had a highly respectable classical pedigree going back to Galen, but what is significant when fast-forwarding to the mid-eighteenth-century developments surveyed in Chapter 5 is the extent to which arguments of *this* kind came to the fore while the argument of imposture declined in significance. It is perhaps hardly surprising that this was the case with medical men like Richard Mead and Sir Hans Sloane, who were in the forefront in explaining away magical beliefs as the 'dreams of people awake', whose victims could 'be cured just as well as those suffering from pleurisy, colic or other similar illness'.[35] But it is striking to find comparable arguments in the writings of liberal clerics like Conyers Middleton and Anthony Ashley Sykes on early Christian miracles and on the supposedly supernatural feats recorded in the Bible, since, although both of them used the argument of fraud, they were also inclined to a medical, psychological view of why people were prone to false beliefs. In both cases a significant accommodationist element also entered into their argument – the claim that allowance needed to be made for the conditions of thought in a historical period when assessing the plausibility of belief systems that prevailed in it: in Middleton's case, as we saw, he used the example of witchcraft to illustrate how phenomena that had once been universally credited came to seem implausible. This is also significant, and it represents a further departure from the Deist position, in this case with roots largely in seventeenth-century erudition; it was again to prove influential in the following years.[36]

Moreover, the reason for these developments is arguably as follows. In fact, the Deists' 'priestcraft' argument, and the ancillary evocation of fraud in the sense of conscious manipulation by the powers that be, is ultimately hard to prove. As Peter Harrison has pointed out in relation to religion, orthodox spokesmen like William Warburton could argue strongly in response to such claims how implausible it was that established religions were a tissue of lies promoted for pecuniary gain.[37] Similarly, with witchcraft and related beliefs, the argument of fraud was hard to sustain when it was contested by those who wanted to assert the reality of the phenomena involved: as we saw in Chapter 4, a case in point is provided by the long-running debate over the 'Drummer of Tedworth', since while sceptics claimed that the whole episode was a fraud, they were no more able to prove this than those, like John Beaumont, who asserted its validity. By comparison, the argument that magical beliefs were due to physiological or psychological defects on the part of those who succumbed to them was much more plausible. As we have seen, this might complement the more conspiratorial view of magic championed by the Deists, but it could equally easily stand on its own. Superstitious beliefs were thus not the result of imposture but of error, indeed potentially well-intended or even completely unconscious error, and in the long term this was to prove a more comfortable, if no less dismissive, explanation for the phenomena in question.

Hence, as we saw in Chapters 5 and 6, such views became increasingly predominant among late Enlightenment spokesmen like John Ferriar, and it is revealing of the state of opinion among the intelligentsia at that point that even those who continued to find magic plausible often felt the need to be discreet about this. This has been well illustrated by Jonathan Barry in his exploration of the dilemma of 'public infidelity and private belief' in the context of eighteenth-century Bristol – in other words, the extent to which people continued to harbour a private commitment to the reality of magical phenomena although they were diffident about admitting this in public for fear of ridicule.[38] The same point has been made by Alex Sutherland in relation to attitudes to second sight in Scotland in the same period, who similarly notes a tension between 'private belief and public disclosure'.[39] In this connection, he invokes the earlier example of Robert Boyle, whose sensitivity to the fashionable attitudes of the London intelligentsia made him initially demur from publishing his collection of supernatural phenomena for fear of being labelled credulous.[40] But Boyle was rare in his squeamishness at a time when other orthodox apologists were impelled by the link of sadducism with 'atheism' to adopt a more aggressively assertive view of the reality of witchcraft and related phenomena. The state of affairs that Barry surveys, on the other hand, is revealing of how far the preponderance of opinion had shifted by the mid-eighteenth century in comparison with the situation half a century earlier.

Yet Barry's study also illustrates a continuing proclivity to believe, and this book has no reason to deny that. At a popular level, as we saw at the outset, magical beliefs continued to be prevalent throughout this period and beyond; indeed, the fact that a magical outlook was a quintessentially popular one had been a commonplace since classical times.[41] It may be true that a more rigid polarisation between popular and educated belief than hitherto was coming into place during the period with which this book has been concerned, but here it is perhaps worth reiterating the point made in Chapter 6 concerning second sight, namely how the association of such ideas with the 'vulgar' seems not to have been a causal factor in educated rejection of them but a corollary of it.[42] As for the educated, to some extent a belief in magic might now subsist in the world of fantasy and make-believe, with ghosts, witches and prophets being seen as the fit subject for realms where belief could be suspended, such as poetry (as we saw at the end of the last chapter), or drama (as was revealed in the aftermath of the Cock Lane affair), or the novel: in this respect, Horace Walpole is a classic case in point.[43] There was also a continuation of the rather salacious tradition of retailing stories of supposedly supernatural occurrences, often aimed at a more middle-brow audience, in the tradition of Defoe.[44] In parallel with this, and at the same time, there were stirrings of a more serious revival of esoteric ideas among a minority of the educated, heralded by the popularity of Mesmer and his English equivalents and becoming ever commoner as the eighteenth century drew to a close. This has been most effectively demonstrated by Paul Kléber Monod in his *Solomon's Secret Arts: The Occult in the Age of Enlightenment* (2013), following on from the earlier studies of Désirée Hirst and others.[45] Moreover this was merely a harbinger of things to come, particularly in the context of the spiritualist movement which swept the country in the 1840s and the occult revival of the late Victorian period, whose legacy we feel to this day.[46]

The state of affairs may be epitomised by the fortunes of the Tedworth case during the period in question. We left this in Chapter 4 suspended with the sceptical attitude of Charles Mackay in his *Memoirs of Extraordinary Popular Delusions* of 1841. But just at this time, new interest was being taken in the case by spiritualists, one of whom, Robert Dale Owen, reprinted Glanvill's account of the affair in his *Footfalls on the Boundary of Another World* (1860).[47] Subsequently, the episode received renewed attention in connection with the debate over the nature of poltergeists between A. R. Wallace, Frank Podmore and Andrew Lang in the publications of the Society for Psychical Research in the years around 1900, in which a strong case was made for its genuineness.[48] Moreover a similar attitude has underlain interest in it ever since, as seen in the account of the case given by Harry Price in his *Poltergeist over England: Three Centuries of Mischievous Ghosts* (1945), or more recently by Alan Gauld and A. D. Cornell in their *Poltergeists* (1979).[49] Indeed, as is noted in Appendix I, each of these students of the affair published various significant documents relating to it. But these receptive accounts of the episode were balanced by sceptical ones which echo the attitude of Mackay. In the Victorian period it was lampooned along with comparable cases by the graphic satirist, George Cruikshank, in his *Discovery concerning Ghosts, with a Rap at the 'Spirit-Rappers'* (1863).[50] And the tendency since the early twentieth century in historical accounts of witchcraft and related phenomena such as Wallace Notestein's classic *History of Witchcraft in England* (1911) or, more recently, Rossell Hope Robbins's *Encyclopaedia of Witchcraft and Demonology* (1959) – in which it merits a full-length entry – has been to treat the case as fraudulent.[51]

Similarly conflicting tendencies have been in evidence concerning second sight, including the reductive approach to such phenomena which we encountered in Chapter 6.[52] Indeed, quite apart from the sometimes rather sensationalist literary evocations of the phenomenon referred to at the end of Chapter 6, the late nineteenth century also saw intense investigation of it by the Society for Psychical Research, which has continued since.[53] Overall one might conclude that, in this entire area, a state of affairs has existed since the late eighteenth century that could be summed up as a 'balance of Antagonisms', a phrase first deployed by the Victorian savant, Thomas Carlyle. He used it in a review of John Wilson Croker's edition of Boswell's *Life of Johnson,* published in *Fraser's Magazine* in 1832, to epitomise the balance between 'the respective merit of the Conservator and the Innovator' which he saw as typifying his own age as he looked back at Dr Johnson's heroic stance in relation to the 'Contradictions' that he confronted in his.[54] But Carlyle's phrase has been taken up, particularly by the twentieth-century Brazilian intellectual, Gilberto Freyre, and from him by Peter Burke in the second volume of his *Social History of Knowledge* (2012), in the slightly adapted form, 'equilibrium of antagonisms', to describe a typical aspect of the modern world, namely its ability to tolerate 'the coexistence and interaction of contrary or countervailing trends'.[55] This perfectly describes the pluralism that we saw at the end of Chapter 5 as characterising the Enlightenment and that has arguably been equally characteristic of Western culture ever since. Above all, it epitomises the attitude to magic among British thinkers since the eighteenth century in that, while the dominant culture rejects it, minorities vociferously espouse it.

Yet what is significant about the current book is the exploration that it has given to the roots of the sceptical attitude that has become predominant since the period which has here seen examined in detail. This was given classic expression by William Hogarth in his much-reproduced *Credulity, Superstition and Fanaticism* of 1762 (Plate 16).[56] Fascinating as it is to learn about those who were prone to beliefs of the kind that he there so effectively ridiculed, what is more important is to understand the complex means by which sceptical attitudes like his came to the fore. That is what it is hoped this book has achieved.

Let us end on a lighter note – in this case with an envoi provided by John Aubrey, who in many ways stands above his period in his ambivalence concerning magic, his mixed outlook on this and other subjects helping to explain his appeal to modern readers. Though he collected supernatural phenomena in his *Miscellanies* (1696), Aubrey also showed an element of scepticism on such topics. His account of 'Apparitions' in his *Natural History of Wiltshire* includes the following deflationary story:

> To conclude Sir Ralph Bankes had a Valet de Chambre, a briske young fellow: who riding late over Badbury warren, he discern'd something looke black, which, as he approacht towards, it became bigger & bigger: Feare came upon him, and he protested his haire stood on end: but thought he, I have but a life to lose, & I will see it, be it spirit or not: He spurres his Horse, and came to the place: And it was onely a heap of Horse-dung.[57]

# THE 'DRUMMER OF TEDWORTH'

## A NOTE ON SOURCES

The best-known account of the Tedworth case is that by Glanvill, initially published in *A Blow at Modern Sadducism. In some Philosophical Considerations about Witchcraft* (1668), and adapted in his *Saducismus Triumphatus: or, Full and Plain Evidence Concerning Witches and Apparitions* (1681) in ways that were elucidated in Chapter 4. These, and particularly the latter, are the source of almost all subsequent accounts of the affair.[1]

However, as also explained in Chapter 4, these accounts derive closely from the letters that John Mompesson wrote to the Oxford professor, William Creed, in 1662–3, and associated documents. Comparison of these texts with Glanvill's published account suggests that he relied on copies that he was given of various of Mompesson's letters to Creed, which the printed versions follow closely, particularly for their factual content, though Glanvill's commentary on the events often differs, as we have seen. The implication is that Glanvill followed a directly parallel set of texts in the form of Mompesson's retained copies of these letters, which do not otherwise survive. The extant items comprise copies made by the Oxford antiquary, William Fulman, which are now in the archive of Corpus Christi College, Oxford.[2] They comprise three letters from Mompesson to Creed dated 6 and 26 December 1662 and 4 January 1663 (hereinafter documents 1, 3 and 4), together with three associated documents: a commentary on the events at Tedworth in January 1663, evidently also by Mompesson (document 6); a letter on the subject to him from his cousin, the Wiltshire MP Sir Thomas Mompesson, dated 11 December 1662 (document 2); and a letter of 6 January 1663 from William Maton, a gentry neighbour of Mompesson's who was to act as a deponent concerning the case when it came to the assizes later that year, to his nephew, Francis Parry, a Fellow of Corpus Christi College, Oxford (document 5).[3] (One possibility is that it could have been through Parry that Fulman, also a Fellow of Corpus, obtained the whole group of manuscripts.)

The first of Mompesson's letters to Creed also survives in other copies. One is in the collection of another Oxford antiquary, Anthony Wood, where it is given the title 'The Demon or Devill of Tidworth in Wilts, in the house there of Mr ... Mompesson'.[4] A second is known only through a text published by Harry Price in 1945 from a manuscript then in the hands of Mr H. Fetherstonhaugh-Frampton, which cannot now be traced. This appears in Price's book, *Poltergeist over England: Three Centuries of Mischievous Ghosts* (1945), and it is perhaps worth commenting here on the manner in which it is there presented. The book includes a chapter on the Tedworth case based exclusively on *Saducismus Triumphatus*. However, this was complemented by the new text in the form of an appendix, and Price explains how he had learned of its existence only 'as this monograph is passing through the press'.[5] At the end of the appendix, he also noted the other documents copied by Fulman, to which his attention had been drawn at this very late stage by Bodley's Librarian, H.H.E. Craster, reproducing a photograph of part of one of them (document 6, the narrative of events in January 1663) – the only photograph of any part of them that has yet been published. However, Price made no further attempt to divulge the content of the Corpus texts.[6] Poor Harry Price! He was very unlucky not to have found this material earlier and to have been able to make better use of it in his account of the Tedworth episode, since, had he done so, it would have done something to allay his reputation as a rather slipshod scholar.[7]

Subsequently, the bulk of the material was published by Alan Gauld in his co-authored work with A. D. Cornell, *Poltergeists* (1979). However, Gauld entirely ignored one item – the letter from Sir Thomas Mompesson – and he omitted significant passages from others, many of them forming the basis of key conclusions in the text above.[8] A complete text was provided in Michael Hunter, 'New Light on the "Drummer of Tedworth": Conflicting Narratives of Witchcraft in Restoration England', *Historical Research*, 78 (2005), 311–53, also available in Birkbeck ePrints. To the Mompesson documents was added an unsigned account of the affair written by a visitor to the Mompessons' house which survives among the State Papers: although filed under 1667, it clearly dates from very early in 1663 (document 7).[9] As we saw in Chapter 4, at one point the experiences recorded overlap with Glanvill's as recorded in his later, published account of the case; indeed, the manuscript throughout overlaps with Glanvill's work, although it is differently worded and the events are set out in a different order. It is thus likely, as we saw above, that this is Glanvill's own earliest account of the case, the differences between it and his later published one being explicable in terms of its being out of his hands when he came to write *A Blow at Modern Sadducism*. Since they are readily available online in *Historical Research* and Birkbeck ePrints, it has not seemed appropriate to reprint these documents here: instead, they are referred to by document or page number within the *Historical Research* edition of them.

Since 2005, a further copy of most of the Mompesson letters of 6 and 26 December 1662 (documents 1 and 3) has come to light at the Dorset History Centre. These texts are to be found in the Sheridan of Frampton Archive, in a commonplace book compiled by Thomas Browne of Frampton, merchant and MP (*c.* 1620–80), which was elaborately rebound in calf by his descendant, Richard Brinsley Sheridan, in the nineteenth century.[10] In this volume, Browne made brief notes on all sorts of topics but he seems to have been particularly interested in magic and witchcraft, copying into it extensive sections from Glanvill's 'Some Considerations About Witchcraft'.[11] He then included copies of Mompesson's first two letters to Creed. The texts are substantively the same as those copied by Fulman and (in the case of document 1) the Wood and Fetherstonhaugh-Frampton copies, but the orthography differs throughout, as very occasionally does the wording, perhaps due to careless or arbitrary copying. In addition, the copyist regarded the last two paragraphs of Mompesson's first letter as irrelevant to his purposes and omitted both, though he included the postscript (these are the paragraphs which are most revealing of Mompesson's perplexed and anxious reaction to the affair; Alan Gauld also omitted the concluding one). The end of the second letter is also truncated, lacking the final four lines and postscript: this is due to the fact that this is the last page in the volume with seventeenth-century pagination, and it is likely that some leaves are missing at this point, which might have contained more of the letters.[12] The new copy thus further illustrates the degree of contemporary interest in the events at Tedworth, but does not add to our detailed knowledge of the affair.

In Chapter 4, recourse to these documents has been supplemented by all relevant sources, including brief references in contemporary diaries, letters and the like. However, two other sources may be singled out here, which have been known to those interested in the Tedworth case since they were first published by Andrew Lang in his article, 'The Poltergeist, Historically Considered', in the *Proceedings of the Society for Psychical Research* in 1903. One is the ballad about the case by Abraham Miles that evidently came out in February 1663, the only extant copy of which was also preserved by

Anthony Wood. It is entitled *A Wonder of Wonders; Being A true Relation of the strange and invisible Beating of a Drum, at the house of John Mompesson, Esquire, at Tidcomb* [sic] *in the County of Wilt-shire.*[13] In addition, a report on the case appeared in two newspapers in April that year, *Mercurius Publicus* and *The Kingdoms Intelligencer*, of which Lang published the version in the former.[14] Here, it is worth noting that the drummer's name is known only from the report in the newspapers, being nowhere given by Mompesson or Glanvill; this also reveals that he hailed from the hamlet of Uffcott in the parish of Broad Hinton near Swindon.[15]

## APPENDIX II

# JOSHUA WALKER'S PAPER
# ON SECOND SIGHT

In *The Occult Laboratory*, I noted that in 1686 Joshua Walker of Brasenose College gave a paper to the Oxford Philosophical Society 'of Second Sighted Men in Scotland' but that the paper did not appear to survive; on the other hand, a clue to its content was provided by the index to the society's minutes, which recorded that second-sighted men abhorred 'Women combing their heads'.[1] In fact, it turns out that the same paper was read to the Royal Society twelve years later and it survives in the society's Classified Papers, vol. 7 (1) 55, with a scribal copy in the society's original Register Book.[2] The Classified Papers version is endorsed 'Read Nov: 16: 98', and the society's original Journal Book does indeed record that at the meeting on 16 November 1698 'A paper was read concerning the Scotch second sighted people foretelling things to come'; it also notes that this stimulated a Fellow, William Bridgeman, to comment that 'he knew one matter foretold by a second sighted Scoch [sic] woman that came to pass according to her prediction'.[3] The text of the paper is printed here: its identity with the paper read by Walker in 1686 is confirmed by its reference to the unsettling effect of women combing their hair.

Classified Papers 7 (1) 55[4]

*Of Apparitions in the N. of Scotland*
*Communicated by Mr. Walker*

    Mr Mack-enzy A.M of Ch. Ch. in Oxford,[5] did seriously affirm, in the presence of several grave persons; that several of his School fellows in the North of Scotland, sayd that they saw apparitions allmost every week: & upon his knowledge they did very frequently fortel the death of Persons, which allways succeeded accordingly: they used to tell the day when such a person would die, 6 or 8 days before they did dye: & he never heard that they faild in their prædictions, but they allways prov'd true. He pitied the boys much, for they were very much frighted, when they saw the apparitions, & if they chanc'd to be alone, when the thing appeared, they used to run to company. He was told that the Apparition did not speak to them, but appeared in the likenesse of the person that died soon after. He sayd this was very common in the Island of Lewis, North of the[6] Hebrides, and in the Highlands, where they used to call the persons that could see these apparitions, secondsighted[7] men. This property of seeing apparitions is peculiar to some families. Not onely boys but persons of all ages had this property, & some of them, are serious, discreet, credible persons. He sayd he was present when a secondsighted man, who was a Scholler & a Gentleman of good credit, & was a Kinsman of his, told one in the company that his wife was dead: upon this the man went home, which was about 10 or 12 miles off, & found his wife dead: she die'd suddenly. There were several Gentlemen in company, when his Kinsman spoke this: & they all concluded that he understood it by some apparition, for they could not[8] finde that he could learn it any Ordinary way. He sayd the 2[d] sighted boys were much disorder'd when they saw a woman combing her head, or with her hair hanging down, because the apparitions came in that dresse commonly. He thinks Sir Geo. Mackenzy Register of the Rolls at Edenborough (not the Advocate)[9] has writ a Collection of all that he could meet with, of this kinde. Sometimes one 2[d] sighted man could see an apparition, which another 2[d] sighted man of an other family could not see. They could see the Apparitions in the dark. Mr Dâl-Garno told one of this Society that a sister in law of his, ‹who› had liv'd amoung some 2[d] sighted persons, gave an account that they did frequently tell what was done at that time, at places several miles distant from them, & upon Enquiry what they sayd was found to be true.[10]

# ENDNOTES

## INTRODUCTION: THE SUPERNATURAL, SCIENCE AND 'ATHEISM'

1. See Max Weber, *The Protestant Ethic and the Spirit of Capitalism* (English translation by Talcott Parsons, London, 1930, from the German original, *Die Protestantische Ethik und der Geist des Kapitalismus*, published in *Archiv für Sozialwissenschaft und Sozialpolitik* in 1904–5), pp. 105, 117, 149 and passim. For a helpful discussion see Alexandra Walsham, 'The Reformation and "The Disenchantment of the World" Reassessed', *Historical Journal*, 51 (2008), 497–528, esp. p. 498.
2. See Keith Thomas, *Religion and the Decline of Magic: Studies in Popular Beliefs in Sixteenth- and Seventeenth-century England* (London, 1971).
3. See, for instance, the topics listed by the late eighteenth-century antiquary Francis Grose in the section of his *Provincial Glossary* (London, 1787) which he devoted to 'superstitions', the summary of which on p. 6 almost reads like the contents list of the core sections of *Religion and the Decline of Magic*, except that it adds second sight. On the concept of 'superstition' see Dale B. Martin, *Inventing Superstition: From the Hippocratics to the Christians* (Cambridge, MA, 2004), and S. A. Smith and Alan Knight (eds), *The Religion of Fools? Superstition Past and Present* (*Past & Present Supplement* no. 3, Oxford, 2008).
4. The exception is Paul Kléber Monod, *Solomon's Secret Arts: The Occult in the Age of Enlightenment* (New Haven and London, 2013), which is even wider than Thomas's in its terms of reference: see pp. 5–6 and passim. Though one might feel reservations about Monod's reification of 'occult thinking', this arguably becomes more appropriate in relation to the later part of the period with which he deals. On his book, see below, pp. 122, 142, 160 and 178. For studies of astrology see n. 20.
5. See below, pp. 73–4, 78–9 and 84. For my earlier work see Michael Hunter and Annabel Gregory (eds), *An Astrological Diary of the Seventeenth Century: Samuel Jeake of Rye, 1652–1699* (Oxford, 1988), and Michael Hunter, 'Science and Astrology in Seventeenth-century England: An Unpublished Polemic by John Flamsteed', in Patrick Curry (ed.), *Astrology, Science and Society: Historical Essays* (Woodbridge, 1987), pp. 260–300, reprinted in Hunter, *Science and the Shape of Orthodoxy: Intellectual Change in late Seventeenth-century Britain* (Woodbridge, 1995), pp. 245–85.
6. See especially Michael Hunter, 'Alchemy, Magic and Moralism in the Thought of Robert Boyle', *British Journal for the History of Science*, 23 (1990), 387–410, reprinted in Hunter, *Robert Boyle (1627–91): Scrupulosity and Science* (Woodbridge, 2000), pp. 93–118, and Hunter, *Boyle: Between God and Science* (New Haven and London, 2009), esp. chapter 11. For alchemy see also n. 17.
7. Thomas, *Religion and the Decline of Magic*, chapters 18 (pp. 570–83) and 22 (pp. 641–68). One should perhaps also note chapter 21, 'Some Interconnections' (pp. 631–40).

8. Alan Macfarlane, *Witchcraft in Tudor and Stuart England: A Regional and Comparative Study* (London, 1970), p. xiv.

9. Thomas, *Religion and the Decline of Magic*, p. 570 (he was there referring specifically to witchcraft, but the comment is equally applicable to magical ideas as a whole).

10. For a survey of and commentary on the major reviews of Thomas's book, see Jonathan Barry, 'Introduction: Keith Thomas and the Problem of Witchcraft', in Barry, Marianne Hester and Gareth Roberts (eds), *Witchcraft in Early Modern Europe: Studies in Culture and Belief* (Cambridge, 1996), pp. 1–45.

11. Thomas, *Religion and the Decline of Magic*, p. 666.

12. See esp. Owen Davies, *Witchcraft, Magic and Culture 1736–1951* (Manchester, 1999) and *Cunning-Folk: Popular Magic in English History* (London, 2003). For a broader perspective see Willem de Blécourt, 'On the Continuation of Witchcraft', in Barry, Hester and Roberts, *Witchcraft in Early Modern Europe*, pp. 335–52, Marijke Gijswijt-Hofstra, 'Witchcraft after the Witch-trials', in Gijswijt-Hofstra et al., *The Athlone History of Witchcraft and Magic in Europe, V: The Eighteenth and Nineteenth Centuries* (London, 1999), pp. 95–189 and Owen Davies and Willem de Blécourt (eds), *Beyond the Witch Trials: Witchcraft and Magic in Enlightenment Europe* (Manchester, 2004) and *Witchcraft Continued: Popular Magic in Modern Europe* (Manchester, 2004).

13. In this respect, the key study was Peter Burke's *Popular Culture in Early Modern Europe* (London, 1978).

14. Ian Bostridge, *Witchcraft and its Transformations, c. 1650–c. 1750* (Oxford, 1997).

15. See esp. Michael MacDonald, 'Religion, Social Change and Psychological Healing in England, 1600–1800', *Studies in Church History*, 19 (1982), 101–25, and Peter Elmer, 'Towards a Politics of Witchcraft in Early Modern England', in Stuart Clark (ed.), *Languages of Witchcraft: Narrative, Ideology and Meaning in Early Modern Culture* (Basingstoke, 2001), pp. 101–18, and his *Witchcraft, Witch-Hunting, and Politics in Early Modern England* (Oxford, 2016). See also the studies by Mark Knights and Andrew Sneddon referred to in Chapter 2.

16. See below, especially Chapter 2, passim, and pp. 173–5.

17. Brian P. Copenhaver, *Magic in Western Culture: From Antiquity to the Enlightenment* (Cambridge, 2015), esp. chapter 14. For a comparable approach see Wouter J. Hanegraaff, *Esotericism and the Academy: Rejected Knowledge in Western Culture* (Cambridge, 2012), esp. chapter 3. On alchemy see especially William R. Newman and Lawrence M. Principe, *Alchemy Tried in the Fire: Starkey, Boyle, and the Fate of Helmontian Chymistry* (Chicago, 2002), and Lawrence M. Principe, *The Secrets of Alchemy* (Chicago, 2013). Other important studies include Charles Webster, *From Paracelsus to Newton: Magic and the Making of Modern Science* (Cambridge, 1982), and John Henry, 'The Fragmentation of Renaissance Occultism and the Decline of Magic', *History of Science*, 46 (2008), 1–48; the latter makes the case that the nature of magic was changed by the colonisation of some of its key elements by the new, experimental science.

18. Euan Cameron, *Enchanted Europe: Superstition, Reason, and Religion, 1250–1750* (Oxford, 2010), part 4. This work is also very patchy in its attention to the existing historiography of the subject. For a superior example of a comparable approach, which is appropriately alert to the secondary literature, see Roy Porter's masterly essay, 'Witchcraft and Magic in Enlightenment, Romantic and Liberal Thought', in Gijswijt-Hofstra et al., *Athlone History of Witchcraft and Magic, V*, pp. 191–282, summarised in Porter, *Enlightenment: Britain and the Creation of the Modern World* (London, 2000), pp. 219–29.

19. E. P. Thompson, 'Anthropology and the Discipline of Historical Context', *Midland History*, 1 (1972), 41–55, on pp. 50–1.

20. It is almost invidious to try to summarise this literature, but as far as witchcraft is concerned, helpful recent overviews are provided by Jonathan Barry and Owen Davies (eds), *Palgrave Advances in Witchcraft Historiography* (Basingstoke, 2007) and Brian Levack (ed.), *The Oxford Handbook of Witchcraft in Early Modern Europe and Colonial America* (Oxford, 2013). On Scotland see esp. Christina Larner, *Enemies of God: The Witch-Hunt in Scotland* (London, 1981), Julian Goodare (ed.), *The Scottish Witch-Hunt*

*in Context* (Manchester, 2002) and Brian P. Levack, *Witch-Hunting in Scotland: Law, Politics and Religion* (New York and London, 2008). On astrology, the now slightly dated work of Patrick Curry, *Prophecy and Power: Astrology in Early Modern England* (Cambridge, 1989) may be supplemented, e.g., by Ann Geneva, *Astrology and the Seventeenth-century Mind: William Lilly and the Language of the Stars* (Manchester, 1995), Lauren Kassell, *Medicine and Magic in Elizabethan London: Simon Forman, Astrologer, Alchemist, and Physician* (Oxford, 2005), and 'Casebooks in Early Modern England: Medicine, Astrology and Written Records', *Bulletin of the History of Medicine*, 88 (2014), 595–625, and Louise H. Curth, *English Almanacs, Astrology and Popular Medicine: 1550–1700* (Manchester, 2007).

21. Stuart Clark, *Thinking with Demons: The Idea of Witchcraft in Early Modern Europe* (Oxford, 1997), pp. viii–ix and passim.
22. See esp. Martin, *Inventing Superstition*.
23. Robert Bartlett, *The Natural and the Supernatural in the Middle Ages* (Cambridge, 2008).
24. Clark, *Thinking with Demons*, esp. chapters 10–11, 14, 16–17. On the preternatural, see also Loraine Daston, 'Preternatural Philosophy', in Daston (ed.), *Biographies of Scientific Objects* (Chicago, 2000), pp. 15–41.
25. See Walter Stephens, *Demon Lovers: Witchcraft, Sex, and the Crisis of Belief* (Chicago, 2002).
26. See the classic study of D. P. Walker, 'The Cessation of Miracles', in Ingrid Merkel and Allen G. Debus (eds), *Hermeticism and the Renaissance: Intellectual History and the Occult in Early Modern Europe* (Washington DC, 1988), pp. 111–24.
27. See Peter Dear, 'Miracles, Experiments, and the Ordinary Course of Nature', *Isis*, 81 (1990), 663–83. On the doughty defence of biblical miracles by, for instance, Robert Boyle, see J. J. MacIntosh (ed.), *Boyle on Atheism* (Toronto, 2005), pp. 200ff., 261ff.
28. On providence, see the brilliant discussion in Thomas, *Religion and the Decline of Magic*, chapter 4, and more recently Alexandra Walsham, *Providence in Early Modern England* (Oxford, 1999).
29. Thomas, *Religion and the Decline of Magic*, passim, and see, for instance, Christopher Marsh, *Popular Religion in Sixteenth-century England* (Basingstoke, 1998), pp. 146ff. On the continuing appeal of the miraculous at a popular level see Walsham, *Providence*, chapter 5, and Jane Shaw, *Miracles in Enlightenment England* (New Haven and London, 2006).
30. See Stephen Brogan, *The Royal Touch in Early Modern England: Politics, Medicine and Sin* (Woodbridge, 2015).
31. On the former, see especially the classic study of George Huntston Williams, *The Radical Reformation* (London, 1962); on the latter see Christopher Hill, *The World Turned Upside Down: Radical Ideas during the English Revolution* (London, 1972).
32. See Clark, *Thinking with Demons*, pp. 543–5, and, e.g., Gary Waite, 'Demonic Affliction or Divine Chastisement? Conceptions of Illness and Healing among Spiritualists and Mennonites in Holland, *c.* 1530–*c.* 1630', in Marijke Gijswijt-Hofstra, Hilary Marland and Hans de Waardt (eds), *Illness and Healing Alternatives in Western Europe* (London, 1997), pp. 59–79, or, on England, Thomas, *Religion and the Decline of Magic*, p. 571.
33. Ibid., pp. 375–6; Hill, *World Turned Upside Down*, pp. 70–2, 231ff. For a useful edition of texts relating to the Webster–Ward debate to which Thomas alludes in the passage cited, see Allen G. Debus, *Science and Education in the Seventeenth Century: The Webster-Ward Debate* (London, 1970).
34. The secondary literature on possession is huge. For an overview see Brian P. Levack, *The Devil Within: Possession and Exorcism in the Christian West* (New Haven and London, 2013).
35. See Copenhaver, *Magic in Western Culture*; see also the pioneering study by D. P. Walker, *Spiritual and Demonic Magic from Ficino to Campanella* (London, 1958).
36. See especially Walter Pagel, *Paracelsus: An Introduction to Philosophical Medicine in the Era of the Renaissance*, revised edn (Basel, 1982), and Charles Webster, *Paracelsus: Medicine, Magic and Mission at the End of Time* (New Haven and London, 2008) and Webster, *From Paracelsus to Newton*.

37. See especially Nicholas H. Clulee, *John Dee's Natural Philosophy: Between Science and Religion* (London, 1988). More recently see Stephen Clucas (ed.), *John Dee: Interdisciplinary Studies in English Renaissance Thought* (Dordrecht, 2006) and Glyn Parry, *The Arch-Conjurer of England: John Dee* (New Haven and London, 2011).

38. Francis Hutchinson, *An Historical Essay concerning Witchcraft*, 2nd edn (London, 1720), sig. A6v.

39. For a recent study of Scot's influence, see S. F. Davies, 'The Reception of Reginald Scot's Discovery of Witchcraft: Witchcraft, Magic, and Radical Religion', *Journal of the History of Ideas*, 74 (2013), 381–401. For his ongoing significance, see Jonathan Barry, *Witchcraft and Demonology in South-West England, 1640–1789* (Basingstoke, 2012), pp. 262ff.

40. See Michael Heyd, *'Be Sober and Reasonable': The Critique of Enthusiasm in the Seventeenth and Early Eighteenth Centuries* (Leiden, 1995).

41. On More see ibid., pp. 92–4. On Casaubon, see Stephen Clucas, 'Enthusiasm and "Damnable Curiosity": Meric Casaubon and John Dee', in R.J.W. Evans and Alexander Marr (eds), *Curiosity and Wonder from the Renaissance to the Enlightenment* (Aldershot, 2006), pp. 131–48.

42. See Roy Porter, 'The Patient's View: Doing Medical History from Below', *Theory and Society*, 14 (1985), 175–98, esp. p. 184.

43. See Clark, *Thinking with Demons*, pp. 198ff., esp. p. 200n on the historiography, and see also Peter Elmer, 'Science, Medicine and Witchcraft', in Barry and Davies, *Palgrave Advances in Witchcraft Historiography*, pp. 33–51, esp. pp. 35ff.

44. Michael MacDonald, *Mystical Bedlam: Madness, Anxiety, and Healing in Seventeenth-century England* (Cambridge, 1981), esp. chapter 5.

45. Michael MacDonald (ed.), *Witchcraft and Hysteria in Elizabethan London: Edward Jorden and the Mary Glover Case* (London, 1991), though, in correcting the earlier, rather Whiggish historiography of the episode, he perhaps goes unduly far in emphasising Jorden's political motives, echoing his argument in 'Religion, Social Change and Psychological Healing': see above, n. 15.

46. Cf. MacDonald, *Witchcraft and Hysteria*, p. xliii (and the appended text of John Swan's *True and Briefe Report, of Mary Glovers Vexation* (1603), p. 68), and, more generally, Paul H. Kocher, *Science and Religion in Elizabethan England* (1953; reprinted New York, 1969), chapters 12 ('The Physician as Atheist') and 13 ('God in Medicine').

47. Francis Bacon, *The Instauratio Magna Part II: Novum Organum and Associated Texts*, ed. Graham Rees with Maria Wakely, Oxford Francis Bacon, vol. 11 (Oxford, 2004), pp. 454–5.

48. See his paper 'Concerning Spirits' in BL Add MS 38856, fols 165–6 (see further below, Chapter 4, n. 97).

49. See Peter Anstey and Michael Hunter, 'Robert Boyle's "Designe about Natural History"', *Early Science and Medicine*, 13 (2008), 83–126.

50. For a brief summary see Michael Hunter, *Boyle: Between God and Science* (New Haven and London, 2009), chapter 7.

51. For an intriguing rumination along such lines see Michel Wasser, 'The Mechanical World-View and the Decline of Witch-Beliefs in Scotland', in Julian Goodare, Lauren Martin and Joyce Miller (eds), *Witchcraft and Belief in Early Modern Scotland* (Basingstoke, 2008), pp. 206–26.

52. Boyle, *Works*, ed. Michael Hunter and Edward B. Davis, 14 vols (London, 1999–2000), vol. 11, p. 429. For a full account of *Strange Reports* and its background, see Hunter, *Scrupulosity and Science*, chapter 10. Concerning the planned further volumes of *Experimenta et Observationes Physicae*, see Hunter, *Boyle Studies: Aspects of the Life and Thought of Robert Boyle (1627–91)* (Farnham, 2015), pp. 184n., 185.

53. Hunter, *Scrupulosity and Science*, pp. 230–31.

54. See ibid., pp. 230, 245–50.

55. Ibid., pp. 227–30, and see Michael Hunter, *The Occult Laboratory: Magic, Science and Second Sight in Late Seventeenth-Century Scotland* (Woodbridge, 2001).

56. Michael Hunter and Charles Littleton (eds), *The Workdiaries of Robert Boyle*, available at www.livesandletters.ac.uk/wd/index.html, WD 36–102 and passim. See also Hunter, *Boyle Studies*, pp. 163–4, 180–82.

NOTES to pp. 12–15 191

57. Lawrence M. Principe, *The Aspiring Adept: Robert Boyle and his Alchemical Quest* (Princeton, 1998), esp. chapter 6 (though for a complication see Hunter, *Boyle Studies*, p. 173n.).
58. Boyle, *Works*, vol. 1, pp. 13–39. See further below, Chapter 4, n. 88.
59. Ibid., vol. 8, p. 292, vol. 10, pp. 492–3.
60. For useful accounts of the genre, see Neal C. Gillespie, 'Natural History, Natural Theology, and Social Order: John Ray and the "Newtonian Ideology"', *Journal of the History of Biology*, 20 (1987), 1–49, and John Brooke, ' "Wise Men Nowadays Think Otherwise": John Ray, Natural Theology and the Meanings of Anthropocentrism', *Notes and Records of the Royal Society*, 54 (2000), 199–213.
61. Henry More, *An Antidote against Atheism* (London, 1653), p. 105. For his usage of 'supernatural' see pp. 112, 114, 115, 116, 118, 121, 122, 140, 142.
62. See, for example, Sarah Hutton, *British Philosophy in the Seventeenth Century* (Oxford, 2016), which refers to this aspect of More's work only in the biographical note on Glanvill, p. 232; or C. A. Patrides's anthology, *The Cambridge Platonists* (London, 1969), which prints Books I and II of the *Antidote* but merely gives the chapter headings of Book III (pp. xxv, 286–7).
63. More, *Antidote*, esp. p. 108. For More's concept of a 'natural history of spirits' see Robert Crocker, *Henry More, 1614–87: A Biography of the Cambridge Platonist* (Dordrecht, 2003), p. 128 and chapter 9, passim. The project is pursued in his *Immortality of the Soul* (1659), but the *Antidote* is the main repository of such material.
64. This includes *Saducismus Triumphatus* (London, 1681 and subsequent editions). See Clare Fitzpatrick, ' "Miraculous and Supernaturall Effects" in the Works of Henry More' (London Ph.D. thesis, 2019), esp. chapter 3. See also Allison Coudert, 'Henry More and Witchcraft', in Sarah Hutton (ed.), *Henry More (1614–1687): Tercentenary Studies* (Dordrecht, 1990), pp. 115–36.
65. Boyle to Glanvill, 18 September 1677, in Michael Hunter, Antonio Clericuzio and Lawrence M. Principe (eds), *The Correspondence of Robert Boyle*, 6 vols (London, 2001), vol. 4, pp. 455–7, on p. 457. See also Boyle to Glanvill, 10 February 1678, ibid., vol. 5, pp. 20–21. Interestingly, 'supernatural' is a word that Glanvill himself hardly used in his writings on demonology (for the only instance, see *A Blow at Modern Sadducism*, 4th edn (London, 1668), pp. 104–5), possibly due to his proneness to conflate the natural and the supernatural through the 'analogy of nature': see below, p. 171.
66. Glanvill, *A Blow*, pp. 113ff. and passim. For an account of the various seventeenth-century recensions of Glanvill's work and their mutual relationship, see Joseph Glanvill, *Saducismus Triumphatus* (London, 1689), reprinted with an introduction by C. O. Parsons (Gainesville, 1966), pp. xix–xxiii; see also below, Chapter 4, n. 2, and pp. 103–4. Here and throughout the book the 1689 edition of *Saducismus Triumphatus* is used because of its convenient, continuous pagination.
67. Glanvill, *A Blow*, pp. 5, 13–14 and passim.
68. *Saducismus Triumphatus*, p. [58].
69. Ibid., Part II, passim. For background on the network that supplied this material see Jonathan Barry, 'Robert Hunt and the Somerset Witches', in his *Witchcraft and Demonology in South-West England*, chapter 2; Peter Elmer, *The Miraculous Conformist: Valentine Greatrakes, the Body Politic, and the Politics of Healing in Restoration Britain* (Oxford, 2013), chapter 5; and Elmer, *Witchcraft, Witch-Hunting, and Politics in Early Modern England* (Oxford, 2016), pp. 216ff.
70. Ralph Cudworth, *The True Intellectual System of the Universe* (London, 1678), pp. 700–715.
71. Isaac Barrow, *Theological Works*, ed. Alexander Napier, 9 vols (Cambridge, 1859), vol. 5, pp. 266–89, esp. pp. 275–6. On Barrow, see Mordechai Feingold (ed.), *Before Newton: The Life and Times of Isaac Barrow* (Cambridge, 1990).
72. On Baxter, see esp. William Lamont, *Puritanism and Historical Controversy* (London, 1996), chapter 9. See also below, pp. 99–100, 107–8 and 112. On Mather see Michael Winship, *Seers of God: Puritan Providentialism in the Restoration and Early Enlightenment* (Baltimore, 1996), esp. chapter 3, and below, p. 112.

73. George Sinclair, *The Hydrostaticks* (Edinburgh, 1672), pp. 238ff.; *Satans Invisible World Discovered* (Edinburgh, 1685), title page and pp. 75ff. See also below, p. 112.

74. Sinclair, *Hydrostaticks*, pp. 117ff., 146ff. and passim, and see Boyle, *Works*, vol. 1, p. lxxvi, vol. 5, p. xxii, and vol. 7, p. xvii and 185ff.

75. Cudworth, *True Intellectual System*, p. 150.

76. For the best account of this dispute see John Henry, 'Henry More versus Robert Boyle: The Spirit of Nature and the Nature of Providence', in Hutton, *Henry More*, pp. 55–76.

77. Boyle, *Works*, vol. 10, pp. 437–571.

78. John Ray, *Synopsis Methodica Stirpium Britannicarum* (London, 1690), 'Præfatio', translated in C. E. Raven, *John Ray: Naturalist*, 2nd edn (Cambridge, 1950), p. 251.

79. Raven, *John Ray*, pp. 69–70, commenting on Ray to Lhwyd, 22 January 1693/4, in R.W.T. Gunther (ed.), *Further Correspondence of John Ray* (London, 1928), pp. 242–3.

80. Most recently, see Kenneth Sheppard, *Anti-Atheism in Early Modern England 1580–1720: The Atheist Answered and his Error Confuted* (Leiden, 2015). See also Michael Hunter and David Wootton (eds), *Atheism from the Reformation to the Enlightenment* (Oxford, 1992), Michael Hunter, 'The Problem of "Atheism" in Early Modern England', *Transactions of the Royal Historical Society*, 5th series 35 (1985), 135–57, and Hunter, 'Science and Heterodoxy: An Early Modern Problem Reconsidered', in David C. Lindberg and Robert S. Westman (eds), *Reappraisals of the Scientific Revolution* (Cambridge, 1990), pp. 437–60, reprinted in Hunter, *Science and the Shape of Orthodoxy*, pp. 225–44, which is closely echoed in the argument put forward in the pages that follow. Older studies include Don Cameron Allen, *Doubt's Boundless Sea: Skepticism and Faith in the Renaissance* (Baltimore, 1964).

81. John Edwards, *Some Thoughts concerning the Several Causes and Occasions of Atheism* (London, 1695), p. 132. For his definition of the real thing, see pp. 133–4 and passim.

82. Alan Charles Kors, *Atheism in France, 1650–1729: The Orthodox Sources of Disbelief* (Princeton, 1990) and Kors, *Naturalism and Unbelief in France, 1650–1729* (Cambridge, 2016).

83. Barlow to Boyle, 29 November 1684, in Boyle, *Correspondence*, vol. 6, p. 93.

84. See David Berman, *A History of Atheism in Britain: From Hobbes to Russell* (London, 1988), esp. pp. 110ff.

85. Francis Gastrell, *The Certainty and Necessity of Religion in General* (London, 1697), pp. 201, 245.

86. Royal Society Boyle Papers 2, fol. 108, printed in MacIntosh, *Boyle on Atheism*, p. 375; Boyle Papers 7, fol. 213.

87. See Michelle O'Callaghan, *The English Wits: Literature and Sociability in Early Modern England* (Cambridge, 2007). On the Restoration period see John Spurr, *England in the 1670s: 'This Masquerading Age'* (Oxford, 2000), pp. 102ff., and on this and the early eighteenth century see Roger D. Lund, *Ridicule, Religion and the Politics of Wit in Augustan England* (Farnham, 2012). For the relationship of this phenomenon to the Habermasian public sphere, see the comments in Hunter, *Scrupulosity and Science*, p. 236.

88. Boyle, *Works*, vol. 11, pp. 283, 294.

89. Glanvill, *A Blow*, p. 172; Samuel Clarke, *A Demonstration of the Being and Attributes of God* (London, 1705), p. 12.

90. Cudworth, *True Intellectual System*, 'To the Reader', sig. ***1.

91. John Harris, *Immorality and Pride, The Great Causes of Atheism* (London, 1698), pp. 8ff. He went on to take issue with Charles Blount.

92. Edwards, *Some Thoughts*, p. 129.

93. Wallis to Tenison, 30 November 1680, Bodleian Library, Oxford, MS Add D 105, fols 70–71. On Hobbes's influence see Samuel I. Mintz, *The Hunting of Leviathan: Seventeenth-century Reactions to the Materialism and Moral Philosophy of Thomas Hobbes* (Cambridge, 1962), esp. chapter 7; Jon Parkin, *Taming the Leviathan: The Reception of the Political and Religious Ideas of Thomas Hobbes in England 1640–1700* (Cambridge, 2007), esp. chapter 5.

94. *The Character of a Coffee-House, With the Symptomes of a Town-Wit* (London, 1673), p. 5.

95. Stuart Piggott, *William Stukeley: An Eighteenth-century Antiquary*, revised edn (London, 1985), p. 84; Molyneux to Locke, 27 May 1697, in E. S. de Beer (ed.), *The Correspondence*

*of John Locke*, 8 vols (1976–89), vol. 6, pp. 132–3. On Toland, see further Chapter 2, below.

96. On Rochester see especially Vivian de Sola Pinto, *Enthusiast in Wit: A Portrait of John Wilmot, Earl of Rochester 1647–80* (London, 1962). See also J. H. Wilson, *The Court Wits of the Restoration* (Princeton, 1948), chapter 2, and, more recently, J. W. Johnson, *A Profane Wit: The Life of John Wilmot, Earl of Rochester* (Rochester, 2004), and Matthew C. Augustine and Steven N. Zwicker (eds), *Lord Rochester in the Restoration World* (Cambridge, 2015). On Aikenhead, see Michael Hunter, ' "Aikenhead the Atheist": The Context and Consequences of Articulate Irreligion in the Late Seventeenth Century', in Hunter and Wootton (eds), *Atheism from the Reformation to the Enlightenment*, pp. 221–54, reprinted in Hunter, *Science and the Shape of Orthodoxy*, pp. 308–32, and Michael F. Graham, *The Blasphemies of Thomas Aikenhead: Boundaries of Belief on the Eve of the Enlightenment* (Edinburgh, 2008).

97. Bentley to Edward Bernard, 28 May 1692, in C. Wordsworth (ed.), *The Correspondence of Richard Bentley*, 2 vols (Cambridge, 1842), vol. 1, p. 39. Bentley's allusion may be to the view that Socrates had brought philosophy from heaven to earth, to which Addison alludes in a more positive manner in *The Spectator*, no. 10 (ed. D. F. Bond, 5 vols, Oxford, 1965, vol. 1, p. 44).

98. Phillip Harth, *Contexts of Dryden's Thought* (Chicago, 1968), p. 81; Robert E. Sullivan, *John Toland and the Deist Controversy: A Study in Adaptations* (Cambridge, MA, 1982), p. 211, referring to the views of T. E. Jessop.

99. Harth, *Contexts of Dryden's Thought*, pp. 82ff. More recently see Harold Love, *The Culture and Commerce of Texts: Scribal Publication in Seventeenth-century England* (Amherst, 1998).

100. Carlo Ginzburg, *The Cheese and the Worms: The Cosmos of a Sixteenth-century Miller* (English trans., London, 1980), p. 155 and passim.

101. See Clark, *Thinking with Demons*, especially Parts I and V. See also his earlier, seminal article, 'Inversion, Misrule and the Meaning of Witchcraft', *Past and Present*, 87 (1980), 98–127.

102. Boyle, *Works*, vol. 10, p. 439.

103. See John Marshall, 'The Ecclesiology of the Latitude-men 1660–1689: Stillingfleet, Tillotson and "Hobbism" ', *Journal of Ecclesiastical History*, 36 (1985), 407–27.

104. Harris, *Immorality and Pride*, p. 13. For an important study of upper class immorality and its implications, see Anna Bryson, *From Courtesy to Civility: Changing Codes of Conduct in Early Modern England* (Oxford, 1998), chapter 7.

105. See D.W.R. Bahlman, *The Moral Revolution of 1688* (New Haven, 1957) and T. C. Curtis and W. A. Speck, 'The Societies for the Reformation of Manners: A Case Study in the Theory and Practice of Moral Reform', *Literature and History*, 3 (1976), 45–64. For a recent appraisal, see Brent S. Sirota, *The Christian Monitors: The Church of England and the Age of Benevolence 1680–1730* (New Haven and London, 2014), esp. pp. 92ff.

106. Glanvill, *A Blow*, sigs B1v–2. Glanvill's opening '*There is NO GOD*' alludes to Psalms 14:1.

107. Boyle to Glanvill, 18 September 1677, in Boyle, *Correspondence*, vol. 4, p. 456; Richard Ward, *The Life of Henry More, Parts 1 and 2*, ed. Sarah Hutton et al. (Dordrecht, 2000), p. 247 and pp. 242ff., passim.

108. Edwards, *Some Thoughts*, pp. 100–101. For Scottish views, see above, n. 20. For Addison, see below, pp. 60–1.

109. Michael Hunter, 'The Witchcraft Controversy and the Nature of Free-Thought in Restoration England: John Wagstaffe's *The Question of Witchcraft Debated* (1669)', in Hunter, *Science and the Shape of Orthodoxy*, pp. 286–307, reprinted by permission of Boydell & Brewer Ltd. For other scholars' use of this essay, see Clark, *Thinking with Demons*, pp. 242, 598–600; Peter Elmer (ed.), *English Witchcraft 1560–1736, IV: The Post-Restoration Synthesis and its Opponents* (London, 2003), pp. xiff.; Barry, *Witchcraft and Demonology in South-West England*, esp. Conclusion.

110. Some of its content derives from 'The Decline of Magic: Challenge and Response in Early Enlightenment England' (based on the Roy Porter Memorial Lecture delivered at the Wellcome Library, 20 June 2011), *The Historical Journal*, 55 (2012), 399–425: © Cambridge

University Press; reprinted with permission. Other sections derive from a talk on 'The Deists and the Decline of Magic' given at the conference on 'Priestcraft: Early Modern Variations on Sacerdotal Imposture', organised by CRASSH at Cambridge on 1–2 September 2016, and at Newcastle University on 4 October 2017.

111. Originally published as 'The Royal Society and the Decline of Magic', *Notes & Records of the Royal Society* (2011), 65, 103–19 (doi: 10.1098/rsnr.2010.0086). This has been emended and expanded at various points, not least to include a summary of my more recent article, 'John Webster, the Royal Society and *The Displaying of Supposed Witchcraft* (1677)', *Notes & Records: The Royal Society Journal of the History of Science*, 71 (2017), 7–19.

112. This is a revised version of 'New Light on the "Drummer of Tedworth": Conflicting Narratives of Witchcraft in Restoration England', *Historical Research*, 78 (2005), 311–53. However, the texts printed on pp. 338–53 of that article are not here reprinted since readers can consult them for themselves in the relevant volume of *Historical Research* (and in some cases elsewhere too, as is indicated by Appendix I). Instead, slightly longer quotations are included from them in the main text than was the case with the original article, particularly in the description of the poltergeist that caused the furore in the first place, and the text has been reordered. It is perhaps worth noting that the final section of the chapter is hitherto unpublished and draws on an overlapping paper, 'The Role of Fraud in the Decline of Magic', which I delivered to audiences at various universities in 2011–12.

113. This chapter is based on the Dacre Lecture given at Oxford on 14 November 2014. Some use is made in it of the introductory material to my *Magic and Mental Disorder: Sir Hans Sloane's Memoir of John Beaumont* (Robert Boyle Project, 2011) (available online at http://www.bbk.ac.uk/boyle/media/pdf/magic_and_mental_disorder.pdf).

114. This is based on a talk given at the Second Sight and Prophecy Conference held at the University of Aberdeen, 14–16 June 2013. In addition, a few portions of the text derive from 'The Discovery of Second Sight in late Seventeenth-century Scotland', *History Today*, June 2001, 48–53. Also relevant is the introduction to my edited collection of texts, *The Occult Laboratory*.

### 1  JOHN WAGSTAFFE, WITCHCRAFT AND THE NATURE OF RESTORATION FREE-THOUGHT

1. See below, pp. 96–7.
2. For the quotation from Baxter see below, pp. 107–8.
3. Glanvill, *A Blow at Modern Sadducism*, 4th edn (London, 1668), pp. 166–7, 175–6 and 159–83, passim.
4. *The Character of a Coffee-House, With the Symptomes of a Town-Wit* (1673), p. 5. I am sceptical of claims that *The Character* is by Glanvill, based largely on its borrowings from *A Blow*: see Samuel A. Weiss, 'Joseph Glanvill and "The Character of a Coffee-House"', *Notes and Queries*, 197 (1952), 234–5, and Jackson I. Cope, *Joseph Glanvill, Anglican Apologist* (St Louis, 1956), p. 36 and n. 111.
5. Glanvill, *A Blow*, sig. B4; Reginald Scot, *The Discoverie of Witchcraft*, ed. Brinsley Nicholson (1886; reprinted East Ardsley, Yorks., 1973).
6. Hobbes, *Leviathan*, ed. Richard Tuck (Cambridge, 1996), pp. 440ff. On Hobbes and the witchcraft controversy see Samuel I. Mintz, *The Hunting of Leviathan: Seventeenth-century Reactions to the Materialism and Moral Philosophy of Thomas Hobbes* (Cambridge, 1962), pp. 102ff., and Ian Bostridge, *Witchcraft and its Transformations c. 1650–c. 1750* (Oxford, 1997), chapter 2.
7. L. B. Wright (ed.), *Advice to a Son; Precepts of Lord Burghley, Sir Walter Raleigh and Francis Osborne* (Ithaca, NY, 1962), pp. 107–8. On the complaints about Osborne's book see Andrew Clark (ed.), *The Life and Times of Anthony Wood*, 5 vols (Oxford, 1891–1900), vol. 1, p. 257. On Osborne see also S.E.A. Betz, 'Francis Osborne's *Advice to a Son*',

in Robert Shafer (ed.), *Seventeenth Century Studies, Second Series. By Members of the Graduate School, University of Cincinnati* (Princeton, 1937), pp. 1–67.

8. See Wallace Notestein, *A History of Witchcraft in England from 1558 to 1718* (1911; reprinted New York, 1968), chapter 12; Moody E. Prior, 'Joseph Glanvill, Witchcraft and Seventeenth-century Science', *Modern Philology*, 30 (1932–3), 167–93; Cope, *Joseph Glanvill*, chapter 4; Thomas H. Jobe, 'The Devil in Restoration Science: the Glanvill-Webster Witchcraft Debate', *Isis*, 72 (1981), 343–56; Charles Webster, *From Paracelsus to Newton: Magic and the Making of Modern Science* (Cambridge, 1982), chapter 4, esp. pp. 96–8; Peter Elmer, *The Library of Dr John Webster: the Making of a Seventeenth-century Radical* (*Medical History*, Supplement no. 6, London, 1986), pp. 7ff.; Allison Coudert, 'Henry More and Witchcraft', in Sarah Hutton (ed.), *Henry More (1614–87): Tercentenary Studies* (Dordrecht, 1990), pp. 115–36; and Lindsey Fitzharris, 'A Committed Helmontian: The Life and Works of Dr John Webster (1611–1682) after the Restoration' (Oxford Ph.D. thesis, 2009), chapter 5.

9. Jobe, 'Devil in Restoration Science', and see the comments in Elmer, *Library of Dr John Webster*, pp. 9–10; Coudert, 'Henry More and Witchcraft', pp. 117–18; and Fitzharris, 'Committed Helmontian', pp. 282ff. For Webster's Interregnum role see Introduction, n. 33.

10. Benjamin Camfield, *A Theological Discourse of Angels, and their Ministries* (London, 1678), pp. 169–70. See also ibid., 'Appendix', passim, and Glanvill, *Saducismus Triumphatus*, 3rd edn (London, 1689), esp. pp. 267ff.

11. John Webster, *The Displaying of Supposed Witchcraft* (London, 1677), sig. a1v; Glanvill, *Saducismus Triumphatus*, p. 54.

12. E.g. Webster, *From Paracelsus to Newton*, p. 96. For other references, see Notestein, *History of Witchcraft*, pp. 294–5; H. R. Trevor-Roper, *Religion, the Reformation and Social Change*, 2nd edn (London, 1972), p. 168; Keith Thomas, *Religion and the Decline of Magic* (London, 1971), pp. 509, 570, 578, 580, 646n.; B. J. Shapiro, *Probability and Certainty in Seventeenth-century England* (Princeton, 1983), pp. 217–18; Bostridge, *Witchcraft and its Transformations*, p. 69–70.

13. Glanvill, *Saducismus Triumphatus*, pp. 271, 273, 275, 276, 285, 291, 295, 304; but these references are trivialised by the concentration on Webster in pp. 267ff. as a whole.

14. See below, p. 44.

15. John Wagstaffe, *The Question of Witchcraft Debated*, 2nd edn (London, 1671), p. 144. I have used the 1671 edition throughout since, as explained below, it reprints the 1669 edition verbatim as well as adding new material.

16. Meric Casaubon, *Of Credulity and Incredulity; In things Divine & Spiritual* (London, 1670), p. 177. On Casaubon and witchcraft see Bostridge, *Witchcraft and its Transformations*, chapter 3.

17. Anthony Wood, *Athenae Oxonienses*, ed. P. Bliss, 4 vols (London, 1813–20), vol. 3, cols 1113–14. On Wagstaffe's gentle status see also below, p. 35. Further brief accounts of Wagstaffe will be found in *ODNB*, Joseph Foster, *Alumni Oxonienses 1500–1714*, 4 vols (Oxford, 1891–2), vol. 4, p. 1152, and Sir Michael McDonnell, *The Registers of St Paul's School, 1509–1748* (London, 1977), p. 198.

18. Wood, *Athenae Oxonienses*, vol. 3, col. 1114. For a recent discussion of *Sundry Things from Several Hands*, the pamphlet which in Wood's opinion Wagstaffe did not write, see Charles Webster, *The Great Instauration: Science, Medicine and Reform, 1626–1660*, 2nd edn (Bern and Oxford, 2002), pp. 175–8.

19. John Aubrey to Anthony Wood, 7 August 1680, Bodleian Library, Oxford, MS Wood F 39, fol. 343. That Wood had other sources of information is suggested by the fact that he added to the letter a note concerning Wagstaffe's place of death.

20. Joseph Glanvill, *Seasonable Reflections and Discourses In Order to the Conviction, & Cure of the Scoffing, & Infidelity Of a Degenerate Age* (London, 1676), pp. 5, 14.

21. Roger North, *General Preface and the Life of Dr John North*, ed. Peter Millard (Toronto, 1984), p. 111.

22. Ibid., p. 112, and see J. and J. A. Venn, *Alumni Cantabrigienses* [to 1751], 4 vols (Cambridge, 1922–7), vol. 1, p. 64, and G. E. Cokayne, *Complete Baronetage 1611–1714*, 6 vols (Exeter, 1900–1909), vol. 3, pp. 241–2.

23. Wagstaffe, *Question*, p. 121 (misleadingly placed commas in the original have been omitted). On the context of this comment, see below, p. 42.
24. *Britannia Rediviva* (Oxford, 1660), sig. Dlv.
25. Wagstaffe, *Question*, p. 152 and pp. 149–98. Wagstaffe explains that he had originally intended to translate the dialogue himself, before discovering that an English version – by More – already existed (p. 149): see below, p. 41. For views on Lucian, see below, n. 53.
26. Wood, *Athenae*, vol. 3, col. 1114; John Wagstaffe, *Historical Reflections on the Bishop of Rome* (Oxford, 1660), pp. 11, 15, 34, 38 and passim.
27. Wagstaffe, *Question*, pp. 54ff.
28. Ibid., pp. 1ff., 12, 55, 66, 89ff., 129, 135 and passim.
29. Casaubon, *Of Credulity*, p. 189.
30. R. T., *The Opinion of Witchcraft Vindicated. In an Answer to a Book Intituled the Question of Witchcraft Debated* (London, 1670), pp. 2, 6; cf. Casaubon, *Of Credulity*, p. 180.
31. Richard Bentley, *The Folly of Atheism, And (what is now called) Deism; Even with Respect to the Present Life . . . Being the First of the Lecture Founded by the Honourable Robert Boyle, Esquire* (London, 1692), p. 4.
32. Wagstaffe, *Question*, pp. 120, 147–8 and passim ('trifle' is misspelt 'triffle' in this edition).
33. Wagstaffe, *Historical Reflections*, pp. 6, 26; Wagstaffe, *Question*, pp. 51, 152 (due to a misprint, 'a' and 'and' are transposed three words from the end of the sentence).
34. Ibid., p. 95; Wagstaffe, *Historical Reflections*, pp. 18–19.
35. Wagstaffe, *Question*, title page, p. 44 and passim.
36. Ibid., p. 130.
37. Ibid. sig. A6; Michael Hunter, *John Aubrey and the Realm of Learning* (London, 1975), p. 169 and n., and see also Kelsey Jackson Williams, *The Antiquary: John Aubrey's Historical Scholarship* (Oxford, 2016), chapter 5.
38. Wagstaffe, *Question*, pp. 144–5.
39. Ibid., p. 64. On the earlier literature on witchcraft see above, p. 35, and Introduction, pp. 4–6.
40. Wagstaffe, *Question*, pp. 21, 25, 52.
41. Ibid., pp. 87ff., 115ff., 121–2, 146.
42. Ibid, pp. 54ff., 65ff. and 125ff.
43. Glanvill, *Seasonable Reflections*, pp. 6–7. In the anti-witchcraft literature, the nearest precedent is perhaps to be found in Reginald Scot's virulent anti-Catholicism, which sometimes verges on hostility to priestcraft as a whole: see Scot, *Discoverie of Witchcraft*, passim.
44. Wagstaffe, *Question*, pp. 125ff.
45. Ibid., pp. 1–2, 43–4, 120.
46. Ibid., pp. 35, 133–5, 137, 140 and 125ff., passim.
47. Ibid., pp. 125–6.
48. Ibid., pp. 112–13.
49. Ibid., pp. 85–6; R. T., *Opinion*, p. 47.
50. See David Wootton, *Paolo Sarpi: Between Renaissance and Enlightenment* (Cambridge, 1983); David Berman, 'Anthony Collins and the Question of Atheism in the Early Eighteenth Century', *Proceedings of the Royal Irish Academy*, 75, sect. C (1975), 85–102, reprinted in his *A History of Atheism in Britain: From Hobbes to Russell* (London, 1988), chapter 3. For more general discussion of this issue, see David Wootton, 'New Histories of Atheism', and David Berman, 'Disclaimers as Offence Mechanisms in Charles Blount and John Toland', in Michael Hunter and David Wootton (eds), *Atheism from the Reformation to the Enlightenment* (Oxford, 1992), pp. 13–53 (esp. pp. 32ff.) and 255–72.
51. Casaubon, *Of Credulity*, p. 183 (in the original, 'not' is accidentally included after 'must').
52. Wagstaffe, *Question*, sigs A2–3. For a comment on the imputation of polytheism, see Glanvill, *Saducismus Triumphatus*, p. 285.
53. Wagstaffe, *Question*, p. 151. See Christopher Robinson, 'The Reputation of Lucian in Sixteenth-century France', *French Studies*, 29 (1975), 387–94, and, for an example of English views, e.g. Samuel Clarke, *A Mirrour or Looking-Glasse both for Saints, and*

*Sinners*, 2nd edn (London, 1654), p. 181. For translators see Francis Hickes, *Certaine Select Dialogues of Lucian* (Oxford, 1634), sig. B3; Jasper Mayne, *Part of Lucian made English from the Original* (Oxford, 1664), sigs A5v–6.

54. Wagstaffe, *Question*, pp. 151–2.
55. Glanvill, *Seasonable Reflections*, p. 17. For Blount and Toland, see Berman, 'Disclaimers as Offence Mechanisms'.
56. Wagstaffe, *Question*, pp. 111ff., 122–3, and see above, p. 34. On the Tedworth case see Glanvill, *A Blow*, pp. 113ff. and below, Chapter 4.
57. Wagstaffe, *Question*, p. 113. See Glanvill, *A Blow*, pp. 176–7; Casaubon, *Of Credulity*, pp. 170–1, 191.
58. Wagstaffe, *Question*, pp. 12–13. Cf. ibid., pp. 24, 51–2.
59. Ibid., pp. 104–5.
60. Ibid., pp. 84–5, 104. For Scot see his *Discoverie of Witchcraft*.
61. Wagstaffe, *Question*, sig. A3, pp. 142, 146–7.
62. Ibid., p. 143 ('Policies' is misspelt 'Polices' in this edition).
63. R. T., *Opinion*, p. 63 and passim; Casaubon, *Of Credulity*, pp. 177ff. For a commentary on the debate see [Thomas Ady], *The Doctrine of Devils, proved to be the grand Apostacy of these later Times* (London, 1676), pp. 157ff.
64. Wagstaffe, *Question*, sig. A3, pp. 144ff. and passim; Bodleian Library shelfmark 8° P 248 Th.
65. Wagstaffe, *Question*, pp. 48, 103.
66. Ibid., pp. 21ff., 65ff., 137ff.
67. R. T., *Opinion*, pp. 56–7, 62.
68. Casaubon, *Of Credulity*, pp. 182, 184ff.
69. R. T., *Opinion*, pp. 3, 8–9, 43–4, 53–4, 58–9; Casaubon, *Of Credulity*, pp. 178–9.
70. R. T., *Opinion*, pp. 15, 19–20. Cf. Wagstaffe, *Question*, pp. 119–20.
71. See above, Introduction. For a statement of an almost uncannily similar view to that expressed above, which I discovered only after writing it, see W.E.H. Lecky, *History of the Rise and Influence of the Spirit of Rationalism in Europe*, 2nd edn, 2 vols (London, 1865), vol. 1, pp. 9–13. Cf. ibid., pp. 118–20. The sophistication of Lecky's historical analysis is often underrated by those who refer to him without ever having read him.
72. Wagstaffe, *Historical Reflections*, p. 27.
73. For the Wenham case, see below, pp. 63–4; *The Protestant Post-Boy*, issues 92–6 (1–12 April 1712). For *The Impossibility of Witchcraft* (London, 1712), and its 2nd edition see *ESTC* T71989, N733; the sequel, *The Impossibility of Witchcraft Further Demonstrated* (London, 1712), largely comprises the same dialogue by Lucian that Wagstaffe appended to his work. It is perhaps worth noting that the variant version of the 1st edition of *The Impossibility of Witchcraft* that appears on *ECCO*, a copy held by the Houghton Library, Harvard (*ESTC* N16847), is almost certainly a hybrid combining the 1st edition title page (which has been detached and reinstated in this copy at some point) with the 2nd edition text, including exactly the same errors of pagination, etc. I am grateful to John Overholt for his help in this matter. On the authorship of this version, see Phyllis Guskin, 'The Context of Witchcraft: The Case of Jane Wenham (1712)', *Eighteenth-century Studies*, 15 (1981), 48–71, on p. 66n., citing Francis Bragge, *The Witch of Walkern* (London, 1712), sig. A3v (this concerns *The Impossibility of Witchcraft Further Demonstrated*, but since that clearly states on its title page that it was 'By the Author of the Impossibility of Witchcraft, &c.', the same conclusion can be applied to that). On Pittis see T. F. M. Newton, 'William Pittis and Queen Anne Journalism', *Modern Philology*, 33 (1935–6), 169–86, 279–302. Guskin provides a full account of the Wenham case and the controversy over it.
74. See *A Discourse on Witchcraft. Occasioned by a Bill now Depending in Parliament* (London, 1736).
75. For citations of the 1736 reprint without any recognition of Wagstaffe's authorship, see Roy Porter, *Enlightenment: Britain and the Creation of the Modern World* (London, 2000), p. 223; Malcolm Gaskill, *Crime and Mentalities in Early Modern England* (Cambridge, 2000), p. 96, n. 69. For citations of the 1712 reprint which fail to acknowledge its debt to

Wagstaffe, see ibid., p. 96, n. 67; James Sharpe, *Instruments of Darkness: Witchcraft in England 1550–1750* (London, 1996), pp. 343 (n. 29) and 349; and Bostridge, *Witchcraft and its Transformations*, p. 132, n. 65 and p. 135, n. 79. Paul K. Monod, *Solomon's Secret Arts: The Occult in the Age of Enlightenment* (New Haven and London, 2013), p. 203, correctly attributes the 1736 reprint but his account of the 1712 book on p. 153 implies that it was less fully derived from Wagstaffe than is in fact the case.

76. It is also worth noting that in 1711 a German translation of Wagstaffe's book was published at Halle, where a translation of Webster's *Displaying of Supposed Witchcraft* was to come out in 1719. Halle was a centre of controversy on such subjects following the publication of Christian Thomasius's *De crimine magiae* (1701): see Trevor-Roper, *Religion, the Reformation and Social Change*, p. 175n.

77. Thomas, *Religion and the Decline of Magic*, p. 580.

78. Mark Goldie, 'Priestcraft and the Birth of Whiggism', in Nicholas Phillipson and Quentin Skinner (eds), *Political Discourse in Early Modern England* (Cambridge, 1993), pp. 209–31, esp. pp. 216, 218, 219–20.

79. See S. P. Lamprecht, 'Hobbes and Hobbism', *American Political Science Review*, 34 (1940), 31–53, esp. pp. 32–3; Mintz, *Hunting of Leviathan*, passim; Berman, *History of Atheism*, chapter 2; Jon Parkin, *Taming the Leviathan: The Reception of the Political and Religious Ideas of Thomas Hobbes in England 1640–1700* (Cambridge, 2007).

## 2 FROM THE DEISTS TO FRANCIS HUTCHINSON

1. On this facet of Deism see esp. Frank E. Manuel, *The Eighteenth Century Confronts the Gods* (1959; reprinted New York, 1967), chapter 2, and 'Deists on True and False Gods', in Manuel, *The Changing of the Gods* (Hanover, NH, 1983), pp. 27–51. For a valuable recent study see Sarah Ellenzweig, *The Fringes of Belief: English Literature, Ancient Heresy, and the Politics of Freethinking, 1660–1760* (Stanford, 2008).

2. [Anthony Collins], *A Discourse of Free-thinking, Occasion'd by the Rise and Growth of a Sect call'd Free-thinkers* (London, 1713), pp. 27ff.

3. Maximillian E. Novak, 'Defoe, the Occult, and the Deist Offensive during the Reign of George I', in J. A. Leo Lemay (ed.), *Deism, Masonry, and the Enlightenment* (Newark, 1987), pp. 93–108. See also his *Daniel Defoe: Master of Fictions* (Oxford, 2001), pp. 653ff., and Rodney M. Baine, *Defoe and the Supernatural* (Athens, GA, 1968*)*.

4. [Robert Wightman], *Specimen of Peculiar Thoughts upon Sublime, Abstruse and Delicate Subjects* (London, 1738), p. 20.

5. ['A Physician in *Hertfordshire*'], *A Full Confutation of Witchcraft: More Particularly of the Depositions against Jane Wenham* (London, 1712), p. 4. For a different reading of this passage, which associates it with Whiggism, see Ian Bostridge, *Witchcraft and its Transformations c. 1650–c. 1750* (Oxford, 1997), pp. 134–5. However, this is characteristic of the manner in which that book ignores the free-thinking tradition on which emphasis is laid here: see below, pp. 174–5.

6. For helpful recent discussion, see Wayne Hudson, Diego Lucci and J. R. Wigelsworth, 'Introduction: Atheism and Deism Revived', and Wayne Hudson, 'Atheism and Deism Demythologized', in Hudson, Lucci and Wigelsworth (eds), *Atheism and Deism Revalued: Heterodox Religious Identities in Britain, 1650–1800* (Farnham, 2014), pp. 1–11, 13–23. See also the March 2018 special issue of *Intellectual History Review*, 28 (2018), 1–224, devoted to 'Priestcraft: Early Modern Variations on the Theme of Sacerdotal Imposture'.

7. Here the classic study is J.G.A. Pocock, *The Machiavellian Moment: Florentine Political Thought and the Atlantic Republican Tradition* (Princeton, 1975).

8. On priestcraft and anti-popery see Mark Goldie, 'Priestcraft and the Birth of Whiggism', in Nicholas Phillipson and Quentin Skinner (eds), *Political Discourse in Early Modern England* (Cambridge, 1993), pp. 209–31, and his 'Ideology', in Terence Ball, James Farr and Russell L. Hanson (eds), *Political Innovation and Conceptual Change* (Cambridge, 1989), pp. 266–91. On More and Casaubon and 'enthusiasm' see above, p. 8.

9. See the telling comments in Kristine Haugen, *Richard Bentley: Poetry and Enlightenment* (Cambridge, MA, 2011), pp. 195ff. (much of it overlapping with her 'Transformations of the Trinity Doctrine in English Scholarship: From the History of Beliefs to the History of Texts', *Archiv für Religionsgeschichte*, 3 (2001), 149–68). For the seventeenth-century background, see Dmitri Levitin, *Ancient Wisdom in the Age of the New Science: Histories of Philosophy in England, c. 1640–1700* (Cambridge, 2015), pp. 447–8 and passim.

10. Phileleutherus Lipsiensis, *Remarks upon a Late Discourse of Free-Thinking* (London, 1713), pp. 63ff. See further below, pp. 80–1.

11. Haugen, *Richard Bentley*, p. 196.

12. See Winfried Schröder, 'The Charge of Religious Imposture in Late Antique Anti-Christian Authors and their Early Modern Readers', *Intellectual History Review*, 28 (2018), 23–34, and Sundar Henny, 'Caught in the Crossfire of Early Modern Controversy: Strabo on Moses and his Corrupt Successors', ibid., pp. 35–59. See also Justin Champion, *Republican Learning: John Toland and the Crisis of Christian Culture, 1696–1722* (Manchester, 2003), esp. part 3.

13. On Van Dale see Anthony Ossa-Richardson, *The Devil's Tabernacle: The Pagan Oracles in Early Modern Thought* (Princeton, 2013), esp. chapter 4. On his influence on Fontenelle and Bekker see also Jonathan Israel, *Radical Enlightenment: Philosophy and the Making of Modernity, 1650–1750* (Oxford, 2001), chapters 20–1. He is cited, for instance, by Toland in *Letters to Serena* (London, 1704), sigs c1–2 and p. 106, and in *Adeisidaemon & Origines Judaicae* (Hagae Comitis, 1709), p. 41. See also below, p. 58.

14. Charles Blount, *Anima Mundi* (London, 1679), pp. 37–8 and passim; see also *Religio Laici* (London, 1683), e.g. p. 41 for sceptical remarks on John Dee and Edward Kelly. On Blount see J.A.I. Champion, *The Pillars of Priestcraft Shaken: The Church of England and its Enemies, 1660–1730* (Cambridge, 1992), pp. 140ff.; Wayne Hudson, *The English Deists: Studies in Early Enlightenment* (London, 2009), chapter 4.

15. Blount (ed. and trans.), *The Two First Books of Philostratus, Concerning the Life of Apollonius Tyaneus* (London, 1680), pp. 3, 32–3 and passim.

16. Ibid., pp. 28–9, citing *Leviathan*, chapter 2.

17. [Charles Blount], *Miracles No Violations of the Laws of Nature* (London, 1683). For Boyle's views on such subjects, see Michael Hunter, *Boyle Studies: Aspects of the Life and Thought of Robert Boyle* (Farnham, 2015), pp. 121, 166–7, and above, Introduction, n. 27. For his response to a 'Deist' who might be Blount see ibid., p. 183, and *The Works of Robert Boyle*, ed. Michael Hunter and Edward B. Davis, 14 vols (London, 1999–2000), vol. 10, pp. lviii–lxi.

18. Philip McGuinness, Alan Harrison and Richard Kearney (eds), *John Toland's Christianity not Mysterious* (Dublin, 1997), pp. 88–91. For perhaps the best accounts of Toland's thought see Robert E. Sullivan, *John Toland and the Deist Controversy: A Study in Adaptations* (Cambridge, MA, 1982) and Champion, *Republican Learning*.

19. Toland, *Letters to Serena*, pp. 4–6, 106–7 and passim. It is perhaps also worth noting that in the synopsis for his unpublished *Christopaedia*, Toland included the allegation that Christ wrote a treatise on magic: BL Add MS 4295, fols 69–70; this volume also includes synopses for works on priestcraft, superstition and related topics. See also the important recent work of Katherine A. East: '*Superstitionis Malleus*: John Toland, Cicero and the War on Priestcraft in Early Enlightenment England', *History of European Ideas*, 40 (2014), 965–83, and *The Radicalisation of Cicero: John Toland and Strategic Editing in the Early Enlightenment* (Basingstoke, 2017).

20. Toland, *Adeisidaemon*, p. 31 and passim. For an English translation, see John Rylands Library, Manchester, 3 f.38: I am grateful to Justin Champion for allowing me to consult the transcript of this made by him and Tristan Dagron. It is cited here by folio reference, in this case fol. 36v.

21. Shaftesbury, *Characteristicks of Men, Manners, Opinions, Times*, ed. Lawrence E. Klein (Cambridge, 1999), pp. 23–4, 40–2, 354ff. and passim. This edition unfortunately omits the vignettes, first included in the second edition of 1714. On these, see Felix Paknadel, 'Shaftesbury's Illustrations of *Characteristics*', *Journal of the Warburg and Courtauld*

*Institutes*, 37 (1974), 290–312, and Justin Champion, 'Decoding the *Leviathan*: Doing the History of Ideas through Images, 1650–1714', in Michael Hunter (ed.), *Printed Images in Early Modern Britain: Essays in Interpretation* (Farnham, 2010), pp. 255–75, on pp. 268–72.

22. Shaftesbury, *Characteristicks*, p. 68.

23. Ibid., pp. 5–6; for Fowler's response see his *Reflections upon a Letter Concerning Enthusiasm, To my Lord \*\*\*\*\** (London, 1709).

24. See Glanvill, *Saducismus Triumphatus*, 3rd edn (London, 1689), pp. 413ff. Moses Pitt's *Account of one Ann Jefferies* (1696) was dedicated to Fowler and published at his behest: see Jane Shaw, *Miracles in Enlightenment England* (New Haven and London, 2006), pp. 147ff., and Peter Marshall, 'Ann Jeffries and the Fairies: Folk Belief and the War on Scepticism in Later Stuart England', in Angela McShane and Garthine Walker (eds), *The Extraordinary and the Everyday in Early Modern England* (Basingstoke, 2010), pp. 127–41. For further evidence of Fowler's interest in material of this kind see Peter Elmer, *The Miraculous Conformist: Valentine Greatrakes, the Body Politic, and the Politics of Healing in Restoration Britain* (Oxford, 2013), pp. 139–40, and Elmer, *Witchcraft, Witch-Hunting, and Politics in Early Modern England* (Oxford, 2016), pp. 219–21, 285–6. For the letter to him dated 4 September 1703 about the case of Thomas Perks, of which various copies survive, see Jonathan Barry, *Raising Spirits: How a Conjurer's Tale was Transmitted across the Enlightenment* (Basingstoke, 2013), pp. 3, 26–31 and passim.

25. See Champion, *Pillars of Priestcraft Shaken*, esp. pp. 22–3, 135 and 160–61.

26. John Trenchard, *The Natural History of Superstition* (London, 1709), pp. 10–11, 20, 35 and passim. For an Italian edition with commentary see Paola Zanardi, *John Trenchard (1662–1723), Storia naturale della religione. Testo e contesto* (Ferrara, 1993). See further below, pp. 123–4.

27. John Trenchard and Thomas Gordon, *Cato's Letters, or Essays on Liberty, Civil and Religious, and other Important Subjects*, ed. Ronald Hamowy, 2 vols (Indianapolis, 1995), vol. 2, pp. 562, 575, 581–2 and 562ff., 842ff., passim. On Trenchard and Gordon, see Marie P. McMahon, *The Radical Whigs, John Trenchard and Thomas Gordon: Libertarian Loyalists to the New House of Hanover* (Lanham, MD, 1990).

28. *The Independent Whig*, no. 52 (31 December 1720); [Thomas Gordon], *The Humourist* (London, 1720), p. 70 and pp. 66ff., 78ff., and 202ff., passim.

29. See Michael Hunter, *The Occult Laboratory: Magic, Science and Second Sight in Late Seventeenth-century Scotland* (Woodbridge, 2001), pp. 29–31, and Justin Champion, 'Enlightened Erudition and the Politics of Reading in John Toland's Circle', *Historical Journal*, 49 (2006), 111–41.

30. See the copy of Martin's *A Description of the Western Islands of Scotland*, 2nd edn (London, 1716) in the British Library, C.45.c.1, Molesworth's annotations to pp. 309, 312, 315.

31. Ibid., p. 305.

32. Ibid., pp. 313, 334.

33. Ibid., p. 313.

34. Ibid., pp. 321, 335.

35. 9 George II, c. 5 (1736), printed in Danby Pickering (ed.), *The Statutes at Large . . . to 1761*, 24 vols (Cambridge, 1762–9), vol. 17, pp. 3–4. On the statute and its background see Owen Davies, 'Decriminalising the Witch: The Origin of and Response to the 1736 Witchcraft Act', in John Newton and Jo Bath (eds), *Witchcraft and the Act of 1604* (Leiden, 2008), pp. 207–32.

36. Martin, *Description*, p. 303. He added: 'the Royal Society were much to blame to admit such a person among them as a Philosopher, who was the farthest from that Character that coud possibly be. *Nullius in Verba* was no Motto for him'.

37. The 21 August encounter is cited in Hunter, *Occult Laboratory*, p. 29, and from there in Marshall, 'Ann Jeffries and the Fairies', p. 136. It is also cited in Stephen Snobelen, 'Lust, Pride, and Ambition: Isaac Newton and the Devil', in James E. Force and Sarah Hutton (eds), *Newton and Newtonianism: New Studies* (Dordrecht, 2004), pp. 155–81, on p. 173.

38. Ralph Thoresby, *Diary*, ed. Joseph Hunter, 2 vols (London, 1830), vol. 2, p. 159.

39. Ibid., vol. 2, pp. 118–19.
40. They now comprise BL Harleian MSS 6468–78. Most are commonplace books comprising notes on classical antiquities from authors like J. G. Graevius, J. A. Gronovius, G. J. Vossius and Jacob Perizon, interspersed by more miscellaneous material, but Harleian 6478 comprises 'Epigrammata Graeca' (it is so lettered on the spine). See also below, nn. 44–5, 47. On the edition of Dio see Thomas Hearne, *Remarks and Collections*, ed. C. E. Doble, D. W. Rannie and H. E. Salter, 11 vols (Oxford, 1885–1921), esp. vol. 1, pp. 97, 222; vol. 2, pp. 8, 11–12, 101; vol. 3, p. 41; vol. 7, p. 303; vol. 10, p. 91; Bodleian Library, Oxford, Rawl. Lett. 8, fols 316, 320; and Oddy to Henry Sike, 20 June [no year], in Trinity College, Cambridge, MS R.4.41, item 3. For Oddy's plans to publish a collection of Greek epigrams see Hearne, *Remarks and Collections*, vol. 3, p. 470; vol. 7, p. 303; vol. 8, p. 56. On Oddy and Bentley see esp. Rawl. Lett. 8, fols 314–15, 316. I am indebted to Kristine Haugen for her advice on Oddy.
41. Hearne, *Remarks and Collections*, vol. 1, pp. 222–3 and passim. Rawl. Lett. 8, fols 306–20 (letters to Hearne, [10] April 1708 to 5 December 1714 and n.d., some of them summarised in Hearne, *Remarks and Collections*); 15–16, fols 320–21 (letter to Hearne, 12 January 1709), and 108, fols 115–20 (letters to Samuel Gale, 15 July, 30 September 1714).
42. Rawl. Lett. 8, fol. 309, printed in Hearne, *Remarks and Collections*, vol. 2, p. 101. Cf. ibid., vol. 4, p. 403; Rawl. Lett. 8, fols 310, 312.
43. Hearne, *Remarks and Collections*, vol. 3, p. 370. Cf. ibid., vol. 1, pp. 222–3. A hint of the vestiges of a religiosity not unlike Thoresby's, to which we will be coming shortly, appears in a rather affecting account that Oddy gave Hearne of an episode when 'scoundrels' made a 'shipwrack of my Papers' in February 1712: Rawl. Lett. 8, fol. 316.
44. For the episode when Oddy seemed sympathetic to the favourable view of the Koran of Henry Sike, the German orientalist who was Regius Professor of Hebrew at Cambridge, and for Sike's later suicide, which Hearne associated with his 'Latitudinarian, and indifferent Principles', see Hearne, *Remarks and Collections,* vol. 3, p. 368. See also ibid., vol. 11, pp. 313–14. For Oddy's suicide, see ibid., vol. 3, p. 370; vol. 7, p. 303; vol. 11, p. 314. Thoresby, too, was aware of Oddy's manner of death, making what was evidently a retrospective addition to his note on his dramatic encounter with him in the diary, 'after felo de se': see York Minster MS Add 21, p. 34 (this is an almost illegible note at the end of the entry concerning 13 June, as in Thoresby, *Diary*, vol. 2, p. 119). At the end of Harleian MS 6469 are some verses concerning death by Dryden which possibly throw light on his suicide (fols 62–3). On the libertarian overtones of suicide, see S. E. Sprott, *The English Debate on Suicide From Donne to Hume* (La Salle, IL, 1961), chapter 4, and Michael MacDonald and Terence R. Murphy, *Sleepless Souls: Suicide in Early Modern England* (Oxford, 1990), chapter 5.
45. See the MSS cited in n. 40, esp. MS 6468, fols 113ff. (notes from John Gregory); MS 6470, fols 33ff. (extracts from G. F. Gemelli Careri); MS 6471, fols 16ff. (notes from Van Dale); MS 6475, fols 30ff. (extracts from Dryden's verse, with special attention to his sceptical and anti-clerical opinions).
46. See above, p. 51.
47. See BL Harleian MS 6470, fols 6ff. See also the notes from John Harris's *Lexicon Technicum* (1704), which include topics like gravity, infinite space and Newton's three laws of motion, in Harleian MS 6473, fols 155ff. For Pufendorf see Harleian MS 6473, fols 161ff. Note also Oddy's support for the Hanoverian succession: see Rawl. Lett. 8, fol. 210, quoted in Hearne, *Remarks and Collections*, vol. 4, p. 404.
48. Rawl. Lett. 8, fol. 306 (quoted in Hearne, *Remarks and Collections*, vol. 2, p. 163), Rawl. Lett. 15–16, fol. 320 (partly cited in ibid., vol. 2, p. 166).
49. The Thoresby–Toland letter survives only in *A Collection of Several Pieces of Mr John Toland*, 2 vols (London, 1726), vol. 2, pp. 439–40. For the letter to which it responds see ibid., pp. 436–8 (from which it is reprinted with Thoresby's reply in T. D. Whitaker's edition of the *Ducatus* (Leeds and Wakefield, 1816), pp. xvi–xvii, and from there in D. H. Atkinson, *Ralph Thoresby, the Topographer; his Town and Times*, 2 vols (Leeds, 1885–7),

vol. 2, pp. 270–2; a slightly different version survives in Yorkshire Archaeological Society, Leeds (hereinafter YAS) MS 9 (I am grateful to Peter Meredith for his help in this connection). This exchange is not noted in accounts of Toland such as Sullivan, *Toland and the Deist Controversy*, or Champion, *Republican Learning*.

50. Thoresby continued: 'he shewed me several original letters from eminent prelates to himself, soft and mild, which if writ with more freedome and authority would in my poor opinion have conduced more to his reduction, considering the use he made of them in his conversation with me': see *Ralph Thoresby's Review of His Life, 1658–1714*, ed. Peter Meredith (Leeds, 2015), p. 211 (from YAS MS 26, p. 249); the equivalent passage in the diary is: 'met with Mr Whiston, a learned person, but wretchedly heterodox': Thoresby, *Diary*, vol. 2, p. 158. For Thoresby and autograph collecting see A.N.L. Munby, *The Cult of the Autograph Letter in England* (London, 1962), p. 3. For Whiston's career, see James E. Force, *William Whiston, Honest Newtonian* (Cambridge, 1985); for his views on supernatural phenomena see below, p. 142.

51. Thoresby, *Review*, p. 205 (from YAS MS 26, p. 243). The passage in Thoresby, *Diary*, vol. 2, pp. 102–3, is as follows: 'after dinner I repeated to his lordship, from the original papers, what I had in general told of before, which were so agreeable that his lordship earnestly desired me to publish them in the Appendix, and gave it me under his hand, that he thought it might be of good use to convince the sceptical in an infidel age'. It is perhaps worth noting that this work is not to be confused with the Appendix, 'Of unusual *Accidents* that have attended some *Persons*', in *Ducatus Leodiensis* (London, 1715), pp. 601ff.

52. See, for example, Wesley as quoted in Michael MacDonald, 'Religion, Social Change, and Psychological Healing in England, 1600–1800', *Studies in Church History*, 19 (1982), 101–25, on p. 111. See also above, pp. 5, 11.

53. This is the wording in the *Review*, pp. 205–6: for that in the diary, see n. 51 (it is here that he refers to the gift of narratives). In the *Review*, Thoresby goes on: 'se his letter to me before my collections of that nature, since drawn up' (see also Thoresby's index to his letters in YAS MS 18, p. 33, which gives the date of the letter as 26 May 1712, thus tallying with the date of the diary entry concerning this encounter: this means, incidentally, that the decision to commence the work preceded the encounters of 13 June and 21 August).

54. See YAS MS 17, pp. 41–2 (Turner, with notes on pp. 16 and 42 from the additions to Turner by Jonathan Priestley, Heywood's trustee; on Turner's book and its background see William E. Burns, *An Age of Wonders: Prodigies, Politics and Providence in England 1657–1727* (Manchester, 2002), pp. 132ff.); BL Add MS 4460, fols 18v–24 (Heywood; cf. J. Horsfall Turner (ed.), *The Rev. Oliver Heywood, BA, 1630–1702: His Autobiography, Diaries, Anecdote and Event Books*, 4 vols (Brighouse and Bingley, 1882–5)) and 40v–80 (Sampson, including fol. 54 for Fowler). See also Thoresby, *Ducatus Leodiensis*, pp. 535, 537, 542 and 601ff. (which has various citations of these MSS). As far as Thoresby's collection is concerned, I have searched for it without success in the main repositories of Thoresby's manuscripts, the Yorkshire Archaeological Society at Leeds, the Cornwall Record Office and the British Library, and in other scattered locations. However, I hope that it may one day come to light. I am grateful to David Wykes and Laura Sangha for their advice in this connection.

55. See Peter Meredith, 'From Grand Design to Scribbled Note: Ralph Thoresby's Presence in the Society's Library', in Ann Alexander and David Thornton (eds), *A Celebration of Ralph Thoresby: The Thoresby Society's Ducatus Tercentenary Volume 1* (Leeds, 2015), pp. 151–81, on pp. 169–70, citing Thoresby Society, Leeds, MS Box SD 9, items c (1–2), d, e, f, g, i, j and k (Peter Meredith kindly informs me that the correct reference is SD 9, not SD 2, as there stated; cf. the 'Appendix' to the same volume, p. 208). See also below, chapter 3, n. 20.

56. See D. L. Wykes, 'Dissenters and the Writing of History: Ralph Thoresby's "Lives and Characters"', in Jason McElligott (ed.), *Fear, Exclusion and Revolution: Roger Morrice and Britain in the 1680s* (Farnham, 2006), pp. 174–88; Elspeth Findlay, 'Ralph Thoresby the

Diarist: the late Seventeenth-century Pious Diary and its Demise', *The Seventeenth Century*, 17 (2002), 108–30; and Laura Sangha, 'Ralph Thoresby and Individual Devotion in Late Seventeenth and Early Eighteenth-century England', *Historical Research*, 92 (2019), 139–59.

57. A. C. Guthkelch (ed.), *The Miscellaneous Works of Joseph Addison*, 2 vols (London, 1914), vol. 1, pp. 423–90; see also W.E.A. Axon, 'The Literary History of the Comedy of "The Drummer"', *Manchester Quarterly*, 14 (1895), 172–81, and Donald C. Baker, 'Witchcraft, Addison and *The Drummer*', *Studia Neophilologica*, 31 (1959), 174–81.

58. *The Spectator*, ed. D. F. Bond, 5 vols (Oxford, 1965), vol. 1, pp. 479–82 (no. 117), on pp. 479, 480. For an elaborate commentary on this passage in the context of the 'political' thrust of his book, see Bostridge, *Witchcraft and its Transformations*, pp. 128ff.

59. See *The Spectator*, vol. 3, pp. 535–82 (nos. 411–21), esp. pp. 570–73 (no. 419). See also below, pp. 163ff., 178.

60. Guthkelch, *Miscellaneous Works of Addison*, vol. 1, pp. 441–2, 474.

61. *The Protestant Post-Boy*, no. 94 (5–8 April 1712). The quotation, from Horace, *Epistles*, ii.2, 208–9, is as used in *The Spectator*, no. 7 (vol. 1, p. 31): see next note. In fact, the author wrongly cites Addison's views on witchcraft as appearing in no. 110 of *The Spectator*, in which Addison dealt with apparitions (*Spectator*, vol. 1, pp. 453–6), rather than no. 117 (pp. 479–82), where they actually appear, his confusion evidently being due to the fact that Addison took a similar line in both, as he did in the few other cases where comparable phenomena are dealt with, e.g. vol. 4, pp. 291–4, 364–9 (nos. 505, 524), vol. 5, pp. 64–7 (no. 604). For the authorship of the articles in *The Protestant Post-Boy*, and of the pamphlet, *The Impossibility of Witchcraft*, which stemmed from them, see above, chapter 1, n. 73. It is perhaps worth noting here that if the Tory Pittis was indeed the author, it further weakens the association of sadducism with Whiggism, as does the fact that a comment to the editors of the journal suggests that the devotion of four successive issues to sadducist sentiments was unpopular with the journal's predominantly Whig readership, implying that this was a personal hobby horse on Pittis's part: see Phyllis Guskin, 'The "Protestant Post-boy" and "An Elegy on the Death of Pamphlets"', *Notes and Queries*, 223 (1978), 40–41.

62. *The Spectator*, vol. 1, pp. 31–5 (no. 7), on pp. 33, 34; interestingly, an editorial note points out the element of overlap with Trenchard's *Natural History of Superstition*.

63. Hutchinson to Sloane, 4 February 1707, 3 April 1712, BL Sloane MS 4040, fol. 302, Sloane MS 4043, fol. 38. I should note that I am sceptical concerning Mark Knights's suggestion that Hutchinson was the author of *The Case of the Hertfordshire Witchcraft Consider'd* (London, 1712): see Mark Knights, *The Devil in Disguise: Deception, Delusion, and Fanaticism in the Early English Enlightenment* (Oxford, 2011), pp. 238 and 266 n. 92. From Hutchinson's 1712 letter to Sloane it is clear that it was an existing work that he thought might be appropriate for publication in this context, which he explicitly described as 'some historical Collections & Observations I had made upon this Subject', whereas *The Case* is a detailed discussion of the Wenham case in which medical arguments are prominent and historical ones hardly appear.

64. MS Sloane 4040, fol. 302. For the 'studied evasion' in Archbishop Tenison's reported response, see the quotation in Bostridge, *Witchcraft and its Transformations*, pp. 34–5 and n. On Hutchinson and the Union see Andrew Sneddon, *Witchcraft and Whigs: The Life of Bishop Francis Hutchinson, 1660–1739* (Manchester, 2008), pp. 64–8.

65. Sneddon, *Witchcraft and Whigs*, pp. 99–100; Hutchinson, *Historical Essay*, pp. 60–61, 79ff.

66. Sloane MS 4043, fol. 38. Cf. Hutchinson, *Historical Essay*, pp. 163ff. See also Sneddon, *Witchcraft and Whigs*, pp. 93ff.; Guskin, 'Context of Witchcraft'.

67. See esp. Bostridge, *Witchcraft and its Transformations*, chapter 5; Knights, *Devil in Disguise*, pp. 213ff.

68. Collins, *Discourse of Free-thinking*, p. 30. See above, p. 49.

69. Hutchinson, *A Short View of the Pretended Spirit of Prophecy* (London, 1708), p. 44 and passim. Cf. Sneddon, *Witchcraft and Whigs*, chapter 4 (by comparison, Bostridge says

surprisingly little on the subject: *Witchcraft and its Transformations*, pp. 147–8). On the French Prophets see also Hillel Schwartz, *The French Prophets: The History of a Millenarian Group in Eighteenth-century England* (Berkeley and Los Angeles, 1980); Schwartz, *Knaves, Fools, Madmen, and that Subtile Effluvium: A Study of the Opposition to the French Prophets in England, 1706–1710* (Gainesville, 1978); and Lionel Laborie, *Enlightening Enthusiasm: Prophecy and Religious Experience in Early Eighteenth-century England* (Manchester, 2015). It is perhaps worth noting that the French Prophets clearly had a significant influence on Shaftesbury's thought: see Shaftesbury, *Characteristicks*, p. xxx, and Shaw, *Miracles in Enlightenment England*, pp. 150–1; they are also referred to by Lord Molesworth in his annotations to Martin's *Description*, p. 306.

70. This point is well made by Jane Shaw in her account of the group in *Miracles in Enlightenment England*, pp. 149ff., esp. p. 154. For the social profile of support for the Prophets, see esp. Laborie, *Enlightening Enthusiasm*, chapter 2; see also Schwartz, *Knaves, Fools, Madmen*, pp. 60–1. Sneddon, by contrast, is inclined to take Hutchinson's attack on the Prophets as subversive at face value: Sneddon, *Witchcraft and Whigs*, esp. pp. 88ff.

71. Schwartz, *Knaves, Fools, Madmen*, pp. 42–4 and passim.

72. Hutchinson, *Short View*, chapter 3. Sneddon makes no reference to this section.

73. Francis Hutchinson, *An Historical Essay concerning Witchcraft*, 2nd edn (London, 1720), sigs a6v–7 and pp. 228ff.

74. Ibid., pp. 68–9, 74ff., 287 and passim. Cf. Sneddon, *Witchcraft and Whigs*, pp. 118ff. For background see Peter R. Anstey (ed.), *The Idea of Principles in Early Modern Thought: Interdisciplinary Perspectives* (London, 2017).

75. David Wootton, 'Hutchinson, Francis (1660–1739)', in Richard M. Golden (ed.), *Encyclopaedia of Witchcraft: The Western Tradition*, 4 vols (Santa Barbara, 2006), vol. 2, pp. 531–2. For a comparable instance of the use of historical argument to critique an established belief system of the period, the royal touch, see William Becket, *A Free and Impartial Enquiry into the Antiquity and Efficacy of Touching for the Cure of the King's Evil* (London, 1722), pp. 4–6 and passim. See below, pp. 82–3, 141.

76. Hutchinson, *Historical Essay*, p. 190.

77. For the alternative view to that expressed here see Bostridge, *Witchcraft and its Transformations*, and Sneddon, *Witchcraft and Whigs* (cf. my review of the former in *Eighteenth-century Life*, 22 (1998), 139–47, on pp. 144ff., and of the latter in *Journal of British Studies*, 48 (2009), 175–6).

78. Hutchinson, *Historical Essay*, pp. 286–8.

79. Ibid., pp. 286, 288 and passim.

80. Ibid., sig. A6. Cf., e.g., p. 74 and the passage cited at n. 76, above.

81. Ibid., title page and pp. 288, 322, and 289ff., passim.

82. Trenchard and Gordon, *Cato's Letters*, vol. 2, p. 577.

83. See especially Bostridge, *Witchcraft and its Transformations*, but also the works of Knights and Sneddon referred to in nn. 63–4.

84. For the potential implications of the book for Hutchinson's career see Sneddon, *Witchcraft and Whigs*, pp. 121–2, 125. For the possibility that Hutchinson wrote a response to Richard Boulton's reply to him which is now lost, see ibid., p. 124.

85. Hutchinson to Arthur Charlett, 17 July 1718, Bodleian Library, Oxford, Ballard MS 38, fol. 27, partially quoted in Sneddon, *Witchcraft and Whigs*, p. 122. The final passage quoted by Sneddon interspersed by elisions actually reads: 'If ever experience doth shew the Contrary, I have no Interest to tempt me to shut my Eyes against it, & I hope in such a Case I shoud have Virtue enough to make me follow Mr Chillingworth' Example & change Notions as he did: but at present I am of the same mind with my Book' (Sneddon's elisions underlined). The allusion which Sneddon elides is to the divine, William Chillingworth (1602–1644), who converted to Roman Catholicism and then back to Protestantism, the implication being that cases like the Tedworth one, which Charlett evidently raised in his letter (see below, Chapter 4, n. 105, though this is also ignored by Sneddon), might have made Hutchinson reconsider the thrust of his book.

## 3. THE AMBIVALENCE OF THE EARLY ROYAL SOCIETY

1. Sir Henry Lyons, *The Royal Society 1660–1940: A History of its Administration under its Charters* (Cambridge, 1944), p. 41.

2. Thomas Sprat, *The History of the Royal Society of London* (London, 1667), pp. 37–8, 97, 340. Cf. ibid., pp. 362–5.

3. Michael Hunter, 'Latitudinarianism and the "Ideology" of the Early Royal Society: Thomas Sprat's *History of the Royal Society* (1667) Reconsidered', in Hunter, *Establishing the New Science: The Experience of the Early Royal Society* (Woodbridge, 1989), pp. 45–71, esp. pp. 63ff., also available in Richard Kroll, Richard Ashcraft and Perez Zagorin (eds), *Philosophy, Science and Religion in England 1640–1700* (Cambridge, 1992), pp. 199–229, esp. pp. 215ff.

4. K. T. Hoppen, 'The Nature of the Early Royal Society', parts 1 and 2, *British Journal for the History of Science*, 9 (1976), 1–24, 243–73. For a comparable view see Christopher Carter, '"A Constant Prodigy"? Empirical Views of an Unordinary Nature', *The Seventeenth Century*, 23 (2008), 265–89.

5. See Michael Hunter, 'Robert Boyle and the Early Royal Society: A Reciprocal Exchange in the Making of Baconian Science', *British Journal for the History of Science*, 40 (2007), 1–23, esp. pp. 13–14, reprinted in Hunter, *Boyle Studies: Aspects of the Life and Thought of Robert Boyle (1627–91)* (Farnham, 2015), chapter 3, esp. pp. 67–8.

6. For a transcript of the journal books up to 1687, see Thomas Birch, *The History of the Royal Society of London*, 4 vols (London, 1756–7) (see also the Hooke Folio: http://www.livesandletters.ac.uk/projects/hooke-folio-online). After 1687 one is dependent on the Original and Copy Journal Books and Council Minutes preserved in manuscript at the Royal Society, the former hereinafter referred to as JBO and JBC.

7. See Marie Boas Hall, *Henry Oldenburg: Shaping the Royal Society* (Oxford, 2002); Michael Hunter, 'Promoting the New Science: Henry Oldenburg and the Early Royal Society', *History of Science*, 26 (1988), 165–81, reprinted in Hunter, *Establishing the New Science*, pp. 245–60.

8. Steven Shapin and Simon Schaffer, *Leviathan and the Air-Pump: Hobbes, Boyle, and the Experimental Life* (Princeton, 1985); Peter Dear, '*Totius in verba*: Rhetoric and Authority in the Early Royal Society', *Isis*, 76 (1985), 145–61, reprinted in Dear (ed.), *The Scientific Enterprise in Early Modern Europe: Readings from Isis* (Chicago, 1997), pp. 255–72; William T. Lynch, *Solomon's Child: Method in the Early Royal Society of London* (Stanford, 2001).

9. See T. F. Gieryn, 'Boundary-Work and the Demarcation of Science from Non-Science: Strains and Interests in Professional Ideologies of Scientists', *American Sociological Review*, 48 (1983), 781–95; Barry Barnes, David Bloor and John Henry, *Scientific Knowledge: a Sociological Analysis* (London, 1996), chapter 6; John Henry, 'The Fragmentation of Renaissance Occultism and the Decline of Magic', *History of Science*, 46 (2008), 1–48, esp. p. 6.

10. See Michael Hunter, *Science and Society in Restoration England* (Cambridge, 1981), chapter 2, esp. p. 32. For further evidence of demarcation on the society's part in its early years, see, e.g., ibid., p. 144; Hunter, *Establishing the New Science*, pp. 56, 312–14; Michael Hunter, 'The Early Royal Society and the Shape of Knowledge', in Donald R. Kelley and Richard H. Popkin (eds), *The Shapes of Knowledge from the Renaissance to the Enlightenment* (Dordrecht, 1991), pp. 189–22, reprinted in Michael Hunter, *Science and the Shape of Orthodoxy: Intellectual Change in Late Seventeenth-Century Britain* (Woodbridge, 1995), pp. 169–79.

11. See above, Introduction, esp. pp. 10ff.

12. Francis Bacon, *The Instauratio Magna, Part 2: Novum organum and Associated Texts*, ed. Graham Rees with Maria Wakely (Oxford, 2004), pp. 298–9, 454–5, 458–9. It is perhaps also worth making the point that I am not talking here about vitalist cosmologies that flourished in the period alongside, and sometimes in opposition to, the mechanical philosophy: see, for instance, the article by Anna Marie Roos and Victor D. Boantza,

'Mineral Waters across the Channel: Matter Theory and Natural History from Samuel Duclos's Minerallogenesis to Martin Lister's Chymical Magnetism, c. 1666–86', *Notes & Records: The Royal Society Journal of the History of Science*, 69 (2015), 373–94, which cites the original version of this chapter and claims to problematise it (pp. 373–4), though in my view it does not.

13. Alan Taylor, 'An Episode with May-Dew', *History of Science*, 32 (1994), 163–84.
14. Birch, *Royal Society*, vol. 2, pp. 97, 99, 105, 109, 113; vol. 3, p. 455; Michael Hunter, *Boyle: Between God and Science* (New Haven and London, 2009), pp. 149, 179–80; L. M. Principe, *The Aspiring Adept: Robert Boyle and his Alchemical Quest* (Princeton, 1998), pp. 155ff. and passim. Also worth noting here is the society's brief interest in divining rods in 1663 (Birch, *Royal Society*, vol. 1, pp. 231–2, 234), in the Glastonbury thorn in 1686 (ibid., vol. 4, p. 483), in the repeal of the statute against multiplication of metals in 1689 (JBO, vol. 8, p. 268: transcribed from JBC, vol. 7, pp. 213–14, and commented on in Michael Hunter, *Robert Boyle 1627–91: Scrupulosity and Science* (Woodbridge, 2000), pp. 112–13), and in Plot's alchemical projects in 1698 (JBO, vol. 10, p. 67). Note also its interest in second sight in 1698: JBO, vol. 10, p. 88, and see further below, pp. 79, 185–6. See also Simon Schaffer, 'Godly Men and Mechanical Philosophers: Souls and Spirits in Restoration Natural Philosophy', *Science in Context*, 1 (1987), 55–85, which explores comparable evidence of the way in which the society's Fellows sought to illustrate the role of 'spirit' in laboratory conditions, though Schaffer is often frustratingly imprecise both about the phenomena involved and about the distinction between evidence deriving from the writings of the Fellows in question and what was divulged at the society's meetings.
15. Greatrakes, *A Brief Account of Mr Valentine Greatrak's* (London, 1666), esp. pp. 43ff.; Hunter, *Between God and Science*, pp. 149–52.
16. *The Correspondence of Robert Boyle*, ed. Michael Hunter, Antonio Clericuzio and Lawrence M. Principe, 6 vols (London, 2001), vol. 3, pp. 93–107, on p. 101. See also Hunter, *Boyle Studies*, pp. 169–70.
17. Jane Shaw, *Miracles in Enlightenment England* (New Haven and London, 2006), chapter 4. The most recent commentator on the case, Peter Elmer, *The Miraculous Conformist: Valentine Greatrakes, the Body Politic, and the Politics of Healing in Restoration Britain* (Oxford, 2013), is more circumspect from this point of view.
18. Henry Stubbe, *The Miraculous Conformist* (Oxford, 1666), p. 8; Greatrakes, *Brief Account*, p. 95.
19. Birch, *Royal Society*, vol. 2, pp. 65ff.
20. *Philosophical Transactions*, 1 (1666), 206–9. Only in 1699 did a paper explicitly on Greatrakes appear, in the form of a letter from Dublin communicated by Ralph Thoresby: ibid., 21 (1699), 332–4. There are copies of letters concerning Greatrakes from Lionel Beacher dated 18 May 1665 and from Thomas Mall dated 28 July 1665 in RS Early Letters B.1.106 and M.1.36: these are evidently the items referred to in Beale to Boyle, 7 September 1665, *Correspondence of Boyle*, vol. 2, p. 522 (though this link is not there made). See also ibid., p. 506n.
21. Glanvill, *Saducismus Triumphatus*, 3rd edn (London, 1689), title page, pp. 72–3, 334–5 and passim. For background to this trope, see Steven Shapin, *A Social History of Truth: Civility and Science in Seventeenth-century England* (Chicago, 1994), and see below, pp. 104, 147.
22. Glanvill, *A Blow at Modern Sadducism* (London, 1668), pp. 93–4. (This recurs in the 4th edition of 1668, pp. 115–16, but not in any of the editions of *Saducismus Triumphatus*: see below, p. 110.)
23. Charles Webster, *From Paracelsus to Newton: Magic and the Making of Modern Science* (Cambridge, 1982), p. 93 and chapter 4, passim. See above, pp. 11ff.
24. For a full account of the affair, of which this paragraph represents a summary, see Michael Hunter, 'John Webster, the Royal Society and *The Displaying of Supposed Witchcraft* (1677)', *Notes and Records: The Royal Society Journal of the History of Science*, 71 (2017), 7–19. This includes a transcription of the unpublished dedication to the Royal Society on pp. 11–12.

25. JBO, vol. 8, pp. 196–7. For a full transcript from the version in JBC, vol. 7, pp. 100–1, see Hunter, *Scrupulosity and Science*, p. 243.

26. Royal Society draft minutes 1689–96, MS 561, meeting of 11 March 1691. There is a problem with the records at this point, and the relevant passage does not appear in JBO, vol. 9, p. 33, or JBC, vol. 8, pp. 46–7

27. For an account, see Patrick Curry, *Prophecy and Power: Astrology in Early Modern England* (Cambridge, 1989), pp. 67–72.

28. *Correspondence of Boyle*, vol. 4, p. 247, vol. 5, pp. 4–5, 95–6, 376, vol. 6, p. 392; Bodleian Library, Oxford, MS Ashmole 368.

29. Birch, *Royal Society*, vol. 3, pp. 454–5.

30. Ibid., vol. 4, p. 481. The copy is still in the library.

31. See Michael Hunter, 'Science and Astrology in Seventeenth-century England: An Unpublished Polemic by John Flamsteed', in Patrick Curry (ed.), *Astrology, Science and Society: Historical Essays* (Woodbridge, 1987), pp. 260–300, esp. pp. 264–6, reprinted in Hunter, *Science and the Shape of Orthodoxy*, pp. 245–85, esp. pp. 249–51.

32. For these, see Curry, *Prophecy and Power*, pp. 72ff. and chapter 3, passim, though Curry, like other commentators, is prone to reify the society in this connection.

33. JBO, vol. 10, p. 14. Cf. ibid., p. 15. The author in question was possibly Robert Godson, whose *Astrologia Reformata* (London, 1697) is indeed dedicated to 'The Most Illustrious Brotherhood of Wisdom, the Royal Philosophical Society of London'. See also JBO, vol. 9, p. 120 (3 May 1693): 'There was addressed to the Society a printed Latin Letter asserting that the late Earthquakes at Sicily, and Jamaica were plainly indicated by the Rules of Astrology, and predicted by Dr Goad'. See *Epistola ad Regiam Societatem Londinensem; Qua de nuperis Terræ-Motibus disseritur, & Veræ eorum Causæ eruuntur* (London, 1693). I am most grateful to Monica Assolini for this reference.

34. *Correspondence of Boyle*, vol. 2, p. 549 (cf. p. 506n.); *The Correspondence of Henry Oldenburg*, ed. A. R. and M. B. Hall, 13 vols (Madison, Milwaukee and London, 1965–86), vol. 5, pp. 490, 497.

35. Ibid., e.g. vol. 2, pp. 523, 648. Cf. John Henry, 'Essay Review: The Origins of Modern Science: Henry Oldenburg's Contribution', *British Journal for the History of* Science, 21 (1988), 103–9, on pp. 107–8. For recent study of a letter to Oldenburg with magical content see Anna Marie Roos, ' "Magic Coins" and "Magic Squares": the Discovery of Astrological Sigils in the Oldenburg Letters', *Notes and Records of the Royal Society*, 62 (2008), 271–88, including p. 282 on Oldenburg's probably negative attitude.

36. For letters between Winthrop, Brereton and Haak, see Birch, *Royal Society*, vol. 2, pp. 473–4; R. C. Winthrop (ed.), *Correspondence of Hartlib, Haak, Oldenburg and others of the Founders of the Royal Society, with Governor Winthrop of Connecticut, 1661–72* (Boston, 1878), esp. pp. 45–6. See also Hunter, *Boyle Studies*, p. 172n.

37. See John Henry, 'Robert Hooke, the Incongruous Mechanist', in Michael Hunter and Simon Schaffer (eds), *Robert Hooke: New Studies* (Woodbridge, 1989), pp. 149–80; Penelope M. Gouk, *Music, Science and Natural Magic in Seventeenth-century England* (New Haven and London, 1999), chapter 6. For alternative views see M. E. Ehrlich, 'Mechanism and Activity in the Scientific Revolution: The Case of Robert Hooke', *Annals of Science*, 52 (1995), 127–51, and Michael Hunter, 'Hooke the Natural Philosopher', in Jim Bennett et al., *London's Leonardo: The Life and Work of Robert Hooke* (Oxford, 2003), pp. 105–62, on pp. 145–9.

38. Robert Hooke, *Lampas: or, Descriptions of Some Mechanical Improvements of Lamps & Waterpoises* (London, 1677), pp. 33–4, and pp. 28ff., passim.

39. Robert Hooke, *Posthumous Works*, ed. Richard Waller (London, 1705), pp. 203ff., on p. 205; JBO, vol. 8, p. 305. On the diaries see Deborah E. Harkness, *John Dee's Conversations with Angels: Cabala, Alchemy, and the End of Nature* (Cambridge, 1999), esp. chapter 3 (and pp. 223–4 on Hooke). Though Hooke cited Trithemius concerning the use of code, he ignored the fact that Trithemius saw this as a means to highly occultist ends: see Harkness, *John Dee*, pp. 111ff., and D. P. Walker, *Spiritual and Demonic Magic from Ficino to Campanella* (London, 1958), pp. 86–90.

40. See Hunter, 'Hooke the Natural Philosopher', p. 161 n. 104.

41. H. W. Robinson and W. Adams (eds), *The Diary of Robert Hooke 1672–80* (London, 1935), p. 204. See also ibid., p. 386: 'Astrology vaine'.

42. For the concept of 'grandees' see John Collins's letter to Newton of 19 July 1670 in H. W. Turnbull, J. F. Scott, A. R. Hall and Laura Tilling (eds), *The Correspondence of Isaac Newton*, 7 vols (Cambridge, 1959–77), vol. 1, p. 36, and Hunter, *Establishing the New Science*, pp. 322, 336 and chapter 9, passim. For the society's active nucleus and the way this evolved, see Michael Hunter, *The Royal Society and its Fellows 1660–1700: The Morphology of an Early Scientific Institution*, 2nd edn (Oxford, 1994), pp. 33–4, 130–31; for Council members and office holders see ibid., pp. 78–82.

43. Another sceptic was John Wallis: see his comments on a magical amulet in Bodleian MS Ashmole 1813, fol. 341v. For Petty, see Hunter, 'John Webster', p. 12. For an ambivalent attitude to Greatrakes like Oldenburg's on the part of Sir Robert Moray, see *Correspondence of Oldenburg*, vol. 2, p. 561. For contrasts in Fellows' magical beliefs, see Michael Hunter, *John Aubrey and the Realm of Learning* (London, 1975), pp. 140–42.

44. For the anti-magical stance of such members of the Oxford group (and later the Royal Society) as John Wilkins and Seth Ward, see A. G. Debus, *Science and Education in the Seventeenth Century: The Webster-Ward Debate* (London, 1970). The relationship between the position of John Webster in that debate and his stance in the 1670s further complicates matters: see the critiques of Thomas H. Jobe, 'The Devil in Restoration Science: the Glanvill-Webster Witchcraft Debate', *Isis*, 72 (1981), 343–56, referred to in chapter 1, n. 9, above.

45. Michael Hunter and Edward B. Davis (eds), *The Works of Robert Boyle*, 14 vols (London, 1999–2000), vol. 11, p. 429.

46. See Hunter, *Scrupulosity and Science*, pp. 233–4 and chapter 10, passim.

47. See Hunter, *Establishing the New Science*, p. 229 and chapter 6, passim.

48. See Samuel Butler, *Satires and Miscellaneous Poetry and Prose*, ed. René Lamar (Cambridge, 1928), pp. 3ff., 31–3, 167–8, 341–3; Thomas Shadwell, *The Virtuoso*, ed. Marjorie Hope Nicolson and David Rodes (London, 1966).

49. Sprat, *History*, p. 417.

50. For Michel Gauquelin's attempt at a statistical appraisal of astrology, see especially his *The Truth about Astrology* (Oxford, 1983) and *Neo-Astrology: A Copernican Revolution* (London, 1991).

51. For Boyle see above, pp. 11–12; JBO, vol. 10, p. 88. For the paper in question see below, pp. 185–6.

52. Henry Baker to Archibald Blair, 10 February 1749, John Rylands Library, Manchester, Baker Correspondence, vol. 4, fol. 67. On this episode, see further below, pp. 155–6. For a critical attitude on the part of the society to overtly supernaturalist material from New England (echoing Oldenburg's attitude to similar concerns that had intrigued the correspondents of Brereton and Haak in the late seventeenth century: see above, p. 75), see the abstract of the letters sent by Cotton Mather published in *Philosophical Transactions* in 1714, from which certain sections were omitted or curtailed on the grounds that they 'relate little to Natural Philosophy' (these dealt with people dreaming of substances which cured them, and with visitations by the dead). See the letters in Early Letters M.2, 21–33, and the abstract in 34, printed in *Phil. Trans.*, 29 (1714–16), 62–71, on pp. 65, 67. See also G. L. Kittredge, 'Cotton Mather's Scientific Communications to the Royal Society', *Proceedings of the American Antiquarian Society*, n.s., 26 (1916), 18–57, and Michael Winship, *Seers of God: Puritan Providentialism in the Restoration and Early Enlightenment* (Baltimore, 1996), esp. chapter 5 (though neither mention this censorship).

53. Quoted in Ian Bostridge, *Witchcraft and its Transformations c. 1650–c. 1750* (Oxford, 1997), p. 126.

54. Anthony Collins, *A Discourse of Free-thinking* (London, 1713), pp. 27ff. See above, p. 49.

55. Phileleutherus Lipsiensis [Richard Bentley], *Remarks Upon a late Discourse of Free-thinking* (London, 1713), p. 33.

56. See Keith Thomas, *Religion and the Decline of Magic* (London, 1971), p. 579n.; Barbara Shapiro, *Probability and Certainty in Seventeenth-century England* (Princeton, 1983), p. 220; Stuart Clark, *Thinking with Demons: The Idea of Witchcraft in Early Modern Europe* (Oxford, 1997), pp. 295–6; Webster, *From Paracelsus to Newton*, p. 99 (though he wrongly conflates this pamphlet with Bentley's Boyle Lectures); Jonathan Israel, *Radical Enlightenment: Philosophy and the Making of Modernity 1650-1750* (Oxford, 2001), p. 377; David Wootton, *The Invention of Science: A New History of the Scientific Revolution* (London, 2015), pp. 468–9.

57. For Boyle, see Introduction, pp. 11ff. For Sydenham, see his 'Theologia Rationalis' in Kenneth Dewhurst, *Dr Thomas Sydenham (1624-89): His Life and Original Writings* (London, 1966), pp. 145–59, and the letter to him from Charles Blount in Blount's *Oracles of Reason* (London, 1693), p. 87, showing his interest in 'the Deists Arguments'. However, for his support for Greatrakes's claims, see Elmer, *Miraculous Conformist*, p. 205, and *Correspondence of Boyle*, vol. 2, pp. 522, 533–4. His views on witchcraft are unclear, as are Radcliffe's, though on the latter's outlook as a whole see below, p. 132. Newton's private (but not public) views on religious topics have, of course, been the subject of intense study. For his move towards a psychological view of the Devil, see Frank E. Manuel, *Isaac Newton: Historian* (Cambridge, 1963), pp. 149–50; Manuel, *The Religion of Isaac Newton* (Oxford, 1974), pp. 63–4; and Stephen Snobelen, 'Lust, Pride, and Ambition: Isaac Newton and the Devil', in James E. Force and Sarah Hutton (eds), *Newton and Newtonianism: New Studies* (Dordrecht: Kluwer, 2004), pp. 155–81. See also Rob Iliffe, *Priest of Nature: The Religious Worlds of Isaac Newton* (Oxford, 2017), pp. 21, 240 and passim. For orally expressed scepticism on his part see below, p. 113.

58. Wootton, *Invention of Science*, p. 469, and pp. 466ff., passim (the latter quotation clearly alludes to his earlier book, *Bad Medicine: Doctors Doing Harm since Hippocrates* (Oxford, 2006)).

59. See above, pp. 62ff.

60. Francis Hutchinson, *An Historical Essay concerning Witchcraft*, 2nd edn (London, 1720), sig. A6.

61. Winship, *Seers of God*, p. 131. Cf. Webster, *From Paracelsus to Newton*, p. 99 (though this passage of his book is unfortunately garbled by a misprint); Thomas, *Religion and the Decline of Magic*, p. 579n.; Shapiro, *Probability and Certainty*, p. 221.

62. Hutchinson, *Historical Essay*, pp. 169–70.

63. Ibid, pp. 179–81. The passage is cited by Hutchinson from the Latin edition of Redi's *Experimenta naturalia* (Amsterdam, 1675), pp. 23ff.; for the original Italian see *Esperienze intorno a diverse cose naturali* (Florence, 1671), pp. 18ff.

64. Boulton, *A Compleat History of Magick, Sorcery, and Witchcraft*, 2 vols (London, 1715–16), vol. 1, sigs A3–B3 and passim. For an assessment both of the *Compleat History* and of Boulton's later response to Hutchinson, *The Possibility and Reality of Magick, Sorcery, and Witchcraft, Demonstrated. Or, a Vindication of a Compleat History of Magick, Sorcery, and Witchcraft* (London, 1722), see James Sharpe (ed.), *English Witchcraft 1560-1736, VI: The Final Debate* (London, 2003), pp. xff., citing the appraisal of Boulton's work on Boyle in Michael Hunter (ed.), *Robert Boyle by Himself and his Friends* (London, 1994), pp. lv–lvi.

65. That Boulton compiled his edition of *The Theological Works of the Honourable Robert Boyle, Esq., Epitomiz'd* (1715) at the booksellers' bidding is confirmed by his undated, begging letter to Sir Hans Sloane, BL Sloane MS 4058, fol. 47. Boulton receives a perhaps rather inflated assessment in Bostridge, *Witchcraft and its Transformations*, pp. 95–7 and chapter 6; see also Andrew Sneddon, *Witchcraft and Whigs: The Life of Bishop Francis Hutchinson 1660-1739* (Manchester, 2008), chapter 5.

66. C. R. Weld, *A History of the Royal Society*, 2 vols (London, 1848), vol. 1, pp. 87ff. The reference to Hutchinson is on pp. 88–9. See also ibid., pp. 111–12, 126.

67. Ibid., pp. 89–90; William Becket, *A Free and Impartial Enquiry into the Antiquity and Efficacy of Touching for the King's Evil* (London, 1722). This is a further instance of the use of historical argument to critique an established belief system of the period which is

comparable in some ways to Hutchinson's. See Stephen Brogan, *The Royal Touch in Early Modern England: Politics, Medicine and Sin* (Woodbridge, 2015), esp. pp. 206ff.

68. Weld, *History*, p. 93.
69. Lyons, *Royal Society*, p. 41.
70. See Weld, *History*, vol. 1, p. 126, and J. A. Paris, *The Life of Sir Humphry Davy, Bart.* (London, 1831), p. 371n.
71. See Sprat, *History*, pp. 347, 371: in addition, the syntax of both phrases is altered. Though Weld was responsible for the alterations and additions to Sprat, it was Lyons who conflated two phrases from the second charter of 1663 together to produce the formula 'the improving Natural Knowledge by experiment': in fact, the reference to experiment comes later.
72. Walter Scott, *Letters on Demonology and Witchcraft* (London, 1830), pp. 344ff., esp. 349–50. Cf. Weld, *History*, p. 93n. (and Paris, *Life of Davy*, p. 371n.).
73. 'Philomath' literally means 'a lover of learning'; it was a term often adopted by astrologers to describe themselves (*OED*).

## 4 THE 'DRUMMER OF TEDWORTH': CONFLICTING INTERPRETATIONS AND THE PROBLEM OF FRAUD

1. Colin Wilson, *Poltergeist! A Study in Destructive Haunting* (London, 1981), p. 120.
2. See Glanvill, *A Blow at Modern Sadducism* (London, 1668) [hereinafter *Blow*], in which his narrative of the events at Tedworth appears on pp. 91ff. In this chapter I have used this edition, since it is Glanvill's initial printed account of the affair, although it lacks the separate title page to the sequel, Glanvill's letter to Henry More commenting on the Tedworth case – *A Whip for the Droll, Fiddler to the Atheist* – which appears in the 4th edition of the same year (the editions otherwise differ only in the addition to the 4th of section divisions both in this and in the main account of Tedworth, and the addition of a few sections of text in 'Some Considerations About Witchcraft', the opening part of the book, the section numbers in which are rationalised). For *Saducismus Triumphatus* I have used the 3rd edition (London, 1689), largely because of its convenient, continuous pagination. See further above, Introduction, n. 66, and below, pp. 103–4.
3. See Christopher Carter, '"A Constant Prodigy"? Empirical Views of an Unordinary Nature', *The Seventeenth Century*, 23 (2008), 265–89, esp. pp. 279–80. See also above, pp. 11ff.
4. See Natalie Zemon Davis, *Fiction in the Archives: Pardon Tales and their Tellers in Sixteenth-century France* (Stanford, 1987); Diane Purkiss, *The Witch in History: Early Modern and Twentieth-century Representations* (London, 1996); Malcolm Gaskill, 'Reporting Murder: Fiction in the Archives in Early Modern England', *Social History*, 23 (1998), 1–30; Marion Gibson, *Reading Witchcraft: Stories of Early English Witches* (London, 1999); Stuart Clark (ed.), *Languages of Witchcraft: Narrative, Ideology and Meaning in Early Modern Culture* (Basingstoke, 2001).
5. The quotation is from Mompesson to William Creed, 4 January 1663, in Michael Hunter, 'New Light on the "Drummer of Tedworth": Conflicting Narratives of Witchcraft in Restoration England', *Historical Research*, 78 (2005), 311–53, on p. 347. The letters from Mompesson to Creed preserved in a copy by William Fulman that now comprises Corpus Christi College, Oxford, MS 318, fols 160–64, from which the details that follow are chiefly derived, are published in full on pp. 338–50 of that article, which is hereinafter cited as 'New Light' with document and/or page number. The article also includes on pp. 350–52 the text of an account of the events in the State Papers, PRO SP 9/230, no. 177. See Appendix I.
6. Boyle to Glanvill, 10 February 1678, in Michael Hunter, Antonio Clericuzio and Lawrence M. Principe (eds), *The Correspondence of Robert Boyle*, 6 vols (London, 2001), vol. 5, p. 20.

7. Throughout this chapter, the spellings 'Tedworth' and 'Tidworth' are used interchangeably. The received spelling of the place name is 'Tidworth', and this was sometimes used in the seventeenth century; but Glanvill's usage of 'Tedworth' has become so familiar that it is frequently echoed here. The fact that Mompesson was 'a *Commission Officer* in the *Militia*' is stated in *Blow*, p. 97; it is omitted in *Saducismus*, p. 321, but there is no reason to consider this omission significant.

8. See A. G. Matthews, *Walker Revised* (Oxford, 1948, reprinted 1988), p. 377. See also *Wiltshire Visitation Pedigrees 1623* (Harleian Society, 1954), p. 134.

9. David Underdown, *Royalist Conspiracy in England 1649-60* (New Haven, 1960), pp. 150–53; A. H. Woolrych, *Penruddock's Rising 1655* (London, 1955), p. 18; B. D. Henning, *The House of Commons 1660-90*, 3 vols (London, 1983), vol. 2, pp. 71–3.

10. See Wiltshire and Swindon Record Office (hereinafter WSRO), 212B/6557. His widow also remembered the local poor in her will, the evangelical tone of which is notable: WSRO Cons Sarum Wills P1/M/364.

11. 'New Light', pp. 339–40.

12. Ibid., pp. 340, 341, 342, 345, 346. A 'bed-teeke' or bedtick was a bag or case in which feathers were put to form a bed (*OED*).

13. Anthony Wood, *Athenae Oxonienses*, ed. Philip Bliss, 4 vols (London, 1813–20), vol. 3, cols 637–8; Creed's wife was Mompesson's 'Cosen' ('New Light', p. 342).

14. Ibid., pp. 340–42.

15. See H. E. Rollins (ed.), *The Pack of Autolycus* (Cambridge, MA, 1927), pp. 114–21, 240. See also Appendix I.

16. Wood, *Life and Times*, ed. Andrew Clark, 5 vols (Oxford, 1891–1900), vol. 2, pp. 53–4. For his ownership of a copy of the first of Mompesson's letters to Creed (and the unique extant copy of the ballad), see Appendix I.

17. See Michael McKeon, *Politics and Poetry in Restoration England: The Case of Dryden's 'Annus Mirabilis'* (Cambridge, MA, 1975), chapters 6–8, who brings out this ambivalence better than William E. Burns, *An Age of Wonders: Prodigies, Politics and Providence in England 1657-1727* (Manchester, 2002), chapter 1. On Wood's attitude, see also Burns, *Age of Wonders*, p. 34.

18. For the witch cries, see 'New Light', pp. 348, 349, 351. For the ashes, see ibid., pp. 344, 352 and *Blow*, p. 110–11.

19. 'New Light', pp. 346–7.

20. Ibid., pp. 341, 345, 347.

21. *Mercurius Publicus*, 16–23 April 1663, no. 16, pp. 252–6, on p. 256; *The Kingdoms Intelligencer*, 20–27 April 1663, no. 17, pp. 257–61, on p. 261 (the text is identical).

22. PRO ASSI 2/1, fol. 95v.

23. *Mercurius Publicus* and *Kingdoms Intelligencer*, pp. 253–4/258–9.

24. Ibid., p. 256/261.

25. Ibid., pp. 254, 255/259, 260.

26. Ibid., 253/258. Drury's imprisonment in the gaol at Fisherton Anger is referred to in WSRO A1/110, E 1663, fol. 159, and T 1663, fol. 141. Cf. *HMC Various Collections*, 1 (1901), p. 145.

27. Mompesson to Collins, 8 August 1674, in *Saducismus*, sig. R4v. For the date of the assizes, see PRO ASSI 24/22, fol. 101.

28. ASSI 2/1, fol. 103v. The pardons on which both sentences of transportation must have relied cannot be traced in the privy seal warrants or dockets books, PRO C82, C231/7. I am indebted to Christopher Whittick and Cynthia Herrup for their help in this connection.

29. 'New Light', document 2.

30. See Ian Bostridge, *Witchcraft and its Transformations c. 1650-c. 1750* (Oxford, 1997), chapter 3; J. A. Sharpe, *Instruments of Darkness: Witchcraft in England 1550-1750* (London, 1996), chapter 1; Peter Elmer, *Witchcraft, Witch-Hunting, and Politics in Early Modern England* (Oxford, 2016), chapter 5.

31. Aubrey, *Remaines of Gentilisme and Judaisme*, in his *Three Prose Works*, ed. John Buchanan-Brown (Fontwell, 1972), p. 201.

32. 'New Light', p. 343.
33. Ibid., p. 344.
34. See Keith Thomas, *Religion and the Decline of Magic* (London, 1971), pp. 606ff.; Diane Purkiss, *Troublesome Things: A History of Fairies and Fairy Stories* (London, 2000), esp. chapter 4.
35. 'New Light', pp. 344–5.
36. Ibid., p. 346.
37. Ibid., p. 344.
38. Ibid., pp. 341, 344, 345.
39. Ibid., p. 342. For Pierce's purchase, see WSRO, 212B/6557, a feoffment dated 2 April 1662.
40. 'New Light', p. 348 and document 6.
41. Ibid., pp. 342, 344, 345.
42. Ibid., pp. 347–8.
43. Abraham Hill, *Familiar Letters* (London, 1767), p. 92. See also ibid., pp. 95, 104–5, 109. The case of an apparition at Driffield in Yorkshire is also discussed: see J[ohn] S[trype] (ed.), *Some Genuine Remains of . . . John Lightfoot* (London, 1700), pp. liff.
44. John Aubrey, *The Natural History of Wiltshire*, ed. John Britton (London, 1847; reprinted Newton Abbott, 1969), p. 121. See also Royal Society MS 92, fols 363–4. The fact that Wren had a companion whose name Aubrey denoted by an ellipsis (and Britton therefore omitted) is taken from the MS.
45. 'New Light', p. 345. See below, pp. 114, 115.
46. *Conway Letters*, ed. Marjorie Hope Nicolson (1930; reprinted ed. Sarah Hutton, Oxford, 1992), pp. 215–16. For John Carr, a medical man who was subsequently Fellow of the College of Physicians, see J. and J. A. Venn, *Alumni Cantabrigienses* [to 1751], 4 vols (Cambridge, 1922–7), vol. 1, p. 295.
47. Samuel Butler, *Hudibras*, ed. John Wilders (Oxford, 1967), pp. 104 (ii.1.131–2), 371; for the date of composition see ibid., pp. xlvi–xlvii.
48. *The Diary of Samuel Pepys*, ed. Robert Latham and William Matthews, 11 vols (London, 1970–83), vol. 4, pp. 185–6. By 'books of it', Pepys must mean the ballad. On Sandwich's heterodox religious views, see ibid., esp. vol. 1, pp. 141, 201, 261, 271. Unfortunately Sandwich's ten-volume journal, now at Mapperton House, Dorset, provides little evidence of his views on such topics, though there are occasions when he showed a robust scepticism about supposed miracles, e.g. vol. 2, pp. 68–70, 74–6; vol. 6, pp. 297–8.
49. Joseph Glanvill to Henry More, 25 September [no year], Pierpont Morgan Library, New York, MS MA 4322. I am grateful to Rhodri Lewis for a transcript of this letter. Though it is there dated '[1668]', 1667 seems more likely. The work by Charleton to which Glanvill refers is his *The Immortality of the Human Soul, Demonstrated by the Light of Nature* (London, 1657). For Charleton's views on religion and related topics see especially Bodleian Library, Oxford, MS Smith 13, various items in which show an idiosyncratic and somewhat cynical viewpoint, tinged by Stoic ideas. Hints of similar views are to be found scattered through his published works, for which see Emily Booth, 'A Subtle and Mysterious Machine': The Medical World of Walter Charleton (1619–1707)* (Dordrecht, 2005), pp. 223–40 and passim.
50. British Library Add. MS 19253, fols 206v, 207v, printed in *Letters of Philip, Second Earl of Chesterfield* (London, 1829), pp. 11–16. These events occurred in 1652–3.
51. British Library Add. MS 19253, fol. 201v, printed in *Letters of Chesterfield*, pp. 24–5. The account appears under the year 1664.
52. Dr Williams Library, London, Baxter Letters, v. 177–8. For a summary see N. H. Keeble and G. F. Nuttall, *Calendar of the Correspondence of Richard Baxter*, 2 vols (Oxford, 1991), vol. 2, p. 37.
53. See Baxter, *Certainty of the Worlds of Spirits* (London, 1691), passim. For passages on apparitions and the like in Baxter's earlier books, see *The Saints Everlasting Rest* (London, 1650; 10th edn, 1669), pp. 252ff.; *The Unreasonableness of Infidelity* (London, 1655), part 3, pp. 82–113; *The Reasons of the Christian Religion* (London, 1667), pp. 147ff.

54. 'New Light', document 7.
55. See above, p. 90.
56. See Joseph Glanvill, *The Vanity of Dogmatizing* (London, 1661), sig. A4, pp. 22, 38, 199–200.
57. *HMC Eliot Hodgkin*, pp. 300–301; *Conway Letters*, pp. 215–16. Cf. ibid., p. 208.
58. Ibid., pp. 215–16. He adds, 'It is part of a letter from that party to me'. On More's interest in such topics, see Introduction, pp. 13–14.
59. See above, p. 95.
60. *HMC Eliot Hodgkin*, p. 52 (the year is there given as [1662?], but this cannot be correct in view of the direct echo of this letter in Henry More to Anne Conway, November–December 1663, in *Conway Letters*, pp. 218–19); *Blow*, p. 117.
61. Ibid., pp. 110–11 (this presumes that the Bible episode is the same one as that described in ibid., p. 105, and 'New Light', p. 344, which may not be the case), 113–15.
62. Ibid., p. 115.
63. *HMC Eliot Hodgkin*, p. 52.
64. The letter of 13 March is published from the MS at Harvard in Georges Edelen, 'Joseph Glanvill, Henry More, and the Phantom Drummer of Tedworth', *Harvard Library Bulletin*, 10 (1956), 186–92, on p. 188; the second quotation is taken from a letter from Glanvill to More dated 25 September in the Pierpont Morgan Library: see above, n. 49. See also *Blow*, pp. 95–6, for the reluctance as stemming from 'a person intimately concerned in it' who advised Mompesson that he should not 'meddle any more with Relations' lest his '*troublesome guest*' returned.
65. Ibid., pp. 93–6. This is quoted at length in M. E. Prior, 'Joseph Glanvill, Witchcraft and Seventeenth-century Science', *Modern Philology*, 30 (1932–3), 167–93, on p. 182, and more briefly on pp. 71–2 above.
66. *Blow*, p. 142, and pp. 137ff., passim; for the title page, see *A Blow at Modern Sadducism*, 4th edn (London, 1668), p. 159 (see also above, n. 2). For background, see above, Introduction, pp. 19, 23–4, and chapter 1, esp. pp. 28–9.
67. *Blow*, p. 104. Cf. 'New Light', p. 344.
68. *Blow*, pp. 117ff.
69. See esp. Steven Shapin and Simon Schaffer, *Leviathan and the Air-Pump: Hobbes, Boyle, and the Experimental Life* (Princeton, 1985); Michael Hunter, *The Occult Laboratory: Magic, Science and Second Sight in Late Seventeenth-century Scotland* (Woodbridge, 2001), Introduction.
70. *Blow*, pp. 100, 102, 119. Cf. 'New Light', pp. 340–1.
71. Ibid, p. 100. It is interesting that he echoes Sir Thomas Mompesson's concept of 'Rendezvous'. Cf. ibid., pp. 101–2, 111.
72. Ibid., pp. 105–7. Compare 'New Light', pp. 344, 346, 350.
73. E.g., *Blow*, pp. 101, 104, 109, 111; *Conway Letters*, pp. 218–19. In his letter of 26 December, Mompesson speaks of 'unlucky trickes' ('New Light', p. 344).
74. Cf. Quintilian, *Institutio oratoria*, VI.iii.18–19.
75. *Blow*, p. 137. It is interesting that Alan Gauld and A. D. Cornell, *Poltergeists* (London, 1979), pp. 61–2, quote them at length in this connection.
76. *Blow*, pp. 138ff.
77. *The Drummer of Tedworth* (London, 1716), pp. 25–6. The only clue to the authorship of this anonymous work is on p. 16, where it is divulged that Glanvill was 'great Unkle to the Writer of this History'.
78. *Blow*, pp. 138–9; *Saducismus*, sig. R3v.
79. See Vivian de Sola Pinto, *Enthusiast in Wit: A Portrait of John Wilmot, Earl of Rochester 1647–80* (London, 1962), pp. 81–90; Harold Love (ed.), *The Works of John Wilmot, Earl of Rochester* (Oxford, 1999), pp. xxxviii, 112–17, 437–40, 612–15.
80. See the letter in the Pierpont Morgan Library cited in n. 49 above; Pepys, *Diary*, vol. 7, p. 382 (but see vol. 8, p. 589, for a more appreciative comment); Aubrey, *Natural History of Wiltshire*, p. 121.
81. *Saducismus*, sig. R2.

82. Dr Williams Library, Baxter Letters, ii. 138–9: see Keeble and Nuttall, *Calendar*, vol. 2, p. 101. For Baxter's publication of such material, see above, n. 53.

83. See above, p. 99. The confession is also reported by John Beaumont: see below, p. 115.

84. See G. L. Kittredge, *Witchcraft in Old and New England* (1929; reissued New York, 1958), p. 323 and chapter 17, passim, esp. pp. 318ff. On the Gunther case, see also James Sharpe, *The Bewitching of Anne Gunther* (London, 1999), chapter 8.

85. *Saducismus*, sig. R3v.

86. Ibid., sig. R2.

87. See *The Letters of John Wilmot, Earl of Rochester*, ed. Jeremy Treglown (Oxford, 1980), p. 147.

88. *Correspondence of Boyle*, vol. 5, pp. 15, 20–1. See also ibid., vol. 4, pp. 455–7, 460–1; vol. 5, p. 37. On Boyle and *The Devil of Mascon*, see above, p. 12. It is perhaps worth noting that Samuel Butler had made a satirical allusion to that work in *Hudibras*: Butler, *Hudibras*, pp. xlvii, 157 (ii.3.161–2), 391, and More also alludes to it in connection with Tedworth: *Conway Letters*, pp. 215–16. For recent studies of the Mascon case, which has some similarities to the Tedworth one, see P. G. Maxwell-Stuart, *Poltergeists: A History of Violent Ghostly Phenomena* (Stroud, 2011), chapter 6, and Kathryn A. Edwards, 'The "Antidemons" of Calvinism: Ghosts, Demons, and Traditional Belief in the House of François Perrault', in Edwards (ed.), *Everyday Magic in Early Modern Europe* (Farnham, 2015), pp. 147–60.

89. See above, Introduction and chapters 1–2.

90. It is worth noting a dating error introduced in the 1688 and subsequent editions (though not those of 1681–2) which has caused much confusion. Perhaps owing to a failure to allow for the traditional start of the year on 25 March, the events of the latter part of 1662 are mistakenly placed in 1661: *Saducismus*, pp. 323, 325. The 1681 edition omitted the letter to More, *A Whip for the Droll*, but this was reinstated in the edition of 1682 and all subsequent editions.

91. All the passages noted in n. 71 above are omitted (pp. 323, 324, 328), and that noted in n. 72 is severely curtailed (pp. 325–6).

92. *Blow*, p. 143.

93. E.g. Mr Hill and Dr Compton on pp. 333–4. On these men and the Somerset connection see Jonathan Barry, *Witchcraft and Demonology in South-West England, 1640–1789* (Basingstoke, 2012), pp. 53–6. For the possibility that it was Mr Hill, who Glanvill specifically states 'was with me at the House', rather than Glanvill, who wrote the State Papers account, see Andrew Pickering, *The Devil's Cloister: Wessex Witchcraft Narratives* (Devizes, 2017), p. 143. However, the fact that the State Papers account's usage of 'I' is so clearly echoed in *Blow* and *Saducismus* (although the details differ slightly) makes this seem to me unlikely.

94. *Saducismus*, pp. 328–31.

95. See John Spurr, *The Restoration Church of England, 1646–89* (New Haven, 1991), esp. chapter 6; Isabel Rivers, *Reason, Grace and Sentiment: a Study of the Language of Religion and Ethics in England 1660–1780*, 2 vols (Cambridge, 1991–2000), vol. 1, chapter 2.

96. Increase Mather, *Remarkable Providences Illustrative of the Earlier Days of American Colonisation*, ed. George Offor (London, 1890), pp. 111–12; George Sinclair, *Satans Invisible World Discovered* (Edinburgh, 1685), pp. 55–75.

97. Baxter, *Certainty of the Worlds of Spirits* (London, 1691), pp. 41–2. An interesting echo of this is to be found in the view of the divine, John Lightfoot, who wrote of the Tedworth case: 'tho by most now Counted a Cheat, yet servs to bring in my mind the many times of our Saviour on Earth. No doubt all Scholars wer infinitely desirous, as well as Herod, to see a miracle, yet theirs wer least gratified. & might not they return & Cry, a meer Cheat. a delusion.' BL Add MS 38856, fol. 165v.

98. Morgan to Hooke, 17 January 1675/6, BL Sloane MS 1039, fols 96–7. See Hooke, *Diary*, ed. H.W. Robinson and W. Adams (London, 1935) pp. 215–16, and above, pp. 75–6.

99. Abraham de la Pryme, *Diary*, ed. Charles Jackson, Surtees Society, vol. 54, 1870 (for 1869), pp. 39–42.

100. Ibid., p. 42. The episode is noted in Richard S. Westfall, *Never at Rest: A Biography of Isaac Newton* (Cambridge, 1980), p. 502, and in Stephen Snobelen, 'Lust, Pride, and Ambition: Isaac Newton and the Devil', in James E. Force and Sarah Hutton (eds), *Newton and Newtonianism: New Studies* (Dordrecht: Kluwer, 2004), pp. 155–81, on p. 165.
101. Webster, *The Displaying of Supposed Witchcraft* (London, 1677), p. 278 and chapter 14, passim.
102. Balthasar Bekker, *Der Betoverde Weereld*, 4 vols (Amsterdam, 1691–3). For a commentary see Andrew Fix, *Fallen Angels: Balthasar Bekker, Spirit Belief and Confessionalism in the Seventeenth-century Dutch Republic* (Dordrecht, 1999), and Jonathan Israel, *Radical Enlightenment: Philosophy and the Making of Modernity, 1650–1750* (Oxford, 2001), chapter 21. On the non-publication in England of all but the first part of Bekker's work, see Andrew Fix, 'What Happened to Balthasar Bekker in England? A Mystery in the History of Publishing', *Church History and Religious Culture*, 90 (2010), 609–31, though Fix overlooks the possibility that the translation might have failed to materialise because it seemed redundant in light of the existing tradition of sadducism.
103. Bekker, *Betoverde Weereld*, vol. 4, pp. 176ff., esp. pp. 179–82. I have preferred to use the French translation, which Bekker read over and endorsed (Fix, 'What Happened', p. 613): *Le Monde Enchanté*, 4 vols (Amsterdam, 1694), vol. 4, pp. 423ff., esp. pp. 430–4.
104. In Bekker's Dutch original, the word is 'groll', i.e. modern 'grol'.
105. See, for instance, Euan Cameron, *Enchanted Europe: Superstition, Reason, and Religion 1250–1750* (Oxford, 2010), p. 267 and chapter 16, passim. It is perhaps worth noting that, although a line similar to Bekker's was taken by the English equivalent of his book, Francis Hutchinson's *Historical Essay concerning Witchcraft* (1718), the Tedworth case is not there mentioned. However, for Hutchinson's views on it see his letter to Arthur Charlett, 17 July 1718, Bodleian Library Ballard MS 38, fol. 27 (endorsed by Charlett, 'about Mr Mompesson's Case'), in which he writes concerning the Tedworth episode (evidently in response to an enquiry by Charlett in a letter that is no longer extant): 'Mr Mompesson's Case was as Surprising as any that happen'd in our age, But I think that the Principles that I lay down, shew, that no safe Prosecution coud have been grounded upon it: & as I hope the Principles are true & right as well as safe & Prudential, I am apt to think that time will confirm them' ('be' is deleted before 'have been'). See also above, chapter 2, n. 85, and, for Mompesson's attempted prosecution of Drury, above, pp. 91ff.
106. Richard Bovet, *Pandæmonium*, ed. Montague Summers (Aldington, Kent, 1951, reprinted East Ardsley, Yorks., 1975), pp. 36–8. For Jonathan Barry's recent revisionist account of this curious work and its author, see his 'The Politics of *Pandæmonium*', in John Newton and Jo Bath (eds), *Witchcraft and the Act of 1604* (Leiden, 2008), pp. 181–206, reprinted in Barry's *Witchcraft and Demonology in South-West England*, pp. 103–23.
107. John Beaumont, *An Historical, Physiological and Theological Treatise of Spirits, Apparitions, Witchcrafts, and other Magical Practices* (London, 1705), pp. 306–11. Beaumont also attacks Bekker elsewhere in his book, esp. chapter 12. On Beaumont see below, pp. 123ff., 152, 163.
108. See Henry D. Rack, *Reasonable Enthusiast: John Wesley and the Rise of Methodism*, 3rd edn (London, 2002), pp. 59–60, including references to Wesley's publication of material relating to the episode in the *Arminian Magazine* in 1784. See also ibid., pp. 387–8, 431ff.
109. *Arminian Magazine*, 8 (1785), 155–7, 202–6, 250–54: the reprint of Glanvill's account is accompanied by an envoi by Wesley which more briefly summarises the journal entry quoted in the text.
110. Wesley, *Letters and Journals*, ed. W. R. Ward and R. P. Heitzenrater (Nashville, 1988– [in progress]), vol. 5, p. 136, including the editors' important note on the passage.
111. Ibid., pp. 135–6, 238.
112. A. C. Guthkelch (ed.), *The Miscellaneous Works of Joseph Addison*, 2 vols (London, 1914), vol. 1, pp. 423–90; see also above, pp. 60–1; *The Drummer of Tedworth*, p. 4 and passim.

113. For the interpretation of this image, and especially its relationship with Hogarth's earlier, suppressed work, 'Enthusiasm Delineated', see Bernd Krysmanski, 'We see a Ghost: Hogarth's Satire on Methodists and Connoisseurs', *Art Bulletin*, 80 (1998), 292–310 (see esp. pp. 296–7 concerning Tedworth). See also Ronald Paulson, *Hogarth's Graphic Works*, 3rd edn (London, 1989), pp. 175–8.

114. For the Cock Lane affair, see Douglas Grant, *The Cock Lane Ghost* (London, 1965); E. J. Clery, *The Rise of Supernatural Fiction, 1762–1800* (Cambridge, 1995), pp. 13ff.; and Paul Chambers, *The Cock Lane Ghost: Murder, Sex and Haunting in Dr Johnson's London* (Stroud, 2006).

115. John Ferriar, 'Of Popular Illusions, and Particularly of Medical Demonology', *Memoirs of the Literary and Philosophical Society of Manchester*, 3 (1790), [23]–116, on pp. 65–6; Charles Mackay, *Extraordinary Popular Delusions and the Madness of Crowds*, reprinted with foreword by B. M. Baruch (London, 1956), pp. 601ff. (the second component of the title was added to the second edition of 1852).

116. See above, p. 55.

117. Gilbert Geiss and Ivan Bunn, *A Trial of Witches: A Seventeenth-century Witchcraft Prosecution* (London, 1997), pp. 224–5. For further commentary on this episode see Bostridge, *Witchcraft and its Transformations*, pp. 79ff.

118. Samuel Harsnett, *A Discovery of the Fraudulent Practises of John Darrel* (London, 1599), pp. 179–84, 294–6; Marion Gibson, *Possession, Puritanism and Print: Darrell, Harsnett, Shakespeare and the Elizabethan Exorcism Controversy* (London, 2006), pp. 113–14, 116. An analogous instance is provided by *The Disclosing of a late Counterfeyted Possession by the Devyl in Two Maydens within the Citie of London* (London, 1574), which juxtaposes an account that has all the verisimilitude of a genuine possession narrative with the record of the subsequent examination of those involved in the presence of the authorities, at which they are said to have confessed to fraud, as if the latter simply trumped the former. For a commentary on this case which does not really confront this issue, see Kathleen R. Sands, *Demon Possession in Elizabethan England* (Westport, CT, 2004), chapter 6. For a further example of a 'manufactured' confession, see below, p. 151.

119. Edward Bever, *The Realities of Witchcraft and Popular Magic in Early Modern Europe: Culture, Cognition, and Everyday Life* (Basingstoke, 2008): see pp. 244ff., 264, 331, 419, 425ff. and index s.v. 'Fraud'.

### 5 THE ENLIGHTENMENT REJECTION OF MAGIC: MID-CENTURY SCEPTICISM AND ITS MILIEU

1. John Ferriar, 'Of Popular Illusions, and Particularly of Medical Demonology', *Memoirs of the Literary and Philosophical Society of Manchester*, 3 (1790), [23]–116.

2. See *ODNB*.

3. Ferriar, 'Of Popular Illusions', pp. 41, 55–6, 91ff. and passim. On Hoffmann and witchcraft see Lester S. King, *The Philosophy of Medicine: The Early Eighteenth Century* (Cambridge, MA, 1978), pp. 202ff. On the Saint-Médard case see B. Robert Kreiser, *Miracles, Convulsions, and Ecclesiastical Politics in Early Eighteenth-century Paris* (Princeton, 1978).

4. Ferriar, 'Of Popular Illusions', pp. 96–7, 114–16. On Mesmer see especially Robert Darnton, *Mesmerism and the End of the Enlightenment in France* (Cambridge, MA, 1968); on English developments see Patricia Fara, 'An Attractive Therapy: Animal Magnetism in Eighteenth-century England', *History of Science*, 33 (1995), 127–77, and Alison Winter, *Mesmerized: Powers of the Mind in Victorian Britain* (Chicago, 1998). On the Lukins case, see Jonathan Barry, 'Methodism and Mummery: The Case of George Lukins', in his *Witchcraft and Demonology in South-West England, 1640–1789* (Basingstoke, 2012), chapter 7. Ferriar's source was probably a note added to the 2nd edition of Francis Grose's *Provincial Glossary* (London, 1790): see Barry, p. 206.

5. John Ferriar, *An Essay towards a Theory of Apparitions* (London, 1813), pp. 19, 64 and passim. For the view of it as pioneering see, e.g., Terry Castle, *The Female Thermometer: Eighteenth-Century Culture and the Invention of the Uncanny* (Oxford, 1995), pp. 163–4; Shane McCorristine, *Spectres of the Self: Thinking about Ghosts and Ghost-Seeing in England, 1750-1920* (Cambridge, 2010), chapter 1; Roger Clarke, *A Natural History of Ghosts* (London, 2012), pp. 148, 308.

6. Paul K. Monod, *Solomon's Secret Arts: The Occult in the Age of Enlightenment* (New Haven and London, 2013); John V. Fleming, *The Dark Side of the Enlightenment: Wizards, Alchemists, and Spiritual Seekers in the Age of Reason* (New York, 2013).

7. See above, pp. 115–16. For a recent full account of Beaumont see Jonathan Barry, 'John Beaumont: Science, Spirits and the Scale of Nature', in Barry, *Witchcraft and Demonology in South-West England*, pp. 124–64.

8. See Beaumont, *Historical, Physiological and Theological Treatise of Spirits, Apparitions, Witchcrafts, and other Magical Practices* (London, 1705), pp. 91–4, 393–7, and Michael Hunter (ed.), *Magic and Mental Disorder: Sir Hans Sloane's Memoir of John Beaumont* (London, 2011), pp. 6–7. For the final quotation, see n. 23 below. For further references, see Beaumont, *Treatise*, pp. 197–8, 200, 251.

9. See above, p. 54. It is perhaps interesting to note that, in the annotations to Martin Martin's *A Description of the Western Islands of Scotland* (see above, pp. 54–5), Toland refers on p. 300 to Beaumont as 'the greatest visionary of the three', also referring to Martin and to James Garden (see below, pp. 149, 153–5). For Beaumont's role in relation to second sight, see below, pp. 152, 163.

10. [John Trenchard], *The Natural History of Superstition* (London, 1709), pp. 11, 15 and passim.

11. Including Sloane's diagnosis, on which see below; Beaumont, *Treatise*, p. 396.

12. Hunter, *Magic and Mental Disorder*, pp. x and 7–8. Buckingham's views are evidenced by his annotations to his copy of Cudworth's *True Intellectual System of the Universe* (London, 1678), now British Library 676.g.17. I am indebted to Dmitri Levitin for drawing my attention to this volume.

13. See Kate Loveman, *Reading Fictions, 1660-1740: Deception in English Literary and Political Culture* (Aldershot, 2008), chapter 3. It is interesting that the Rochester 'Dr Bendo' hoax is mentioned on pp. 78n., 81: see above, p. 107.

14. Ferriar, *Theory of Apparitions*, pp. 67–8, 69–75.

15. Hunter, *Magic and Mental Disorder*, passim. See also James Delbourgo, *Collecting the World: The Life and Curiosity of Hans Sloane* (London, 2017), esp. 278ff., who summarises the text of Sloane's memoir at length and also provides ancillary references documenting such attitudes on his part.

16. See, for example, Monod, *Solomon's Secret Arts*, p. 177; Barry, 'John Beaumont', p. 126.

17. It is probably now Sloane MS 2731: see Hunter, *Magic and Mental Disorder*, p. xiii.

18. For background information on the Ashmole episode, see ibid., pp. xii–xiii.

19. It is possibly significant that Sloane wrote the text in French for a French recipient, since he may have perceived French savants as more receptive to such views than English ones. For a comparably sceptical attitude, see the Abbé St Pierre's 'Discours . . . Pour expliquer physiquement certaines apparitions' in *Mémoires de Trévoux*, January 1726, pp. 119–45, of which Sloane probably owned a copy although his run of the journal (now British Library PP4261b) no longer contains this particular issue. He corresponded with St Pierre in 1714 concerning his plan for a universal peace in Europe (St Pierre to Sloane, 14, 30 April 1714, BL MS Sloane 4043, fols 246, 249; Sloane to St Pierre, 27 May 1714, MS Sloane 4068, fol. 89). Ferriar summarised and extended St Pierre's findings in his *Theory of Apparitions*, pp. 118ff.

20. Hunter, *Magic and Mental Disorder*, passim. For Sloane's medical correspondence see British Library MSS Sloane 4075–8. For a rare example of a consultation concerning someone suffering from a mental disorder in 1707, Sir John Bolles, see Sloane 4078, fol. 303.

21. E.g. Thomas Morgan, *Philosophical Principles of Medicine*, 2nd edn (London, 1730), pp. 392–4. Trenchard similarly speaks of 'Melancholy and Hypochodriack Men' and his overall diagnosis is similar: *Natural History*, p. 14 and passim.

22. Archibald Pitcairne, *The Philosophical and Mathematical Elements of Physick* (London, 1718), p. 186.

23. Hunter, *Magic and Mental Disorder*, passim. For the further comment, see a fragment filed at the very end of Sloane's correspondence which appears to be part of the draft of Sloane's response to the letter from the Abbé Bignon acknowledging the memoir quoted in ibid., pp. xxii–xxiii (Sloane MS 4069, fol. 271, kindly drawn to my attention by Arnold Hunt). The original French of this sentence, including the section quoted on p. 123 above, reads: 'Il m'a souvent parlé de cet état de conversations avec ces esprits comme de ‹la› chose le plus chagrinant du monde & qu'il estoit bien heureux d'estre quitté par les vomissemens & purgatiffs naturels que l'avoient delivrés'. Sloane also corrected Bignon's misidentification of Buckingham: see Hunter, *Magic and Mental Disorder*, p. xxiii. (Accents and apostrophes have been added as appropriate in this sentence and that quoted in n. 24.)

24. Loc cit. The original French reads: 'il me racontoit peu d'années avant sa mort que dans un secte nouvel qu'on nommoit Philadelphians il y avoit un bassin d'airain qui estant mis en dessous de Chevett du lit ne manqueroit jamais produire de tels (songes ou) conversations' (within this, 'd'années' replaces 'temps' deleted, which is itself inserted to replace 'd'années'; the entire phrase 'nouvel qu'on nommoit Philadelphians' is inserted, as is 'du lit'; after 'jamais', 'de' is deleted).

25. Although ideas about fluids and receptacles are common in Jane Leade's writings (*A Fountain of Gardens*, vol. 1 (London, 1696), p. 59, even speaks of 'a sanctified Vessel meetly prepared', while vol. 2 (London, 1697) refers to golden vessels on pp. 256 and 305), I have not found anything answering to Beaumont's statement. But for related ideas in Beaumont's own writings, see his *Treatise of Spirits*, pp. 200ff., and in his *Gleanings of Antiquities* (London, 1724), pp. 118ff. and 139ff. For the Philadelphians, see esp. Julie Hirst, *Jane Leade: Biography of a Seventeenth-Century Mystic* (Aldershot, 2005).

26. See above, Introduction, p. 8.

27. See above, p. 64 and see also Hillel Schwartz, *Knaves, Fools, Madmen, and that Subtile Effluvium: A Study of the Opposition to the French Prophets in England, 1706–10* (Gainesville, 1978), esp. pp. 43ff., and Lionel Laborie, *Enlightening Enthusiasm: Prophecy and Religious Experience in Early Eighteenth-century England* (Manchester, 2015), chapter 6. For Trenchard's view, see *Natural History*, p. 29; on pp. 30–32 he instances the Quakers at greater length.

28. More, *Enthusiasmus Triumphatus* (London, 1656), p. 51; Trenchard, *Natural History*, esp. p. 45. See above, p. 9. It is interesting that Sloane cited certain seventeenth-century precursors in his memoir of Beaumont: see Hunter, *Magic and Mental Disorder*, pp. 15–16 (Edward Tyson) and 17 (Peter Barwick). See further Peter Elmer, *Witchcraft, Witch-Hunting, and Politics in Early Modern England* (Oxford, 2016), pp. 251ff.

29. Robinson, *A New System of the Spleen, Vapours and Hypochondriack Melancholy* (London, 1729), pp. 406–7. Cf. ibid., pp. 247–8. For background see Roy Porter, *Mind-forg'd Manacles: A History of Madness in England from the Restoration to the Regency* (London, 1987).

30. Mead, *Medical Precepts and Cautions*, trans. Thomas Stack (London, 1751), pp. 74ff.

31. Peter Templeman (ed.), *Select Cases, and Consultations, in Physick. By the late Eminent John Woodward M.D.* (London, 1757), pp. 20ff., 279ff., 420.

32. Ibid., p. 288.

33. John Friend, *Emmenologia* (English trans., 1729), sig. A6.

34. See, e.g., Friend, *Emmenologia*, sig. A7 and passim; Richard Mead, *A Mechanical Account of Poisons* (London, 1702). For Chirac see esp. Nicholas Purcell, *A Treatise of Vapours*, 2nd edn (1707).

35. Pitcairne, *Philosophical and Mathematical Principles*, passim. For accounts of this tradition see R. E. Schofield, *Mechanism and Materialism: British Natural Philosophy in an Age of Reason* (Princeton, 1970), chapter 3; Arnold Thackray, *Atoms and Powers: An Essay on Newtonian Matter-Theory and the Development of Chemistry* (Cambridge, MA, 1970), chapters 3 and 5; Andrew Cunningham, 'Sydenham versus Newton: the Edinburgh Fever Dispute of the 1690s between Andrew Brown and Archibald Pitcairne', in W. F. Bynum and V. Nutton (eds), *Theories of Fever from Antiquity to the Enlightenment* (London,

1981), pp. 71–98; T. M. Brown, 'Medicine in the Shadow of the *Principia*', *Journal of the History of Ideas*, 48 (1987), 629–48; R.J.J. Martin, 'Explaining John Freind's *History of Physick*', *Studies in History and Philosophy of Science*, 19 (1988), 399–418; Anita Guerrini, 'Newtonianism, Medicine and Religion', in Ole Peter Grell and Andrew Cunningham (eds), *Religio Medici: Medicine and Religion in Seventeenth-century England* (Aldershot, 1996), pp. 293–312; Akihito Suzuki, 'Psychiatry without Mind in the Eighteenth Century: The Case of British Iatro-Mathematicians', *Archives Internationales d'Histoire des Sciences*, 48 (1998), 119–46; and Roy Porter, *Flesh in the Age of Reason* (London, 2003), pp. 305ff.

36. Mead, *Mechanical Account of Poisons*, sigs A4v–5; Robinson, *A New Theory of Physick and Diseases, Founded on the Principles of the Newtonian Philosophy* (London, 1725).

37. See his comment in the Beaumont memoir on 'attraction' as 'still a little shadowy': Hunter, *Magic and Mental Disorder*, p. 3.

38. King, *Philosophy of Medicine*, pp. 109ff., on pp. 110, 114, 115.

39. See, e.g., Robinson's vitriolic attack on Blackmore, Cockburn and Woodward in *New Theory*, p. 244 and passim, or Morgan, *Philosophical Principles*, esp. preface. See also the accounts cited in n. 35.

40. Mead, *Mechanical Account of Poisons*, 3rd edn (London, 1745), pp. v–vi, xxxiv–xxxv and passim. See also Thomas Stack's 'Life' of Mead in Mead, *Medica Sacra* (English trans., 1755), p. 14 and passim. Of course, this is partly due to the slow 'drip' of Newton's views into eighteenth-century intellectual life: for a useful table see Thackray, *Atoms and Powers*, p. 12. For modern accounts of Mead see Ludmilla Jordanova, 'Richard Mead's Communities of Belief in Eighteenth-century London', in Simon Ditchfield (ed.), *Christianity and Community in the West: Essays for John Bossy* (Aldershot, 2001), pp. 241–59, and Craig Ashley Hanson, *The English Virtuoso: Art, Medicine and Antiquarianism in the Age of Empiricism* (Chicago, 2009), chapter 5.

41. For the claim concerning quacks see esp. Mead, *Mechanical Account of Poisons*, p. xv; Morgan, *Philosophical Principles*, p. xii.

42. Sir Hans Sloane, *Voyage to . . . Jamaica*, 2 vols (London, 1707, 1725). For comments on Sloane in this regard see Michael Hunter, 'Introduction', in Alison Walker, Arthur MacGregor and Michael Hunter (eds), *From Books to Bezoars: Sir Hans Sloane and his Collections* (London, 2012), p. 7; for further information, see *From Books to Bezoars*, passim; Arthur MacGregor (ed.), *Sir Hans Sloane: Collector, Scientist, Antiquary, Founding Father of the British Museum* (London, 1994); and Delbourgo, *Collecting the World*.

43. *Pharmacopoeia Radcliffeanæ, or Dr Radcliff's Prescriptions Faithfully gather'd from his Original Recipe's* (London, 1716) and *Pharmacopoeia Radcliffeanæ, Pars Altera* (London, 1716).

44. See [William Pittis], *Some Memoirs of Dr John Radcliffe*, 2nd edn (London, 1715), William MacMichael, *The Gold-headed Cane* (London, 1827), pp. 1–55. For modern accounts see Ivor Guest, *Dr John Radcliffe and his Trust* (London, 1991) and the biography in Eveline Cruikshanks, Stuart Handley and D. W. Hayton (eds), *The House of Commons, 1690–1715*, 5 vols (Cambridge, 2002), vol. 5, pp. 245–51, which is to be preferred to that in *ODNB*. On Richard Bentley's reference to Radcliffe in his response to Collins, Phileleutherus Lipsiensis, *Remarks Upon a Late Discourse of Free-thinking* (London, 1713), p. 33, see above, pp. 80–1.

45. Mead, *Medica Sacra; or, a Commentary On the most remarkable Diseases, Mentioned in the Holy Scriptures* (English trans., 1755), passim.

46. See R. M. Burns, *The Great Debate on Miracles: From Joseph Glanvill to David Hume* (Lewisburg, 1981), esp. chapters 4–5; Jane Shaw, *Miracles in Enlightenment England* (New Haven and London, 2006), chapter 7. On the broader background, see Introduction, p. 6.

47. The literature is huge, but, in addition to the references in the previous note see Sir Leslie Stephen, *History of English Thought in the Eighteenth Century*, 2 vols, 3rd edn (London, 1902), vol. 1, pp. 228–77; William H. Trapnell, *Thomas Woolston: Madman and Deist?* (Bristol, 1994); Roger D. Lund, 'Irony as Subversion: Thomas Woolston and the Crime of

Wit', in Lund (ed.), *The Margins of Orthodoxy: Heterodox Writing and Cultural Response, 1660–1750* (Cambridge, 1995), pp. 170–94, and Lund, *Ridicule, Religion and the Politics of Wit in Augustan England* (Farnham, 2012), pp. 201ff.; James A. Herrick, *The Radical Rhetoric of the English Deists: The Discourse of Skepticism, 1680–1750* (Columbia, SC, 1997), chapters 4, 7, 8; Laura M. Stevens, 'Civility and Skepticism in the Woolston-Sherlock Debate over Miracles', *Eighteenth-century Life*, 21 (1997), 57–70; Michael Suarez, ' "The Most Blasphemous Book that ever was Published": Ridicule, Reception and Censorship in Eighteenth-century England', in Wallace Kirsop (ed.), *The Commonwealth of Books* (Melbourne, 2007), pp. 46–77; Wayne Hudson, *Enlightenment and Modernity: The English Deists and Reform* (London, 2009), chapter 3; Hugh Trevor-Roper, 'From Deism to History: Conyers Middleton', in his *History and the Enlightenment*, ed. John Robertson (2010), pp. 71–119; R. G. Ingram, ' "The Weight of Historical Evidence": Conyers Middleton and the Eighteenth-century Miracles Debate', in Robert D. Cornwall and William Gibson (eds), *Religion, Politics and Dissent, 1660–1832* (Aldershot, 2010), 85–109; Ingram, *Reformation without End: Religion, Politics and the Past in Post-revolutionary England* (Manchester, 2018), part 2; and Brian Young, 'Conyers Middleton: the Historical Consequences of Heterodoxy', in Sarah Mortimer and John Robertson (eds), *The Intellectual Consequences of Religious Heterodoxy, 1600–1750* (Leiden, 2012), pp. 235–65.

48. By comparison, the literature is very meagre, really only comprising H. C. Erik Midelfort, 'The Gadarene Demoniac in the English Enlightenment', in Emily Michelson (ed.), *A Linking of Heaven and Earth* (Aldershot, 2012), pp. 49–66, which develops the discussion of the topic in his *Exorcism and Enlightenment: Johann Joseph Gassner and the Demons of Eighteenth-Century Germany* (New Haven and London, 2005), pp. 91–2, 106–7, 179–80 and 190–92. For a brief account see Brian P. Levack, *The Devil Within: Possession and Exorcism in the Christian West* (New Haven and London, 2013), pp. 46–8; there are also relevant remarks in Anthony Ossa-Richardson, 'Possession or Insanity? Two Views from the Victorian Lunatic Asylum', *Journal of the History of Ideas*, 74 (2013), 553–75. It is interesting to note Sykes's comment in a letter to Cox Macro of 13 October 1737: 'I will let you into one secret, & that is, *The Enquiry* was design'd & wrote so long ago as Mr Woolstons controversy was on foot. But I was unwilling to raise a controversy at that time: & it had laid by still, had not some to whom I lent it, extorted it from me', BL Add MS 32556, fol. 241v.

49. Church, *A Vindication of the Miraculous Powers, Which Subsisted In the First Three Centuries of the Christian Church . . . With a Preface Containing Some Observations on Dr Mead's Account of the Demoniacs in his New Piece entituled, Medica Sacra* (London, 1750). At times in his text, Church interestingly defers to Mead on professional grounds (pp. xi–xii and passim). It is also, of course, true that, in contrast to the other controversial works referred to here, Mead's book was originally written in Latin: but the translation by Thomas Stack seems as 'authorised' as the other translations of works by Mead that he did at this time.

50. See Mead, *Medica Sacra*, esp. pp. ivff. For the view that 'From the intense puritan piety of his youth Mead seems to have travelled to a more deistic religion', see Anita Guerrini in *ODNB*. For a slightly complacent account of Mead and of this work, see Jordanova, 'Richard Mead's Communities of Belief'.

51. See Robert E. Sullivan, *John Toland and the Deist Controversy: A Study in Adaptations* (Cambridge, MA, 1982), and more recently, Jeffrey R. Wigelsworth, *Deism in Enlightenment England: Theology, Politics and Newtonian Public Science* (Manchester, 2009). Cf. also Hudson, *Enlightenment and Modernity*, where Mead appears briefly, but only for Thomas Morgan's criticism of him (p. 76).

52. For the pious protestations of his will, see Delbourgo, *Collecting the World*, p. 271. See also ibid., pp. 303–4.

53. Ibid., p. 271, citing Basnage de Beauval to Sloane, 9 November 1696, MS Sloane MS 4036, fol. 273 (which makes it clear that Sloane did indeed send a copy of the book); Ann Thomson, *Bodies of Thought: Science, Religion, and the Soul in the Early Enlightenment* (Oxford, 2008), pp. 104–6; Arnold Hunt, 'Sloane as a Collector of Manuscripts', in *From*

*Books to Bezoars*, pp. 190–207, on p. 198. It is perhaps also worth noting that both Sloane and Mead owned presentation copies of Archibald Pitcairne's heterodox *Epistola Archimedis*: see Michael Hunter, 'Pitcairneana: An Atheist Text by Archibald Pitcairne', *Historical Journal*, 59 (2016), 595–621, on p. 598 n. 12.

54. See Richard Parkinson (ed.), *Private Journal and Literary Remains of John Byrom*, 2 vols in 4 parts (Chetham Society, 1854–7), vol. 2, part 1, p. 27. For Folkes's views on religion and William Stukeley's alarmed reaction to them, see David B. Haycock, *William Stukeley: Science, Religion and Archaeology in Eighteenth-century England* (Woodbridge, 2002), p. 227.

55. See *The Works of John Wesley*, 14 vols (London, 1872, reprinted Grand Rapids, Michigan, 1958–9), vol. 4, pp. 194–5: entry for 22 December 1780. For an earlier visit by Wesley see ibid., vol. 2, p. 520: entry for 12 December 1759 (also printed in Wesley, *Letters and Journals*, ed. W. R. Ward and R. P. Heitzenrater (Nashville, 1988– [in progress]), vol. 4, p. 236).

56. For references to Mead in relation to attitudes to magic, see James Sharpe, *Instruments of Darkness: Witchcraft in England 1550–1750* (London, 1996), p. 271, and Roy Porter, 'Witchcraft and Magic in Enlightenment, Romantic and Liberal Thought', in Marijke Gijswijt-Hofstra et al., *Athlone History of Witchcraft and Magic*, vol. 5: *The Eighteenth and Nineteenth Centuries* (London, 1999), pp. 191–282, on p. 230. It is interesting that he owned the copy of Martin's *Description* annotated by Molesworth and Toland (and a copy of the *Treatise of the Three Impostors*): see Justin Champion, 'Enlightened Erudition and the Politics of Reading in John Toland's Circle', *Historical Journal*, 49 (2006), 111–41, on p. 117.

57. Mead, *Medica Sacra*, pp. xiii–xv and passim.

58. Ibid., pp. 28ff.

59. Ibid., pp. 80–82 and pp. 75ff., passim.

60. Ibid., pp. xi, 75, 89 (where he also cites Sykes), 96–7 and passim; Ferriar, 'Of Popular Illusions', p. 39.

61. For the controversies in which he was involved see John Disney, *Memoirs of the Life and Writings of Arthur Ashley Sykes, D.D.* (London, 1785); *ODNB*. See also above, n. 48.

62. Sykes, *Enquiry*, pp. 20ff.; *Further Enquiry*, pp. 69–70, 93.

63. Sykes, *Enquiry*, pp. 28, 61; *Further Enquiry*, pp. 66–7, 96, 97.

64. Sykes, *Enquiry*, pp. 60–61; *Further Enquiry*, pp. 24, 68, 72, 96, 98. I thus disagree with Brian Levack's view that medical views were less significant than biblical scholarship: *The Devil Within*, p. 49.

65. Sykes, *Enquiry*, p. 77; *Further Enquiry*, pp. 75, 84, 105ff. On accommodationism see Midelfort, 'Gaderene Demoniac'. It is worth noting here that the medical arguments are also prominent in John Douglas, *The Criterion: or Miracles Examined* (London, 1754), in which Mead is repeatedly cited.

66. John Jackson, *Remarks on Dr Middleton's Free Enquiry*, 2nd edn (London, 1749), p. 59. It is perhaps worth noting that Sykes was also moving towards distrust of the Fathers.

67. Middleton, *Free Inquiry*, p. ii; Trevor-Roper, 'From Deism to History'. For other modern studies see above n. 47.

68. See Hudson, *Enlightenment and Modernity*, pp. 61ff. For the Deists' attitude to magic, see above, Chapter 3.

69. Middleton, *Free Inquiry*, p. viii.

70. Ibid., pp. 76, 79, 80, 185. It is perhaps worth noting that in a letter to Lord Hervey of 12 March 1734 Middleton wrote, concerning health, 'I formerly made some study of it, & thought myself so strong, as to venture on a quarrel even with the Physicians', Suffolk Record Office AC941/47/8.

71. Middleton, *Free Inquiry*, pp. 92, 184–5, 197. Cf. Sykes, *Further Enquiry*, p. 86: the ventriloquist in question is presumably James Bick (d. 1734), of whom there is a mezzotint by John Faber the Elder (British Museum 1851,0308.47).

72. Middleton, *Free Inquiry*, pp. 221–3. He then went on to deal with the St Médard case: see above, p. 121.

73. Ibid., pp. 228–9 and passim.
74. Toll, *A Defence of Dr Middleton's Free Enquiry, against Mr Dodwell's Free Answer* (London, 1749), p. 73.
75. Toll, *Defence*, pp. 64, 73. Cf. Toll, *Some Remarks upon Mr Church's Vindication of Miraculous Powers, &c.* (London, 1750), pp. 42–5. On changing attitudes to the royal touch see Stephen Brogan, *The Royal Touch in Early Modern England: Politics, Medicine and Sin* (Woodbridge, 2015), esp. chapter 6.
76. Sykes to Sloane, 17 April 1715 and no date, Sloane MS 4076, fols 379–80. See also Sykes to Sloane, 18 May 1739, Sloane MS 4056, fol. 98.
77. Sykes, *Enquiry*, p. 47.
78. See above, p. 62, and the letters to Sloane there cited.
79. Sykes to Birch, 19 November 1749, Add. MS 4319, fol. 74 (quoted in Disney, *Memoirs*, p. 218).
80. See Middleton to Hervey, 22 February, 9 March 1738, Add. MS 32458, fols 36–7 (he also consulted Radcliffe), and Middleton to Sloane, 1 September 1728, Sloane MS 5049, fol. 225.
81. See Trevor-Roper, 'From Deism to History', pp. 77–9.
82. See esp. Woodward's letter to Middleton of 14 November 1726, BL Add MS 32457, fols 49–50. On medical rivalry, see e.g. Roy Porter, *Bodies Politic: Disease, Death and Doctors in England 1650–1900* (London, 2001), pp. 209ff., and above, nn. 35 and 39.
83. Middleton to Heberden, 3 April 1749, 4 February 1750, Add MS 32457, fols 184 (after 'used', 'to enjoy' is deleted), 185. Cf. Middleton to Heberden, 18 August 1746, ibid., fols 168–9, commenting on a doctor whose religious zeal exposed Middleton as 'the only natural man in the company'.
84. W. S. Lewis (ed.), *The Yale Edition of Horace Walpole's Correspondence*, 48 vols (New Haven, 1937–83), vol. 15, pp. 293, 309–11. Gordon evidently also had links with Sloane: see the letters of 29 September 1728 and 12 March 1739, BL Sloane MS 5050, fols 10, 63, assuming that the 'T. Gordon' who sent them is the same man.
85. For Pitcairne, see Hunter, 'Pitcairneana', and Alasdair Raffe, 'Archibald Pitcairne and Scottish Heterodoxy, *c.* 1688–1713', *Historical Journal*, 60 (2017), 633–57; for Morgan, see esp. Wigelsworth, *Deism in Enlightenment England*, esp. chapter 5. Among earlier examples one might mention Walter Charleton (see above, p. 98) and Thomas Sydenham (see above, p. 81). For a further example of heterodoxy in a medical context, see the case of Henry Layton as discussed in Ann Thomson, *Bodies of Thought*, chapter 4.
86. For Hogarth's print see above, p. 118, and Plate 16.
87. See Lewis, *Yale Edition of Walpole's Correspondence*, vol. 15, p. 315.
88. Sykes to Macro, 13 October 1737, Add MS 32556, fol. 241 (the word in question was 'Fetfa' or perhaps 'Tetfa'). For Macro's medical training see *ODNB*.
89. Church, *Vindication of the Miraculous Powers*, pp. 344ff. For Addison's view, see above, pp. 24, 60–1. It is interesting that Ferriar was particularly scathing about this: 'Of Popular Illusions', pp. 111–12.
90. See, for instance, Joseph Juxon's *A Sermon upon Witchcraft Occasion'd by a Late Illegal Attempt to Discover Witches by Swimming* (London, 1736), which has sometimes been cited as a significant text in the growing rejection of the possibility of witchcraft by the educated (e.g. Sharpe, *Instruments of Darkness*, pp. 273–4), but which echoes Hutchinson's *Historical Essay* in its continuing ambivalence on aspects of the topic. See also above, pp. 65–6. It is perhaps worth noting the view of David Katz (*The Occult Tradition: From the Renaissance to the Present Day* (London, 2005), p. 63) that the Bible is 'the ultimate esoteric writing'.
91. Becket, *A Free and Impartial Enquiry* (London, 1722), pp. 53, 61–2 and passim; Mead, *Medica Sacra*, p. 30. See also Brogan, *Royal Touch*, pp. 206ff.
92. Turner, *The Art of Surgery*, 2 vols (London, 1722), vol. 1, pp. 158ff.; Freind, *History of Physick*, 2 vols (London, 1725–6), vol. 1, p. 305, vol. 2, pp. 274ff. (and see Martin, 'Explaining', pp. 412–13).
93. Whiston, *An Account of the Dæmoniacks, and of the Power of Casting out Dæmons, both in the New Testament, and in the First Four Centuries* (London, 1737) (though this

engages surprisingly little with Sykes's book), and Whiston, *Mr Whiston's Account of the Exact Time when Miraculous Gifts Ceas'd in the Church* (London, 1749), p. 39 and passim. Also highly revealing are his *Memoirs*, 2nd edn, 2 vols (London, 1753).

94. On Sykes and Newton's papers see Rob Iliffe, 'A "connected system"? The Snare of a Beautiful Hand and the Unity of Newton's Archive', in Michael Hunter (ed.), *Archives of the Scientific Revolution: The Formation and Exchange of Ideas in Seventeenth-Century Europe* (Woodbridge, 1998), pp. 137–57, on pp. 141, 143, 144; on his defence of Newton against Warburton see Disney, *Memoirs*, pp. 251ff., and Jed Z. Buchwald and Mordechai Feingold, *Newton and the Origin of Civilization* (Princeton, 2013), p. 397. For his quota- tion of Newton, see his *Further Enquiry*, pp. 22–4. Middleton also cited Newton in his *Free Inquiry*, pp. 177–8n. (see also Buchwald and Feingold, *Newton*, pp. 390ff.); for Newtonian clichés in his correspondence see e.g. his analogy between reason in man and gravity in the universe in his letter to Lord Hervey of 31 July 1733, Suffolk Record Office AC941/47/8.

95. Sykes, *Further Enquiry*, p. 97. The claim referred to is made in Whiston's *Account of a Surprizing Meteor* (London, 1716), esp. pp. 68ff. (on this episode, see Patricia Fara, 'Lord Derwentwater's Lights: Prediction and the Aurora Polaris', *Journal of the History of Astronomy*, 27 (1996), 239–58). For Sykes's low view of Whiston see also Sykes to Macro, 13 October 1737, Add. MS 32556, fol. 241 ('Mr Whiston's Pamphlet is more contempt- ible, than you can imagine: but just of a peice with his late performances'), and Sykes to Birch, 22 October 1749, Add. MS 4319, fol. 78, where he wrote of Whiston's *Memoirs* how '[I] now think Him to be, neither that *sincere*, nor *honest* man, nor *religious* one, that he pretends'.

96. Monod, *Solomon's Secret Arts*, chapter 5; Katz, *The Occult Tradition*, p. 67.

97. See, e.g., Genevieve Lloyd, *Enlightenment Shadows* (Oxford, 2013); Anthony Pagden, *The Enlightenment and Why It Still Matters* (Oxford, 2013); William J. Bulman and R. G. Ingram (eds), *God in the Enlightenment* (Oxford, 2016).

98. Church, *A Reply to the Farther Enquiry into the Meaning of the Demoniacks in the New Testament* (London, 1737), pp. 7n., 27, 75, 93; on p. 57 he cites Van Dale.

99. See above, n. 5.

## 6  SECOND SIGHT IN SCOTLAND: BOYLE'S LEGACY AND ITS TRANSFORMATION

1. By contrast, it is interesting to note Thomas Kirk's brief account of second sight in his account of his tour of Scotland in 1677, which stimulated no follow-up at all: P. Hume Brown (ed.), *Tours of Scotland 1677 and 1681 by Thomas Kirk and Ralph Thoresby* (Edinburgh, 1892), pp. 34–5.

2. See Michael Hunter (ed.), *The Occult Laboratory: Magic, Science and Second Sight in Late Seventeenth-century Scotland* (Woodbridge, 2001) (hereinafter *Occult Laboratory*). Tarbat's letter was first published in full in the edition of *The Secret Commonwealth* printed at the behest of Sir Walter Scott in 1815 (see ibid., p. 40), though for John Beaumont's publication of its substance without acknowledging his source, see below, p. 152. In fact, a tiny hint of Boyle's interest had appeared at an intermediate date in the form of a reference, 'concerning the second Sight, Relations communicated', in connec- tion with the unpublished part of his *Strange Reports* (see above, pp. 11–12) as listed by Thomas Birch in his 1744 edition of Boyle: see Michael Hunter and Edward B. Davis (eds), *The Works of Robert Boyle*, 14 vols (London, 1999–2000), vol. 14, p. 357. This is noted (from the 1772 reprint of Birch's edition) by Arthur Sherbo in 'The Text of Johnson's "Journey to the Western Islands of Scotland": "Bayle" or "Boyle"', *Notes and Queries*, 197 (1952), 182–4, on pp. 183–4. For relevant material that has come to light since *Occult Laboratory* was published, see below, pp. 185–6, and nn. 13 and 31. It is also worth noting here an account of second sight that appeared in parallel with mine, Shari A. Cohn, 'A Historical Review of Second Sight: The Collectors, their Accounts and Ideas', *Scottish*

*Studies*, 33 (1999), 146-85, and a further, more accessible edition of one key text in the form of Robert Kirk, *The Secret Commonwealth of Elves, Fauns, and Fairies. Introduction by Marina Warner* (New York, 2007).

3. *Occult Laboratory*, pp. 51-3.

4. Ibid., pp. 90-94, 165-9; it is also printed in Michael Hunter, Antonio Clericuzio and Lawrence M. Principe (eds), *The Correspondence of Robert Boyle*, 6 vols (London, 2001), vol. 5, pp. 127-31.

5. Michael Hunter, *Boyle Studies: Aspects of the Life and Thought of Robert Boyle (1627-91)* (Farnham, 2015), chapter 9, on p. 185.

6. See Peter Anstey and Michael Hunter, 'Robert Boyle's "Designe about Natural History"', *Early Science and Medicine*, 13 (2008), 83-126, esp. pp. 102ff.

7. Boyle, *Works*, vol. 6, p. 14.

8. *Occult Laboratory*, p. 51.

9. See above, pp. 11-12.

10. Quoted above, p. 15.

11. *Occult Laboratory*, pp. 10-12, 35-8 and 54-76. On the descent of the MS see also Eiluned Rees and Gwyn Walters, 'The Dispersal of the Manuscripts of Edward Lhuyd', *Welsh History Review*, 7 (1974-5), 148-78, esp. p. 161.

12. See *Occult Laboratory*, pp. 21-2, and below, pp. 185-6.

13. On Lhuyd, see *Occult Laboratory*, pp. 25-6, 205ff.; see also J. L. Campbell and Derick Thomson, *Edward Lhuyd in the Scottish Highlands, 1699-1700* (Oxford, 1963). For Garden's letters to Aubrey see *Occult Laboratory*, pp. 22-4, 42-4 and 118ff., and for their adaptation for *Miscellanies* see Aubrey, *Three Prose Works*, ed. John Buchanan-Brown (Fontwell, 1972), pp. 111ff., 392ff. Since *Occult Laboratory* was published, I have kindly been informed by Kelsey Jackson Williams of a further letter from Garden to Aubrey dated 27 May 1697, Bodleian Library MS Rawl. Lett. 107, fol. 224: though it provides no further information on second sight, it mentions a young man, Hugh Grant, whom Garden had located to help Lhuyd concerning linguistic matters in the Highlands (presumably nothing came of this, however, as he is not mentioned in Campbell and Thomson, *Edward Lhuyd*; the Grant family is referred to in *Three Prose Works*, p. 399, but not a member of it called Hugh).

14. See Michael Hunter, *John Aubrey and the Realm of Learning* (London, 1975), chapter 3. On Aubrey's 'Templa Druidum' see also Kelsey Jackson Williams, *The Antiquary: John Aubrey's Historical Scholarship* (Oxford, 2016), chapter 1.

15. Hunter, *John Aubrey*, chapter 2. On county natural histories see also Stan A. E. Mendyk, '*Speculum Britanniae*': *Regional Study, Antiquarianism, and Science in Britain to 1700* (Toronto, 1989) and Elizabeth Yale, *Sociable Knowledge: Natural History and the Nation in Early Modern Britain* (Philadelphia, 2016).

16. Hunter, *John Aubrey*, pp. 124ff. For the preternatural, see above, pp. 5, 11.

17. Hunter, *John Aubrey*, pp. 102-4; Aubrey, *Three Prose Works*, pp. 1ff.

18. Ibid., pp. 5-6.

19. Robert Latham and William Matthews (eds), *The Diary of Samuel Pepys*, 11 vols (London, 1970-83), vol. 6, p. 48, quoted in A. Rupert Hall's commentary in ibid., vol. 10, pp. 361ff., on p. 364. Cf. ibid., pp. 381ff., e.g. pp. 383-5, and (for instance) Claire Tomalin, *Samuel Pepys: The Unequalled Self* (London, 2002), pp. 252, 256. For *Hydrostatical Paradoxes* see *Diary*, vol. 8, pp. 250-1, 258, 351, 400.

20. See Boyle, *Works*, vol. 1, p. lxxxiv; Robert Latham (ed.), *Catalogue of the Pepys Library at Magdalene College, Cambridge*, 7 vols (Cambridge, 1978-94), vol. 7 part 2, pp. 13-30. Cf. Kate Loveman, *Pepys and his Books: Reading, Newsgathering, and Sociability, 1660-1703* (Oxford, 2015), p. 268, though this area of Pepys's book collecting does not receive as much attention as it might in this otherwise valuable book.

21. *Occult Laboratory*, pp. 24-5, 44-6, 160-86.

22. Ibid., p. 185.

23. See above, pp. 98, 107, and the commentary in Pepys, *Diary*, vol. 10, pp. 388-90; Edwin Chappell (ed.), *The Tangier Papers of Samuel Pepys*, Navy Records Society, 73 (1935),

pp. 10, 14–15, 21. (Pepys's notes on his Spanish visit in the same volume are commonsensical and inquisitive but, sadly, say nothing about the *saludadores*.)

24. For a useful recent account of the *saludadores*, see María Tausiet, 'Healing Virtue: *Saludadores* versus Witches in Early Modern Spain', *Medical History Supplement*, 29 (2009), 40–63.

25. Evelyn, *Diary*, ed. E. S. de Beer, 6 vols (Oxford, 1955), vol. 4, pp. 468–70.

26. *Occult Laboratory*, p. 170. Cf. p. 25.

27. See *Occult Laboratory*, p. 12, including n. 41 for what could be a record of a conversation between the two. For Boyle's earlier initiatives see Michael Hunter, *Boyle: Between God and Science* (New Haven and London, 2009), chapter 12.

28. *Occult Laboratory*, pp. 17–18, 90ff.

29. For examples of such documents see Ruth Paley, Cristina Malcolmson and Michael Hunter, 'Parliament and Slavery 1660–c. 1710', *Slavery and Abolition*, 31 (2010), 257–81, esp. p. 265. For texts in the hand of Boyle's amanuensis, Robin Bacon, surviving in archives other than the Boyle Papers see, e.g., BL Add MS 72897, fols 79–80 (Petty MSS); Petworth House MS 13222 (13) (Orrery MSS) and Boyle, *Works*, vol. 12, p. xviii.

30. A further example of the transmission of such copied documents illustrating a shared interest in second sight is provided by the survival of a copy of Garden's letters to Aubrey on the subject among the papers of John Locke (interestingly, this evidently derives from an intermediate version between the original letters and the published version in *Miscellanies*: see *Occult Laboratory*, pp. 42–3, and Aubrey, *Three Prose Works*, pp. 395–6). Magic was a topic which interested Locke but on which he was publicly discreetly ambivalent.

31. *Occult Laboratory*, p. 10 and n.; Beaumont, *Treatise* (London, 1705), pp. 94–101 for the quotation of the Tarbat letter, pp. 91–4 for Beaumont's own experiences, and 84–129 for his account of second sight as a whole, also utilising Aubrey's *Miscellanies*, Martin's *Description* (see below), a 1581 Venetian work containing 'somewhat which seems ally'd to this Gift of the Second Sight' and other relevant material. It is appropriate here to supplement *Occult Laboratory* by citing additional evidence concerning Beaumont's claim that the account in question was sent 'to a Lady, by a Person of whom she had desired it' (p. 94; cf. p. 101), which was there linked with the interest in the subject of Elizabeth Stillingfleet (*Occult Laboratory*, pp. 10n., 20 and n., and 77n.). In the course of a discussion of second sight by Robert Wodrow in his *Analecta*, 4 vols (Edinburgh, 1842–3), vol. 3, pp. 262–5, he speaks of a letter on the subject that he had been told about that was said to be from Lord Tarbat to Mrs Stillingfleet (pp. 264–5), citing two instances from it which are in fact the very two from Tarbat's interview with and letter to Boyle that are summarised on p. 145 above. The significance of this is unclear: possibly Tarbat sent a version of his letter to Boyle to Mrs Stillingfleet; possibly both Wodrow and Beaumont saw the copy of *The Secret Commonwealth* that we know was sent to her and ignored all its content except Tarbat's letter to Boyle; or possibly confusion arose in the course of manuscript transmission. On Beaumont, see above, pp. 115ff., 123ff.

32. *Occult Laboratory*, pp. 17–18.

33. Ibid., p. 80 and pp. 77–106, passim.

34. See Michael Hunter, 'Alchemy, Magic and Moralism in the Thought of Robert Boyle', *British Journal for the History of Science*, 23 (1990), 387–410, reprinted in Michael Hunter, *Robert Boyle (1627–91): Scrupulosity and Science* (Woodbridge, 2000), chapter 5.

35. For the first publication of Kirk's work, see above, n. 2. For recent studies see, e.g., Julian Goodare, 'Between Humans and Angels: Scientific Uses for Fairies in Early Modern Scotland', in Michael Ostling (ed.), *Fairies, Demons and Nature Spirits: 'Small Gods' at the Margins of Christendom* (London, 2018), pp. 169–90.

36. *Occult Laboratory*, p. 100 and passim. For the copy whose title page makes explicit the book's apologetic purpose, see ibid., p. 77n. (this is the copy that makes the association with Elizabeth Stillingfleet: see n. 31).

37. See *Occult Laboratory*, pp. 26–7, 47, 187–204.

38. Martin Martin, *A Description of the Western Islands of Scotland*, 2nd edn (London, 1716), pp. ix, xii and passim. The reprints were edited by Donald J. Macleod (Stirling, 1934) and Charles W. J. Withers (Edinburgh, 1999).

39. Ibid., pp. 300ff., esp. pp. 307, 335.

40. Ibid., pp. xii–xiii.

41. Ibid., p. 308–9. For Boyle, see above, pp. 11–12, 146–7; for Glanvill, see p. 15.

42. 'Theophilus Insulanus', *Treatise on the Second Sight* (Edinburgh, 1763), p. 84 and passim. For the attribution to William Macleod rather than Donald McLeod, see Thomas Jemiely, 'Samuel Johnson, the Second Sight and his Sources', *Studies in English Literature 1500–1900*, 14 (1974), 403–20, on pp. 407–8. For a further, fully accepting account of second sight, see *A Voyage to Shetland, the Orkneys, and the Western Isles of Scotland* (London, 1751), pp. 56ff.

43. Baker to Blair, 15 August, 27 October 1747, John Rylands Library, Manchester, Baker Correspondence, vol. 3, fols 119, 162, and see other letters in the same volume and in vol. 4, and those in vol. 2 referred to in the next note. On this episode, see also above, p. 79. On Baker see G. L'E. Turner, 'Henry Baker F.R.S.: Founder of the Bakerian Lecture', *Notes and Records of the Royal Society*, 29 (1974), 53–79.

44. Baker to Blair, 4 November 1746, and Blair to Baker, 4 December 1746, Baker Correspondence, vol. 2, fols 281, 291.

45. See Rodney M. Baine, *Daniel Defoe and the Supernatural* (Athens, GA, 1968), esp. chapter 5; see also ibid., chapter 7, on the works concerning Duncan Campbell that are evidently not by Defoe but by William Bond. On Defoe's later publications on magic see also Maximillian E. Novak, 'Defoe, the Occult, and the Deist Offensive during the Reign of George I', in J. A. Leo Lemay (ed.), *Deism, Masonry and the Enlightenment* (Newark, 1987), pp. 93–108, and his *Daniel Defoe: Master of Fictions* (Oxford, 2001), chapter 27.

46. Richard B. Schwartz, *Samuel Johnson and the New Science* (Madison and Milwaukee, 1971), p. 79 and chapter 3, 'The Baconian Legacy', passim.

47. James Boswell, *The Life of Samuel Johnson: together with Boswell's Journal of a Tour to the Hebrides and Johnson's Diary of a Journey into North Wales*, ed. George Birkbeck Hill, rev. L. F. Powell, 6 vols (Oxford, 1934–64), vol. 1, p. 450 (21 July 1763), vol. 5, p. 13n. I am indebted to Fred Lock for his advice on matters Johnsonian.

48. Samuel Johnson, *A Journey to the Western Islands of Scotland*, ed. J. D. Fleeman (Oxford, 1985), pp. 89–91. For the reading 'Boyle' rather than 'Bayle' see Sherbo, 'Text of Johnson's "Journey to the Western Islands of Scotland"'. In a note to this passage on p. 212 of his edition, Fleeman cites a passage from Bacon's *Sylva Sylvarum* about a premonitory dream, but this is barely relevant.

49. Boswell, *Life of Johnson*, vol. 5, p. 159. Cf. Boswell's defence of second sight as no more superstitious than electricity or magnetism: ibid., vol. 5, p. 391.

50. Johnson, *Journey*, pp. 89, 91. It is perhaps interesting that John Brand, in his *Observations on Popular Antiquities* (his extended edition of Henry Bourne's 1723 *Antiquitates Vulgares*) (Newcastle, 1777), pp. 381ff., deals with second sight by quoting Johnson's account, thus illustrating its canonical status.

51. John Ferriar, *An Essay towards a Theory of Apparitions* (London, 1813), pp. 28, 41, 63ff., and passim.

52. John Ferriar, 'Of Popular Illusions, and Particularly of Medical Demonology', *Memoirs of the Literary and Philosophical Society of Manchester*, 3 (1790), [23]–116, on p. 34. See also pp. 32–4, passim.

53. Samuel Hibbert[-Ware], *Sketches of the Philosophy of Apparitions*, 2nd edn (Edinburgh, 1825), pp. 133, 212ff., on p. 215. A comparable view is taken in John Abercrombie, *Inquiries concerning the Intellectual Powers and the Investigation of Truth* (Edinburgh, 1835), esp. p. 296.

54. Hibbert, *Sketches*, pp. 226n., 232 and passim. In conflating second sight with stories of monitory dreams and apparitions, Hibbert invoked Wesley as a key advocate of their apologetic role (pp. 213–14), citing the passage quoted on p. 117 above in connection with the Tedworth case. The only reference I have found to an interest in second sight on Wesley's part is a rather neutral one in his *Letters and Journals*, ed. W. R. Ward and R. P. Heitzenrater (Nashville, 1988– [in progress]), vol. 4, p. 486 (19 August 1764), but it is interesting that, when Boswell 'made some remark that seemed to imply a belief in *second sight*' in 1773, his interlocutor, the Duchess of Argyle, replied: 'I fancy you will be a *Methodist*' (Boswell, *Life of Johnson*, vol. 5, p. 358).

55. See above, pp. 54–5. See also *Occult Laboratory*, pp. 29–31.
56. Burt, *Letters from a Gentleman*, 2nd edn, 2 vols (London, 1759), vol. 2, pp. 212–13, 285–8.
57. Ibid., vol. 1, pp. 279ff., 333ff.
58. McNicol, *Remarks on Dr Samuel Johnson's Journey to the Hebrides* (London, 1779), pp. 191ff. For the Cock Lane ghost see ibid., p. 198. For Johnson's involvement in the case see Douglas Grant, *The Cock Lane Ghost* (London, 1965), Emma Clery, *The Rise of Supernatural Fiction 1762–1800* (Cambridge, 1995), pp. 14ff. and Paul Chambers, *The Cock Lane Ghost* (Stroud, 2006). It is perhaps worth noting that McNicol was also critical of Johnson for his indecision as to whether second sight was a faculty or a power: *Remarks*, pp. 192–3.
59. Pennant, *A Tour in Scotland and Voyage to the Hebrides, MDCCLXXII* (Chester, 1774), p. 323 (see also his *Tour in Scotland, MDCCLXIX* (Chester, 1771), pp. 154–5); MacCulloch, *A Description of the Western Islands of Scotland*, 3 vols (London, 1819), vol. 2, pp. 32–3.
60. Jacob Pattison, *A Tour Through Part of the Highlands of Scotland in 1780*, National Library of Scotland, MS 6322, fols 14, 21 (formerly pp. 24, 38). The final quotation, which slightly echoes *The Spectator*, no. 604 (8 October 1714) (ed. D. F. Bond, 5 vols, Oxford, 1965, vol. 5, p. 65), is quoted in Martin Rackwitz, *Travels to Terra Incognita: The Scottish Highlands and Hebrides in Early Modern Travellers' Accounts c. 1600 to 1800* (Münster, 2007), p. 509, who quotes other accounts of second sight on pp. 505ff. Pattison died in 1782: for his memorial see Andrew Duncan, *Elogiorum Sepulchralium Edinensium Delectus* (Edinburgh, 1815), p. 14.
61. Boswell, *Life of Johnson*, vol. 5, p. 227.
62. Paul K. Monod, *Solomon's Secret Arts: The Occult in the Age of Enlightenment* (New Haven and London, 2013), esp. p. 340. Cf. ibid., pp. 7, 261–2 and passim.
63. Boswell, *Life of Johnson*, vol. 5, p. 227. Cf. Johnson's comment in *Journey*, p. 90, that the ministers 'universally deny it, and are suspected to deny it, in consequence of a system, against conviction'.
64. McNicol, *Remarks*, pp. 192, 196. A similar statement concerning second sight as a vulgar belief occurs in Beattie's letter to Mrs Montague of *c.* 1772, in Sir William Forbes, *An Account of the Life and Writings of Dr James Beattie*, 2nd edn, 3 vols (Edinburgh, 1807), vol. 1, p. 286.
65. See above, Chapter 2, and below, pp. 174–5.
66. See *Occult Laboratory*, p. 9 and passim; below, p. 186. For background see the influential study of Steven Shapin, *A Social History of Truth: Civility and Science in Seventeenth-century England* (Chicago, 1994).
67. In making this claim I am departing from a standard trope of the historiography of the period, exemplified (for example) by Patrick Curry, *Prophecy and Power: Astrology in Early Modern England* (Cambridge, 1989) or Lorraine Daston and Katharine Park, *Wonders and the Order of Nature 1150–1750* (New York, 1998), chapter 9, esp. pp. 343ff. See also above, p. 3. It is perhaps worth noting that 'Theophilus Insulanus' was particularly insistent in refuting this association: *Treatise*, pp. 84–5.
68. Boswell, *Life of Johnson*, vol. 5, p. 159; Scott, *The Lady of the Lake: A Poem* (Edinburgh, 1810), notes to Canto 1, p. viii. It is perhaps worth noting here that Letter 1 of Scott's *Letters on Demonology and Witchcraft* (London, 1830) is very much indebted to the views of Ferriar and Hibbert.
69. See, for example, Judith V. Grabiner, 'Maclaurin and Newton: The Newtonian Style and the Authority of Mathematics', in Charles W. J. Withers and Paul Wood (eds), *Science and Medicine in the Scottish Enlightenment* (East Linton, 2002), pp. 143–71; Paul Wood (ed.), *Thomas Reid on the Animate Creation* (Edinburgh, 1995), p. 5 and passim.
70. See, e.g., M. A. Stewart and John P. Wright (eds), *Hume and Hume's Connexions* (Edinburgh, 1994).
71. See Alan E. Shapiro, 'Newton's "Experimental Philosophy"', *Early Science and Medicine*, 9 (2004), 185–217.
72. For a brief exposition of this contrast see Michael Hunter, 'Newton's Style of Science', in Denis R. Alexander (ed.), *The Isaac Newton Guide Book* (Cambridge, 2012), pp. 27–33. It

should be stated that what is at issue here is the eighteenth-century image of Newton rather than the man himself: on his complex views, see the references cited in chapter 3, n. 57.

73. Hibbert, *Sketches*, pp. 132, 231. Cf. Abercrombie, *Intellectual Powers*, p. 296, where a 'principle' is invoked to explain second sight.

74. See above, pp. 121–2, 143.

75. See above, pp. 128–9.

76. Scott, *Lady of the Lake*, notes to Canto 1, pp. viii–xii. For an analogous sentiment, see the essay on 'General Principles of Taste' appended to John Stoddart, *Remarks on Local Scenery and Manners in Scotland during the Years 1799 and 1800*, 2 vols (London, 1801), vol. 2, pp. 323ff., which is critical of the way in which 'we enthrone the science of material objects in the seat of mental knowledge, and transfer the strict definitions, the analytical distinctions, and the logical deductions of the one, to the undefinable, and complex sensations of the other' (p. 325).

77. See Thomas Campbell, *Gertrude of Wyoming; a Pennsylvanian Tale. And Other Poems* (London, 1809), pp. 117ff. To this was added in the 3rd edition of 1810 a set of 'Notes' which include on 228ff. an account of second sight from Martin's *Description* which is similar to but not identical with Scott's; at one point (p. 234) Martin is described as a 'credulous author'. For Carr, see his *Caledonian Sketches* (London, 1809), pp. 456ff. Carr almost exactly paraphrased the arguments of Beattie that we will encounter in the next but one paragraph by way of answering Johnson's affirmative attitude, though adding a modish allusion to belief in animal magnetism, to which he was equally hostile.

78. See above, pp. 61 and 156.

79. William Collins, 'Ode on the Popular Superstitions of the Highlands of Scotland, Considered as the Subject of Poetry' of *c*. 1749, in Richard Wendorf and Charles Ryskamp (eds), *The Works of William Collins* (Oxford, 1979), pp. 56–63 and 161ff. Another early literary allusion to second sight, which is cited by Ferriar in his 'Of Popular Illusions', p. 33, appears in James Thomson's *Castle of Indolence*, canto 1, stanza 30: see James Thomson, *Liberty, The Castle of Indolence and Other Poems*, ed. James Sambrook (Oxford, 1986), p. 183.

80. Wendorf and Ryskamp, *Works of Collins*, pp. 57, 62: for the commentary, see Peter Womack, *Improvement and Romance: Constructing the Myth of the Highlands* (Basingstoke, 1989), pp. 87ff.; see also ibid., chapter 4, passim.

81. Beattie, *Essays* (Edinburgh, 1776), pp. 181–3 and 183–5n. Beattie had earlier expressed his views on the subject in a letter to Mrs Montague, probably of 1772: see Forbes, *Account of the Life and Writings of Beattie*, vol. 1, pp. 285–9: this seems to be a commentary on Theophilus Insulanus's book.

82. Beattie, *Essays*, pp. 182–3.

83. Gilpin, *Observations, Relative chiefly to Picturesque Beauty, Made in the Year 1776, On several parts of Great Britain, Particularly the High-Lands of Scotland*, 2 vols (London, 1789), vol. 2, p. 133. For background see Malcolm Andrews, *The Search for the Picturesque: Landscape Aesthetics and Tourism in Britain, 1760–1800* (Aldershot, 1989), chapter 8.

84. Beattie, *Essays*, p. 185n. This is also cited in Scott, *Letters on Demonology*, p. 43.

85. See Coleman O. Parsons, *Witchcraft and Demonology in Scott's Fiction* (Edinburgh, 1964), pp. 151ff. and passim.

86. See *Occult Laboratory*, p. 40.

87. See Alex Sutherland, *The Brahan Seer: The Making of a Legend* (Bern and Oxford, 2009), esp. chapter 6.

88. On the interest in the topic of continental authors such as Georg Conrad Horst, see A.J.L. Busst, 'Scottish Second Sight: The Rise and Fall of a European Myth', *European Romantic Review*, 5 (1994), 149–77 (though his reasons for the decline in interest in the topic are somewhat questionable). See also Womack, *Improvement and Romance*, and Elsa Richardson, *Second Sight in the Nineteenth Century: Prophecy, Imagination and Nationhood* (London, 2017).

## CONCLUSION: THE 'DECLINE OF
## MAGIC' RECONSIDERED

1. See particularly my comments on the debate between Wagstaffe and his opponents on pp. 45–6. See also pp. 140–1.
2. See above, p. 21.
3. See Michael Hunter, 'A New Theory of Intellectual Change', in Hunter, *Science and the Shape of Orthodoxy: Intellectual Change in Late Seventeenth-Century Britain* (Woodbridge, 1995), pp. 11–18, and the exemplification in Hunter, 'How Boyle Became a Scientist', in *Robert Boyle (1627–91): Scrupulosity and Science* (Woodbridge, 2000), pp. 15–57, esp. pp. 49–50.
4. See above, pp. 24–5 and 137–8.
5. Joseph Glanvill, *Saducismus Triumphatus*, 3rd edn (London 1689), p. 448 (More's editorial note), and see above, p. 111.
6. For helpful accounts of the Society for Psychical Research see Alan Gauld, *The Founders of Psychical Research* (London, 1968), Ronald Pearsall, *The Table-Rappers* (London, 1972) and Shane McCorristine, *Spectres of the Self: Thinking about Ghosts and Ghost-Seeing in England, 1750–1920* (Cambridge, 2010). See also below, pp. 178, 179.
7. On Boulton, see above, p. 82, including n. 65 on his appraisal by Ian Bostridge in his *Witchcraft and its Transformations c. 1650–c. 1750* (Oxford, 1997). On Defoe, see above, pp. 49, 156, and ibid., passim. Also interesting are Bostridge's remarks in his essay, 'Witchcraft Repealed', in Jonathan Barry, Marianne Hester and Gareth Roberts (eds), *Witchcraft in Early Modern Europe: Studies in Culture and Belief* (Cambridge, 1996), pp. 309–34, on pp. 314–15. See also below, n. 44.
8. Glanvill, *A Blow at Modern Sadducism*, 4th edn (London, 1668), p. 38. For Boyle, see above, p. 87.
9. Quoted in J. J. MacIntosh (ed.), *Boyle on Atheism* (Toronto, 2005), pp. 260–1. Of course, these comments, though prescient, preceded the findings of Edmond Halley, to which Boyle would doubtless have accommodated himself. For Glanvill's comparable arguments, see above, p. 104.
10. Webster, *The Displaying of Supposed Witchcraft* (London, 1677), pp. 267–8 (perhaps predictably, he saw the findings of the Royal Society as supporting his case). This point is well made by Coudert, 'Henry More and Witchcraft', in Sarah Hutton (ed.), *Henry More (1614–87): Tercentenary Studies* (Dordrecht, 1990), pp. 115–36, on p. 129. See also Jacqueline Broad, 'Margaret Cavendish and Joseph Glanvill: Science, Religion and Witchcraft', *Studies in History and Philosophy of Science*, 38 (2007), 493–505, on p. 502, though she perhaps fails fully to understand the rationale of Glanvill's supernaturalist endeavour. For the Glanvill quotation, see above, p. 14.
11. Boyle, *Works*, ed. Michael Hunter and Edward B. Davis, 14 vols (London, 1999–2000), vol. 8, p. 108.
12. See above, p. 70, and see Michael Hunter, *Boyle Studies: Aspects of the Life and Thought of Robert Boyle* (Farnham, 2015), pp. 169–70.
13. Boyle, *Works*, vol. 8, pp. 295–313; Glanvill, *A Blow*, pp. 9, 48, 51 and passim. On this aspect of Glanvill's work, see esp. Julie A. Davies, 'Poisonous Vapours: Joseph Glanvill's Science of Witchcraft', *Intellectual History Review*, 22 (2012), 163–79. (Her monograph, *Science in an Enchanted World: Philosophy and Witchcraft in the Work of Joseph Glanvill* (New York, 2018) unfortunately appeared too late to be taken into account in the current volume.) On Glanvill's pioneering status in relation to 'the analogy of nature', see J. E. McGuire, *Tradition and Innovation: Newton's Metaphysics of Nature* (Dordrecht, 1995), pp. 76–7, and Simon Schaffer, 'Newtonian Angels', in Joad Raymond (ed.), *Conversations with Angels: Essays towards a History of Spiritual Communication, 1100–1700* (Basingstoke, 2011), pp. 90–122, on p. 111. On the eighteenth-century fortunes of the concept see E. R. Wasserman, 'Nature Moralized: The Divine Analogy in the Eighteenth Century', *English Literary History*, 20 (1953), 39–76.
14. Glanvill, *A Blow*, pp. 177ff.; above, p. 42.

15. John Trenchard and Thomas Gordon, *Cato's Letters, or Essays on Liberty, Civil and Religious, and Other Important Subjects*, ed. Ronald Hamowy, 2 vols (Indianapolis, 1995), vol. 2, p. 566.

16. Wootton, *The Invention of Science: A New History of the Scientific Revolution* (London, 2015), chapter 13. Wootton does, of course, acknowledge the complexities of the situation, citing my work (see esp. pp. 459–60), but his overall conclusion that 'Bentley was right' (p. 471) is unacceptable.

17. See above, pp. 80–1.

18. See especially his *Paolo Sarpi: Between Renaissance and Enlightenment* (Cambridge, 1983). Considering the context, it seems odd that on p. 473 of *The Invention of Science* Wootton singles out Blount's *Philostratus* to exemplify unbelief without noting its explicitly anti-magical thrust: see above, pp. 51–2.

19. Charles Webster, *From Paracelsus to Newton: Magic and the Making of Modern Science* (Cambridge, 1982), p. 100. Unfortunately, this is the last page of the book and Webster does not pursue the matter.

20. Peter Elmer, *Witchcraft, Witch-Hunting, and Politics in Early Modern England* (Oxford, 2016), p. 1. He combines this with acknowledging the influence of Stuart Clark, *Thinking with Demons* (Oxford, 1997), on which see above, Introduction, pp. 4–5.

21. Bostridge, *Witchcraft and its Transformations*, chapter 5 and passim.

22. See above, Chapter 2, nn. 5, 58, 61, 67, 69, 77 and 83 (see also the citations there of the related works of Andrew Sneddon and Mark Knights); above, n. 7. For a more sustained critique of Bostridge's book, see my review essay, 'Witchcraft and the Decline of Belief', *Eighteenth-century Life*, 22 (1998), 139–47, on pp. 144ff.

23. Morrab Library, Penzance, MOR/MAN/54. The volume, in which the MS follows a printed pamphlet, *A True Account of a Strange and Wonderful Relation of one John Tonken of Penzans in Cornwall* (London, 1686), reached the library with the Borlase Papers; it was purchased by W. C. Borlase in 1882. See Jenny Dearlove, 'The Pretended Crime of Witchcraft', in June Palmer (ed.), *Treasures of the Morrab* (Penzance, 2005), pp. 21–30. I am indebted to Jonathan Barry and Peter Elmer for drawing my attention to this item and to Alex Higlett for her help in my study of it. For a brief and slightly noncommittal account of it see Elmer, *Witchcraft, Witch-Hunting, and Politics*, p. 290. For the likelihood that Rawlinson was the author based on the fact that Samuel Weller states that he was a contemporary of his at St John's College, Oxford, see Dearlove, 'Pretended Crime', pp. 28–9. This may be confirmed by the similarity between the handwriting of the Morrab MS and various MSS of similar date of Thomas Rawlinson in the Bodleian Library, Oxford: e.g. MS Rawl B 250, fol. 77 (letter to Hearne of 4 February 1717/18), B 415 (church notes, 1717), C 930, fol. 12 (letter to Hearne, 1 May 1718). In addition, his notes on Leland, referred to in the next note, are written in a similar format to the Morrab MS, going through the text making notes by page.

24. See the life of Rawlinson by his brother, Richard, in Bodleian Library MS Rawl. J 4° 4, fols 148–50, esp. fols 148v–9, and the fulsome acknowledgments of Rawlinson in Michael Maittaire, *Annales typographici*, 5 vols (The Hague, 1719–41), I, pp. 128n., 374n., and Thomas Hearne (ed.), *Walteri Hemingford, Historia de rebus gestis Edvardi I, Edvardi II & Edvardi III*, 2 vols (Oxford, 1731), vol. 1, pp. civ–v. See also Rawlinson's extant notes on Leland, compiled for Hearne, in Bodleian MS Rawl. Lett. 15–16, fols 335–43. For further information see *ODNB*.

25. The text on fols 4–8 comprises notes on H. F., *A True and Exact Relation . . . of the Late Witches, Arraign'd & Executed in the County of Essex* (London, 1645) and John Davenport, *The Witches of Huntingdon, their Examinations and Confessions* (London, 1646); the former includes ancillary information from John Stearne, *A Confirmation & Discovery of Witchcraft* (London, 1648), p. 15, while in the latter Rawlinson compared the details of two of the cases given there with those in 'R. B.' [Nathaniel Crouch], *The Kingdom of Darkness* (London, 1688), pp. 159–62.

26. MOR/MAN/54, fol. 1v.

27. Ibid., fols 1–3 and passim.

28. The debate stemmed from Margaret C. Jacob's influential *The Newtonians and the English Revolution, 1689–1720* (Hassocks, 1976), and the riposte by Anita Guerrini, 'The Tory Newtonians: Gregory, Pitcairne, and their Circle', *Journal of British Studies*, 25 (1986), 288–311. For a more recent contribution see John Friesen, 'Archibald Pitcairne, David Gregory and the Scottish Origins of English Tory Newtonianism, 1688–1715', *History of Science*, 41 (2003), 163–91, who usefully lists relevant writings in nn. 1–5.

29. Bostridge, *Witchcraft and its Transformations*, pp. 155–7. Cf. p. 235 for a further reference to Collins and p. 173 to Gordon, and p. 93n. for a quotation from *Cato's Letters*.

30. Elmer, *Witchcraft, Witch-Hunting, and Politics*, pp. 287–9.

31. See J. H. Plumb, *The Growth of Political Stability in England 1675–1725* (London, 1967); John Brewer, *The Sinews of Power: War, Money and the English State, 1688–1783* (London, 1989).

32. R. E. Sullivan, *John Toland and the Deist Controversy: A Study in Adaptations* (Cambridge, MA, 1982), p. 277.

33. On the Enlightenment influence of Toland and other Deists see, e.g., Ernst Cassirer, *The Philosophy of the Enlightenment*, English trans. (Princeton, 1951), esp. pp. 171ff.; Franco Venturi, *Utopia and Reform in the Enlightenment* (Cambridge, 1971), pp. 49ff.; Jonathan Israel, *Radical Enlightenment: Philosophy and the Making of Modernity, 1650–1750* (Oxford, 2001), esp. chapter 33.

34. See above, pp. 51, 54, 55, 123–4; Toland, *Adeisidaemon* (Hagae Comitae, 1709), pp. 46–7 (English trans., fols 47v–8) (see above, p. 53 and n. 20).

35. See above, pp. 129, 135.

36. On its roots see the crucial study of Dmitri Levitin, *Ancient Wisdom in the Age of the New Science: Histories of Philosophy in England, c. 1640–1700* (Cambridge, 2015), esp. chapter 3. On its legacy see Erik Midelfort, 'The Gadarene Demoniac in the English Enlightenment', in Emily Michelson (ed.), *A Linking of Heaven and Earth* (Aldershot, 2012), pp. 49–66, on pp. 51, 57–8, and Anthony Ossa-Richardson, 'Possession or Insanity? Two Views from the Victorian Lunatic Asylum', *Journal of the History of Ideas*, 74 (2013), 553–75, on pp. 559–63.

37. Peter Harrison, *'Religion' and the Religions in the English Enlightenment* (Cambridge, 1990), pp. 77ff., esp. p. 79.

38. Jonathan Barry, 'Public Infidelity and Private Belief? The Discourse of Spirits in Enlightenment Bristol', in Barry, *Witchcraft and Demonology in South-West England, 1640–1789* (Basingstoke, 2012), chapter 6: a preliminary version appeared in Owen Davies and Willem de Blécourt (eds), *Beyond the Witch Trials: Witchcraft and Magic in Enlightenment Europe* (Manchester, 2004), pp. 117–43.

39. Alex Sutherland, *The Brahan Seer: The Making of a Legend* (Oxford and Bern, 2009), p. 117, and see Chapter 4, passim.

40. Ibid., pp. 93–4, citing Hunter, *Scrupulosity and Science*, chapter 10. However, it is worth stressing that Boyle would probably have overcome his scruples had death not intervened, a point that Sutherland overlooks: see above, p. 11.

41. See above, p. 3. For classical attitudes, see Dale Martin, *Inventing Superstition: From the Hippocratics to the Christians* (Cambridge, MA, 2004).

42. See above, pp. 160–1. For the growing alienation between educated and popular culture at this point see the comments of Alexandra Walsham, 'Recording Superstition in Early Modern Britain: The Origins of Folklore', in S. A. Smith and Alan Knight (eds), *The Religion of Fools? Superstition Past and Present (Past and Present Supplement* no. 3, Oxford, 2008), pp. 178–206, on p. 196. Here I should point out that I have reservations about some of the conclusions of Thomas Waters, 'Magic and the British Middle Classes, 1750–1900', *Journal of British Studies*, 54 (2015), 632–53, who arguably plays down the extent of change in the eighteenth century as part of his case for an abnormal level of hostility towards magic among middle-class journalists in the early nineteenth.

43. See above, pp. 163ff. On the Cock Lane affair and its aftermath, including the responses of Garrick, Walpole and others, see esp. E. J. Clery, *The Rise of Supernatural Fiction, 1762–1800* (Cambridge, 1995). A further important study of related themes is Sasha

Handley, *Visions of an Unseen World: Ghost Beliefs and Ghost Stories in Eighteenth-century England* (London, 2007). There is also some helpful information in Bostridge, *Witchcraft and its Transformations*, esp. pp. 170ff.

44. See Jonathan Barry, 'News from the Invisible World: The Publishing History of Tales of the Supernatural *c.* 1660–1830', in Jonathan Barry, Owen Davies and Cornelie Usborne (eds), *Cultures of Witchcraft in Europe from the Middle Ages to the Present* (London, 2018), pp. 179–203. See also C. O. Parsons, 'Ghost-Stories before Defoe', *Notes & Queries*, 201 (July 1956), 293–8.

45. Paul K. Monod, *Solomon's Secret Arts: The Occult in the Age of Enlightenment* (New Haven and London, 2013); Désirée Hirst, *Hidden Riches: Traditional Symbolism from the Renaissance to Blake* (London, 1964); and, e.g., R.D. Stock, *The Holy and the Daemonic from Sir Thomas Browne to William Blake* (Princeton, 1982); Joscelyn Godwin, *The Theosophical Enlightenment* (New York, 1994); and John V. Fleming, *The Dark Side of the Enlightenment: Wizards, Alchemists, and Spiritual Seekers in the Age of Reason* (New York, 2013).

46. See especially Ronald Pearson, *The Table-Rappers* (London, 1972).

47. R. D. Owen, *Footfalls on the Boundary of Another World* (Philadelphia, 1860), pp. 214–24.

48. A. R. Wallace, 'Mr Podmore on Clairvoyance and Poltergeists', *Journal of the Society for Psychical Research*, 9 (1899–1900), 22–30, on p. 25; Frank Podmore, 'Clairvoyance and Poltergeists', ibid., 37–45, on p. 39 (see also the report on the general meeting of the Society for Psychical Research, 26 January 1900, in the same volume, pp. 206–7); Andrew Lang, 'The Poltergeist, Historically Considered', *Proceedings of the Society for Psychical Research*, 17 (1901–3), 305–26, with remarks by Podmore and Lang in ibid., pp. 327–36. See also Andrew Lang, *Cock Lane and Common Sense* (London, 1894), pp. 92–4; Lang, *The Book of Dreams and Ghosts* (London, 1897), pp. 220–1; Frank Podmore, *Modern Spiritualism: A History and a Criticism*, 2 vols (London, 1902), vol. 1, pp. 26–7. See also Ferris Greenslet, *Joseph Glanvill: A Study of English Thought and Letters in the Seventeenth Century* (New York, 1900), p. 155ff.; H. Addington Bruce, *Historic Ghosts and Ghost Hunters* (New York, 1908), pp. 17–35; H. Stanley and I.M.L. Redgrove, *Joseph Glanvill and Psychical Research in the Seventeenth Century* (London, 1921), chapter 6.

49. Harry Price, *Poltergeist over England: Three Centuries of Mischievous Ghosts* (London, 1945), chapter 5 and appendix A; Alan Gauld and A. D. Cornell, *Poltergeists* (London, 1979), pp. 42–62. See also Sacheverell Sitwell, *Poltergeists* (London, 1940), pp. 113–24, 214–29 (Sitwell's account on pp. 113ff. is focused on Edith Sitwell's poem inspired by this case, 'The Drum', which also appears on pp. 9–10 of his book and in her *Collected Poems* (London, 1957, reprinted 1993), pp. 110–12); A.R.G. Owen, *Can We Explain the Poltergeist?* (New York, 1964), pp. 93, 145–7; Raymond Bayless, *The Enigma of the Poltergeist* (West Nyack, NY, 1967), pp. 11–13; Brian Inglis, *Natural and Supernatural: A History of the Paranormal from the Earliest Times to 1914* (London, 1977), pp. 120–2; Colin Wilson, *Poltergeist! A Study in Destructive Haunting* (London, 1981), pp. 120–3, 135; John and Anne Spencer, *The Poltergeist Phenomenon: An Investigation into Psychic Disturbance* (London, 1996), pp. 15–17, 84–5, 101–2, 112, 151, 261; Roger Clarke, *A Natural History of Ghosts: 500 Years of Hunting for Proof* (London, 2013), pp. 72–83.

50. George Cruikshank, *Discovery concerning Ghosts, with a Rap at the 'Spirit-Rappers'* (London, 1863), pp. 18–19.

51. Wallace Notestein, *A History of Witchcraft in England from 1558 to 1718* (1911; reprinted, New York, 1965), pp. 273–6; R. H. Robbins, *The Encyclopaedia of Witchcraft and Demonology* (New York, 1959; reprinted 1981), pp. 140–3. Cf., e.g., C. L'E. Ewen, *Witchcraft and Demonianism* (London, 1933), pp. 338–9; R. C. Finucane, *Appearances of the Dead: A Cultural History of Ghosts* (London, 1982; reprinted as *Ghosts: Appearances of the Dead and Cultural Transformation*, Amherst, NY, 1996), pp. 141–3 and 210; P. G. Maxwell-Stuart, *Poltergeists: A History of Violent Ghostly Phenomena* (Stroud, 2011), pp. 136ff.

52. For instance, for a riposte to Hibbert's *Sketches of the Philosophy of Apparitions* (see above, pp. 157–8), see the anonymous *Past Feelings Renovated; or, Ideas Occasioned by the*

*Perusal of Dr Hibbert's 'Philosophy of Apparitions'. Written with the View to Counteracting Any Sentiments Approaching Materialism, which that Work, However Unintentional on the Part of the Author, may have a Tendency to Produce* (London, 1828). On nineteenth-century attitudes to second sight see above, p. 166.

53. See especially John L. Campbell and Trevor H. Hall, *Strange Things* (London, 1968), and the rather more sympathetic account in Elsa Richardson, *Second Sight in the Nineteenth Century* (London, 2017), chapters 5–6. Andrew Lang also took an interest in the topic, producing an edition of Kirk's *Secret Commonwealth* in 1893 and writing about it in *Cock Lane and Common Sense*, pp. 226ff. For more recent investigations see Shari A. Cohn, 'A Historical Review of Second Sight: The Collectors, their Accounts and Ideas', *Scottish Studies*, 33 (1999), 146–85. For a recent edition of Kirk's book by a New Age devotee, see R. J. Stewart, *Robert Kirk: Walker between Worlds* (Shaftesbury, 1990).

54. Thomas Carlyle, 'Boswell's Life of Johnson', in his *Critical and Miscellaneous Essays*, 4 vols (London, 1839), vol. 3, pp. 114–94, on pp. 145ff., 179.

55. Peter Burke and Maria Lúcia G. Pallares-Burke, *Gilberto Freyre: Social Theory in the Tropics* (Oxford and Bern, 2008), pp. 64–6 (they there explain how Freyre cross-fertilised the phrase with the concept of 'equilibrium' that he derived from Herbert Spencer's *First Principles* and from his mentor, Franklin Giddings); Peter Burke, *A Social History of Knowledge, II: From the Encyclopédie to Wikipedia* (Cambridge, 2012), pp. 2, 250. I am most grateful to Peter Burke and Maria Lúcia G. Pallares-Burke for their assistance in this matter, partly for pointing me to Carlyle's original usage and partly for explaining how 'equilíbrio de antagonismos' would be the natural way of expressing the concept in Portuguese. I have preferred Carlyle's original phrase, which seems best to express my meaning. I should perhaps point out that in earlier publications I invoked the concept of 'schizophrenia' to indicate the state of affairs that I am now using this phrase to describe: see my *Robert Boyle: Scrupulosity and Science*, p. 244, echoed in my Roy Porter Lecture, *Historical Journal*, 55 (2012), 399–425, on p. 425.

56. See above, pp. 118, 140.

57. See above, p. 149, and John Aubrey, *The Natural History of Wiltshire*, ed. John Britton (London, 1845), pp. 120–22. The Bankes story is not printed by Britton and is taken from the MS copy of Aubrey's work at the Royal Society, MS 92, p. 366 ('Sir' is given as 'S.' and, in the last line, 'dunging of a horse' is written in smaller script above the line as an alternative to 'heap of Horse-dung'). For Bankes see above, p. 97. For Aubrey's ambivalence, see above, pp. 97, 107, and Michael Hunter, *John Aubrey and the Realm of Learning* (London, 1975), pp. 129–30 and chapter 2, passim.

## APPENDIX I: THE 'DRUMMER OF TEDWORTH': A NOTE ON SOURCES

1. For bibliographical details of these works, see Chapter 4, n. 2, and Introduction, n. 66. For a reprint of the relevant part of *Blow*, see John Ashton, *The Devil in Britain and America* (London, 1896; reprinted Hollywood, CA, 1972), pp. 47–59.

2. Corpus Christi College, Oxford, MS 318, fols 160–64. For further details, see Hunter, 'New Light on the "Drummer of Tedworth": Conflicting Narratives of Witchcraft in Restoration England', *Historical Research*, 78 (2005), 311–53, esp. 338–50.

3. For Maton's role as a deponent, see Mompesson to Collins, 8 August 1674, *Saducismus*, sig. R4v.

4. The manuscript copy in Wood's hand is bound into a collection of printed pamphlets in his collection now in the Bodleian Library, Wood 467, following item 2 (i.e. effectively forming item 3, since the next item is no. 4, though the flyleaf following this refers back to item 2). For further discussion see Hunter, 'New Light', n. 17.

5. Price, *Poltergeist over England: Three Centuries of Mischievous Ghosts* (London, 1945), p. 393 and pp. 393–8; see also chapter 5 (pp. 43–61) and appendix A (pp. 388–99), passim.

His description of the case in the text of his book, derived from *Saducismus*, appears on pp. 45–59. A typescript of the text is preserved with seven letters from Fetherstonhaugh-Frampton to Price, dating from 22 May to 1 August 1944, in the Harry Price archive in the University of London Library, HPC/4B/296.

6. Price, *Poltergeist*, facing p. 52, a photograph of part of fol. 160 of the Corpus MS captioned 'John Mompesson's journal'. See also p. 399, where Price quotes Craster's letter to him, dated 28 June 1944, in which he drew his attention to his article, 'The Drummer of Tedworth', *Bodleian Quarterly Record*, 4 (1923–5), 100–1, in which he had noted the existence of the Wood manuscript, and also outlined the content of the Corpus MS.

7. See Trevor H. Hall, *Search for Harry Price* (London, 1978), chapter 18 and passim. For a slightly more sympathetic account see Richard Morris, *Harry Price: The Psychic Detective* (Stroud, 2006).

8. Alan Gauld and A. D. Cornell, *Poltergeists* (London, 1979), pp. 44–55. In addition to the complete omission of document 2, 22 lines are there omitted from document 1 (the final paragraph of the letter), 22 from document 3 (the final two paragraphs of the letter and the first paragraph of the postscript), 26 from document 4 (the first paragraph and the first sentence of the second, which refers back to document 2, as also the last 4 sentences of the letter and the postscript), and 1 from document 5 (the final salutation).

9. PRO State Papers 29/230, no. 177. Abstracted in *Calendar of State Papers Nov. 1667–Sept. 1668* (1893), pp. 149–50.

10. See the entry relating to Browne in Henning, *The House of Commons, 1660–90*, vol. 2, pp. 734–5. The Browne family was related to that of the Somerset witch-hunter, Robert Hunt: Jonathan Barry, *Witchcraft and Demonology in South-West England, 1640–1789* (Basingstoke, 2012), pp. 26, 28, 33.

11. Dorset History Centre D/SHE/5, pp. 460–77. This comprises a transcript of 'Some Considerations' from *A Philosophical Endeavour Towards the Defence of the Being of Witches and Apparitions* (London, 1666), omitting the first paragraph; it continues to section 8, omitting sections 9–20 (pp. 2–35, omitting pp. 35–62): that the text comes from the 1666 edition rather than from those of 1668 has been confirmed by collation, since, insofar as there are tiny additions to the latter, these are here lacking. I am grateful to Peter Elmer for sharing his findings concerning this volume; cf. his *Witchcraft, Witch-hunting, and Politics in Early Modern England* (Oxford, 2016), p. 218–19n.

12. D/SHE/5, pp. 479–84. The final sentence of the postscript to document 1 is also missing, as is its date and the salutation to document 3 (which instead appears at the head of the first letter). The last words of the final page are 'being of spirits by', with the catchword 'by'; p. 485 is of later paper and has quite different content (a nineteenth-century obiter dictum about 'Gratitude').

13. The original is in Bodleian Wood 401 (no. 98, fol. 193). See Andrew Lang, 'The Poltergeist, Historically Considered', *Proceedings of the Society for Psychical Research*, 17 (1901–3), 305–26, on pp. 310–13; it was reprinted from there in Price, *Poltergeist over England*, pp. 390–93. An edition with commentary appears in *The Pack of Autolycus*, ed. Hyder E. Rollins (Cambridge, MA, 1927), pp. 114–21, 240.

14. See Lang, 'The Poltergeist', pp. 308–9, from where it was reprinted in Price, *Poltergeist over England*, pp. 388–9. This article was apparently first noticed by Lord Braybrooke in his edition of Pepys's diary (*Memoirs of Samuel Pepys, Esq.*, 2 vols, 1825, vol. 1, p. 227). See also Rollins, *Pack of Autolycus*, p. 240, where both newspapers are cited.

15. That Drury lived at Broad Hinton is confirmed by document 3.

### APPENDIX II: JOSHUA WALKER'S PAPER ON SECOND SIGHT

1. Michael Hunter, *The Occult Laboratory: Magic, Science and Second Sight in Late Seventeenth-century Scotland* (Woodbridge, 2001), p. 22. The meeting in question occurred on 23 March. For the minutes see R. T. Gunther (ed.), *Early Science in*

*Oxford, volume 4: The Philosophical Society* (Oxford, 1925), pp. 175–6; for the index entry see p. 258.

2. RS Original Register Book, vol. 7, pp. 241–2. This has minor differences from the Classified Papers version in capitalisation, spelling and punctuation. More substantively, it lacks 'they' and 'very' in line 4 and '6 or 8 days before they did dye:' in line 6; in lines 21–2 it inserts 'the' before 'company' and has 'knew' instead of 'understood'; and in the final sentence it has 'me' for 'one' and omits 'had' before 'liv'd'.

3. RS Original Journal Book, vol. 10, p. 88. For the FRS and government official, William Bridgeman, see Michael Hunter, *The Royal Society and its Fellows, 1660–1700: The Morphology of an Early Scientific Institution*, 2nd edn (Oxford, 1994), pp. 200–1 (F357).

4. The number '(123)' appears at the top right-hand corner of the document, which is endorsed on its verso: 'Mr. Walker of Apparitions in the North of Scotland' and '103' or '163' (the central digit does not appear to be '2').

5. This is evidently Simon Mackenzie, nephew of Sir George Mackenzie of Rosehaugh (1636–91), king's advocate for Scotland. I am grateful to Kelsey Jackson Williams for informing me of a letter in the University of St Andrews archives, msdep 75, box 3, bundle 3, item 36, directed to one 'Mr Simon Mackenzie att Oxford student in Christ Church'. This man does not, however, appear in Joseph Foster, *Alumni Oxonienses 1500–1714*, 4 vols (Oxford, 1891–2), whose only relevant record is for George Mckenzie, son of Sir George Mackenzie, who matriculated at University College, Oxford, in 1702; see vol. 3, p. 957. From the other letters in msdep75/3/3, it appears that Simon Mackenzie was at Christ Church in 1685–6 and that in 1687 he went to Holland, where he stayed for about three years. I am also grateful to Michael Riordan for his help in this connection.

6. There is a gap at this point, probably because of an existing blot on the paper. This is ignored in the version in the Register Book.

7. 'sighted' repeated and deleted. Six words later, 'apparitions' altered in composition.

8. Followed by 'finen' [?] deleted.

9. Walker is careful to distinguish Sir George Mackenzie (1630–1714), created 1st Viscount Tarbat in 1685 and 1st Earl of Cromarty in 1703, from Sir George Mackenzie of Rosehaugh, as referred to in n. 5, above. The former was of course Boyle's informant on second sight, and the 'collection' of which Walker had heard was evidently Tarbat's letter to Boyle as printed in *Occult Laboratory*, pp. 90–4, 165–9.

10. There is a cross in the margin beside this sentence, within which the word 'who' is an insertion. George Dalgarno (?1626–87), a schoolmaster who hailed from Scotland, was active in Oxford scholarly circles from the mid-1650s onwards: see Rhodri Lewis, *Language, Mind and Nature: Artificial Languages in England from Bacon to Locke* (Cambridge, 2007), esp. pp. 85ff. Assuming that Walker's paper as read to the Royal Society in 1698 is identical with that read to the Oxford Philosophical Society, 'this Society' presumably refers to the latter.

# INDEX